The Strange Case
of Thomas Quick

The Strange Case of Thomas Quick

The Swedish Serial Killer
and the Psychoanalyst Who Created Him

DAN JOSEFSSON

Translated from the Swedish by Anna Paterson

Portobello

Published by Portobello Books 2015

Portobello Books
12 Addison Avenue
London
W11 4QR

Originally published in Swedish as *Mannen som slutade ljuga: berättselsen om Sture Bergwall och kvinnan som skapade Thomas Quick* in 2013 by Lind & Co, Stockholm

The cost of this translation was defrayed by a subsidy
from the Swedish Arts Council, gratefully acknowledged.

A CIP catalogue record for this book
is available from the British Library.

1 3 5 7 9 10 8 6 4 2

ISBN 978 1 84627 576 0 (trade paperback)
ISBN 978 1 84627 577 7 (ebook)

Typeset by M Rules

Printed and bound by CPI Group (UK) Ltd, Croydon, CR0 4YY

www.portobellobooks.com

Loneliness seems to be such a painful, frightening experience
that people will do practically everything to avoid it.

Psychoanalyst Frieda Fromm–Reichmann

Contents

PART 3: THE WORLD OF THOMAS QUICK

Translator's note

The reader should expect some variation in voice and style in the translation of the supporting documents: this is an extraordinary story and, in evidence, Dan Josefsson has used extracts from a wide range of sources. The documents include interviews, conducted by himself or others – letters and diaries, broadcasts, newspaper articles and books, medical case notes, police reports and notes, court records and other legal documents. His careful reporting has been reflected in the authenticity of the translation, which has retained some quirks of phrasing and style. Respect for the original source has also meant that some passages written in unconventional English (e.g. letters from native Swedish speakers) have been kept with only very minor changes. Passages originally written in English have been italicised in the text. All other quotations have been translated.

PART 1

The Psychological Enigma

1

Prologue in Örje Forest, summer 1997

'I don't have the courage to know that at this point.'
Thomas Quick, statement when questioned
(July, 1997) about where he had hidden
Therese Johannessen's head.

Half the day was gone by the time the Swedish contingent arrived at Örje Forest, near the Swedish border in south-east Norway. The minibus and the police cars parked just inside the forest, as instructed by the Norwegian police. One of the men climbing out of the minibus was over six feet tall, with thinning hair, a short beard and steel-rimmed glasses. He was the serial killer known as Thomas Quick, a name he had adopted late in the summer of 1992, just before he began to confess to his horrific crimes. Previously he was known as Sture Bergwall.

Quick was accompanied by a small group of people who knew him well. Seppo Penttinen, the senior investigating officer (SIO) from the Sundsvall police force was there, as was Quick's psychotherapist Birgitta Ståhle, his solicitor Claes Borgström and a couple of psychiatric nurses who were in charge of his medication. They were accompanied by Sven Å Christianson, an expert on memory function. Christianson, a psychologist from Stockholm University, was writing a book about Thomas Quick. That morning, they had driven from Säter psychiatric hospital, located about two and a half hours by car from Stockholm.

The serial killer had been taken to Norway to help him remember. He had hidden the remains of Therese Johannessen, a nine-year-old girl from Drammen in Norway, somewhere in Örje Forest. In 1988, nine years earlier, Quick had picked up Therese, and killed and

3

dismembered her. The murder had been such a traumatic experience that he repressed the memory of it immediately afterwards. For years, he had been unaware of the fact that he had murdered the little girl. A court had sentenced him for other crimes to be held in the secure unit of the regional psychiatric hospital in Säter, and his psychiatric treatment included psychotherapy. The 'talking cure' had helped him to recover repressed memories of the murder of Therese and several other killings, but the recovery process was slow and the emerging memories caused the patient a great deal of anguish. The painstaking therapy had gradually excavated a catalogue of memory fragments, adding up to a terrifying body of knowledge. Over the course of twenty-five years, he had murdered one person after another, whilst a merciful repression mechanism meant that all the murders had been forgotten. He had no idea how many people he had killed, or how. So far, the police had opened some fifteen investigations based on his confessions. Four investigations had reached trial in regional courts, and they had found him guilty every time. This trip to Norway would, it was hoped, unearth evidence in support of a fifth murder conviction.

By now Quick had remembered how he had killed Therese but he lacked a last, crucial fact. He was unable to reveal where he had hidden the body. Therese had disappeared from her home without a trace. The investigation desperately needed to identify her remains. Without this last piece in the jigsaw, it would be difficult to bring the case to trial. This was a new challenge for the team that had formed around Quick. The bodies in the four prior murder convictions had been found long before Quick's confessions.

The media had pursued Thomas Quick for years and journalists were keen to get a glimpse of him. But the Swedes needed peace and quiet to do their work. The Norwegian police had declared Örje Forest off-limits and had forbidden access to the airspace above it. All routes into the forest were closed by police road blocks. No effort was spared to help Quick make this important breakthrough.

The previous year, Quick had made an attempt to show the way to the place where the girl's body was hidden. At that time his mental image was of the body lying near a disused gravel quarry.[1] But in the forest, in a state of great distress, he had led the team to a small lake. He had dismembered the body of the nine-year-old on the banks of the lake, then dropped the pieces of her body in the water.

That summer, the Norwegians had launched the country's biggest crime investigation since the Second World War. Approximately 35,000 cubic metres of the forest lake was drained. The silt layer was dredged and then sieved. The mud was explored to such a depth that experts identified decayed material some 10,000 years old.[2] Sadly, no trace of a body was found.

This investigation told its own story about Thomas Quick's seriously problematic memory. It was not until the police had informed him of the unproductive pond operation that Quick remembered he had only taken pieces of the girl's flesh while swimming. Those pieces would have rotted by now. As more memories emerged, he had vivid visions of the girl's pink lungs, which had seemed almost to glow as they floated on the dark surface of the lake.[3] He had hidden the dismembered skeleton inside mysterious cavities that he called 'caches'. His caches were sacred places, built up with stones and camouflaged. Just thinking about the caches caused Quick such profound anguish that he had so far been unable to lead the police to a single one of them.

In the year following that abortive operation Quick had undergone continuous and intense psychotherapy. Now, the whole team returned to Norway for another attempt. His story of how he dealt with the flesh and the skeleton might be true; on the other hand, it might be something he had dreamed up because the truth was too painful to tell. The team knew that their man sometimes had to avoid telling the truth, but that did not, they thought, diminish his overall trustworthiness. The recovery of certain memories caused him extreme distress, and sometimes he could find relief only by providing false information. He knew that he lied 'so that that his mind would not be wrecked by the anguish he felt during the ongoing investigation', as the lead police interviewer Seppo Penttinen put it in an article.[4]

Regardless of the ins and outs of the lake story, Quick's latest bid was that the bones of the child's body were to be found somewhere in Örje Forest and that he was ready to lead the way to the caches.

After a swift lunch, brought by the Norwegian police and eaten on the side of the road, everyone piled into the vehicles and drove deeper into the forest. Quick was in a minibus, accompanied by the senior investigating officer, the psychotherapist, the lawyer, the memory expert, a senior officer from the Norwegian violent crime squad and a sound technician who taped every word Quick uttered. The Swedish prosecutor in charge of the investigation, Christer van der Kwast, was in the next car. He had decided to travel to Norway, not because he had to, but because he wanted to be there when they unearthed what was left of the corpse. Van der Kwast wore headphones so that he, too, could hear everything Quick said. A team of Norwegian police dog handlers went in their own car.

The caravan rolled slowly along the track. Soon, Quick called a halt. He wanted to reconnoitre. They had arrived at the once-drained lake and, for a while, he stood looking at the water. He didn't speak. Then he returned to the minibus.

After a few hundred metres they reached a gravelled area surrounded by trees. Quick wanted to get out and walk. He explained where the cars should park and then wandered off among the trees to have a pee. According to a Norwegian police report, he was heard repeating to himself, 'We've arrived, we've arrived.' The party's expectations rose. A cache must be nearby.

Christianson, the memory expert, had talked with Quick several times in the patient's small room at Säter. Christianson, who was an expert witness for the prosecution, was gathering material for his book *Inside the Mind of a Serial Killer*. It had been hoped that where the therapy sessions and the police interviews had failed he might be successful in extracting information from Quick. And Christianson succeeded. In time for the journey to Norway, he had found out about the kind of tools needed to open the enigmatic caches. His report suggested that the police should bring 'an implement for breaking the ground, e.g. a pick, a small spade or similar'.[5] Also, Quick might want to open a cache himself and, if so, he would say something along the lines of, 'I'm now going to open this place of burial', or, 'Would you open it . . . lift it so I can have a feel inside.' The memory expert recommended that the police should promise Quick 'a private moment' alone with 'a bone fragment, e.g. a rib' once the cache had been opened. If allowed this he might be persuaded to overcome his immense reluctance to hand over his relics, a reaction which, in Christianson's experience, was typical of serial killers.

Christianson had also included a list of important items to bring on the journey: 'Coffee, water/soft drinks. Sandwiches, chocolate bars (sweets) and cigarettes. Medication: xanol (?), dosage as required by TQ.' Actually he got the name of the medicine slightly wrong. He meant Xanax (alprazolam, banned in some countries), one of the many controlled substances prescribed for Thomas Quick. He needed large doses because, as the group was well aware, without medication he didn't have a hope of dealing with the terrible anxiety that accompanied his memory recovery. The psychiatric nurses were on permanent high alert, ready to provide tablets whenever he asked. The party, led by Quick, left the gravelled area and walked into the forest. A Swedish police report noted that Quick was soon 'in great distress and [asking] for help'. This was the sign they had all hoped for. Quick was on the brink of the kind of mental trip back in time which the team knew to call 'regression' or 'time shift'.

Anna Wikström, a police constable, later reported: 'At that moment, Thomas Quick screams out his anguish in the words "nomis come and help me". Thomas Quick shouts this phrase out loudly across the area. *Nomis* is the name Simon reversed. *Simon* is a frequently occurring theme in the therapeutic work with Thomas Quick's inner world.'[6]

The police constable knew that the serial killer had regressed to 1954 or, rather, had become four years old. Here, in the middle of the forest, he was reliving the dreadful event that the staff at Säter hospital had identified as the primary cause of his impulse to kill. The so-called 'Simon event' was a trauma so appalling that few horror films could touch it. Four-year-old Sture, sexually abused since infancy, was being assaulted by his father when his heavily pregnant mother entered the bedroom, naked from the waist down. As she stood by the bed, she had a late miscarriage. Sture watched his prematurely born brother dangling on the umbilical cord between his mother's legs and decided

7

to call the baby Simon. His mother accused Sture of causing the miscarriage because he had aroused his father's libido. Next, the bedroom became the scene of a violent orgy. His father ran to the kitchen for a knife and, while Sture looked on, his parents carved up the baby's body as part of a sex act. They forced Sture to eat parts of its flesh.[7]

Everyone in the Quick team knew about the 'Simon event' and that the entire Bergwall family had been deeply dysfunctional. The police interviews with Thomas Quick's six siblings confirmed this belief, precisely because of the way they all categorically denied that their parents had been abusive. They also insisted that their mother had not been pregnant in 1954. Clearly Quick's brothers and sisters had repressed their traumatic childhood experiences.

It was obvious to the party in Örje Forest that Quick was now mentally reliving the emotionally charged 'Simon event'. He had a vision of his little brother, which made him call out his name. As so often in the past, Quick used 'Nomis', because saying the name backwards caused him less pain. The regression into the past was a good omen, since Quick would recover memories of his murders during these episodes.

After a while, Quick managed to pull himself together. He said that they were now close to a cache, but asked to be driven to another area, a bit further away. He wanted to find out if the other cache would be psychologically easier to reveal.[8] Once there, he left the gravelled track and started to climb a slope.

By now, Quick showed what senior investigating officer Penttinen described as 'evident anguish' and his behaviour grew eccentric. Penttinen says that Quick, 'while climbing, clasps his hands into a ball shape which he appears to carry close to his body'.[9] Wikström's report takes up the narrative:

Quick then continues, powerfully anxious, to walk a little further into the forest where he kneels near a tree trunk. Here he examines the smell and taste of the bark on the tree. [...] Thomas Quick also puts his hand under a stone and feels underneath it and, at this point in time, curls up in a foetal position in a small hollow. Thomas

Quick's mind is in powerful turmoil and members of staff intervene. He states that he is near a hiding place but that he lacks the strength to go there.[10]

That members of staff 'intervene' meant that Thomas Quick was given more Xanax. After swallowing the tablets, he told Claes Borgström, his solicitor, that they were within 20–25 metres of a cache and that he would later indicate exactly where it was located.[11] The party moved on again and the serial killer soon recognized the place. The police constable reports:

> Thomas Quick [...] looks up into the sky. He raises his voice and counts five different areas several times. Penttinen and myself ask what these five signify. After a while, with a hint of irritation, Thomas Quick states, loudly and clearly, [...] it represents five kinds of internal organs: one, the heart, two, the kidneys, three, the liver, four, probably the stomach and five, something else that I at present cannot recall. Thomas Quick shouts out these five items several times.

Of course, Quick had revealed that Therese's organs had not been sunk into the pool but deposited in five separate caches. Soon afterwards, he suffered another anxiety attack and set out at a run. Constable Wikström describes it: 'Penttinen manages to grab hold of his sweater but Thomas Quick tears himself free and continues along a narrow track that follows the ridge. Keeping pace with him but staying about one metre behind, I allow him to run freely.'[12]

They ran until Quick stumbled and fell head first into a pile of stones. Two police officers grabbed hold of him to break the fall. For a few minutes, he lay there, apparently out cold. Then he suddenly came to and said: 'I'm so close now.'

Wikström's account again:

> He tells us in an anguished voice about place number one, i.e. the first place sought in today's re-enactment, where we will find the torso, including the ribs. Place number two, i.e. the place for

Therese's head, is located in the gravel and sand quarry further along the ridge. As for place number three, where we were at that point in time, it is where Therese's thighs, feet and arms are buried. He says, 'I chopped her feet off.'[13]

The re-enactment exercise continued all afternoon but despite several attempts Thomas Quick could never quite locate a cache. At the end of the day, the team brought him to a place where a birch had stood until the Norwegian police cut it down and carried it off for forensic examination. They suspected that a mark in the bark might have been carved by Quick at the time of the murder in 1988. Quick had not been able to find the birch on his own, but now that he was taken to the right place, he recognized it and confirmed that he had carved that mark. The memory of a gruesome ritual came back to him. The senior investigating officer wrote in his report that he 'had understood the description as foll[ows]: T Q had held the girl's chopped-off hand in his own, as well as a knife and [at the same time] carved the symbol into the tree bark.'[14]

By then, it was after six in the evening and the re-enactment had lasted for more than five hours. Quick was getting tired. So far, he hadn't been able to approach any of the caches, but there was still hope. He announced that one of Therese's hands was in a small cache of its own near the felled birch. He was even ready to reveal how it was constructed. The girl's hand was surrounded by several small stones arranged in a cross-shape. He had placed bigger stones on top of the cross and then sealed it with something that he didn't care to speak about. When asked if he could show the police the place, he said that he had no energy left.[15] In the end, though, the group managed to persuade him to try. Penttinen describes how Quick took on his own repression mechanisms in the last arduous struggle of that day: 'After the felled birch had been indicated to him, Quick goes to stand just a few metres from it. He then outlines a sector with his hands. The area stretches uphill and away from the road. Quick also tries to show where the "cache" is by walking slowly from his original position and in the direction shown by his hands.'[16]

But the attempt failed. The Norwegian police reported: 'After being urged to find the cache, TQ began walking in the direction of the area that he had previously indicated as the hiding place. He moved extremely slowly and looked stiff and uneasy. After some 15–20 metres, TQ burst into tears. He said that he could not make it.'[17]

The Quick team would not see him open any cache that day. However, before the re-enactment was over for the day, he carried out a ritual near the stump of the birch tree: 'Quick demands a moment of solitude near the tree and staggers towards it. He crouches, pats the stump with his hands, pulls off a handful of leaves and thin twigs, and removes a sliver of wood from the trunk. Then he returns to the road and strolls along to the minibus provided by the Swedish national police.'[18]

No immediate breakthrough, then, but Penttinen was feeling hopeful all the same. After all, Quick had described where in the forest the cache with the hand was to be found: 'At an earlier stage, Quick had stamped on the ground and explained that it was similar to the earth where the hand had been buried. The ground where Quick stood was soft, mossy and had a certain amount of give.'[19]

Next, the Norwegians would undertake major excavations in Örje Forest. Penttinen accompanied Quick in the minibus that took them back to Säter hospital. He would later report on the journey to his Norwegian colleagues, saying that Quick had been terse but convinced that the police would find what they were looking for in the sites he had shown them. The intense media scrutiny meant that the Norwegians decided to delay the digging for three weeks.[20]

In the end they found no trace of Therese Johannessen.

On Friday 4 July, Anna Wikström, Seppo Penttinen's assistant, talked with Thomas Quick, alone with him in his room at Säter, about the disappointing result. The serial killer, worried about it himself, had asked for the meeting. He had just retrieved a memory of how he had returned to Örje Forest, in 1989 or 1990, collected all the body parts and taken them away. To the bitter end, he kept hoping that the police would find a 'finger bone' that he thought he might have left behind. He was also quite sure that the girl's head was still in the forest. He could now reveal that he had dug a pit for it in a 'secret place'. Wikström cautiously asked how deep the pit was. Quick replied: 'I don't have the courage to know that at this point.'[21]

The Norwegians gave up searching for the five caches in Örje Forest but, a year later, Thomas Quick was convicted of the murder of Therese Johannessen. There were no witness statements and no forensic data that linked him to the missing girl. He had never been able to reveal where he had hidden her body. However, none of this affected his credibility. The doctors and psychotherapists at Säter explained that all Quick's murders were enacted by his subconscious as symbolic narratives about the abuse he had been subjected to as a child but had later repressed. This was why Quick found it so difficult to remember his deeds. He was convicted of Therese's murder solely on the basis of his confession, which was accepted as truthful – as was the case in all his eight court convictions for murder between 1994 and 2001.

Providence had been good to the Quick team. If they had not been informed early on about how memory repression works, everyone might have jumped to the conclusion that the serial killer was lying. Without that special insight, the first murder investigation would have closed a few months after the first police interview with Quick in 1993. This didn't happen, of course. The team had acquired the essential expert knowledge in the nick of time and understood that Quick really was a credible serial killer even though he tended not to remember what his victims looked like, where he had killed them or how he had gone about hiding their remains.

What was the source of the expertise the team had benefited from? The answer was quite straightforward. The knowledge flowed from a stylish Art Nouveau apartment block on Norrtull Street in Stockholm and, more precisely, from a tastefully redecorated top-floor flat.[22] A private psychoanalytic practice could be reached through a door round the corner on Vidar Street, which patients were advised to use when they came to see the psychoanalyst, a white-haired old lady who spent her days at work in an armchair, listening.

When the Örje Forest excavations were in full swing during the summer of 1997, this analyst was eighty-three years old. She worked full-time, however, and had no intention of retiring.

This was Thomas Quick's real psychotherapist. The Säter hospital psychologists were her tools; they thought that she had a positively superhuman capacity for insight into the psychological connections between past and present. It was this woman who had established that Quick's murders were symbolic narratives that retold forgotten episodes of childhood abuse. Only she could interpret Quick's dreams. Overall, she regarded Thomas Quick as the most important case she had come across in her forty years as a psychoanalyst.

Every week, Quick's hospital psychologist made the round trip between Säter and Stockholm to see the analyst and discuss what the serial killer had said and done during the therapy sessions. This routine was established from the start of the therapy in November 1991, and so it would continue until 2002, when the therapy was ended at the request of the patient.

The analyst was compiling a massive manuscript which included the most interesting reports on Quick, as well as her analysis. It was to become a book: 'The World of Thomas Quick'. She believed that this book, her magnum opus, might fundamentally change our understanding of human psychology. Indeed, she believed that the case of Thomas Quick would become more significant than Sigmund Freud's case study of 'The Wolf Man'. She spent all her free time working on the book. Everyone who knew her agreed that she was obsessed with Thomas Quick.

However, she never called him Thomas Quick.

She called him Sture.

2

The funeral of an investigator

'Stories generated at the intersection of law and human psychology are irresistible.'
Interview with the journalist Hannes Råstam,
summer 2011

Masthugg Church stands on a hill high above Gothenburg, the second largest city in Sweden. The panoramic view from outside the church door takes in the harbour and a glimpse of the North Sea. Skagen, the northernmost tip of Denmark, lies some 80 kilometres straight to the west. The Norwegian border is about 150 kilometres to the north – as is Örje Forest.

It was at Masthugg that my investigation of the Quick scandal would begin, but I had no idea at the time. I had travelled to Gothenburg to attend the funeral of a friend of mine, the investigative journalist Hannes Råstam. In 2008, Hannes had interviewed Sture Bergwall and persuaded him to admit that he was not a serial killer. Although Bergwall had confessed to thirty-nine murders and had been found guilty of eight of them, the truth was that he was not a killer at all. This remarkable revelation led to a series of retrials unprecedented in Swedish legal history.

That day, the church was full of mourners. Hannes was only fifty-six years old when he died. Next to his white coffin someone had placed a small framed photograph of him surrounded by his children. They all looked very happy together. He cared deeply about his work, and had hoped to resist the cancer long enough to be around when Bergwall's last sentence for murder was torn up in court. He didn't come close.

I liked Hannes. He was a very unusual journalist. When he was thirty-six he gave up a successful career as bass player in a well-known rock band and went off to take a college course in journalism. He turned out to be their oldest ever student. Much later, he edited a couple of TV documentaries that I had produced and we became friends. Then he started producing his own documentaries with outstanding success. In the few years of his career as a journalist, he was behind some major scoops. His secret was his ability to analyse huge quantities of paperwork. When something captured Hannes's interest, he would keep at it round the clock, reading everything he could find and remembering most of what he read. It was no accident that he had exposed the Quick verdicts for what they were: arguably Sweden's biggest legal scandal in modern times.

As I waited in my pew for the funeral service to begin, I thought about Hannes and his revelations about Quick. The events leading up to the conviction of the criminal known as Thomas Quick began in April 1991, when a mixed substance abuser called Sture Bergwall was convicted for aggravated robbery and sentenced to treatment at Säter, a forensic psychiatric hospital that specializes in treating criminal offenders. From the autumn of that year he received regular psychotherapy. Another year at Säter and Bergwall confessed to murder. Six months later, the police were informed. Over the following nine years the police reopened a number of old investigations, all focused on Bergwall, who had changed his name to Thomas Quick before the police investigations began. In the end six different courts convicted him of eight murders. The first conviction was in 1994, when the court found him guilty of the murder of fifteen-year-old Charles Zelmanovits in the northern town of Piteå. In 1996, Bergwall was found guilty of the murder of two Dutch tourists, Marinus and Janni Stegehuis, who had been knifed to death while asleep inside their tent near Lake Appojaure in the far north. In 1997, Bergwall was convicted of beating an Israeli tourist called Yenon Levi to death (Levi's body was found in Rörshyttan, some 40 kilometres from Säter) and in 1998 of the abduction and murder of Therese Johannessen. He was tried and found guilty of the murder of two Norwegian women, Gry Storvik and Trine Jensen from Oslo, in 2000, and of the murder of the school-boy Johan Asplund, from Sundsvall, in 2001.

By the time the 2001 sentence was pronounced, chief prosecutor Christer van der Kwast had already told Quick that he was suspected of murders nine and ten. Quick had admitted to killing two missing persons and the police had opened the murder investigations. One of them concerned Marianne Rugaas Knudsen, a seven-year-old Norwegian girl who left her home in Risør in 1981 to buy sweets and never came back. The other alleged victim was Olle Högbom, a Swedish eighteen-year-old youth who vanished in 1983 after leaving a school party in central Sundsvall. The unsolved case of a three-year-old boy whose dead body had been found in a waste bin enclosure in Jönköping was very likely to become the eleventh murder investigation. Quick had already claimed that the little boy was 'one of his'. Once the prosecutor succeeded in getting Quick tried and convicted in these three cases, he could move on down a long list of other confessions. He had every reason to assume that the Quick cases would keep him busy until he retired and a new chief prosecutor took over.

Hannes Råstam was not the first to question Thomas Quick's confessions. There were those who had reservations about him from the start. Leif G. W. Persson, a well-known and respected professor of criminology, warned van der Kwast early on that Quick was likely to be a compulsive liar. As the years went by, some police officers took the same view and a few of them resigned in protest at the way the investigations were carried out. A handful of journalists wrote critical articles, among them Dan Larsson, who in 1998, went to the lengths of listing in a self-published book his reasons for believing that Thomas Quick was a liar.[23] The Quick case was often debated by the media, but Larsson's book had little impact. Jan Guillou, a well-known and popular journalist, was similarly critical. Among those who publicly doubted Quick's confessions were psychologists, lawyers and other notable professionals. On the whole, however, doubters were few and far between.

Quick let it be known that he was deeply pained by all this criticism. His confessions were meant to help his victims' friends and relatives to achieve closure and also to offer new psychological insights into the identification of would-be serial killers. He felt misunderstood and insulted. But his offended tone prepared no one for the slap-down he had in store. In 2001, after his eighth (and last) murder conviction, the serial killer wrote an article which was published in *Dagens Nyheter*, a leading daily newspaper, announcing his decision to take what he called 'time out' – indefinitely. He claimed that he could no longer endure the wounding criticism he was subjected to:

> I intend to take time out for my own sake, hoping to hold on to my will to live. I am a human being, after all, and it is only human to crave confirmation that my story is morally valid and legally important. That I should have to cope, year after year, with the unfounded claims directed at me by a band of false witnesses who say that I am a mythomaniac and stand by while this small group is uncritically offered space in the media, is and will continue to be, too much like hard work.[24]

Having made himself clear, Thomas Quick refused to take part in any more police interviews and ended his ten year course of psychotherapy.

It was another seven years before Hannes Råstam exposed the truth about why Quick stopped collaborating. The driving force had been Göran Källberg, a psychiatrist who had worked at Säter and returned as its medical director after a few years at another hospital. Källberg personally took on the clinical management of Quick. Reviewing his patient's prescriptions, he found much cause for concern. He suspected that Quick's addiction to benzodiazepine tranquillizers might have something to do with his strange confessions. Källberg decided that the patient needed detoxification. He explained his decision in a newspaper interview: 'Benzodiazepines reduce inhibitions and the patient took them in addictive doses. It is beyond any doubt that his statements in court will have been affected. I would not trust anyone who consumed these substances on such a scale.'[25]

Quick's daily intake had been so high that safe withdrawal required a dosage reduction regime carried out over nine months. His first completely drug-free day since his teens in the 1960s was on 22 February 2002. Five days later, he went back to using his given name, Sture Bergwall. Then the serial killer withdrew into a long silence.

Christer van der Kwast knew that without Thomas Quick's cooperation, it would be useless to try to bring the prosecution's cases to court. In February 2002, he reluctantly decided to stop a handful of ongoing murder investigations. By 2008, Sture Bergwall had not been front page news for a long time. Most people had lost interest in this strange man. Not so Hannes Råstam. He made a documentary about false confessions and another that touched on how some forms of psychotherapy can create false memories. Next, he settled down to investigate the case of Thomas Quick.

He soon realized that he had found a challenge worthy of his skills. The long series of murder investigations had generated a huge number of documents: verbatim accounts of police interviews, reports of forensic medical examinations, crime site investigation protocols and so on, folder upon folder, shelf upon shelf. He persuaded the police to let him have access to the tape recordings of interviews and the videos of crime site re-enactments like the operation in the Örje Forest. He worked late into the night, sometimes phoning me from his car at around ten o'clock, on his way to the office after saying goodnight to his family. At this time, Sture Bergwall had spent several years leading an isolated and very tightly scheduled life. Precisely timetabled days had helped him cope with the stressful drug withdrawal programme and, once drug-free, he stuck to his routines. At six o'clock every morning, he went for a brisk hour-long walk, usually in the hospital's largest interior courtyard, a rectangular garden of roughly 20 by 40 metres. To avoid getting dizzy he would walk in a figure of eight. He spent most of the day in his room (about 11 square metres), where he solved crosswords and read books. He had a stereo and TV set. No one, including his immediate family, ever called or phoned, and he refused all interview requests.

And so the years went by.

On the 22 April 2008, Hannes wrote a letter to Sture Bergwall and asked to meet. Bergwall said that he had liked Hannes's TV reportage and agreed to the interview. They met twice that summer.

A couple of months later, Hannes called me. He was on his way back from Säter and wanted to tell me that he had scooped a story so huge he didn't dare say exactly what had happened. Since I knew that his research had led him to believe that Bergwall's confessions were false, I assumed that the alleged killer had retracted them. Over the next eighteen months, Hannes made three hour-long television documentaries which strongly suggested that six unanimous District Courts had convicted an innocent man of eight murders.

The fact that Bergwall had gone back on his confessions did not mean that acquittals would be granted immediately or at any time. In Sweden, confession alone, without independent evidence, is not sufficient for a criminal verdict. Consequently, claiming that your confession was false does not automatically lead to the conviction being quashed. Generally, retrials of murder convictions are extremely rare and have only been granted on a few occasions in the twentieth century. At the time most people considered Bergwall's chances of being freed to be practically non-existent. Certainly, some of the trials may have been flawed – but all of them? It seemed implausible. Then, to general astonishment, in December 2008, a lawyer called Thomas Olsson announced that he would act for Bergwall and lodge retrial applications in all eight murder cases. Because his client was penniless, Olsson undertook to act pro bono. In other words, unless he succeeded in getting Bergwall freed he would not be paid.

Just reading through the mass of paperwork that had accumulated on Quick would take months. More daunting still, Olsson had to put together detailed appeals persuasive enough to give Sture Bergwall a sporting chance of a retrial in at least one of the cases. He had committed himself to years of work without pay while keeping on salaried assistants, without whom the job would be impossible. He was apparently prepared to put his own finances on the line in order to see a multiply convicted man go free.

In April 2009, four months after the broadcast of Hannes's first Quick documentary, Thomas Olsson submitted his first application for retrial. He had decided to begin with the murder of the Israeli tourist Yenon Levi. The application itself consisted of 73 pages, divided into 274 numbered sections. It was backed up by several folders of additional material. Olsson's arguments proved crushingly effective, reviewing each element of van der Kwast's prosecution before grinding it to dust. By the time the reader reached Section 274, the murder verdict had been revealed as a scandalous miscarriage of justice. The conviction of Sture Bergwall seemed nothing short of incredible, since the evidence against him was non-existent and the indications that he had been lying were plentiful. It was as alarming as it was astonishing.

For three months, a senior prosecutor based in Malmö scrutinized the retrial application and the paperwork of the original case. If he refused a retrial after studying the documentation it would be the end of the road for the appeal. But he didn't and the application went to the Svea Court of Appeal for another three months of scrutiny. The outcome was sensational. Sture Bergwall had succeeded with something almost without precedent. Three Appeal Court judges had unanimously decided to grant him a retrial.

The case was handed over to a new chief prosecutor called Eva Finné. She spent another three months going through Thomas Olsson's objections to the murder investigation. If her review revealed any reasonable basis for assuming that Sture Bergwall was guilty, Finné's investigation would have resulted in a new trial against Bergwall. However, she found no grounds for suspicion and cancelled the preliminary investigation in May 2010. Sture Bergwall was officially innocent of the murder of Yenon Levi.

Olsson and his assistants laboured on. One retrial application after another wound its way through the judicial system. New prosecutors examined the applications and arrived at the same conclusion every time: Sture Bergwall had been convicted on profoundly flawed grounds. Thanks to Thomas Olsson, he won case after case. It was astonishing.

The reinvestigations demonstrated that chief prosecutor Christer van der Kwast and his senior investigating officer Seppo Penttinen had managed to persuade the courts that Thomas Quick's accounts of his murders had been much more coherent and plausible than was actually the case. Interrogations had consisted of asking him leading questions and allowing him to change the details over and over again if his answers didn't fit the facts. In spite of this helpful prodding, his final confessions were full of errors. The retrial applications read like catalogues of Quick's mistakes. His convictions were quashed because, in the opinion of all the retrial prosecutors, if the courts had had the slightest idea of how the interrogations were conducted, none of the guilty verdicts would have been returned.

The retrial process took a long time. When the second verdict was torn up in 2011, Hannes phoned Bergwall at Säter to congratulate him. Since the day Bergwall retracted his confessions, they had spoken on the phone almost daily. By then, Hannes was working on a book about the 'Quick affair' but stomach pains made writing difficult. He had no appetite and was losing weight. Three weeks later, Hannes went to see a doctor at Sahlgrenska hospital. The doctors identified metastatic growths in his liver but couldn't find the primary tumour. Hannes had only a few months left to live.

He held out for nine months, but lost the struggle and died in his Gothenburg home on 12 January 2012. Two months later, prosecutor Jonas Almström decided to close the preliminary investigation into the murder of the eleven-year-old boy Johan Asplund. Olsson phoned Bergwall to tell him that he had been acquitted a third time.

This time, there was no call from Hannes.

Eighteen months later Sture Bergwall was cleared of all his murder convictions.

After five years of retrials, eleven prosecutors and fifteen Court of Appeal judges had reviewed the conduct of the investigations and found it wanting in each case. The role played by the group around Sture Bergwall was obvious. The 'Quick team' had persuaded one regional court after another to return guilty verdicts on a drug addict who had confessed to bizarre deeds he knew next to nothing about. The Quick team had been united by a shared creed: the prosecutor Christer van der Kwast, the psychologist Birgitta Ståhle, the police officer Seppo Penttinen, the memory expert Sven Å Christianson – even the lawyer acting for the defence, Claes Borgström. Borgström had practically pleaded for the prosecution; he had been known to argue in his final plea that it would be 'tragic' if his client was *not* convicted of murder.[26]

Why had the Quick team behaved in this way? Hannes knew that he would not have time to answer that question before he died. During what would be the last summer of his life, he put it like this:

> Stories generated at the intersection of law and human psychology are irresistible . . . But . . . even if one arrived at some insight into Quick's mind and his reasons for confessing, another even greater mystery would be waiting: the mentalities of Seppo Penttinen, Christer van der Kwast, Claes Borgström, Birgitta Ståhle and Sven Åke Christianson. How could they keep this circus up and running? They toured crime sites while Quick was as high as a kite and slurred his words, couldn't speak straight, and yet the man was supposed to remember, in detail, what happened fifteen years ago. If you want to talk about a psychological enigma – they're all enigmatic. And all of them are highly educated people.[27]

The group psychology was made still more mysterious by the fact that none of the team members seemed all that troubled by the retrial applications and their outcomes. Penttinen, as well as the (now retired) chief prosecutor van der Kwast, stubbornly insisted that the verdicts had been correct in each case. Christianson agreed and defence advocate Borgström regretted nothing. Neither Birgitta Ståhle nor any of the other Säter therapists who had treated Bergwall ever uttered a word in public. Officially, none of the five people on Hannes's list retracted a single word, even in the face of the overturned convictions, as one experienced prosecutor after another declared that there was no evidence against the defendant. It was truly inexplicable.

Hannes Råstam was given a musician's funeral in Masthugg Church. Globetrotters, the band he had toured with for fifteen years, played a beautiful version of 'When the Bombs Fall', the 1982 protest song by

Björn Afzelius, which Hannes had liked and sometimes listened to while he worked. That day the band performed without their bass player. I cried a little where I sat in my pew, and then spent the evening with some mutual friends. We drank wine and told each other stories about Hannes. I had no idea that, just three days later, I would start working on the same enigma that my friend had been talking about before he died.

3

An even greater mystery

'Paralysed, I observe in the mirror the reflection of a self that does not exist.'
Thomas Quick, quoted in Margit Norell's unpublished
book 'The World of Thomas Quick'.

A couple of nights after I had returned to Stockholm, I woke in the middle of the night. My family was asleep, but I felt restless. I kept thinking about Hannes and about Bergwall, who of course had not been allowed to attend the funeral. I assumed that he must be a deeply unpleasant person and a reckless liar, but I believed that Hannes might have wished for Bergwall to have a chance to say goodbye. I knew that they had talked on the phone almost daily for three and a half years. I climbed out of bed and took my laptop along to the kitchen table. It was a little after three in the morning and the house was silent. I thought I might do Hannes a small, sentimental good turn by trying to give this Sture Bergwall character a kind of second-hand experience of the funeral. His email address was available online, so I wrote to him explaining that I was one of Hannes's friends and went on to tell him about the ceremony in Masthugg Church, adding YouTube links to the music. After that I felt ready to go back to bed.

When I woke in the morning, Bergwall had replied. He wrote that Hannes had spoken about me from time to time, that he was grateful for my message and that he had wept as he read it. Later the same day, his older brother phoned me. Sten-Ove Bergwall, a retired journalist and writer, said that Sture had forwarded my email to him and that he, too, had found the brief account very moving. It had led him to ask for my help with an important but so far unexplored aspect of the

24

Quick scandal. As he saw it, the erroneous verdicts had their origins less in the police investigations and more in his brother's treatment at Säter hospital. Sten-Ove had tried to write a book about the Säter therapy, but hadn't been able to find a publisher. Would I see what I could do? I promised to read the manuscript.

Sten-Ove's manuscript turned out to be an angry tract aimed at Säter's psychotherapists and doctors. The main source of evidence for the accusations was Sture Bergwall himself and his hospital notes. I thought about it and then phoned Sten-Ove to tell him that, in my opinion, his article was not sufficiently well researched to add to Hannes's incisive investigative journalism. It should be possible to identify people who knew what had really happened at Säter, and why. To get to the heart of Säter's secrets, one must find some way of approaching the initiates. He listened, took what I said on board and agreed with me, then asked if I would undertake the investigation. At seventy years of age, and not entirely well, he was not sure that he was up to the task himself. I promised to consider it.

It is true that I am not a complete stranger to the world of psychotherapy. Before I decided to become a journalist, I had worked as an assistant nurse in a closed psychiatric ward. One experimental approach to the care of young psychotic patients had been to offer them talking therapy. In the 1990s, when Sweden was battered by an economic crisis, the ward was shut down as part of health service cuts. This was when I changed careers: I studied journalism at Stockholm University and, afterwards, wrote on social and cultural issues for newspapers and worked as a television producer in investigative journalism. In 2006, I returned to psychology after the birth of my first child, co-writing a book about attachment theory and love relationships that was aimed at a general audience. Ten years had passed since my last investigative job; I was rusty and, besides, I had a family to look after. But Sten-Ove's plea for help had fired my imagination. Even as we were talking, a plan was beginning to take shape. Perhaps I could use my background in psychology as a passport that would allow me to enter the closed world of psychotherapy. But first I had to find out more about the Quick affair and what was known about his psychotherapy.

As it turned out, not that much was known about his treatment. He had been seeing two psychotherapists: one was a doctor, a psychiatrist called Kjell Persson; the other a psychologist, Birgitta Ståhle. Dr Persson treated Quick from the autumn of 1991 until the spring of 1994, when he left his post at Säter. Birgitta Ståhle was primarily responsible for Quick's treatment until 2002, when the psychotherapy was stopped at Quick's request. The information on how these two therapists had managed their patient was not in the public domain. Neither of them had agreed to be interviewed since the first retrial applications were lodged. When journalists contacted them, they invoked professional confidentiality and put the phone down.

During his work on the first retrial application, Thomas Olsson had asked Anna Dåderman, a senior academic expert in forensic psychiatry, to examine Sture Bergwall's medical case history, including his medication regime. Her report was very critical of the practice of allowing Bergwall almost to self-administer substances classed as addictive at dose levels so high that she described them as 'experimental' rather than therapeutic.[28] From the patient's notes, she also concluded that he had been treated with 'recovered memory therapy'. The idea behind this method is to make the patients aware of memories that they have 'repressed', usually of childhood abuse.

In the middle of the 1980s, recovered memory therapy was in vogue, but the method came under increasing scrutiny. Critically, it was not supported in the growing body of new research. That traumatic events could be 'pushed out' of active memory only to return later in life was a construct that had been around since the end of the nineteenth century but had always been controversial. Doubts were expressed in the worlds of psychoanalysis and scientific psychology.[29]

Research into memory function had also demonstrated that it is amazingly easy to create false memories.[30] Although therapists believed that they were trying to help a patient retrieve or 'recover' what until then had been 'repressed' episodes of childhood sexual abuse, they instead ran the risk of creating new, false 'memories' which soon became indistinguishable from the real thing. Obviously this kind of interference might lead to tragedies in the lives of both the patient and their relatives.[31] In her expert's report on Sture Bergwall's treatment, Dåderman pointed out that the risk of accidentally implanting false memories is well known to practitioners and becomes more likely if the patient is prescribed certain classes of drugs while the interventions are carried out.[32]

However, at Säter the clinicians' response was to dismiss Dåderman's criticism. For one thing, they insisted, no one had tried to recover Sture Bergwall's repressed memories. I came across a report from 2009 sent by Ståhle to the social services department. In it, she claims again and again that she had never used the memory recovery approach in her therapy sessions with Sture Bergwall. In fact, she had never even heard of it:

> With regard to the therapeutic method known as Recovered Memory Therapy (induced memory retrieval), Dåderman feels it is based on suggestion and would contribute to implanting false memories. She further believes that this method, in combination with pharmacological treatments carried out in parallel with such therapy, had a direct causal relationship to Sture Bergwall's desire to confess to crimes that he had not committed. [...] Those basic suppositions are completely incorrect. Consequently, Anna Dåderman bases her conclusions on false premises. In my capacity as a professional psychologist, I have never worked with this method and have never encountered it, neither in a clinical nor a theoretical context.[33]

Straight talking, no ifs or buts. Ståhle had also been interviewed by chief prosecutor Björn Ericson and DCI Kjell-Åke Wendt, who had been appointed to scrutinize Sture Bergwall's retrial applications. Ståhle's interview statements were just as unambiguous: 'This retrial application includes an expert's report by Anna Dåderman. In it, she makes certain claims about the therapy and especially about recovered memory therapy. I do not know of any such therapy and it is not a therapeutic methodology practised at Säter.'[34]

The directors at Säter all sang from the same hymn sheet.

In 2012, when Säter's medical director Dr Susanne Nyberg was interviewed on television, she refused to admit any knowledge of recovered memory therapy, though she was somewhat evasive in her responses: 'That kind of therapy is not something . . . I must say, I know nothing about it. In other words, I'd put it like . . . put it like this, I don't even know if it has . . . if it has been done there, as it were. Only the psychologist who has been carrying out the therapy can describe it, of course. I don't know either . . . if what was said was correct . . . But I've never heard of it.'[35]

Ståhle had taken careful notes during her therapy sessions with Bergwall and it would have been exciting to read her observations. However, as she stated to both the chief prosecutor and the social services department, she had destroyed all her notes. Much later on, I actually found a letter from Ståhle to Penttinen, in which she explained that she had 'tidied away' – as she put it – all her notes immediately after Bergwall stopped his psychotherapeutic treatment in 2002.[36]

In the spring of 2012, I phoned Sture Bergwall and we spoke for more than an hour. He had been declared 'Not Guilty' of five of his eight murder convictions. He was entering his twenty-second year at Säter.

Sture sounded calm and friendly. He had nothing to hide, he said. If I wanted to get to the bottom of what had happened at Säter, he would give me permission to view the medical notes, psychiatric reports and all the other documents that had accumulated around him since he was a little boy at school in the 1950s and, later on, a client of various care institutions and courts. He also promised to send me the numerous letters and notes he had saved from his years as Thomas Quick. Hannes had given him a scanner and a stream of documents started to flow into my inbox the very same day.

I asked Sture whom he held responsible for the fact that he had been wrongly convicted, again and again. He replied that, for the most part, he had himself to blame, but that he shared the responsibility with a woman called Margit Norell. 'It's impossible to exaggerate Margit Norell's importance,' he said. 'Without Margit, no Thomas Quick. That's the long and short of it.'

I searched for information about Margit Norell but, at first, found very little: she was born in 1914, ran a private practice as a psychoanalyst and died in 2005. She had never been employed at Säter but had billed them for acting as an external consultant, or supervisor, to some of the people concerned with Thomas Quick's psychotherapeutic treatment, including Kjell Persson and Birgitta Ståhle.

For a practising psychotherapist, the supervisor's advice serves as a professional touchstone. Usually, supervisor and therapist will meet weekly to discuss the patient and decide how to proceed together. The supervisor will be the more experienced practitioner and substantially influence the patient's treatment. It was possible that Norell could have had steered Sture Bergwall's therapy. But her age must surely have been a factor? In 1991, when Sture was sentenced to forensic psychiatric care, Margit Norell was seventy-seven years old, more than ten years past retirement age. The psychotherapy continued for another eleven years, which means that in 2002, when Sture backed out, Birgitta Ståhle's supervisor was eighty-seven. It seemed strange that a woman of such an advanced age would have been in charge of this particular patient.

Another consideration was that Säter's clinical remit is forensic psychiatry. It simply did not seem plausible that one individual, not even on the in-house staff, could have directed Sture's treatment to the extent that he claimed. Clinical practice must, after all, conform to healthcare legislation and social service department regulations.

But as the mystery deepened I learned in phone calls to Sture that Margit Norell had been surrounded by a retinue of psychotherapists who 'adored her' and had been well informed about what happened during his therapy sessions. Birgitta Ståhle was 'one of Margit's' and one of two who were actually working at Säter. The others were all psychotherapists supervised by Norell but based elsewhere, and had no expertise in forensic psychology.

Sture provided me with a clue to the members of the group. He had a book called *A Room to Live In: A study of deep-seated psychotherapeutic processes and object relations therapy*, published in 1999. This was after he had been convicted of five murders. The book was an anthology intended to introduce a Swedish readership to 'object relations theory', based on the experiences of six women contributors who had applied this theory in their psychotherapy practices. They not only shared the same theoretical approach but also the same supervisor who had 'looked after' them, as they put it, 'for a very long time'. The supervisor was Margit Norell and one of the contributors was none other than Birgitta Ståhle. In her chapter 'Traumatic Experiences and Violent Crime' she describes her work with convicted criminals at Säter. She had picked a quote from an unnamed patient to introduce her chapter: 'I know that my rational mind will crumble after just one more step into the anguish. Paralysed, I observe in the mirror the reflection of a self that does not exist.'[37]

Later, I would discover that Sture was the source of the quote.

Ståhle writes that she started her work with criminals on the assumption that their acts of violence are narratives reflecting experiences which are 'hidden' inside them: 'In the crimes they have committed, these patients have already told us about something [. . .] The criminal act is a re-telling, using a subconscious language, which shows what is concealed inside the internal space.'

The aim of this therapeutic approach was 'to express and shape all concealed memories that have not been integrated and digested'. All this sounded very much like the recovered memory therapy that Anna Dåderman had accused Ståhle of practising and about which Ståhle had claimed total ignorance. However, she expressed herself so vaguely that it was impossible to draw any definite conclusions.

At this stage, though, a handwritten dedication on the inside page of Sture's copy interested me more than the contents of the book. It was written by the psychotherapist Cajsa Lindholm:

> *For Sture,*
> *Thanks for sharing your narrative with us*
> *From Cajsa, on behalf of the authors*

Cajsa Lindholm is a psychotherapist with a private practice in Stockholm's Södermalm area. Despite her apparent distance from the case, by 1999 she was so closely involved that she dedicated the book to 'Sture', a name he had changed some seven years before the book was published. This seemed to confirm that there really was a group surrounding Margit Norell, a group that was close to Sture Bergwall.

Sture had yet another clue for me. He said that Margit Norell had wanted to write a book about him and had given him a printed copy of the incomplete manuscript. He had lodged it with his lawyer in Stockholm.

Thomas Olsson, Sture's lawyer, is a partner of Silberskys, one of Sweden's best-known legal practices. The head office, a handsome building from the turn of the last century, is located at Kungsholm Square in central Stockholm. Olsson turned out to be a slim man with a marked Stockholm accent, hair combed straight back and discreet stubble. When I arrived he showed me the Quick files, crammed into a small mountain of boxes on the floor in his office. The practice had moved recently and he had not yet had time to unpack. Two folders marked *Margit's Selection* contained Margit Norell's manuscript, more than 700 pages in all. I copied the lot and took it home. It was a remarkable document.

The text had been written on a computer, but the changing fonts and erratic page numbering showed that it had been worked on at different times and with different word processors. It comprised a collection of documents from several different sources. Some passages had been written by Margit Norell, others were extracts from Birgitta Ståhle's therapy notes. A large part was made up of Sture's own daily notes, a record of his memories, dreams and fantasies in diary format, which he wrote between the routine therapeutic sessions. Norell also quoted from letters written by Sture to his psychotherapists, as well as the trial proceedings. The trial material included parts of the witness statements by the memory expert Sven Å Christianson, the closing pleas by chief prosecutor Christer van der Kwast and addresses to the court by the defence lawyer Claes Borgström.

Margit Norell seemed to have regarded Sture as a co-writer. At one point, she asked him about the title 'The World of Thomas Quick' – was he happy with it? He said that he was. The manuscript begins with Norell describing how Sture came to be sent to Säter, where his psychotherapy sessions with the medical consultant Kjell Persson began in November 1991. Norell writes: '[F]rom that month onwards, I undertook the supervision of Sture's therapy . . .'[38]

That line is stranger than it sounds. A supervisor is always connected to the supervised psychotherapist, not to any one patient receiving therapy. Here Norell spoke of working on 'the supervision of Sture's therapy', implying that she saw herself as tied to a specific patient rather, than a therapist. When I asked around among psychologists and psychotherapists I knew, everyone agreed that it was unheard of. Another baffling feature was Norell's claim that she had decided who would be Sture's therapist: 'Sture chose Kjell Persson and I supported his choice even though Persson is not a trained psychotherapist.' Effectively, then, Dr Persson, a consultant psychiatrist, required her approval. Norell had to give him the nod before he started to treat Sture Bergwall. Norell also says that Dr Persson stopped working at Säter in the spring of 1994 and that the chief psychologist Birgitta Ståhle replaced him as Sture's therapist. Again, Ståhle reported on the progress of her patient and his management was decided during her weekly meetings with Norell.

I had to wonder at the influence exerted by a psychoanalyst in private practice over a state mental hospital. After all, the patient had been sentenced to forensic psychiatric care. What did a psychoanalyst have to do with this kind of organization at all?

The manuscript grew very interesting once Norell began to explain what she intended to achieve with the therapeutic work. Its one central aim was to help Sture recover his repressed memories. As she put it:

Before the therapeutic process began, Sture could not remember anything that happened to him before the age of 12. His memory of the murders he had committed – a series of events that started when he was 14 years old – have emerged for the first time during the therapy. None of these crimes had previously brought him to the attention of the police, either as a suspect or as part of an investigation. When, in the course of the treatment, a murder and some of its contextual details became sufficiently clear, Sture himself would ask for the police to be involved. He collaborated in interviews and generally in the investigations. The murders emerged in an order and at a pace that he was able to cope with but the next step would always be police involvement. In parallel with this aspect of the therapeutic work, retrieval of deeply traumatic memories of other events from the patient's early years – above all, from when he was 4–5 years old – emerged from their repressed state – at times, in very dramatic ways.

Norell insisted that the psychotherapy offered to Sture at Säter was essential: 'Sture could not have endured [reliving] early life experiences had he not encountered therapists he could trust to stay by him throughout these horrible recoveries.'

The manuscript 'The World of Thomas Quick' relies a great deal on Ståhle's notes, made during the actual therapy sessions – exactly the kind of documentation she 'tidied away' in 2002. One set of notes describes a dramatic session on 25 September 1995, when Sture had only one murder conviction. According to Dr Dåderman's analysis, he was maintained on a combination of hard drugs, mainly benzodiazepines: Stesolid (diazepam), Xanax (alprazolam), Rohypnol (flunitrazepam – a powerful hypnotic) and Heminevrin (clomethiazole, a non-benzodiazepine hypnotic).

I knew that their talking therapy was conducted with him lying on his bed and Ståhle sitting on an armchair at his side. Ståhle wrote that Sture was high, almost manic, when the session began. They were speaking about the 'Simon event'. Sture went into a state of regression and journeyed back in time to 1954. As his relived experiences grew more and more intense, he was able to describe in detail how his parents went about carving up Simon's body. In alternating states, he was now Simon being butchered, now the 'Sture-shell', a description he applied to his four-year-old self, watching as the butchery was carried out. This is how Ståhle describes the event:

The Simon event emerges. Sture swings between being inside the Sture-shell and being Simon. Sture is part of the event and role-plays with gestures, body-language and words throughout its course. When he fuses with Simon, Sture closes his eyes and his whole body expresses the pain of dismemberment. The Sture-shell watches the event with wide-open eyes, registering who does what to Simon/Sture. The eyes of the Sture-shell reflect his paralysed state.

His face is contorted in mortal fear, his mouth is gaping. I, Birgitta, can communicate with Sture, which proves that, although certainly in a deeply regressed state, he still is in contact with the present.

The first cut slices through the right side of the torso. The blow is dealt by the mother. Then, the father takes hold of the knife. Again and again, the Sture-shell says 'not his throat, not his throat', then arches his neck. The knife chops and slices the body open. The right leg is cut off. This series of events is demonstrated alternatively as registered by the Sture-shell and by the fused brothers.

M [mother] cuts off some of Simon's flesh and pushes it into the Sture-shell's open mouth. The Sture-shell says: 'I'm not hungry.' M and F [father] are 'hugging' each other, engaged in an act Sture describes as 'nasty'. He then reaches out to hold Simon's hand. He finds that it is loose. He says: 'I've made my baby brother's hand come off.'

By the time I got to Birgitta Ståhle's note, I had already spent half the night working my way through the manuscript of 'The World of Thomas Quick'. I went back to the 2009 report that Ståhle had submitted to the social services ministry and read again what she had written about recovered memory therapy: 'In my capacity as a professional psychologist, I have never worked with this method and have never encountered it, neither in a clinical nor a theoretical context.'

There was nothing else for it: I had to conclude that the former chief psychologist at Säter hospital had been lying. Apparently, Norell rather than Ståhle determined the therapeutic approach. The treatment begun by Dr Persson seemed to have followed the same guidelines: Norell was the common factor. Besides, both Birgitta Ståhle and Kjell Persson lacked accreditation as psychotherapists and, without qualified supervision, would have had no legal right to conduct psychotherapeutic sessions with anyone.

Who was this Margit Norell? I looked for her in the databases. It seemed that she had few publications of any kind to her name and had given next to no interviews. The best chance to find out more about this woman would be to speak to those who had been members of her 'group'. This would be a tough task. If they remained as loyal to her as when they clubbed together to write *A Room to Live In*, they would hardly open up to me and discuss Norell's role in Thomas Quick's psychotherapy. I had to make a plan.

I was going to pretend to be interested in another aspect of their work. I would play the role of an admirer of Margit Norell. I did have plausible credentials. My two books on psychology focused on attachment theory which has similarities to the object relations theory that Margit pioneered in Sweden. If I referred to my books and claimed that I intended to write a history of object relations theory from a Swedish perspective, perhaps some of the past members of Norell's group would be willing to talk to me. It was worth a try.

By way of preparation I deleted all references to Hannes Råstam on my home page, on my Facebook page and on Twitter. However, the 'In Remembrance' note that I had written for the arts pages in *Aftonbladet* could not be removed. It might cause problems since I had called Hannes one of Sweden's all-time finest journalists. I could only hope that none of the people I planned to contact had read that issue of *Aftonbladet*.

The list of contributors to *A Room to Live In* included Tulla Brattbakk-Göthberg, a psychotherapist. Her chapter was not about recovered memory therapy as such but about mothers who had found it difficult to bond with their infants. What she had written was genuinely interesting so I picked her as my first interviewee, phoned her and introduced myself as planned: I was working on a history of object relations theory in Sweden and hoped to speak to her about Margit Norell's pioneering work. I didn't breathe a word about Thomas Quick. Tulla said that I was welcome to interview her. By this time she had retired and gone to live in Vadstena. When I stepped on the train, I still knew very little about Margit Norell and had even less of an idea about what to expect from the interview.

Tulla collected me from the station. She turned out to be a friendly lady in her seventies with a pleasant, easy-going manner, not at all guarded or suspicious. We settled at the kitchen table in her house and chatted a little about object relations theory before I mentioned Norell. Tulla said that she had seen Norell as her psychoanalyst and then as her supervisor back in the 1980s. She had felt very gratified when, in 1990, Norell invited her to join the exclusive group that gathered around her once a month on a Saturday. The group members were qualified psychologists or psychotherapists, or in training for one of these specialties. Many of them had known Norell in some capacity since the 1970s, either as a therapist or a supervisor, often both concurrently and usually on a weekly basis. Norell taught theories of psychoanalysis and conducted group supervision sessions during which the members presented case histories of current patients.

So far, Tulla had told me nothing especially noteworthy. But then she launched into something unexpected. She began to describe a troubling element of the group's relationship with Norell. Each of the apprentice psychologists regarded Norell as his or her 'mother' and she required each one of them to be absolutely obedient to her. 'No one criticized her,' Tulla said. 'If you spoke out of turn, said something that could be misinterpreted, you were attacked by the others. And ran the risk of being expelled from the circle of "siblings".'

Next, Tulla started to speak about Thomas Quick. Things had got out of hand when Margit initiated group discussions about Quick, she said. Norell had been utterly convinced that Sture Bergwall was a serial killer and that the grotesque tales from his childhood were truthful accounts of previously repressed memories. According to Tulla, it was 'unthinkable' to question any of her convictions in the group because it might easily be seen as saying 'something mean about our mother'.

Tulla looked concerned, shook her head and said, 'We were adults, successful professionals. But we became so small.'

Tulla went on to say that Birgitta Ståhle had been a member of the group and that Göran Källberg had joined them. He had been in therapy with, and under the supervision of, Margit Norell at the same time as he was the director of the entire forensic psychiatry establishment at Säter. In other words, the same Göran Källberg who had been regarded as the hero when, in 2001, he returned to Säter and took Quick's medication in hand. But as we talked, it became clear that his role had been more multi-faceted than most people realized. Generally 'Margit's pupils' were heavily emotionally dependent on her. Tulla herself had been unable to break free from the group until the end of the 1990s, when she moved to Norway. And yes, the medical director had been one of the acolytes.

I had stumbled straight into a whole pile of the missing jigsaw pieces needed to complete my picture of the Thomas Quick phenomenon. Even so, I had got nowhere near to a vision of what the whole would look like. It would take a year of research and many interviews with Margit's former acolytes before I fully grasped what Tulla Brattbakk-Göthberg had told me in that first interview. I would hear Margit Norell described, again and again, as a person with an exceptional talent for rendering other people emotionally dependent on her.

When I returned to Stockholm, I copied and scanned everything I could find about Sture Bergwall's life and the Quick trials. Next, I tried to complete the picture of Margit Norell's life, from her birth in 1914 to her death in 2005. I studied the minutes of the group meetings and listened to tapes of her addressing her pupils. The cassettes, still untouched, had been recorded in the 1980s and 1990s. I also read at least a thousand pages of Norell's correspondence with foreign psychoanalysts and built up a timeline on Excel that included some 2,000 events in the lives of Margit Norell and Sture Bergwall and linked to thousands of source documents.

All this added up to the biggest research project of my life. I was slowly beginning to understand what had happened at Säter. Hannes had been wondering until the end about what drove them all: Birgitta

Ståhle, Seppo Penttinen, Christer van der Kwast, Claes Borgström and Sven Å Christianson. Who or what made them believe so blindly in the alleged serial killer Thomas Quick?

Now, finally, I had the answer. It was Margit Norell.

PART 2

Margit and Sture

4

She owned the truth

'The truth was that I was the cause of unlived life and the unfulfilment of my mother's life'
Margit Norell, 1976, in a letter written to an
American psychoanalyst

I found a photo of Margit Norell in the Royal Library reading room. I was there to look up the collected newsletters of a now defunct psychoanalytical society. One issue contained one of the very rare published interviews with Margit. The piece was illustrated by a grainy black and white picture of a smiling woman with large glasses and a perm, seated in a high-backed leather armchair. The caption read 'Margit Norell in her consultation room, autumn 1996'. She was eighty-two years old at the time and had supervised Sture Bergwall's therapy for five years.

She was asked if she was writing anything, a question which probably referred to memoirs, but she answered that she was in 'a difficult situation at present' because she was 'supervising the therapeutic treatment of a murderer'. She went on to say that 'her notes filled three folders' and that she spent 'almost all her free time trying to turn the notes into a book'. Her book would show that this murderer 'was impelled to use murder to deflect his past experiences', meaning by that events that took place when 'he was four or five years old, utterly terrible things'.[39]

Margit's daughter, Annie Norell Beach, lives in a villa near Stockholm. When I met her, she was sixty-two years old and had retired from her job in order to devote herself to her hobby, making blankets from fabrics and fleeces. I was struck by her detachment; she spoke about her mother without denigrating or idealizing her. She kept a sober distance that tends not to come easily to people talking about parents who have disappointed them.

When I called Annie was well prepared. Since Margit's death seven years previously, she had put a great deal of work into trying to understand her mother. She had researched the family background and contacted people who had been close to Margit for a long time but had, at some point, ended up in conflicts so bitter that all communication had ceased. Annie told me that this was a recurring pattern in her mother's life. She could act as a supervisor and therapist to someone for years then suddenly cut off all contact and never mention them again. During Annie's youth, a series of psychotherapists met this fate.

I asked her what her mother was like as a person. 'She was very charismatic in many ways,' Annie said. 'She could enter a room and before long become the centre of attention – even if she didn't say a word. It is hard to put one's finger on how she did it, but she had a kind of presence. No one could remain indifferent to her.'

Annie recognized her mother's many good sides. 'There was so much I respected and admired about her. She was quite rebellious and brave and unconventional, she forged her own path and followed her instincts. She wasn't an opportunist. Human rights and democratic issues were central to her thinking; she was interested in the world and never narrow-minded or conventional. These were aspects of her personality that I truly liked and appreciated and admired.'

But one of Margit's characteristic features was her deep-rooted seriousness: 'She found joy and fun irksome. I sometimes felt that she was drawn to suffering. A little too much jollity and she seemed to think that you weren't quite trustworthy.'

Despite having people around her most of the time, Margit was isolated from them. 'In many ways, she was a lonely woman and her loneliness was self-inflicted. I'm sure it wasn't deliberate, but she was flawed in ways that created her isolation. For instance, she was incapable of small talk. For her, saying something like "Come on, let's go for a coffee" was unthinkable. She had practically no friends. I mean, the mutual kind of friendship that you enjoy on equal terms.

With her, it was always about being with people who somehow depended on her.'

Margit seems to have felt at ease only when she could be the authority figure who enlightened admiring apprentices about psycho-analytical theory. Her approach was always categorical.

'For her, there were actually no grey areas,' Annie explained. 'Only black or white. End of story. I told my husband that today someone would interview me about Margit and asked him what he would've said about her. He replied that *judgemental* was the first word that came to mind. And, yes, there's a lot in that. She was the truth-owner, if you like. She owned the truth. She had a body language to match, she often sat like this . . .' Annie demonstrated how her mother would beat the air with her straight index finger, as if to hammer home each state-ment as she put it into words. 'She didn't compromise, not ever. My husband and I love to discuss things, brain-storm and turn arguments inside-out. Not with her, though. All she would say was "it's like this and like that" and wave her finger at you. That's how she always expressed herself.'

When Margit couldn't assume her role as psychoanalyst with people she met, she often became mute and withdrawn. Annie told me that, in 1991, she and her husband had a human rights activist from Sri Lanka staying with them for several months. He was a Buddhist monk who had grown up in a monastery and never lived with a family before. 'His name was Samita. He was a very nice, friendly person and I learned a lot from him. I was on parental leave with our eldest daugh-ter, so Samita and I saw a lot of each other every day for a couple of months. He had never had to cook or look after babies, and thought learning these things was great fun.'

One evening, Margit came for supper.

'How well I remember that meal. Samita, in his monk's garb, was sitting next to Mum. I went off to the kitchen for a while and when I came back to the dining room, I realized that she hadn't uttered a single word. I won't ever forget that, especially because I felt that he would be just right for her: he was politically active, an intellectual as well as a warm-hearted human being. He had all the characteristics that my mother valued highly. And yet, there she sat, in total silence. Memories like this make me very sad. She missed so much, I say to myself. But she had no idea of how to talk with people. If her own role was ill-defined, she somehow didn't dare to try. Relationships demanding mutuality made her switch off.'

According to Annie, Margit's work was her top priority. She was not particularly interested in her family. When her three children were young, looking after them became the job of the live-in maid, a German woman. Annie admits that 'the maid almost felt more like my mother than my real mother did'. Margit never played with her children because, Annie explained, she didn't know how to go about it.

'As for Margit's own childhood, it's a fact that she only rarely had even one of her parents at home. So, she hardly knew how a parent should behave. She was apparently a very lonely child.'

In 1914, Margit Norell was born to a wealthy family in Uppsala. Her paternal great-great-grandfather was a James Dickson from Scotland, who arrived in Gothenburg in 1809. Over the years, Dickson, together with his older brother, turned the family enterprise into Sweden's first wholesale timber business. As his business grew, Dickson acquired his own fleet of cargo ships. The family became enormously wealthy and recognized as power brokers by the Swedish establishment. Margit's paternal great-grandfather was one of James Dickson's sons. He not only inherited a great fortune, but was also elected to parliament and was a member of King Oscar's personal shooting party.[40]

Margit's paternal grandmother, Florence, had a sad start in life. At the age of four her mother died and the little girl was dispatched to a well-to-do aunt in England who brought her up according to strict Victorian ideals. Florence returned to Sweden at twenty-four and married Oscar Quensel, Margit's paternal grandfather. Quensel came from a wealthy merchant's family in Gothenburg, but he refused to take over his father's business and decided to study theology. He was eventually ordained to pastoral office. Later, he became professor of practical theology at Uppsala University.

In 1881, Oscar and Florence had a son, Percy, Margit's father to be.

He grew up in a grand house just a stone's throw from Uppsala Castle. As a child, he was surrounded by every material comfort, but lacked emotional warmth. His mother, deeply influenced by her own upbringing under the eagle eye of the London aunt, insisted on leading her life as if she were still in Victorian England. This is how Margit's father described his mother in a note found among his posthumous papers:

> Her principles were extremely puritan. Her notions about how to live were drawn from England and no home furnishings deemed acceptable unless ordered from London. [...] She spoke only English with us children and with our father, and saw to it that we were brought up in the English manner. For instance, my sister was never allowed to attend school in Sweden and was instead taught by an appalling English governess. What has stayed in my memory is that I was not allowed to join my schoolmates in sport and play, on Sundays. During all my school years, I endured a very strict regime.[41]

Percy met Margit's mother in Graz in southern Austria, where he had gone to study geology. Annie Weiss, a zoology student, was an Austrian Jewess from the well-to-do family of a senior civil servant. Percy and Annie became fond of each other but any love affair had to be put on hold during Percy's three-year-long scientific expedition to Patagonia and Tierra del Fuego at the southern tip of South America. A mountain range, Cerro Quensel, and a small flowering plant, *Senecio quenselii*, were named after him. Meanwhile, back in Austria, Annie achieved a doctorate in zoology. After his return to Europe, Percy completed his doctorate, went to Vienna to marry Annie and then brought his new wife to Uppsala. Their first child, Margit, was born in 1914. Soon after her birth, the family moved into an opulent apartment in Stockholm's affluent Östermalm district. They had just one more child, Margit's little sister Ella.

A studio photograph of the Quensel family, taken in 1917, shows three-year-old Margit with a white bow in her dark, curly hair. Her parents are a good-looking, well-dressed couple. Annie holds little Ella in her arms and Percy has put his arm around Margit as if to keep her still. She looks gravely into the camera.

A professional photographer was also asked to capture the family apartment in a costly album full of very crisp, black-and-white images. The house is reminiscent of the magnificent home filmed by Ingmar Bergman in *Fanny and Alexander*. One photo shows the Oriental Room, its four-poster bed piled high with cushions and its floor covered in thick rugs. Another room was furnished on a hunting theme, with a display of stuffed birds and exotic souvenirs that must be mementoes from Percy's scientific expeditions. An expertly lit picture shows the huge dining table laid for a party.

As a married woman, Margit's mother gave up her own research but often followed her husband on long journeys all over the world. She wrote up her travels and her 'essays' were published in various Swedish papers, marking the start of a successful career as a roving reporter for the intellectually ambitious magazine *Vecko-Journalen*. I read some of Annie's articles for *Vecko-Journalen* in the late 1920s and early 1930s and found that they are wide-ranging political reports, based on quite intimate interviews with important contemporary politicians or people in their entourage.

Margit's parents were often abroad for months on end, her father on his scientific expeditions and her mother just about anywhere, reporting from Russia, Africa, India and South America. When they were away, Margit and her little sister had to stay with their father's old-fashioned mother Granny Florence.

Annie Quensel was a charming and gregarious woman, who enjoyed a grand social life. She was also a very talented linguist; despite living in Austria until her early twenties she learned to speak and write flawless Swedish in just a few years. Apart from her native German, she also spoke English, French and Spanish fluently. She made several tours in the Soviet Union as a reporter and interviewed, among others, Lenin's wife. In England, Annie interviewed a fascist party leader, in France she met the president and, in Bulgaria, Tsar Ferdinand. She interviewed the chief of the military dictatorship in Siam (now

Thailand) and embarked on a series of travels in India, where she interviewed, among others, Mahatma Gandhi. At the same time she was part of the jet set of the 1920s and 1930s, glamorous, glittering and cosmopolitan.

She reported on visits to splendid palaces, dinners with the wealthy and her travels in the company of the elite. A typical story was headlined THE MONTE CARLO OF THE ORIENT. It begins: 'Nature in Macao, the Portuguese colony in China, is beautiful. Home of Chinese diligence during the day, it becomes a sinful Babel at night.' She offered insights into the goings-on 'behind the curtains of the Royal Palace in Phnom Penh, where the women live in complete isolation from the outside world' but she, 'escorted by King Monivong' was allowed to inspect 'the secret interior of the palace city'.[42] In one of her reports she travelled on 'the longest regular flight in the world, which takes you from Java to Holland in ten days!'. Mostly, she travelled by ship. During one of these long journeys she befriended the mega-star Charlie Chaplin and later followed him to Bali: 'When Charlie looks pleadingly at you and asks you come along, disobeying him is impossible.' The trip was written up in several of her travel pieces, illustrated by photos of a radiantly happy-looking Chaplin and 'his people' on an extended holiday.

In a large, richly gold-framed oil portrait of Annie Quensel that hung on the wall of her home, the striking-looking Austrian Jewess looks searchingly straight into the eye of the beholder. She does not smile openly, but her lips appear to curl in faint amusement. The portrait was painted in 1932 by the British artist Philip de László, who during his active life painted four American presidents and several European kings.[43] Margit's mother had met de László on one of her journeys and he asked to be allowed to paint her.

I try to imagine Margit's childhood. From a young age, she had to manage without her mother for months on end. Like all lonely children, she lived in a constant state of longing. Among her collected letters, I found the following passage, written in the 1970s to an American psychoanalyst who came as close to being her friend as was possible. Margit writes that, of the 'three mothers' she had as a little girl, she felt closest to Florence, her strict grandmother, and then to a housemaid called Hulda. Her biological mother came third.[44] She also speculates that her birth must have been a great disappointment for her mother:

My mother was a beautiful and intelligent Jewish-Austrian woman, who married my father shortly after having gotten to know him as a postgraduate student in Graz and then became impressed by the wealthy home of his parents in Sweden and the way they received her. She was at that time offered a professorship in the US which she then gave up. Photos from their wedding trip show my mother's face as very close to catatonic, which must have been the result of her learning to know my father, who was quite rigid and could have violent outbreaks of aggression. He soon became a professor of geology and certainly understood a lot about stones but very little about human beings. My birth in the social circumstances of that time and my parents meant to my mother, I believe, that her fate could not be changed. [. . .] Not until my father died in 1965 and I looked through all old photographs and realized the distinctly catatonic look on my mother's face during her wedding-trip did I realize the reality this feeling expressed. The truth was that I was the cause of unlived life and the unfulfilment of my mother's life.[45]

Her sense of guilt recurs in another letter:

There was of course [. . .] never an open expression on the part of my mother that I was the cause of unlived life on her part. The only thing she stated directly — as far as I can remember — was that she tried to breastfeed me for a week but that I did not want her milk. And this fact followed me through my childhood and I thought a lot about it and why it could have been so.[46]

Many of the longstanding members of Margit's inner circle have told me that, throughout her life, she felt awkward about her appearance: short, plump and with a stubby nose. In her letters, she often emphasizes how beautiful her mother was. As a girl, she must have constantly compared herself with the glamorous mother who left her daughter behind whenever another opportunity to travel came her way. In a child, such experiences can breed self-contempt. In one of her letters she speaks of her childhood as 'autistic'.[47]

In 1968, aged fifty-four, Margit writes about the people she grew up with in a set of autobiographical notes. She mentions her father the geologist, her Austrian mother, her paternal grandmother who spoke English and her maternal grandmother who spoke only German when she came to stay with them during the war:

> *While at school, I would try to work out whom I was most like among all these people, and I finally decided that it was my grandfather, even though I had no memories of him since he died when I was a year old. But when, in my teens, I was handed his books, letters and diaries, I read with growing interest and with a feeling akin to recognition. My grandfather was, for many years, the professor of practical theology in Uppsala [. . .]. He was regarded as a rather quiet man, but he was thoughtful and observant, and widely travelled. After his death, notes that were found in his desk drawers told of how he had viewed his contemporaries in Uppsala, what he had seen and recorded about people and nature during his travels and much, too, about his thoughts and his life.*[48]

I have a vision of Margit, a lonely teenager, at her desk in her strict grandmother's house in affluent Djursholm. Her mother is partying with Charlie Chaplin in a palace somewhere on the other side of the globe and if her father isn't on an expedition to South America, he is in an inaccessible, crotchety mood. Young Margit looked for solace in her dead grandfather, a man she had never met but had come to imagine as her soulmate.

But, in her teens, Margit also felt for the first time that she was seen by her mother and found worthwhile: '*Not before I could be of some real help to my mother in running errands for her and later reading and delivering the articles she as a journalist sent home from different parts of the world did I feel that I had some real meaning for her.*'[49]

49

One evening, Margit had a crucial revelation: 'I have a distinct memory of being sixteen, sitting at my desk one night, when suddenly an insight of great clarity came to me – I would spend my life listening to people who wanted to talk to me about their problems. At the time, of course, I had no idea of how to make this happen.'[50]

When Margit's mother was forty-six she fell ill and had to have an operation. She didn't require major surgery but antibiotics were unknown at the time. Annie died quickly from sepsis. Now Margit could help her mother with one last act, which she describes much later in a letter: '*When she went to [the] hospital for the operation, which in itself unexpectedly led to her death, she left me her diaries and letters from men she had been close to during later years. I read them all and burned them in the night after her death. I was 19 then.*'[51]

When Margit read about these infidelities, her old feelings of guilt flared up again. She wished that she had been able to help her mother in some way. In a letter, she links her mother's fate with her work as a psychoanalyst:

So a large part of my work – and the part which interests me most, I believe – is working with people with a significant potential for a much richer life for themselves and others – what I would have wished for my mother, but in reality prevented her from through entering into her life. In some sense it is also freeing others for meaningful life in the way I would have wished somebody could have helped free me at an earlier age.

Margit clearly admired and idolized her mother but she showed no inclination to emulate Annie's fast-moving, fashionable life. On the contrary, Annie Norell Beach told me that Margit had hated the upper classes all her life and despised their social milieu. As a young woman, she turned in a very different direction. Her grandfather's learned articles on practical theology awakened her interest in spiritual matters. While still at school, she began to read philosophers like Nietzsche and Kierkegaard. She also followed in his professional footsteps and enrolled to study theoretical theology at the University of Uppsala. Politically, Margit veered to the left; she studied the works of Marx and the history of social democracy, and developed an interest in education for the masses. She took courses at the social democratic institutions known as the 'people's colleges'.[52] In other words, Margit was not tempted by exclusive parties in Macao and, as the years went by, placed more and more of a distance between herself and the moneyed lifestyle her mother had enjoyed.

One evening in 1936, she went along to the Christian Student Union to listen to a lecture by a young, radical clergyman called Curt Norell.[53] He walked her home afterwards and they started meeting regularly. Curt had been a member of the Communist Youth Association in Gothenburg and had also joined the anti-fascist, left-wing organization Clarté. When he studied at the University of Lund, he was a friend of the leader-to-be of the Swedish social democratic party, Tage Erlander, and of the legendary promoter of sex education Elise Ottesen-Jensen. He was passionate about education for the people, psychotherapy and sex education, all areas he would devote himself to for the rest of his life. He never worked as a minister in a church.

According to Annie, the personalities of Margit and Curt were very different. 'I think you'd be hard put to find anyone who won't tell you that it was extremely easy to become fond of Curt,' she said. 'He was in every way a true humanist, very easy to get on with. He had a good sense of humour and a great capacity for enjoying simple things. He loved music. For him, entering a room full of people and immediately finding someone to talk to was easy. Very unlike Mummy, in other words.'

During the financial crisis in the late 1930s, twenty-three-year-old Margit started working as a teacher in the workers' educational association centres in the Ådalen manufacturing communities. This was where the 'Ådalen shootings', a notorious incident during the 1931 strikes that saw the army firing into crowds of striking workers, had taken place. The violence shocked the nation, but the social democrats were keen to reduce the antagonism. The Educational Institute (Studiehem) that the party set up in Kramfors was an important step, based on the idea of bridging class differences by giving the working class access to education.[54] Margit worked for two terms at the

Institute, teaching Swedish, mathematics and psychology. Photos in the family albums show Margit teaching English to five working men in their Sunday best, all seated together around a worn desk. The plainly dressed Margit looks small and unassuming. Money for the enterprise was short and the teachers lived in conditions as Spartan as their pupils, a sharp contrast to the comforts Margit was used to. Curt and Margit married and took on the task of being joint managers of the institute. They moved to Kramfors on the momentous day in 1939 when Germany's invasion of Poland triggered the Second World War. The Norells were housed in two of the institute's four rooms while all the remaining space was earmarked for classrooms.

While the war raged in Europe, Curt and Margit made astonishing efforts to offer the local people educational opportunities. Every year, they set up fifty study circles covering a range of subjects from languages to sex education to child and social psychology. In the summers, Margit would cycle from place to place along the wide valley of the River Ångerman to teach sex education, including contraception. In the winters, she would do the same journeys on skis. She and Curt started crèches, youth clubs and choirs in several communities and invited an unending stream of lecturers to the institute. They arranged socials for people who wanted to dance, play music, read poetry or sing together. In an interview, Margit said: 'In Kramfors, I experienced all that I had missed when I was growing up. I got to meet all kinds of people although I stubbornly refused to socialize with the local elite. If a meeting was held at the rectory, I would send Bojan Myraeus [the institute's housekeeper and maid-of-all-work] instead.'

Margit's real strength turned out to be her therapy-like conversations with people she met on her travels around Ådalen.[55] Her vision as a sixteen-year-old was about to become reality. Curt and Margit managed the institute throughout the Second World War and, during that time, their sons Staffan and Thomas were born. Very little in Margit's life was even faintly reminiscent of her mother's, except when it came to looking after the children. There she followed her mother's example and engaged the factotum Bojan as their nanny.

When the war ended in 1945, Curt was asked to come to

Stockholm with his family and run a so-called 'hemgård'. It was modelled on the English community settlement or social centre, where people from an urban area could meet and learn new skills together. The director had to organize activities similar to those in the Kramfors Institute, with emphasis on lectures, courses, crèches and socials. The Norells accepted and moved into Birkagården, a building on central Karlberg Way.

While Curt established himself as the new director, Margit travelled, displaying more of the awesome energy that she had already displayed in Ådalen. She made several journeys to bomb-blasted Germany where she ran courses for social workers and youth leaders who had set themselves the task of rebuilding the country in line with democratic ideals. She also travelled throughout Germany lecturing on sex education. She brought photos back home from her travels, images of bombed bridges, broken churches and cities in ruins. The poverty and general misery was terrible. Margit was a Jewess and a socialist in a country where, until very recently, Jews and socialists had been persecuted and killed. None of this seemed to affect her decision to try to help the German people after the war.

Margit and Curt's third and last child, Annie, was born in 1950. Margit kept a diary during Annie's first year and from her entries it is clear that, by then, she often saw people who came to her for 'help with internal as well external difficulties'.[56] In other words, she worked as a kind of self-taught psychotherapist. It is not surprising that she decided to train as a psychoanalyst. In the decades that followed she would become a much-mythologized figure, both loved and feared.

Forty years later, Margit Norell's life grew intertwined with that of the hospitalized junkie Sture Bergwall. By then, she had already followed Freud and taken the words from the Gospel of John as her motto: 'Truth shall set ye free.'[57]

5

Sture's childhood and youth

'He felt that no one cares for him. He has been disappointed
by his parents and his siblings.'
From Sture Bergwall's case notes (1966)

On 26 April 1950, Margit gave birth to Annie in the Stockholm
maternity hospital Pro Patria. On the same day, Tyra Bergwall, née
Quick, was taken to the labour ward at Falun Hospital, where the
mother of four gave birth to twins, Sture and his sister Gun. Sture's relatives had not accumulated wealth by trading in timber or anything
else. They owned no banks and did not belong to the king's inner
circle. Though the information held in parish records is sparse, I note
that Sture's paternal grandfather was a factory worker, an engine
greaser, and lived with his wife Johanna and their six children in the
tied accommodation belonging to the Bergvik sulphite plant in
Hälsingland. Sture's maternal grandfather, Per Johan Kvick, was a line
maintenance man, who had fourteen children with his wife Kristina.
Further back in time, I find labourers, smallholders and tenant farm-
ers, sawmill workers, housemaids and farmhands. Some of Sture's
relatives had been born out of wedlock to the housemaid made pregnant by a farmer's son or some casual partner. There was the odd
suicide by drowning, curtly noted in the parish record of births and
deaths. As is often the case with working-class lives, there are hardly
any clues to what these people felt or experienced.

The birth of the twins meant that the Bergwalls were now a family
with six children. They moved into the newly built housing for factory workers in Främby, just outside the old mining town of Falun.
They were allocated two rooms and a kitchen. Sten-Ove, Sture's oldest

brother, describes his tenth birthday in his book *My Brother Thomas Quick*. His birthday present was a cheese sandwich, 'with good white bread and proper slices of cheese on top'. He ate it standing in the street outside their new home. The children didn't starve, but the family was poor.[58]

Their father, Ove, was a factory worker and a member of the Pentecostal Church. Ove was a sad man, and even touched by tragedy. His poor education troubled him and he was prone to sudden outbursts of rage. He dealt with the problem of his education by studying for middle school exams by correspondence. When Ove succeeded, the local paper ran a piece under the headline FATHER OF SIX PASSES EXAMS, illustrated by a photo of him. He carried on afterwards as a private student and eventually passed several subjects at university entrance level. The children grew up with his ambitions for them hanging over them. They were pushed to study and go on to join one of the professions that were now out of his grasp.

But Ove was no household tyrant, despite his tantrums. He lacked authority, at least according to his eldest son. It was Tyra, their mother, who managed the children's upbringing, held the family together and stretched the meagre budget to keep them in food and clothing. When her husband came back from the factory, he was fed and handed clean clothes, just like the children. As Sten-Ove writes:

My father did not dream. He was a man without a future. His studies were just an activity driven by restlessness and never part of a plan. He had no role outside the family, except as a member of the Pentecostal congregation, but his attitude to his church and what it offered was ambivalent. Rather than giving him strength, religion made him more dependent. He sensed this and reacted against it but without realizing why. His intense engagement would suddenly crack as violently and be replaced by doubts. [...] Dad was a creative but inhibited man, depressive by nature and, at best, volatile and hard to reach. He had to carry a heavy burden, some kind of creative urge that never found an outlet. To be half-aware of something like that must be among the worst kind of mental experience:

an uncertain sense that under other and more favourable conditions you might have had a richer life.

Before Sture and Gun were two years old, a seventh sibling joined them – a girl called Eva. There is very little information available about Sture's earliest years but I cannot escape the feeling that in such a large family, the youngest children were unlikely to get the attention they craved. Their father was hardly a comforting figure and their mother would not have had time to provide the children with anything other than immediate necessities.

Sture's earliest memories are from when he was seven. The year before the family had been offered a slightly larger flat in Korsnäs, also near Falun. Sture and his twin sister had just begun primary school when he fell seriously ill with tuberculosis. He was sent to a sanatorium where he spent the best part of a year and was only allowed occasional visits from his parents. He remembers how he would stand alone in the X-ray suite with cold photographic plates pressed against his chest, and his belly full of contrast fluid. He cried when he had to swallow that thick mush, with only a nurse to comfort him.

His father had written to *The Children's Letterbox*, a popular radio programme, and asked for a message of good wishes for Sture. *Dala-Demokraten*, the local paper, got wind of it, paid for a Meccano set and sent a reporter along to record the moment when the gift was handed over and unwrapped. A photograph shows Sture in his hospital bed, looking very sweet, his eyes wide open above his shy, gap-toothed smile. I reflected that, especially at that time, it must have been very hard for a child of his age to handle a potentially fatal disease without the support of his parents.

Tuberculosis is an epidemic disease that has always been difficult to treat. By the late 1940s, however, the antibiotic para-aminosalicylic acid, or PAS, was used with some success. It saved Sture but his year at Högbo Sanatorium left its mark. He had missed his entire first year in school and it is possible that the long separation from his parents was at least a partial explanation of the anxiety that characterized the rest of his childhood. His mother was very pleased to have him back home again, but she showed love by providing food and a roof over her loved ones' heads, rather than with tenderness and hugs. During the summer of 1958, she made sure that Sture studied enough to keep up with the children of his age. Sture, who was quick on the uptake and very verbal, caught up easily enough. The real problem was that he had grown plump during his year in hospital. Before he fell ill, he was a tall boy with a gangly body that was awkward to control. Now, overweight and taller than his classmates, with legs weakened by lengthy bed rest, he was even more awkward. He couldn't keep up with the other children and often fell over, so he was laughed at. Besides, his twin sister Gun consistently achieved higher marks, which mattered in the Bergwall family.

The sanatorium-induced frailty singled him out as an oddball and the other boys picked on him and chased him. His older brother Örjan remembered that Sture's teacher Teodore Kruse called Sture 'a goat', meaning that he could not keep his long arms and legs under control. Kruse also complained that Sture didn't behave himself, was often late to lessons and told fibs when asked to explain why. He struggled with dyslexia and sometimes jumbled his words when he spoke. Eva, Sture's sister, said in a police interview in the 1990s that her brother had been very lonely at school and never had a best friend.

Once Sture had started secondary school in Falun, he realized that he was homosexual when he fell in love with a boy in his class – a secret he had to keep at any cost. Until 1934, homosexual intercourse was illegal in Sweden and carried a penalty of up to two years forced labour. Sexual acts between adults of the same gender were not completely decriminalized until 1944, six years before Sture's birth, after which homosexuality was categorized as a mental aberration. This definition was still in place as late as 1979, when Sture was twenty-nine. He grew up in a society where his sexuality was classed as a perverse product of a diseased mind and hence a psychiatric diagnosis.

The realization that he was one of these 'perverts' hit the fourteen-year-old like a bomb. He couldn't look for help at home. His family subscribed to the strict moral rules of the Pentecostal Church and didn't speak about sex in any case, much less about sexual 'deviancies'.

'Something like that is so central to one's life but I couldn't speak about it to anyone,' Sture said to me. 'I couldn't socialize with other homosexuals. It was a part of my identity and it made me very lonely.'

Sture started using drugs in secondary school as a way to forget his sexuality. He had tried alcohol but his favourite intoxicant was trichloroethylene (TCE), a colourless and sweet-smelling liquid solvent used, among other things, to de-grease tools. Its effects on the nervous system are dangerous and the substance was banned in 1996. In the 1960s, it was still sold in brown glass bottles and stocked by grocers. By the age of fourteen, Sture had acquired the habit of carrying a bottle of TCE in his pocket. When he was on his own, he moistened a cloth from the bottle and pressed it to his nose. Inhaling gave him a high so powerful that he hallucinated and felt 'psychotic'. For a few hours, the whole world would disappear, taking his troubles with it. He sniffed practically every evening until he was twenty-four. High as a kite and completely alone, Sture would wander aimlessly around Falun at night.

His report card noted that Sture was a habitual absentee and his attitude to schoolwork was distracted at best. Despite this, he played an active role in school life. He was the editor of the school magazine and, for a while, chairman of the Pupils' Council. As the chairman, Sture was full of ideas and showed 'certain leadership qualities', the teacher said, but had difficulty controlling his impulses and often became agitated. The minister who supervised Sture's confirmation into the church spoke of how the boy swung between 'joyful energy and utter weariness'.[59] The overall impression is of an adolescent leading a double life. He tried to fit in and be the person his school and his family wanted him to be while harbouring two secrets: his attraction to men, which he considered a sickness, and his substance abuse. But he could not contain his homosexual desires. While at secondary school, Sture was charged with having made sexual overtures to another boy. He was called in for a talk with his class teacher whose notes, kept by the school, state that the boy admitted to a 'homosexual inclination'.[60] He insisted on how important it was that his parents did not find out and the school respected his wish. Sture was sixteen before his brother Sten-Ove, who was ten years older and working as a journalist on *Dala-Demokraten*, learned that his younger brother was gay. A reporter had told him that Sture had been beaten up by other youths for messing around with younger boys. At first, Sten-Ove could not believe his ears; he, too, found homosexuality simply unthinkable.

In March 1966, the school doctor wrote to a psychiatrist at the Child and Adolescent Mental Health Clinic in Falun and asked him to examine a problematic pupil called Sture Bergwall:

> He shocked his fellow pupils with overtly homosexual behaviour. The case has been brought to the attention of the headmaster. The boy is very unhappy about his urges. He in fact seems deeply depressed and wants to be cured. Somatic status without remark. Because the boy wishes his parents to remain unaware of his problem, the appointment details should preferably be sent care of Harald Åkerlund, Headmaster [...].[61]

So, at sixteen, Sture was seen by a psychiatrist and was subjected to a battery of psychological tests. After the consultation, the doctor wrote in his case notes:

> The tall youth was neatly dressed but looked around the long narrow ward in a confused manner. He wore dark sunglasses. He seemed tense throughout the psychometric investigations. Generally, it was easy to get in contact with him. He asked spontaneously: 'Do you enjoy being a psychologist?'
>
> He wants to become a clergyman, just like an older brother who is about to sit his school finals in the summer. The youth participated in all the tests and consistently tried to do his best. However, he seemed to be unimpressed by the process.
>
> In the intelligence test, the patient's performance was well above average. However, he functioned irregularly. With regard to other functional aspects of his personality, we noted that he displayed a pattern similar to people with adjustment issues. Overall, there were

indications of similarities with people coping with poor impulse control and also those who show a certain feminine direction in their interests.

Further comments: the patient spoke with dramatic intensity; [he had] something of an actor's approach to narrative and an extensive verbal range. He showed a tendency to introspection and an apparently uncontrolled flow of impulses which accompanied a lively imagination. The narratives revealed a strong need for self-promotion and a concomitant fear of rivalry in the context of 'being a man'. There was evidence of aggression in confrontational situations and of vivid fantasies about death. His relationship with his peers seemed conflicted. He has sensed the aggression directed towards him from peers and said that he has no friends. His relationship with his family was also full of conflicts. He felt that no one cares for him. He has been disappointed by his parents and his siblings.[62]

These case notes contain many elements that recurred every time Sture was examined by psychiatrists. He usually came across as more than averagely intelligent, spoke well using a wide vocabulary and was given to theorizing about his own situation. His lively imagination was often remarked on, as was his acting talent.

After the examination, the psychiatrist wrote a reassuring letter to the school: 'His homosexuality is probably not innate but rather an expression of a neurotic mind. It would seem that with appropriate psychotherapy, his prognosis is good.'

During 1966 Sture saw a psychologist regularly. He spoke openly about his attraction to boys and about the tension he experienced at home because he had not come out to his parents. He was described in the case notes as a young man 'with several problems such as lack of impulse control, insecurity and a need to self-promote, also aggressive tendencies and a certain dramatic instinct'.[63] His school records note that he sometimes had outbursts of anger directed at teachers as well as other pupils but emphasize that he always apologized afterwards. No one realized that he was addicted to a mind-altering drug likely to account for some of his moodiness. Sture kept the TCE sniffing under wraps and focused on his homosexuality. It was, he said, the biggest problem in his life and he was keen to be cured.

'I've always been fascinated by psychoanalysis,' he admitted to me. 'I had read quite a lot about psychoanalysis and free association, and believed that homosexuality was a consequence of external rather than biological factors. I wanted to work out why I was a queer. Why was I so different from my siblings? To me, that was the crucial question.'

The case notes tell of Sture's hopes: 'Speaks [. . .] spontaneously – pat. is highly verbal – about how he feels his homosexual inclinations have diminished during this past week.'[64]

This was the beginning of Sture's life-long involvement with psychiatry.

The illness that the doctors set out to eradicate was homosexuality.

6

Margit meets Freud

*I would not be surprised if [. . .] we would see that loneliness
in its own right plays a much more significant role in the
dynamics of mental disturbance than we have been ready to
experience so far.*

Frieda Fromm-Reichmann, psychoanalyst

Margit began her training in psychoanalysis in 1951 at the Swedish
Psychoanalytical Society in Stockholm. Her youngest daughter was
one year old, Sture's age.

At the time of Margit's training, psychoanalysis was still a relatively
young discipline, originating some sixty to seventy years earlier in
Austria. Sigmund Freud, arguably 'the father of psychoanalysis', formulated hypotheses that fundamentally changed our views on the
human mind. He argued that we conceal forbidden desires and needs
in a mental compartment he called the 'unconscious'. Though pushed
out of consciousness, the urges still influence thought, emotion and
action. It followed, according to Freud, that repressed, unconscious
desires were often in opposition to conscious wishes, expectations and
moral ideals. People might believe that they strive to reach one goal
while unconsciously wanting something quite different. In the most
conflicted cases, this disjunction could generate mental disorder of a
type Freud called 'hysteria' and, later, 'neurosis'.

At the turn of the nineteenth century, Freud refined his ideas but
also tried to find a way to use them to treat mental disorders. The
approach, which he called 'psychoanalysis', was to assist the patient in
consciously exploring his or her unconscious. Once the patient
became aware of what had been repressed, the inner conflict would

resolve and the mental distresses either disappear or become less troubling. The professional who helped make the patient aware of the unconscious was the psychoanalyst.

In practice, the patient would lie down on a couch or sofa with the psychoanalyst seated at the head. The patient was meant to speak and the psychoanalyst to listen, at least most of the time, neither confirming nor encouraging, only acting as a neutral mirror. But the analyst should also be alert to clues of internal conflict and steer the exchange with the patient in fruitful directions. In this way, the patient would gradually learn what was hidden in his or her unconscious.

Understandably, the process of psychoanalysis was likely to make the patient deeply anxious, since the repressed states of mind were likely to be troubling and could include hatred towards parents, self-contempt, shame, various types of death-wish or forbidden sexual desires. The patient would be strongly motivated to avoid becoming aware of these difficult emotions and try to resist the analyst. Freud developed methods to get around such resistance, such as 'free association': letting the patient talk about anything that came to mind without intervention. This would bring on a mental state that Freud likened to falling asleep or being hypnotized.[65] A skilled psychoanalyst was expected to discern when the patient 'slipped up' and revealed subconscious material. Another technique involved analysis of the patient's dreams. In *The Interpretation of Dreams*, Freud claimed that when we dream, the unconscious is freed from censure and addresses us directly A record of the patient's dreams would provide the analyst with a peephole into the unconscious. By encouraging free association about dreams, the two methods could be used in combination.[66]

Freud's ideas have had a tremendous impact outside the sphere of medicine, influencing popular as well as high culture. In art, Freud's ideas about dreams as a link to the human unconscious gave rise to the surrealist movement and the psychoanalytical models of thought changed literature. For generations it has been taken as read that mental disorders might originate in traumatic experiences in childhood, and that we all suppress wishes and desires that might control our behaviour in mysterious ways. It is now hard for us to imagine how our image of 'the self' looked before Freud's insights into memory and cognition.

Freud did not use any accepted experimental approach when he created the psychoanalytical theory, which was why many researchers in relevant fields reacted negatively when he claimed that he had uncovered revolutionary truths about the human psyche. In 1909, Freud and some of his colleagues travelled to the United States where he gave a lecture about his new findings at Clark University in Massachusetts. It started a near-interminable row. American scientists noted that psychoanalysts did not run control groups and did not base their conclusions on statistical analyses of their data. This made it impossible for other scientists to check the results by repeating their experiments. Freud's research was carried out in a closed room where he talked confidentially with his patients, sometimes for many years. He then presented his conclusions as 'case histories' in which the identity of the patient was hidden behind pseudonyms like 'Little Hans', 'Rat Man' and 'The Wolfman'.[67] Freud and his colleagues elevated their subjective interpretations of what was said on the therapy couch to 'scientific truths' about the functions of the human mind.

Critics insisted that the psychoanalytical interpretations of patients' dreams and free associations were no more than notions pulled out of thin air, given credence by the suggestibility of patients. The analysts responded by saying that they were only prepared to discuss their work with people who were trained in psychoanalysis, convincing many outsiders that the psychoanalysts saw themselves as the priests of a religious sect. An American critic wrote: 'Psychoanalysis, disguised as a branch of science, tries to sneak in and strangle science from the inside.'[68]

In Sweden, the interest in psychoanalysis grew slowly.[69] Nordic pioneers set up joint psychoanalytical societies in 1931, Denmark with Norway, and Sweden with Finland. By that time, societies were already up and running in Austria, Britain, France, Hungary, India, Japan, The Netherlands, Switzerland, and the United States. For several years the Swedish psychoanalytical society barely kept going. In 1950, the year before Margit Norell began to train as a psychoanalyst, the society had six full members, and there were only ten to fifteen psychoanalysts at work around the country. The discipline as a whole was subjected to the same criticism as it received elsewhere.[70] *The House that Freud Built*, a critical work by Joseph Jastrow, became available in translation as early as 1934. Jastrow, an American psychologist, fired with both barrels: '*Freudian argument ignores, distorts and runs the gamut of speculation from the superficially plausible to the completely ridiculous. Freudian argument is so involved, fatuous, specious, cryptic, inconsistent, has been spread so wide and so irresponsibly, that I can do little more than sample its grosser errors and major transgressions.*'[71]

Margit Norell was a couple of years into her long training programme when the doctor and professor of forensic psychiatry Olof Kinberg wrote an article for *Dagens Nyheter* in which he said: 'Psychoanalysis claims to be an empirical science but incorporates nonetheless elements of spiritualism that appeals to adherents of Christian theology and other metaphysical creeds.'[72]

The professor of philosophy Ingmar Hedenius called psychoanalysis a sect analogous with Marxism and Christianity.[73] The editor-in-chief of *Dagens Nyheter*, the liberal Herbert Tingsten, wrote that psychoanalysis had all the characteristics of a 'faith based on salvation'. The intellectual Pehr Henrik Törngren, who was, unusually, a trained psychoanalyst, published an article in which he expressed his disappointment with what had been achieved with psychoanalysis, recognized the parallels with Catholicism and Marxism, and added for good measure that its teachings shared features with homeopathy and astrology. Psychoanalysis was seen as a dogmatic discipline lacking in empirical evidence to support its claims.

When Margit began her training this sort of opposition was taken as par for the course. Like her fellow analysts, she felt that the truths of the psychoanalytical profession did not need to be buttressed by science. Indeed, she would fight her toughest battle, not against outsiders, but against forces within 'the movement', a battle whose outcome directly affected how she would act much later when she supervised Thomas Quick's treatment at Säter.

To understand the nature of these conflicts and the effect they had the Thomas Quick case, it is essential to know a little about how Freud worked. As he went about inventing psychoanalysis from scratch, he frequently changed his mind on crucial points. Every time he modified his ideas about how the psyche functions he had to rethink how to carry out psychoanalytical treatment. One such U-turn concerned the role of early trauma. For a few years towards the end of the 1890s, Freud believed that most mental disturbances could be traced back to traumatic experiences in childhood. Then he abandoned that idea and instead developed his theory of drives. A key element of this theory is that infants are sexually attracted to the parent of the opposite sex, and that this desire could lead to psychological problems both in childhood and adulthood. Freud's theory of drives claimed that mental problems in the adult were caused by the collisions between different, more or less forbidden drives and not by traumatic mental or physical experiences in childhood.

Freud's ideas changed and developed over time and, during the first couple of decades of the twentieth century, the trailblazers of psychoanalysis took on board different elements of his thinking. Several schools of thought formed within the discipline, making an exact definition of 'psychoanalysis' impossible.

It was Freud's theory of drives that generated the most irreconcilable conflict. Margit Norell would man the barricades all her life. The psychoanalysts who kept faith with the so-called 'orthodox' form of the teaching dug themselves in and, in the 1930s, declared the theory Freud had finally adopted to be the one true and scientific basis for psychoanalysis. In the trenches on the opposing side, the Freudians confronted troops made up of those who believed that, one way or the other, personal well-being is determined by the quality of interpersonal relationships rather than conflicting drives within the individual. People on this side were sceptical about the theory of drives and believed that real-life events, especially in childhood, play an important role in the development of personality.

They were the 'neo-Freudians', of whom the best known are Harry Stack Sullivan (1892–1949), Erich Fromm (1900–1980), Karen Horney (1885–1952) and Frieda Fromm-Reichmann

(1889–1957). All of them, except Sullivan, had grown up in Germany and fled from the Nazis to America. They had questioned orthodox Freudian analysis from the 1930s onwards, rejecting the 'neutral' role of the analyst and actually prioritizing emotional engagement with their patients.[74]

Margit's training was supervised by orthodox Freudians. The members of the Swedish Psychoanalytical Society (SPS) were precise and dogmatic adherents to an idea of 'correct' treatment. The theory of drives was one of the corner stones of their version of Freudian analysis. They regarded the neo-Freudians as heretics. However, Margit soon realized that she did not believe in the orthodoxy. Even before her training had begun, she had read works by Erich Fromm and Karen Horney, who believed that neurotic personality disorders were caused by dysfunctional relationships in childhood and youth.[75]

Margit grew sceptical of the orthodox approach to therapy but had to keep her doubts to herself. The SPS was a dogmatic organization that might well have excluded her if she had spoken up.[76] She continued to read neo-Freudian books and articles in secret while treating patients under the supervision of orthodox Freudians. In an autobiographical piece, she describes the difficulty of applying the theory of drives to her analysis as a non-believer: '*I tried to work as a reasonably committed Freudian analyst – but felt at the same time that I never got a proper grip on my patients' most critical problems and emotional experiences.*'[77]

She led an intellectual double-life, pretending to be an orthodox Freudian but studying the forbidden teaching of the neo-Freudians. Frieda Fromm-Reichmann, a German psychoanalyst and the wife of Erich Fromm, made the deepest impression on her. Fromm-Reichmann worked at Chestnut Lodge, a mental care facility just outside Washington, where she offered psychoanalytical treatment to patients suffering from schizophrenia. She thought that even this severe form of mental disorder was influenced by insecure relationships in childhood. Her essays and articles were collected in her book *Psychotherapy and Psychoanalysis*. It made such a powerful impression on Margit that even thirty years later, she would say that it had changed her life.

One of her colleagues lent me Margit's own copy of Fromm-Reichmann's book. It was full of notes and marks, with Margit's Yes!-moments exploding on the page in the form of single or double underlinings and exclamation marks in the margins. She spoke in an interview about a passage in the book that had affected her profoundly. It came from the final chapter, 'On loneliness', and in it Fromm-Reichmann formulates an idea, exceptional at the time: mental disorder could be the outcome of loneliness. She writes that her patients in Chestnut Lodge suffer, perhaps more than anything else, from their inability to be close to others:

> *Loneliness seems to be such a painful, frightening experience that people do practically everything to avoid it. [. . .] Real loneliness [. . .] leads ultimately to the development of psychotic states. It renders people who suffer it emotionally paralysed and helpless. [. . .] I would not be surprised if [. . .] we would see that loneliness in its own right plays a much more significant role in the dynamics of mental disturbance than we have been ready to experience so far.*[78]

Margit had underlined these sentences with thick pencil lines. Generally, she was so impressed that, for the rest of her life, she thought of Frieda Fromm-Reichmann as her 'soul mate' even though they never met.[79] She describes the experience of reading the book in one of her rare interviews:

> I understood what [Frieda Fromm-Reichmann] wrote, understood her approach to therapy, learned something from it and recognized myself in her. [. . .] For one thing, she touched upon a subject that no one had written about before and which she, too, had noted as absent in psychiatric thought and publications. The subject is the importance to both children and adults of loneliness when exposed to traumatic experiences and does not refer to solitude as an expression for something other than being lonely. It is about the immediacy of loneliness, of living in that state and knowing the unbearable reality of it, which children cannot experience because children cannot survive alone.[80]

In the Norell photo album, there is a black and white picture of Margit, taken by her eldest son, Staffan, in 1959, around the same time that she discovered Frieda Fromm-Reichmann. It shows Margit, her dark hair piled up on her head, sitting with her head tilted a little to one side, smiling and looking into the camera. She had just celebrated her forty-fifth birthday, which meant that a shadow that had darkened her life for a long time was fading when the photo was taken. She explained her anxiety in a letter: '*My mother died aged forty-six and not before I myself passed this age did it become clear to me that I had never really counted on living past the age at which she died.*'[81]

She was now standing on the threshold of a world that she had feared she would never see. It might have strengthened her resolve. She had already tried to persuade a group of younger students at the Psychoanalytical Society to read and discuss Frieda Fromm-Reichmann's forbidden book but nobody had dared join the study group. They were too fearful of antagonizing the Psychoanalytical Society's board. By then Margit was ready to do something more radical. She planned to gather a group of pupils and secretly teach them neo-Freudian psychoanalysis. When she considered them ready, they would set up a new organization with herself as its director and battle against the orthodox Freudians.

When Staffan photographed his smiling mother, she had all that ahead of her. She was not to know that the project would cause damage to her in a way that would not heal for the rest of her life.

7

Sture's youth

'The loneliness I felt during those months was enormous.
All my dreams of the future had been ruined and all I could
feel was grief.'
> Sture Bergwall, speaking about the suicide
> of the first man who had returned his love.

By the end of his ninth year at secondary school Sture had reasonably good marks, but since he had not passed all his subjects he could not apply to senior school, which was seen as a major failure by his family. In the summer of 1967, seventeen-year-old Sture got a job as a janitor in the local branch of a bank. One of his tasks was to take mail to the post office and the daily trip meant that he kept meeting and eventually fell for a fourteen-year-old boy. One day, he lured his new friend into the bank's printed paper store, which had its own street entrance. According to later interrogations, Sture had allegedly touched the boy in a way that frightened him, so he had run away and told the police. However, in the end, no charge was brought.

Obviously Sture was still attracted to boys and psychotherapy had not helped. He turned to God instead. He was a member of a church youth group, took Holy Communion every week and had considered himself a Christian for a long time. He decided to apply to a Fjellstedtska, a boarding school for boys who wanted to go on to study divinity and become ordained. His older brother Torvald was already there, well on his way to the ministry. The school records show that Sture's drug abuse had worsened. In addition to his daily TCE sniffing, he drank alcohol, mostly beer and wine. He made sexual advances to his classmates and ended up feeling profoundly anxious and depressed, even making an awkward attempt at suicide. He suffered so badly during the six months he spent there that, in the winter of 1967–8, he was forcibly admitted to the city's mental hospital at Ulleråker. He was given antipsychotic medication and insulin shock treatment, used at the time to manage clinically depressed patients.

Even hospitalization failed to curb Sture's drug addiction. In the Ulleråker case notes, I found entries such as 'quite markedly intoxicated on smuggled alcohol' and 'even found sniffing in the ward'. Another note records that Sture had 'asked another patient to buy trichloroethylene, which he had sniffed. He was strongly affected.'

Sture tended to become addicted to whatever substance he tried. He was fighting depression and could not accept that he was homosexual. One case note describes how 'he felt drawn to a sweet little boy on the ward and touched him at every opportunity. During this period, the patient was in an exalted mood but also anxious and would cry in despair afterwards.'[82]

In February 1968, Sture was kicked out of the boarding school for the following reasons: 'Absent 185 hours. Hence, large gaps in attainment, his knowledge not even reaching entry level for senior school. Also, he has made sexual advances to other pupils, which left the Headmaster with the strong impression that [Sture] would be unable to cope with remaining in an exclusively male boarding school.'

Sture went home to Falun, stayed with his parents and managed to get a nights-only job as nursing auxiliary at Falun Hospital. This was where he met a nursing team leader called Tom, the man Sture still calls his first true love:

It began when I was called in to see him. Tom told me that he thought I had a real aptitude for the job and that he wanted to help me get into nursing college. From that moment, I dared to believe I had a future after all. We began to go out together and, later, had a sexual relationship. I was so much in love. To me, it was a very special experience and a beautiful one.

Tom might have saved him, but when Sture arrived at work one day he was told that Tom had died. He had killed himself. Sture was only eighteen years old. 'Then began the saddest period in my life. The loneliness I felt during those months was enormous. All my dreams of the future had been ruined and all I could feel was grief.'

During 1969 Sture's multiple drug dependency grew. Then a series of events took place that would lead to his first admission to inpatient psychiatric care. As Thomas Quick, many years later, he used this episode to convince his critics that he was a real serial killer, as he appears to have behaved exactly as one might have expected.

On nights when Sture was off-duty, he was at a loss over what to do. He could not bear being at home in Korsnäs and would instead cycle the five kilometres to central Falun to wander the streets aimlessly, drinking fortified wine and sniffing TCE. In this state, he encountered an eleven-year-old boy called Ola on his way home from a school party. Sture dragged the boy into a blacksmith's yard and ordered him to pull his trousers down. According to the court conviction a year later, Sture had masturbated in front of Ola and then tried to push his penis into the boy's anus. Before Ola managed to escape, Sture threatened the boy: bad things would happen to him if he told anyone. The incident took place just before Sture's nineteenth birthday.

Later that summer, he hung out with two queer boys of his own age and had occasional sex with them. He also began to use amphetamine, which was on sale in City Park. Amphetamine quickly became a favourite of his but he didn't dare inject the drug intravenously and absorbed the powder through his mouth instead. At one point, Sture asked for help at the adult psychiatric clinic. His notes say:

The patient has tried to fight his homosexuality. His condition recently felt urgent. [...] He is torn, has difficulties concentrating at work, struggles to stay off alcohol, drinks 2–3 times per week. Drinks to be able to speak about his anxiety but if he consumes more than a certain number of glasses (equiv. 1–2 bottles) he feels morose, then depressed. Has smoked hash occasionally, does not take any addictive substances in tablet form, no opioid injections.[...]

Homosexuality always a burden, but he says that he has now lost control of his actions and that this is something new.[83]

Sture had not mentioned taking amphetamine or sniffing TCE. The doctor prescribed tranquillizers, which his patient promptly incorporated into his growing pharmacological repertoire. In the autumn, his two friends went off to university and Sture was left alone in Falun. It had become hard to get hold of amphetamine but he sniffed TCE and drank fortified wine, topped up with tranquillizers and, when he was not on duty at the hospital, again took to wandering at night in a state of intoxication.

On 22 October 1969, Sture was walking along Svärdsjö Street when thirteen-year-old Anders cycled past. When Sture asked if Anders had 'a nice cock' the boy replied that he must get home. Sture wanted to touch Anders and begged to be allowed. He put his hand on the boy's crotch but Anders protested loudly. Sture also kissed Anders on the cheek, but did nothing else. Three days later, Sture found a new victim, another thirteen-year-old called Karl Göran. He had been walking through Falun with some of his friends and had stopped to tie his shoelace. Sture grabbed Karl Göran by the scruff of his neck, said that he was beautiful and pulled him down into a ditch. The boy called for help and managed to get free. When a car passed, Sture became scared and ran away.

These incidents were reported to the police. Falun is not a big town and by the end of October 1969 a couple of officers were ready and waiting for Sture when he left the hospital at the end of his shift. He was taken to the station and confessed almost at once. He was interviewed briefly but then asked to be allowed to go home to sleep before being more thoroughly interrogated. The police let him go.

What happened next is a good insight into Sture's lack of self-control at this stage, and also illustrates his deeply rooted self-destructiveness. He had been found out and knew that his shameful crimes would be exposed in a court of law but he said nothing to his family. Instead, he went to his room and sniffed TCE alone. Then he cycled back to Falun, where he bought a couple of bottles of wine and beer and drank the lot. Later, he took some of the Largactil tablets (chlorpromazine, an antipsychotic) he had been given at the walk-in psychiatric clinic. At eight o'clock, he attended the late service in Stora Kopparberg church and then went to the hospital even though he was not on duty that night.

Sture took the back door route to the staffroom in ward 51, part of the infectious diseases department where he usually worked. He met a colleague there, a nurse called Maud, who knew him quite well. When questioned, she described him as unhappy and very intoxicated. Sture's drunkenness irritated Maud but she felt sorry for him and promised to fix him a sandwich since he hadn't eaten anything all day. Then the telephone rang and Maud had to take the call. Sture put on a white coat and went to room 4, where a nine-year-old boy called Stefan lay asleep. Sture woke the boy by chatting to him and then began to 'caress Stefan's male organ [. . .]', as the subsequent investigation put it.[84] When Stefan screamed, Sture panicked and tried to silence him, first by covering his mouth and then grabbing the child by the neck. He let go when Stefan's nose started bleeding and he fell out of bed. Sture thought that he had killed the boy and ran from the room. He called the hospital exchange from the nursing station to ask the telephonist to alert the duty doctor and tell him to go to ward 51 where a small boy was dying or dead. Then he called for a taxi, left the hospital and asked to be taken to a clergyman he knew. Hysterical and weeping, he told the minister about the murder he had committed. In despair, Sture showed him blood on his hands. When interviewed later, the minister said that he had felt unsure if this scene was the outcome of intoxication fuelling Sture's dramatic instincts, or if he really had murdered somebody.

Sture used the minister's telephone to call the police and leave an anonymous message about the murder at the hospital. Then he phoned the ward and spoke to his colleague Maud, who told him that Stefan was alive. Maud had found him on the floor with a nose bleed. Stefan said that he had had a nightmare about a doctor coming into his room and kissing him. She put the boy back into bed and he fell asleep.

Accompanied by the minister and still in tears, Sture returned to the hospital. Maud could not understand why he was so upset and took him to see Stefan, who was sleeping peacefully. 'He's really alive,' Sture said and fainted. When he came to, he left the hospital and cycled home. He went to the police station the following day and turned himself in. Stefan was examined and faint strangulation marks were found on his neck. It is unlikely that anyone would have noticed if Sture had not raised the alarm.

The hospital incident was added to Sture's previous confessions of sexual harassment of boys. He was arrested and spent months in the Håga forensic psychiatric institution in Södertälje. A public prosecutor opened court cases against Sture for a string of offences that included sexual abuse of minors and attempted murder of the hospitalized boy. Otto Brundin, an elderly consultant, carried out a full psychiatric examination. His report would be quoted decades later in court.

Dr Brundin stated that Sture had behaved 'in a calm, orderly, polite and constructive manner' throughout the several weeks-long examination and that the patient 'gradually felt his condition improve steadily'. According to Brundin, this was because Sture no longer had access to the drugs he had previously abused: 'It has become obvious that the relatively long period during which Bergwall had been prevented from all use of alcohol-containing drink as well as other neuroactive substances has been beneficial for his health. He had become relaxed and no longer shows dysphoria [distress]. He is not anxious or anguished and has generally no symptoms of depression. He has no disorders of thought or perception.'[85]

It was Brundin's main diagnosis that would be quoted decades later by those who wanted Thomas Quick to be seen as a likely serial killer: 'Bergwall exhibits severe sexual perversion in the form of *paedophilia cum sadismus* [sadistic paedophilia].'

He went on to insist that the hospital incident was the result of 'an intent to murder in order to obtain sexual release, an act typical of sadistic paedophiles'. He went on to state that Sture's drug and alcohol dependency had no part in turning him into someone who kills for pleasure. The explanation was to be found elsewhere: '[it lies in] the genetic code handed down to Bergwall which contains chromosomes with aberrant functions'. He concluded that disturbed chromosome function meant that Sture was a sadistic paedophile by birth.

Brundin felt the appropriate treatment was hormonal castration. However, Sture was afraid that the treatment would dull him. His consultant agreed that there was a risk:

> Bergwall's fears concerning possible effects on the development of his personality are not unfounded. Thus, he recognizes well enough the difference between the bull and the ox, or castrated bull, although it should be remarked at this point that it is in the bull's nature to kill people, while the therapeutic goal in Bergwall's case would be to remove the killer component in the structure of his personality but also to control such changes that would go on to cause a dampening of his personality, *à la* the ox.

Brundin rounded off his report by stating that Sture was a dangerous killer: 'In the view of the examining consultant, Bergwall is not only dangerous but might, under certain circumstances, constitute an exceptional danger to another person's life and limb.'

He recommended inpatient psychiatric care.

The social services department wanted a second opinion from another consultant. They picked Yngve Holmstedt, who represented a new generation of psychiatrists that would take over from people like Otto Brundin. Holmstedt was not interested in genes and chromosomes and instead saw Sture's problems as the product of his upbringing:

> Bergwall is a 20-year-old male. His life since puberty has been dominated by serious problems related to his sexuality. He grew up in a working class home with expectations of academic success, especially relevant given the father's great disappointment at not having had the opportunity to study in his youth, also a background of early free church morality and overt prudery, especially with regard to sexual

morals. The demands made on the children are likely to have considerably outstripped what the parents could offer them by way of emotional warmth and personal interest. Four of the patient's siblings have passed examinations qualifying them for higher education – or soon will, in the case of the fourth.

[Sture's] development also seems to have been further complicated by two features. One is that he is a twin. His twin sister appears even before the age of 10 to have been both physically and mentally stronger than [Sture]. Also, until the end of primary education, the twins continued to attend the same class at school – the sister consistently achieving the better marks, something much lauded by the family as a whole.

The second feature is that [Sture] entered puberty early, thus his sexual problem also became a major concern at an early stage. [...] He has, since puberty, been intensely engaged in an anguished struggle between his drive towards sexual contacts with younger, somewhat feminine boys and his super-ego's and society's condemnation of such acts. [...] Since the age of 15, Bergwall has swung between periods of deep distress, depression and battling with his inclinations followed by recurrences of his attraction to boys with release of tensions on one hand and, on the other, an increasingly troubled conscience as a dual consequence. Notably, he has attempted suicide on several occasions and also had to be admitted to psychiatric care several times.[86]

Holmstedt observed that Sture's crimes had been committed 'under the influence of mental abnormality of such a deep-rooted type that it must be thought of as equivalent to mental illness'. He made it clear that he did not accept Otto Brundin's conclusion that the hospital incident proved his patient's inclination to kill boys for pleasure:

As for the postulated 'intention to kill' in connection with the aggression shown towards the young boy in the hospital, I believe it highly improbably that any such intention was present. [...] More probably – based on experience from other, similar cases –

the violence was a panic response and aimed at silencing the boy, i.e. to stop his screaming and weeping, and nothing else. [. . .] All suggestions that Bergwall 'kills for sexual pleasure' are therefore likely to be groundless.

Holmstedt also wrote that he could find no evidence that Sture was more of a sadist than other homosexuals, and that what he needed was 'a period of being cared for in a mental hospital . . . and radical therapy, e.g. some form of psychoanalysis would be a theoretically worthwhile approach'. Holmstedt ultimately suspected that psychoanalysis would not change the patient's sexuality and rounded off his report with the hope that Sture would find help from God: 'A strong religious conviction can, as one might hope would be the outcome in [Sture's] case, offer considerable means of sublimating his sexual urges.'

The court followed Holmstedt's advice. On 26 May 1970, it convicted Sture of four charges of causing public nuisance, sexual assaults on children and exposure with sexual intent. The murder charge was thrown out; the court did not consider Sture to be someone who killed for pleasure. He was sentenced to secure psychiatric care and was admitted to the Sidsjö mental hospital in Sundsvall. He was twenty years old.

More than two decades later, when Sture had become the serial killer Thomas Quick, many thought it obvious that he as a nineteen-year-old had in fact attempted to murder the boy in the hospital. By that time he was considered responsible for at least four murders even before 1969, so the hospital incident was seen as an attempt to commit murder number five. It all seemed to fit the picture of a ruthless serial killer. No one mentioned that the 1969 investigation report contained several witness testimonies of Sture's hysterical sense of guilt on the night of the incident, and his alerting, first the hospital's telephone exchange, then a clergyman and the police. It was also conveniently forgotten that, the day after the 'attempted murder', he had turned himself in at the police station and confessed to his crime. No one wanted to hear Holmstedt's good arguments for dismissing the notion that Sture took a sadistic pleasure in killing and hardly anyone referred to the court's rejection of the 'attempted murder' charge.

In 1969, Sture Bergwall was a young man facing difficult problems, but there was no evidence that he was a sadistic killer just thwarted of his fifth murder. His personal history from these years had been rewritten to suit the alleged activities of Thomas Quick.

8

The Holistic Institute

'I transferred my fundamental relationship with my mother
to Margit.'
The psychoanalyst Jan Stensson on his psychotherapy
with Margit Norell in the 1960s.

In the early 1960s, Margit was still working under the umbrella of the
Swedish Psychoanalytical Society, feeling increasingly ill at ease. The
patients she saw at her private practice in Birkagården were treated
according to neo-Freudian principles as opposed to the orthodox
Freudianism of her training.

Jan Stensson, a retired psychoanalyst, had been one of her patients
at this time. I arranged to meet him for an interview about his relationship with Margit. He came across as a gentle, sympathetic man
who listened attentively to my questions, as one might expect after
forty-odd years of professional listening. He talked thoughtfully and
carefully, keen to express what he had to say with utter precision.

Jan met Margit in 1962. He was twenty-seven years old and had
moved to Stockholm to study psychology at the university. He wanted
to become a psychotherapist and needed practical experience so he
trained in child and adolescent psychotherapy at the Erica Foundation.
Apart from the Freudian-orientated training offered by the
Psychoanalytical Society, there were hardly any other programmes for
psychotherapists who wanted to work with adults. Margit had reluctantly taken the Society's course but Jan rejected it. He was attracted
to the neo-Freudian theory that what mattered most for mental well-
being was the quality of interpersonal relationships. He was supported
in this by his teacher at the Erica Foundation, a man called Gösta

Harding who was a pioneer of psychoanalysis in Sweden and had once been the chairman of the Society, a post he had left because he detested the dogmatic and illiberal atmosphere. In a letter to a colleague, he had said that there was something fundamentally wrong with the current state of psychoanalysis: 'The movement has split into sects and these have developed systems as rigid as those of any church.'[87]

The training programme required Jan to undergo psychoanalysis but he felt that he needed it anyway. Jan had difficult relationships with both his parents but particularly with his father, a minister. Gösta Harding recommended him to contact Margit Norell, because he knew she believed that early relationships were influential on mental health and disagreed with key aspects of Freud's teachings.

Margit's practice was two flights up in Birkagården and Jan remembers it well. He says that he formed an emotional bond to Margit almost at once: 'Margit had a knack of arousing very strong feelings in people she met. She was very charismatic.'

During the sessions, Jan lay on the bed and Margit sat in an armchair at the head end. She was not the neutral listener who merely reflected what the patient said, as expected from a Freudian analyst; Margit engaged with her patients in quite a different way.

> From the first, I felt that she listened very intently, in a very supportive way. She agreed with everything I said, understood everything I blamed others for. When I revealed how critical I was of my parents or my wife, she always firmly took my side. She questioned nothing I said and I felt she saw things wholly from my point of view. Whatever injustices or upsets I described, she backed me up. And this made me feel seen, appreciated and understood.

Jan soon began to look up to Margit.

> I came to see her as a very wise, very knowledgeable person. A free spirit, aware of the time we lived in and the lives we led. Her attitudes were modern. I kept comparing her to my mother, I suppose.

Both women were married to clergymen, of course, but Margit was a much more evolved person, somehow, and wiser. It meant that my poor mother was overshadowed. She seemed so provincial, a little slow-witted and unsophisticated. Now I realize that I was unfair, but that is how I felt in the beginning.

In psychoanalysis, this is known as 'maternal transference'. While he was her patient, Jan perceived in Margit many positive characteristics which he considered had been lacking in his early relationships with members of his family. The transference meant that he grew emotionally dependent on his analyst. 'I transferred my fundamental relationship with my mother to Margit. Naturally, that was an effect of my own needs at the time and also of what I did in the therapy sessions. But there was another element in my devotion to her and that was Margit's ability to arouse very strong feelings within the framework of the psychoanalytical situation.'

Jan's psychoanalysis lasted ten years. At first, he had one session every week but soon he was spending more time with Margit, first two, then three encounters a week. During an especially intense period, Jan was on the couch four times a week.

When Jan had been her patient for about a year, Margit asked him if he would like to join a neo-Freudian study circle that she planned to start. There were four other members who, like Jan, were Margit's patients. All of them studied psychology with the aim of becoming psychoanalysts and all were over thirty years old, which meant that Jan, at twenty-eight, would be the youngest. The others came from smart and moneyed families; one of them was the son of a famous poet. Jan told me that he felt an outsider and ashamed of his plain, rustic background.

Their primary goal was to learn about neo-Freudian analysis under Margit's tutelage, but they hoped that the study circle would grow into a new, alternative psychoanalytical society. Margit wanted to break the current society's monopoly on training and introduce neo-Freudian theory to a new generation of psychoanalysts.

From 1963 onwards, the group met once a week in one of the

members' homes, or Margit's own, whoever had the space. It was important to keep the meetings secret because Margit risked being excluded from the official society if it became known that she had a sideline training her own analysts. At the meeting she lectured on neo-Freudian theory and her own experiences of treating patients. The group prepared by studying a book from a list of relevant literature she had compiled. The first book they were given to read was *Psychoanalysis and Psychotherapy* by Frieda Fromm-Reichmann. According to Jan, it was obvious that Fromm-Reichmann meant a lot to Margit – she was Margit's 'idol', as he put it.

The book made a deep impression on Jan. The idea that analysts could engage with their patients on a personal level was an intriguing perspective, different from Freud's theory of drives and also from the biologically and genetically oriented approach that dominated Swedish clinical psychiatry in the 1960s. The psychodynamic approach felt modern and radical.

Jan was not alone in responding to Margit as his new mother. They had all exposed their innermost concerns to her and formed emotional bonds with her. He believes that they had all been exceptionally receptive to the dream of the infinitely supportive mother, as each one of them felt that their home had lacked a secure parental figure. This was – or so Jan believes – why they had turned to psychoanalysis in the first place.

Apart from Jan, only one other member of Margit's first study circle is still alive. Her name is Monica von Sydow. I met her in a Stockholm care home in the spring of 2012. She was nearly eighty-four and wheelchair-bound. Her speech was deliberate, but she was keen to talk about her childhood and her experiences with Margit.

Monica's parents, Ingun and Fredrik, were both nineteen and unmarried when Ingun got pregnant. They came from wealthy families and Ingun was sent away to relatives in Italy so that she could give birth abroad and avoid scandal. The plan was that Ingun's daughter Monica would be adopted by an Italian family and the young parents would end their relationship. Instead, they married against their parents' wishes and, two years later, brought Monica back to Sweden, although it meant separating her from her adoptive Italian parents. Fredrik and Ingun had no home of their own, so Monica and her mother lived with Ingun's parents in their apartment on Strand Way in Stockholm.

Two years later, a disaster struck that would cast its shadow over the rest of Monica's life. Late in the afternoon on Monday 7 March 1932, Fredrik's father and two housemaids were found murdered in his apartment on Norr Mälarstrand. The murder weapon appeared to be an iron. At the time of the discovery of the bodies, Fredrik and Ingun had left Monica with Ingun's parents and were out with some friends for a meal. When the police arrived and Fredrik was told that they wanted to speak to him, he whispered a few words in Ingun's ear, pulled out a gun, shot her and then himself in the head. Both died almost immediately.

Four-year-old Monica was simply told that Ingun had gone to Paris and her childhood passed without another mention of her mother. She did not even know her parents had died until she was thirteen years old, when she was sent to the library in her boarding school. There, she happened to come across old newspaper cuttings about the 'von Sydow murders'. It was her first encounter with her own tragic history.

Monica suffered from anxiety all her life. At first, she consulted a Freudian psychoanalyst but, in the late 1950s, by which time she had decided to train as an analyst, she was advised to ask Margit Norell for help. After a whole life filled with longing for a mother, her emotional dependence on Margit grew profound. She began to imitate Margit's body language and movements, just as a child might imitate a parent. They met socially, something that was unthinkable by the standards of orthodox Freudian psychoanalysis. When, in 1963, Margit asked Monica if she would like to join the secret study circle, she was glad to be asked and accepted.

Margit spent five years teaching her 'circle' until, in 1968, she considered them fully qualified psychoanalysts. When she had too many patients herself, she passed them on to members of her group. It meant that, for all of them, each analytical session turned into a cross between psychotherapy and supervision.

In February 1968, Margit announced the establishment of the Institute for Holistic Psychotherapy and Psychoanalysis in an article published in the journal *Läkartidningen*, a medical magazine. The article explained that the new society's role was to 'serve as a focus for people trained in medicine or psychology who have become interested in holistic psychotherapy and that it would, through its membership, train psychoanalysts and psychotherapists and carry out psychotherapist treatments of patients'.[88] Jan Stensson, Monica von Sydow and the other members of the first study circle were known as 'the older group' and made up the core committee of the Holistic Institute. Margit together with the older group would take on about twenty pupils. The newly born institute operated from a rented two-room flat on Bastu Street in Stockholm.

Margit's article was published two weeks before her fifty-fifth birthday. She chaired the new society, was the head of the institute and also selected herself to be its only training analyst: someone regarded as able to offer psychoanalysis to trainees on course to becoming psychoanalysts. It was one of the most prestigious titles in the world of psychoanalysis.

Now, as the leader of her own society, Margit could step onto the international stage. The Holistic Institute was immediately granted membership of the International Federation of Psychoanalytic Societies (IFPS), a worldwide organization for neo-Freudian groups and societies. It was founded in 1962 on Erich Fromm's initiative. During the years that followed, Margit was invited to the large international IFPS congresses in Madrid, New York, Zürich and Berlin where she was greeted with respect.[89] Many of the leading psychoanalysts she met during her travels were invited to come to Sweden and hold seminars at the Holistic Institute. They included major figures in the world of psychoanalysis, like Harold Kelman, Irvin Bieber, Otto Allen Will, Joseph Barnett, Marianne Horney Eckardt, Earl G. Wittenberg, Jorge Silva García and Beatrice Foster.

Margit's star was bright and ascending. But her foreign contacts did not realize there was a serious problem at the heart of the Holistic Institute.

Her control of 'the older group' was almost total. As their psycho-analyst, she knew them intimately, aware of everything from their childhood difficulties to their love lives as adults. She had been told about their infidelities, family problems and every other aspect of their private existence. In her role as supervisor, Margit also had full insight into everyone's professional work. She knew which patients her colleagues found troublesome and exactly what had caused the trouble. Not only did Margit know them through and through, she was also the most important person in their lives. They were like a group of siblings with the same mother and, typically, they competed for their mother's love and attention.

Jan told me that he used to believe that he was Margit's favourite.

In an analytical situation, she was more intimate with me than is usual. She would confide her views and thoughts to me, much more directly than was the normal practice. Of course, it made me feel special, recognized. I perceived her confidences as proof that she trusted me and believed that I had something unique to offer. To me, it was as if she had seen who I really was and thought of me as one of the driving forces within the society she planned to create. Well, that's what I believed. At first, it was a very positive experience.

Once the Holistic Institute had been set up, it became routine for Margit and Jan to discuss the other members of the group in their weekly combined supervision and analysis sessions. She would criticize their colleagues, examine their weaknesses as psychoanalysts, and even give away their secrets. In doing this, Margit broke the duty of confidentiality that should govern all psychotherapy and which ensures that no information uncovered during psychotherapy ever becomes known to outsiders. At first, Margit's indiscretions made Jan proud: 'I was flattered by her confidence in me. But it didn't take long before I felt that it was all quite wrong. It seemed so crazily out of order.'

By 1971, Jan was becoming increasingly uncomfortable with the group. He had to keep pretending that he did not know the private lives of the others. Also, it had begun to dawn on him that his relationship with Margit was not quite as unique as he had believed. Margit was leaking personal information to everyone in the group.

Monica von Sydow told me that she had a strong impression of being especially close to Margit and, just like Jan, she learned things about the other group members that she should not have known. Margit seems to have used these breaches of confidence to make sure the older members felt chosen and bonded with her.

I tried to imagine what it was like when the group gathered for a meeting chaired by Margit. Five people aged between thirty-five and forty, and Margit, approaching sixty, would be seated around the seminar table in the flat. All the younger people saw Margit as a mother figure, wanted to prove themselves worthy of her and her support. Each one of them knew sensitive, personal things about the others, knowledge they imagined was uniquely shared with Margit. As for Margit, she knew practically all there was to know about everyone present while no one had much of an idea about what made her tick.

The atmosphere must have been extraordinary.

'It was very much like a sect,' Jan Stensson admitted. 'The entire show centred on Margit and there were simply no other personalities of note. I have experienced the sectarianism in the Christian free churches in Småland. The similarities are there, the isolation and the madness.'

Margit thought extremely highly of her own ability as a psychoanalyst. She was convinced that her skills were equal to treating people with serious mental illnesses. She thought herself as good as she believed her model analyst, Frieda Fromm-Reichmann, to be and her self-belief was infectious. 'In the beginning, she stimulated us, made us enthusiastic,' Jan said. 'She was utterly self-assured and, somehow, she extended her own self to include us all. And, in turn, this effect was partly an extension of her idolisation of Frieda Fromm-Reichmann.'

This grand self-assurance, coupled with a disdain for her Swedish colleagues, was also evident in some of Margit's letters to her friends abroad: '*[M]y standards and expectations for therapeutic work transcend what is the more mediocre standard in institutions and most analytic work here.*'[90]

Margit's approach to therapeutic treatment entailed her becoming a good parent to every patient. Her theory was that, secure in this new relationship, the patient would dare to examine the connections between disturbing childhood events and their mental state later in life for the first time. The insight, once reached, would make even the most difficult problems disappear. She became known as someone who took on the kind of patient other psychoanalysts felt they could not do anything for. Sometimes, she passed on seriously disturbed patients to her inexperienced colleagues. Jan said:

> We came to believe we were world-class therapists. She told us that, unlike the members of the longer-established society, we were capable of curing patients who were borderline or even diagnosed psychotics. It became an issue of faith that she had imparted to us methods that meant we could help the seriously ill.
>
> The patients she referred to us were often very damaged and very ill. They might've been physically abused by family members, children of parents who had locked them into dark cellars or women with childbirth traumas that had caused psychotic behaviour and deep depression. Several had had psychotic episodes in their past. Margit didn't just ask us to treat the ordinary run of neurotics, but all types of borderline cases.

However, as early as the Holistic Institute's first two years, it became obvious that Margit's approach was ineffective. One after the other, the 'older group' analysts had to cope with patients in therapy committing suicide. 'NN, a woman therapist and older group member, was one of the pillars of the society in the beginning. Then, over a fairly short time, three of her patients killed themselves,' Jan said. 'It was such a terrible thing to happen. For the rest of us as well as for her.'

One of Jan's patients also killed herself. 'The only suicide during my entire professional life. I know that patient shouldn't have been in analysis, she was too ill. At least, I shouldn't have worked with her in the way I did.'

Margit's highly theoretical notions about how to treat the most deeply disturbed patients had collided with an irreconcilable reality. The outcome was catastrophic. Panic broke out among the older group and they turned to their 'mother' for support. They had a shock coming. Even though Margit had trained them all, then allocated patients to them and supervised their therapeutic work, she placed the responsibility for the suicides squarely on the shoulders of her less experienced colleagues. She believed that failed therapy was by definition due to the psychoanalyst not digging deep enough or not working intensively enough with his or her own childhood traumas. When therapy didn't help the patient it was because of the analyst's personal weaknesses. This personal failure would mean that the analyst could not take on the role of secure deputy-parent that the patient needed.

Jan recalled Margit turning on the therapist with the three dead patients and criticizing her severely. 'Margit said that NN hadn't worked hard enough with herself, that she was immature and a flawed personality and so forth. She said things like "You're as stiff as a frozen twig and as easy to snap."' When Jan's patient committed suicide, he too was left without any kind of support and was instead accused of being solely responsible. There was nothing left of the boundless confirmation and encouragement that he had come to expect from the woman who had meant so much to him as his teacher, supervisor, psychotherapist and latter-day mother.

In the wake of their failed therapeutic efforts, the 'older group' members began to hold their own secret meetings to discuss Margit. This was how they came to realize that, over the years, she had dispersed sensitive personal information about all of them. Jan said:

We were furious and disappointed, too. There was something sick about all we had been involved in. Margit's dominant manner – perhaps one could use the word narcissistic – had its own attraction because such self-assurance imparts a kind of charisma. It can be both enticing and seductive. Now, we paid attention to our different

89

experiences of Margit: her way of picking one of us as her 'confidant' at different times; her ill-judged habit of spreading knowledge about us without letting on. We were rather unkind and I wouldn't argue that this process was particularly healthy or good for us, but it was probably necessary at the time.

The discovery triggered a war against Margit that lasted for several years. The antipathy was painful to Margit, who felt utterly alone. Her feelings are plain to see in her letters to foreign psychoanalysts. After 1968 the volume of Margit's correspondence grew fast and it is obvious that she was looking for more than just exchanges on professional matters. Her letters contain many examples of her hesitant attempts to create the mutual trust she apparently lacked in Sweden.

Her husband Curt couldn't help. Just about everyone who knew Margit between the 1960s and the 1990s agrees that she disliked her husband intensely by then. Annie Norell Beach recalled that her mother would often row with Curt and was perpetually dissatisfied with him, even though he had taken on much of the running of the family to let Margit work in her therapy room from early morning until late at night. Annie felt that Curt did his best and his efforts kept the family together, but Margit always disapproved.

I found a typical example of Margit's search for affection in her exchange of letters with the American psychoanalyst Otto Allen Will. He was a kind man who had worked with Frieda Fromm-Reichmann until her death in 1957, when he took over as director of the psychiatric unit Chestnut Lodge in Rockville near Washington. There, he and his colleagues worked on the psychotherapeutic treatment of patients with schizophrenia. Margit got in touch with Otto Allen Will when she visited America in 1966. She invited him to Sweden to lecture on treatment for schizophrenia in the summer of 1968 and, once back in the United States, Otto wrote a friendly thank-you note, mentioning an intimate conversation they'd had during a walk in Haga Park before she drove him the airport: '*I shall never forget the pleasure of sitting at the side of the lake near the airport and being able to talk simply and personally with you.*'[91]

Margit's reply was very emotional:

I was deeply moved on receiving your letter and sensed a form of validation which I seldom have experienced. I also felt that I would never forget the pleasure of sitting at the side of the lake near the airport and talking so simply and personally with you. But I didn't dare to express this directly and openly to you because of my fear of being the only one experiencing it this way and meeting some totally different reaction on the part of the other. I feel this has been a large part of my problem and experience.[92]

A few years later, Otto came back to give another set of seminars. Afterwards, Margit wrote: 'I, for my part, felt something I had not felt before during my entire professional life. Driving home from the airport where we had said goodbye, I realized that, for the first time, I had enjoyed the happy, liberating experience of being with a true colleague.'[93]

Margit was fifty-six years old at the time but what she wrote was no exaggeration. Her first and only experience of collegiate warmth was with a psychoanalyst whom she had met only a few times and who lived across the Atlantic. In her daily work, Margit received patient after patient who were emotionally dependent on her. She must have felt a strong need to be constantly idolized or else she would hardly have chosen the life she led, but it did isolate her from her peers. Margit had no supervisor of her own to support her, presumably because of her exalted view of her own skills and her low opinion of her Swedish fellow practitioners.

In 1970, Margit finally met a man qualified, in her view, to be her supervisor and therapist. He was the seventy-year-old psychoanalyst Erich Fromm, a philosopher and sociologist of world renown who had been married to Margit's idol Frieda Fromm-Reichmann. Fromm was one of the founding members of the neo-Freudian movement and a prolific writer whose work combined his studies of human psychology with radical social criticism aimed at the capitalist consumer society. His books *Escape from Freedom* (1941) and *The Art of Loving* (1956) became international bestsellers and by the time that Margit met him, he had produced practically one book every year for several years. His central theme was his claim that mental ill health is generated, to a large extent, by the alienation and oppression endemic to class-ridden capitalist societies. He had sharp observations to make about the consumerist illusion of happiness and instead emphasized emotional connections as the basis for a happy life.[94]

Fromm was a social democrat and prepared to fight for a more egalitarian society but he also urged psychoanalysts to help their patients rebel against the internal oppression that he believed had been imposed on them since childhood. In Fromm's view, Freud had too readily let parents off the hook. He once expressed the difference between Freud's and his own way of understanding the role of childhood in these terms: 'Basically, Freud's principle was: the child is guilty and not the parents. [. . .] But I think the analyst should be the accuser of the parents.'[95]

Erich Fromm and Margit shared similar outlooks about many professional matters so, in the spring of 1970, she wrote to ask him if he would consider a lecture tour in Sweden. To her delight, he accepted and arrived in July that year, accompanied by his second wife.[96] He spoke at a Holistic Institute seminar with specially invited guests and packed out the Citizens' House in Stockholm for a hugely successful public lecture that Margit had arranged.[97]

When Fromm had returned to Locarno in southern Switzerland, Margit wrote to tell him that the Holistic Institute was causing her trouble because the 'older group' was turning against her. She never mentioned her own breaches of confidentiality or the terrible series of suicides:

> I easily get paralysed in trying to deal with it. My fear of loneliness is a
> decisive factor I feel, and there is the realistic fear of splitting a very young
> society. So I tend to withdraw when obstacles and aggressiveness mount
> and to resort to my work with other patients than candidates – especially
> as these patients to a large extent are politically radical people, with
> positions where they influence our present day Swedish society – and to
> the training and supervision of those candidates who do earnest and
> devoted therapeutic work.[98]

The letter ended with a plea for help. In Sweden, she said, she was alone: '*Would it be possible for me to have a few talks with you in Locarno sometime next summer or fall? I do have the feeling that it would be of great help to me in the situation our Society and I myself are in. It is not so easy to keep a steady course with no one to talk these things through with, and with the complexity of the situation.*'[99]

Fromm said that he would see her for a week in the autumn of 1971. They corresponded often during the six months or so leading up to the meeting, discussing psychoanalytical literature and jointly tearing apart Freud's theory of drives. Margit complained about the ungrateful members of the society's 'older group': '*A few of them have been in analysis with me for a long time and would also admit that I practically saved their lives, but this has not prevented them from leaving me [. . .].*'[100]

Fromm backed her wholeheartedly and, by correspondence, singled her out as a model of a pure and genuine human being:

> *I am sorry that the conflicts in the Society have not been solved, and that they affect you personally. [. . .] I am often struck by the fact [. . .] that people find it so difficult to distinguish between the genuine and the false, the clean and the dirty in people. This is, I believe, a most fundamental category, much more so than psychological categories like being aggressive or authoritarian and so on. It is difficult in psychological terms to even define what cleanliness vs. dirtiness is, but less difficult to define what is genuineness vs. bluff. Psychoanalysts have unfortunately given too little attention to those qualities which make the whole difference between doing harm, or even helping.*[101]

Margit happily took Fromm's analysis to heart and applied it to her rebellious young colleagues: '*I possibly could have been of better help to them by seeing the false and dirty in them and reacting to it at an earlier time. I have been afraid fully to experience disappointment, loneliness and rage I think.*'[102]

In the middle of October, Margit travelled to Locarno. The Swiss town is beautifully situated on the banks of Lake Maggiore near the Italian border. Fromm and his wife went there during the summer months and spent the winters in their home in Mexico. Fromm's secretary had booked a room for Margit in a small hotel and arranged for her to meet her host daily during the six days of her stay for several hours of conversation. A week after her return to Sweden, Margit wrote a deeply enthusiastic thank-you letter, which included a measure of self-criticism that was unlike her:

> *Dear Dr Fromm, to-day a week ago we spent the last evening together at the nice restaurant down by the lake in Locarno and I feel how much I want to thank you both for that evening [Fromm's wife was also present] with all its warmth and good food and the abundance of your personal and historical knowing which you let me share.*
>
> *And then comes that for which it is more difficult to express what I feel – the talks we had during the week. For me they were essentially psychoanalytical sessions in the truest sense I have ever experienced and they meant very, very much to me. They also helped [me] to see some important things clearer. I suddenly saw the risk I at times run of disappearing into the tree as the Chinese painter of the legend, who disappeared into the picture he himself had painted. I feel less inclined for passivity and less frightened even when tired or disappointed and I feel a strong wish that [I] need love and my own need to prove things about myself may get less important and less prevent me seeing people and what is going on clearer.[. . .]*
>
> *Some of the people I like best here expressed their great satisfaction and pleasure when I in a few words told them what my stay in Locarno had meant to me. They said that they had sometimes wondered how I could manage what they feel to be a large amount of hard work and responsibility alone and that they had wished for me it need not always be so. What I at times have felt quite consciously is a tendency to envy my own patients.*[103]

Fromm had given Margit a copy of his 1964 book *The Heart of Man* and she read it during her journey home. Its arguments made a deep impression on her. It is one of the many books in which Fromm develops and comments on his own system for understanding personality disturbances.[104] Among other topics, he defines a biophilous personality, which translates as 'one which loves life', and a necrophilous type, characterized by its 'love of death'. According to Fromm, necrophilous people are emotionally cold and prefer to keep others at a distance. They are also aggressive, narcissistically self-obsessed, generally given to destructive interpersonal relationships, and lack the capacity to love. Instead their goal is to control others. As extreme examples of those belonging to this category, he mentions Hitler and Mussolini, but emphasizes that many necrophilous people can be as deranged as the notorious historical figures without actually being in a position to start a war: *'A necrophilous person loves control, and in the act of controlling he kills life.'*[105]

Margit felt she recognized herself in *The Heart of Man*:

I started reading it with great pleasure on my way home. Different kinds of aggressiveness in me and necrophilic tendencies suddenly came to my mind clearer than I have dared to focus on them earlier and a piece of self-analysis resulted. At the same time I very clearly felt how much I wish for a possibility to continue talking these things through with you if and when that would be possible for 3 weeks or 3 days – whatever would be possible for you. I think this need is so strong in me because of a rather autistic childhood and having to find my way alone to a large extent later also.[106]

During that autumn, Margit wrote several letters emphasizing how much her encounter with Fromm had meant to her: *'The hours I had with you and your great honesty have helped me very, very much in looking at what I have been doing wrong [. . .] A feeling that comes to me much more often now is hope – also in the midst of quite a lot of hard work – and I feel that I am beginning to see other people a lot clearer.'*[107]

Margit hoped to meet Fromm every summer for a week of intensive psychotherapy. It was not to be. Fromm was an exceedingly busy man and his health was poor. He was constantly working to new book deadlines and would dash off at the drop of a hat, leaving Europe for Mexico or New York. He issued half-promises about inviting Margit to Locarno, only to postpone the meeting again and again. It became steadily more obvious that Margit had pinned her expectations of a happier future on a psychotherapist who was even less likely to stay in the same place than her globetrotting mother had been.

In the summer of 1973, all of two years after the first meeting in Locarno, Margit was granted another, much longed-for week of therapy with Erich Fromm. They met daily and Margit was very satisfied. Afterwards, she immediately started a campaign to bring about a third visit, but often long periods would go by without any response from Fromm. At the same time, her conflict with the institute's analysts escalated and her new hope of becoming less lonely began to fade.

9

Margit's defeat

*'I have been calling forth the image of your face many times
when the situation has felt very hard.'*

> Margit, in a letter to David Schecter,
> her only friend (1977).

By 1972, Margit was struggling. The previously adoring group of
younger analysts was so hostile that all its members refused to attend
any therapy or supervision sessions with her. Erich Fromm – from
whom she had expected so much as her own supervisor – barely
replied to her letters. She was terribly lonely but providence was
about to hand her a gift in the form of Barbro Sandin. A couple of
years earlier, Sandin, a forty-four-year-old mother of three, had
started studying at the College for Social Studies in Örebro. She finished her studies in 1972 and landed a traineeship at Säter, the mental
hospital that looked after some of Sweden's most severely ill patients.
Säter included outpatient care as well as wards for inpatients and a
notorious secure pavilion for criminals sentenced to forensic psychiatric care.

Barbro Sandin spent her term of practical work experience on a
ward caring for psychotic patients. She developed a good relationship
with a young man called Elgard Jonsson, a schizophrenic regarded as
chronically ill. Sandin felt very sorry for him and wanted to help him.
The Säter approach to managing schizophrenic patients was typical of
psychiatry at the time and depended mainly on electroconvulsive therapy (ECT) and administration of powerful drugs. But the hospital had
a progressive medical director who encouraged the young trainee
social worker to try treating Elgard Jonsson with 'talking therapy'. A

97

competent supervisor was required and she contacted Margit Norell, who accepted the task.[108] Elgard Jonsson's condition improved, his medication was reduced and he moved in with Sandin's family. He found himself a job as a forestry labourer and, later, studied psychology and qualified as a clinical psychologist. The medical director was so impressed that, in 1973, he offered Sandin a part-time post with special responsibility for treating schizophrenics even though she was a social worker and not a psychotherapist. Margit was retained to provide the backup of psychotherapeutic competence.[109]

From Margit's perspective, the new post was an almost incredible stroke of luck. It had been her dream since the 1950s to follow in her soulmate Fromm-Reichmann's footsteps and use psychotherapy in the treatment of schizophrenic patients. In 1969, she had made a pilgrimage to the legendary psychiatric unit Chestnut Lodge, and spent a day in the small villa inside the precincts where Fromm-Reichmann had lived until her death in 1957.[110] In Sweden, Margit had occasionally supervised doctors who had psychotic patients but had never expanded this side of her practice. Now, thanks to Barbro Sandin, she had a chance to create her own Chestnut Lodge at Säter. As it happened, her new role as Sandin's supervisor created a connection with Säter that would make it possible for Margit to take over the control of Sture's psychotherapy some twenty years later.

Sandin travelled to Stockholm regularly to see Margit. Her hospital workload grew and in 1975 she was given a full-time post. A year later the hospital engaged a few more psychotherapists who would all be supervised by Margit. It was an experimental enterprise that came to be known as 'the Säter model' and eventually it was given its own building.

The Säter model was based on the premise that the cause of schizophrenia in the adult is oppression and abusive control in childhood, usually exerted by parents. To this day, there is no research data to support this hypothesis but it was popular in the 1970s. In the spring of 1975, *Läkartidningen* published an article by Margit, Barbro and the medical director Mats Nyman in which they described their experimental treatment practices. They wrote, among other things:

The initiative to this clinical approach derived from our assumption that schizophrenia is essentially a developmental disturbance, originating during the early years of childhood and that the condition can be understood as a mode of surviving stressors that proved too hard to deal with. [. . .] Reality has limited the patient's striving to expand. He has been forced to accept a compromise that entailed a narrowing down of the persona he might have become. Illness has been an adaptation to oppression, in the hope of saving something from life. It follows that the adaptation, above all, causes the schizophrenic person to experience a 'death of the emotions' but also that the patient carries within herself such resources of self-realization that, although her development has stopped at too early a stage, possibilities of growth still remain.[111]

The therapy focused on helping the schizophrenic patient to understand which traumatic childhood events had caused the illness: 'The patient must reach a clear insight into, as well as an emotional contact with, his or her early, deep feelings of disappointment and all the difficult experiences that once ruined fundamental possibilities of positive functional development.'

Those who read about the Säter model in Swedish newspapers during the 1970s and 1980s would have got a strong impression that the approach was successful. The journalists celebrated Barbro Sandin for her work on rehabilitating schizophrenics and reported that conventional psychiatrists were trying to stop her.

However, I could not find any scientifically conducted studies that validate the Säter model. Sandin and her enthusiastic supporters claimed successes which seem to have only one published confirmation: the collected case histories of the first group of patients Sandin treated. Though these patients improved a great deal, they had been hand-picked by Sandin. It would be rash to draw any general conclusions. Johan Cullberg, professor of psychiatry and Sweden's grand old man of dynamic psychiatry (which focused on emotional processes), carried out a large-scale evaluation of the Säter model and other similar enterprises. The results showed that very few schizophrenics were cured. The patients with the most positive outcomes were probably misdiagnosed and had been over-medicated in the first place. It followed that they felt better once their drug intake was reduced. Cullberg pointed out that the psychobiological basis for schizophrenia is still largely unknown and while he does not deny that Barbro Sandin significantly helped individual patients, he writes that '[Sandin] generalizes on the basis of her successes and assumes that her approach is applicable to a wide range of patients diagnosed with schizophrenia. However, the concept "schizophrenia" covers several different and, in principle, unknown conditions. It follows that they require nuanced and individual treatment.'[112]

The Säter model belonged to the anti-psychiatry movement of the 1970s. It rebelled against standard psychiatric approaches and was a school of thought that appealed to many people all over the world. R. D. Laing, a Scottish psychiatrist, was one of the movement's best-known figures who, in his turn, was strongly influenced by neo-Freudians like Frieda Fromm-Reichmann. In Laing's opinion, the mentally ill were subjected to treatments that were extensions of the oppression exerted within bourgeois families and, on a grander scale, within capitalist society. Laing argued that schizophrenic patients should be regarded as healthier than 'normal people' because their 'illness' was a refusal to go along with hypocritical conventions laid down by the false 'democracy' of families and/or society at large. Laing and his collaborators experimented with so-called 'household communities' free of hierarchical structures but without positive results. Today, it seems very naive to apply radical politics to the treatment of psychotic patients but, as Johan Cullberg writes in his autobiography, the anti-psychiatry movement was an understandable reaction to the poor outcomes of the psychiatry of the day:

One might say that the movement formed as an antithesis to established psychiatry, swollen and ready for someone to prick the balloon. Historically, the accusations lobbied by anti-psychiatry are as comprehensible [in the circumstances] as were Molière's criticisms of the entire medical profession in the 18th century, when he complained of the medics hiding their ignorance about the reasons and treatments of illnesses behind a pompous façade and scientific pretensions.

The media saw the revolution within psychiatry as a part of a wave of radical change that would, it was hoped, reach society as a whole. Hence, the Säter model was widely greeted as a harbinger of salvation even though, as a method of treatment, it was already controversial in the 1970s.

I listened to an archived radio programme broadcast in April 1973, about a 'true story' novel called *I Never Promised You a Rose Garden* (1964). It had been a bestseller in the United States that was due to be published in Sweden. The author, a woman called Joanne Greenberg who wrote under the pseudonym Hannah Green, had written a slightly fictionalized autobiographical account of how the psychiatrist Frieda Fromm-Reichmann cured her of schizophrenia just three years after her admission to the psychiatric facility at Chestnut Lodge.[113]

The radio reporter introduces the topic:

Joanne Greenberg was a diagnosed schizophrenic who recovered completely after being given talking therapy. It is as little recognized today as it was twenty-five years ago, that schizophrenia, a mental illness, can be cured in this way. In fact, there are still very divergent opinions about both what schizophrenia is and how to treat the patients. [...] However, the theoretical basis for Joanne's psychotherapy is that childhood experiences and troubled emotional relationships with the child's immediate guardians are the origin of the condition called schizophrenia and that the schizophrenic state has a backstory that can be understood and made comprehensible to the patient.

Margit is introduced as 'a Swedish pioneer in this area'. Since the 1950s, the presenter says, 'Margit has been following Frieda Fromm-Reichmann's therapeutic approach to severe mental illness. Above all,

Margit Norell has served as supervisor and tutor on talking therapy to psychologists and psychiatrists who, on their own initiative, have sought to find an alternative to such methods such as electroconvulsive therapy and anti-psychotic medication.'

After being introduced, Margit begins to speak. Her Swedish is precisely articulated and carefully formulated, and her delivery reminds me of an earlier generation of actors at Dramaten, the Swedish National Theatre. She sounds a little like Ingrid Bergman in the 1970s, but her voice is shriller and has an argumentative note. I am struck by her complete self-assurance as she pronounces on what exactly schizophrenia is and how the condition must be treated, though even forty years later it remains a multifaceted and enigmatic illness. She tells her listeners about the finer points:

The child who becomes schizophrenic has been prevented from truly exerting its will at some point while growing up. Prevented from feeling truly respected and from truly expressing its own self. Prevented from deciding and acting according to its own needs and wishes. It will have been the child who has always tried to please others, to fulfil *that* person's expectations, *this* person's expectations, *the next* person's expectations. The outcome is often that the schizophrenic individual feels that 'I consist of a collection of gramophone records – there are several different versions of me'.

The programme presenter asks Margit what therapy for a schizophrenic patient would involve. She replies that the therapist should 'offer the patient a new form, an alternative to previous interpersonal relationships, a new experience of human contact that would allow the schizophrenic patient to dare get in touch with the deep, dangerous, forbidden and denied elements. Dare to express these elements, communicate about them, experience them.'

As I listened, I began to understand why Jan Stensson and his colleagues saw Margit as such a great authority that they unhesitatingly took on the treatment of severely ill patients without any real expertise. She comes across as an expert, although her knowledge was likely to be purely theoretical. There is no proof that she had ever met a person with schizophrenia.

Supervising Barbro Sandin and the other therapists working with the 'Säter model' was one of Margit's two most gratifying experiences in the 1970s. The second one was personal: she fell in love.

The man she loved was a psychoanalyst based in New York with his own practice in Manhattan. He was a member of the board of the Alanson White Institute, a neo-Freudian establishment in New York founded by Erich Fromm and Frieda Fromm-Reichmann. His name was David Schecter and he was twelve years younger than Margit.

For several years, David had been in analysis with Erich Fromm, who had also supervised him. Margit and David met at a conference in America in 1972 and started exchanging letters. Professionally and personally they had much in common. Both were trying, often in vain, to meet Erich Fromm and both were very interested in reading and discussing psychoanalytical theory. David was a Jew and Margit felt a long held-back need to talk about her own Jewishness, an identity that had not, she felt, been given enough space in her life. From 1975, their correspondence grew more personal and more intense. David wrote about his severe neck injury in a car accident and about the chronic pain that periodically made him depressed. He was married, with two teenage children, but often felt very alone. It troubled him greatly that he couldn't talk to Erich Fromm, whom he saw as a substitute father.

Margit was moved by his frankness and eventually dared to open up to him. In November 1975, she wrote:

It was when reading your last letter and finding myself crying while doing so, that I realized how much I wish that you would be a bit nearer and that I do have a pretty large burden of work and responsibility to carry here, without ever having a real friend or colleague to talk to. At the moment I have 21 patients or supervisees and 26 of their patients for which I feel responsible – about half of them schizophrenics or other very sick people – I believe I counted them all really for the first time today.[114]

Most of Margit's letters to David were handwritten because she would not allow her secretary to type them. They were often long and intimate, full of insights into her emotionally arid life and her sense of crushing loneliness. She wrote about her childhood with a brutal father and an absentee mother, and confessed that she felt guilty about having ruined her mother's life and about her jealousy of her younger sister, whom her mother seemed to prefer. The correspondence developed into a mutually therapeutic exchange. David had lost both his parents in his youth and grappled with guilt himself. He wrote supportively:

> You, Margit, are only part of [a] causal chain and thus must remove the self-accusation + actively work on self-forgiveness by understanding what went on in the truest human terms. [. . .] You – Margit – could never be the cause of unlived life. That is to externalize the cause to a baby who – as Fromm used to say to me in similar matters – 'didn't ask to be born'.[115]

Margit underlined the last few sentences with her biro.

With time, the tone of their writing grew almost tender. This was especially true of Margit's letters, which by the end of 1975 read more like love letters. But although they occasionally met at conferences arranged by the international society, which had both the Alanson White and the Holistic Institutes as member organizations, there are never any hints that their relationship was anything other than platonic. The only exception to this was one letter from Margit in which she suggests that they go away on a three-week holiday together. David always ignored that kind of suggestion and seems to have regarded Margit as a mother figure.

I have interviewed several people who were part of Margit's life in the latter half of the 1970s and many believed that Margit was in love with David. She seems to have kept her feelings under control and stayed content with their friendship, which was characterized by a mutuality that was rare in her life. They tried to help each other solve difficult problems and their letters prove how very important they were to each other.

In the spring of 1976, Margit wrote about the Holistic Institute rebellion: '*Then I was asked – or more rightly forced – to resign as director of our Institute.*'[116]

The members of her institute had begun to curtail her role by taking crucial tasks away from her. She felt tired, ill and betrayed. David tried to comfort her and she thanked him: '*A healing process is going on – in which you have a large part David, because I never felt I could express myself so freely to anyone before.*'[117]

David wrote to her about his severe pain and Margit wanted to help him. She clearly regarded his bodily ailments as, at least in part, outcomes of childhood traumas, and repeatedly offered to take David on as a patient and become his psychoanalyst.

In August 1976, he wrote warmly about Margit's '*radiant quality of spirit that literally shines through your being*'. It was Margit, he said, who helped him to endure when his pain and depression were at their most unbearable.[118]

In November 1976, Margit wrote to David about the next move by her colleagues. They wanted her to resign from her post as training analyst, her last formal role at the Holistic Institute. David responded with warm praise for her approach to psychoanalysis: '*It is rare and beautifully balanced; gentle and firm, realistic and yet optimistic; looking away from the closed in.*'[119]

Margit told him that her eyes had filled with tears as she read this. She added that she used to comfort herself by recalling all the good she had done for her patients. In one letter, she mentions a bruising meeting at the Holistic Institute and then, the following day, that she had found her morning paper reviewing a book by an author who had received therapy under her supervision '*at a very critical time in her life*'. That very evening, she went to see a film only to discover that the female lead was another ex-patient whose therapy she had supervised.[120] Experiences of this kind made her feel better during the times when her colleagues attacked her and tried to get rid of her.

Margit's letters to David offer us glimpses of her mindset at this time, but also provide insights into what happened many years later, when Margit took charge of Sture Bergwall's treatment at Säter. In a letter from spring 1975 she describes a discovery that she has made: '*It is gradually becoming clear to me that my mind and feeling works freer and more active as a supervisor with difficult patients than when I am the therapist. [T]hose are the patients I am most interested in, but they also awaken most strongly my longing to have someone to share experiences with and sometimes of course also my fear.*'[121]

In 1991, when Margit accepted the responsibility of supervising Sture's therapy, she was following up this discovery: she believed that she functioned at her best when she treated problematic patients at one remove.

Sture was exposed to an approach to therapy that Margit described in a letter to David back in March 1977. She wanted to tell him about a very interesting patient, a well-known feminist called Hanna Olsson:

> *Hanna, age 32 and for the last year one of the most well-known and responsible people here on questions of women's rights and relationships between men and women, came to work with me last November after several years of Freudian analysis [. . .] After a few weeks of our work together she sent me some poems out of which I cite: 'I look at my new mother with wonder in my eyes and ask: do you have the strength, do you have the will to let me be born in your eyes, in your words?' [. . .] And then [she] starts descend into the cleft where she never dared to go with any of her Freudian analysts.*[122]

In a later letter, Margit explains that this therapeutic 'descent' signified Hanna reliving suppressed memories of 'terror and deceit [that] she was exposed to at the age of 2 or 3'. She did not go into exactly what kind of abuse had taken place, but the therapy sessions could be dramatic:

> *Hanna feels she cannot dare to go back to these early experiences and feelings except in double sessions and when she need not go back to her work – which involves much responsibility – the same day. So we have arranged [the therapy] accordingly, and after having worked intensely for more than an hour Hanna is often so tired that she sleeps on my couch for the last half hour – a very deep and refreshing sleep as she says.*[123]

David had never heard of such an outcome of therapy and asked Margit for details: '*What state was the patient in? Did it seem like a day-dream or "hypnagogic" state? i.e. – twilight state?*'[124]

Margit replied that this case was different: '*Hanna's state was not like a day-dream or hypnagogic state, but a twilight-state in the sense that she was in so close contact with early experiences and the whole early surroundings including all senses and some specific bodily sensations, while reaching out for this early material – that she was "there" and could not at the same time be in the here and now.*'[125]

At the end of March 1977, Margit gave a lecture at the Holistic Institute. The day before, she wrote to David to say that she anticipated that this would be her last appearance in front of her colleagues because they wanted to get rid of her.

The subject she had chosen to speak about was her therapeutic work with Hanna Olsson. Margit had said that she found it most interesting to observe '[how] in the course of the therapeutic process, [the patient] reconnects with intense, primary and very early experiences that are recalled complete with the wealth of smells and colours, and with the emotional intensity that surely cannot be greater than in early childhood'.[126]

It is interesting to compare Margit's description of Hanna's therapy with what Birgitta Ståhle wrote some seventeen years later in her case notes on Thomas Quick's recall of childhood events during therapy: 'His memories are extremely intense and stressful, and so sharply detailed that Thomas hears sounds, senses smells and, generally, experiences and feels the entire situation as it once was.'[127]

The therapy Margit spoke about in 1977 was used a couple of decades later to treat Quick. Margit was one of the early practitioners of a form of therapy later called re-enactment or reliving therapy, and also regression or recovered memory therapy. This line of therapeutic work had grown into something of a global phenomenon in the 1980s, but it was also proving dangerous in that it could induce memories of events that had never taken place.[128]

Margit's fears were proven right; this was to be her last lecture to the Holistic Institute. The final confrontation took place that year. She described the whole week to David as '*a bit hellish*'. At the annual general meeting, the entire 'older group' demanded that Margit stop working as a training analyst and a majority voted in favour. Margit responded by resigning. She told David: '*I have been calling forth the image of your face many times when the situation has felt very hard.*'[129]

Still, Margit was not completely without allies: '*Among the therapists I am working with outside the Holistic group, the thought has already come up to form a new group and that the therapy I stand for must have a continuation. At the moment I am so tired of groups and all the work I have put into them, that I can't even start thinking about this.*'

Margit retreated to her practice in Birkagården and concentrated on her patients and admirers outside the Institute. David's letters were full of praise: '*I can conjure up your kindly compassionate yet zesty face when I want to be in touch with you. I think of you in all kinds of situations – with music, patients and in the dark at night. I am truly grateful for your being, Margit!*'[130]

David's problems with pain and depression were growing worse. He needed Margit, he said. She insisted that she would be prepared to be his psychoanalyst, no matter at what cost to herself: '*I also feel I can be in touch with you at any time. I want to and our friendship means very much to me – and will always do so. Nevertheless I would be willing to risk it – or even lose it – if that would be the price to pay for working with you in therapy in a way that could be of real help to you.*'[131]

David was grateful but reasoned that the geographical distance between them was too great and turned down her offer. His attempts to control his pain made him undertake a long series of physical treatments, including an operation on his neck. He normally took strong painkillers and needed occasional periods of detoxification. In the autumn of 1979, Margit travelled to New York to see David and worked with him in a few therapy sessions. Their meeting was a disaster. David was so depressed that he had stopped talking. Later, he wrote to her and apologized. Margit wrote back to say that he had nothing to apologize for. They carried on exchanging letters but David's grew briefer and darker, finally focusing entirely on his depression.

At the end of March 1980, both of them learned that Erich Fromm had died in his sleep. For seven years, Margit had clung to the hope of a third therapy session with Fromm but now it was too late. David was her only remaining friend but his condition was serious. I interviewed one of Schecter's New York friends and he told me that David had been shattered by the news of Fromm's death.

David and Margit had been writing to each other several times a month for years but now his flow of letters was drying up. In April, she begged him to get in touch and let her know how he had been feeling since Fromm's death.[132] David replied that he had been 'drowning in depression' and thanked Margit for her patience and for the times they had spent together. He was already using the past tense, as if that time was now history.[133]

On 10 July 1980, David wrote his last letter to Margit, just one page to tell her that he had been hospitalized for six weeks. He adds that he often thought about her and her generosity towards him. His letter ended:

> I am also quite depressed (keep this between us) and am seeing my analyst daily for double sessions which are painful but hopefully will in the long run aid with the depression.
>   I hope all goes well in your life. Forgive the long delay in my writing but the illness was building before my June hospitalization.
>   I send you all my love, David.

Two days after posting this letter, David saw his psychoanalyst. His wife picked him up and, on the way home, he claimed to have remembered something he had forgotten in his Manhattan practice in an office building on the corner of 87th Street and Lexington. While his wife parked the car, David walked up the stairs to the top floor. He tried to get outside onto the flat roof but the door was locked, so he went into an office on the fifth floor, opened a window and jumped out.

And so the psychoanalyst, husband and father David Schecter died. Margit had lost her only friend four months after losing Erich

Fromm, the only psychotherapist and supervisor who had ever mattered to her, though their time together amounted to just a fortnight in total.

During her remaining thirty-five years she would never again receive supervision or therapy from anyone. For the rest of her life, she would surround herself with devoted pupils so emotionally dependent on her that they treated her as a mother figure, not a friend.

The close relationship she had had with David also proved irreplaceable. With his death, Margit's brief sojourn in the land of close and mutual relationships was finished.

10

Sture in the 1970s

*'Drunk last Friday, also taken tablets bought in the hospital
kiosk. Says he regrets this, promises not to do it again.
Permitted to leave ward again.'*
Case note from Säter about the twenty-three-year-old
patient Sture Bergwall (1973)

I have often wondered at what point people become responsible for
the shape of their lives. I am not a fatalist and am wary of the idea that
everything we do is genetically or socially predetermined. I believe that
we have free will and are responsible for our actions. But I cannot work
out when we become able to make decisions and be responsible for
them. Is it at the age of three? Perhaps ten? When Sture, at fourteen,
molested some of his schoolmates for the first time, did he make an
active choice? Did he choose to start sniffing TCE? When I read the
interview records from 1969 of Sture's assaults on the four boys, I
instinctively regard him as responsible for his actions. He was nineteen
years old. If he had been pestering my child, I would probably have
started to fantasize about killing him. But I feel much less certain when
I look at a Högbo sanatorium photograph from 1956 and examine the
boy in the hospital bed with his large eyes and shy smile. His life had
not been easy, and neither had Margit's. I cannot tell to what extent
they were responsible for their respective destinies.

Sture's case notes add up to a 250-page volume that portrays a paradoxical and enigmatic young man. He was a loner. He had no close
friends and seemed unable to sustain love affairs. On the other hand,
he had obvious social skills. He was fast on the uptake, witty and

knowledgeable about many things. People felt at ease in his company. When he was not high on controlled substances, he had the knack of making others feel seen and appreciated. He was a devout Christian who went to church every week. He enjoyed literature, read widely and was emotionally affected by music and nature. He lied, but often creatively. A schoolteacher once told him that he ought to become a writer and he dreams about it to this day.

When Sture spoke to doctors and psychotherapists he was able to analyse his problems. Minutes after having won a doctor's sympathy by engaging with them on an intellectual and emotional level, he might escape from the ward and take whatever drugs he could lay hands on. He was a hugely tricky customer who also felt genuine anguish and was haunted by depression, states of mind that were made worse by drug abuse.

In May 1970, twenty-year-old Sture was sentenced to secure psychiatric care because he had molested and sexually assaulted four boys. By the end of June, he had been admitted to the Sidsjön mental hospital in Sundsvall.

In the autumn of 1971, when Sture had been at Sidsjön for just over a year, he was allowed to start taking lessons at the Sami College in Jokkmokk, where his twin sister Gun was also studying. Initially he did well. His school reports mention that he was open about his homosexuality and took initiatives such as having religious discussions and evening prayers with his fellow students. It looked very hopeful, but Sture displayed his usual duplicity. He fell in with a couple of homosexual men who were drug addicts. They got stoned together and Sture had sexual relationships with both of them.

After his first year at college, Sture was an amphetamine addict. When he came back to Jokkmokk at the beginning of the autumn term, he ran wild. In October, he was picked up in the street, unconscious after taking a mixture of alcohol, amphetamine, TCE and assorted tranquillizers. The police drove him straight back to Sidsjön and his notes state that he hallucinated when he woke up. His spell as a college student was over.

Soon after Sture's return to the hospital, a group of fellow patients started a collection on behalf of a boy whose father, also a Sidsjön patient, had just died. Sture stole the money they had raised, escaped and bought a train ticket to Stockholm. When I spoke to him about his getaway, he recalled buying a bottle of TCE in a shop on the way to the station and sniffing on the train. In Stockholm he met up with a man called Bjarne, a previous Sidsjön inmate. Bjarne had bought some amphetamine powder and Sture got high at once. Twenty-four hours later, he turned up, dirty and dishevelled, at his brother Sten-Ove's flat in Uppsala, some fifty kilometres north of Stockholm. Sten-Ove let his little brother have a hot bath and persuaded him to take the train to Sidsjön. Back in the hospital, Sture did not dare turn up in the workshop because he risked being beaten up for stealing the collection money.

In January 1973, Sture was moved from Sidsjön to the secure unit at Säter, which was closer to Falun, his home town. The Säter case notes show how chaotic his life had become. He often had suicidal thoughts and asked for psychotherapy. Sture told his doctors about his TCE-induced hallucinations and his other addictions, including that he would sniff paint thinner, drink alcohol, take amphetamine and a banned slimming compound called Preludin (phenmetrazine), which could still be bought on the Swedish black market in the 1970s. Preludin 'made him perk up' at first, he said, but then followed 'a period of indifference and fatigue'.[134]

What struck me as I read his notes was that apparently no one at Säter even tried to wean him off drugs. Instead, he was given a new addiction in the form of prescriptions of neuroactive medication in large doses, for example, the extremely addictive anxiolytic Alepam (oxazepam, a benzodiazepine).[135] He was initially prescribed three 45 mg Alepam tablets and two sleeping tablets (Mogadon, another benzodiazepine) at bedtime. In March, the Alepam dosage was increased to 50 mg three times daily, enough to knock a horse out, according to the doctors I consulted. This happened even though it was known that he procured illicit drugs around the hospital.

At the time, Säter was a small community with services such as a shoemaker, various workshops and a kiosk with an attached cafe. The staff was fully aware that the kiosk was a black–market outlet for drugs as is confirmed in Sture's notes. There are unequivocal references to Sture having bought tablets 'in the kiosk'. He was found to have a stash of methaqualone (a habit-forming central nervous depressant), which has barbiturate-like effects and was used medically before benzodiazepines were widely available. In the 1970s and 1980s, these tablets, under their trade names Mandrax (UK) and Quaaludes (USA), were popular party drugs, as described by the journalist Hunter S. Thompson in *Fear and Loathing in Las Vegas*. Sture also got hold of the now banned sedative Vesparax, a powerful, long-lasting combination of two barbiturates (brallo- and secobarbital, also the antihistamine hydroxyzine which prolongs the sedative effect). In 1970, Jimi Hendrix overdosed on Vesparax and suffocated on his own vomit.[136]

Sture topped up his generous supply of prescription Alepam tablets with a whole catalogue of other controlled substances and managed to stay high most of the time. His case notes confirm this:

29 January: 'Affected yesterday night. Patient's speech blurred.'

02 March: '"Haunted" on Tuesday, began with headache. Thursday, fainted, briefly unconscious. By evening, buzzing and his muscles were slack. Denies having taking any tablets other than as prescribed.'

03 March: 'Clearly affected by something during the evening/night. Walks unsteadily. When asked, patient denies everything, states that he feels dizzy and in a haze [. . .]. Restricted to ward until further notice.'

06 March: 'Drunk last Friday, also taken tablets bought in the hospital kiosk. Says he regrets this, promises not to do it again. Permitted to leave ward again.'

17 March: 'Strongly affected by tablets during the day. Able to walk without support. Admits taking methaqualone (Revonal). Refuses to say how many. Patient staggers out into the ward, then tips over his drink, moved on to ward 4A.'

18 March: 'Back to normal. Says he got hold of 3 tbs. Revonal and 2 tbs. Vesparax. Moved on to ward 30 B.'

Despite being a known junkie, he was seen as something of a model patient: 'Always behaves politely and caringly towards others. Never demanding or insistent. Says that he likes the ward, likes both patients and staff. Often takes walks around the hospital sites after supper to keep fit.'

Sture assured the doctors that he would stop abusing drugs and said that he wanted to take adult university access courses run by the local authority in Uppsala and go on to study comparative literature. I find it hard to believe that the medical staff at Säter could have trusted a young man with such severe drug dependency problems. Still, they must have thought him capable of succeeding with his project because in May he was given a conditional discharge. In August 1973, he moved in with his brother Örjan, who lived in a student residence in Uppsala.

The student lifestyle was liberating for twenty-three-year-old Sture. The party culture made it so much easier to get wasted without drawing attention to himself, Örjan never made a fuss when his brother came home hammered, and Sture could admit to being gay. The National Association for Sexual Equality ran a club for homosexual men and Sture often went there in the evenings. He even brought men back to the flat.

Uppsala was alive with political activism, and the protest movement against America's war in Vietnam was particularly energetic. Sture was drawn in. He had once been a member of the Young Social Democrats but now he joined a Maoist group calling itself the Communist Union of Marxist–Leninists. He had not attended more than a handful of meetings before the union's president declared in a speech that homosexuality was a bourgeois perversion and should be fought. That was enough to make Sture give up on politics.

He did not care much for the university access courses but earned some cash by working for the post office. Throughout this period, he took drugs in astonishing quantities which, he thinks, must have been the cause of the disastrous incident on the night of 7 March 1974. Sture began his evening at the gay club where he met a student called Lennart Höglund, who was about ten years older than him. They chatted over beer and a sandwich, and agreed to go back to Höglund's small flat in a student hall of residence. They were both drunk and Sture had taken some tablets as well as bringing his small bottle of TCE with him, as always.

Lennart Höglund's flat consisted of a bed-sitting room, some three by four metres, a tiny kitchen and a bathroom. They settled down with the alcohol that Sture had brought. In interviews afterwards, Höglund claimed to have noticed that they were both losing control. At some point, Höglund undressed and went to the bathroom. This is how Sture later described what happened next: he went into the kitchenette and sniffed TCE, which had an unexpectedly scary effect – it triggered terrifying hallucinations. As he emerged from the bathroom, Höglund appeared to be a monster. Sture hit Höglund on the head with a frying pan, then grabbed a kitchen knife and stabbed him several times before fleeing.

Two days later, when he was at work sorting mail, the police came for him. He remembered the details of the hallucination and was aware that he had stabbed a man, but he had no idea of how he had got out of the flat or what state he had left Höglund in. He soon learnt that his companion had been close to death from blood loss but had somehow managed to call the emergency services, crawling on his hands and knees to let the ambulance crew in. Photos of the crime scene show Höglund's room and the corridor outside covered in blood. Against all odds, he survived, after some time in intensive care.

Sture lied like a trooper in the police interviews. At first, he said he had never met Höglund, then he admitted being in Höglund's room when a third man had forced his way in and demanded that Sture pay him to sleep with Höglund. But Höglund was able to describe how a heavily intoxicated Sture had had a hysterical outburst and slashed wildly at his surroundings.

Once the investigators realized that Sture was on a conditional discharge from Säter, he was compulsorily re-admitted in March 1974. His crime was classified as attempted manslaughter but because he was already sentenced to psychiatric care, no prosecution was instigated. A condition of this decision was that Säter must commit to keeping Sture 'in a secure ward for a lengthy period in consideration of the nature of the crime and its connection to Bergwall's severe mental abnormality'.[137]

Not only did this not happen, but the incident had remarkably few consequences for Sture. His discharge was curtailed and he was held in a secure ward for a while but after only a few months he was again free to roam the hospital precinct. When I asked Sture to explain why the worst act of violence in his life didn't lead to a harsher punishment, he speculated that the hospital's discharge committee probably wanted to tone the whole affair down. They were, after all, sharing the responsibility for letting him out in the first place. 'The way I see it, it all goes to show that psychiatrists shouldn't be in charge of criminals. If you commit a crime you should go to prison.'

During the months he stayed at Säter, Sture fell back into his old routine of getting high every other day. Looking through the spring 1974 case notes, I read things like 'partied on hair tincture' and 'drunk at night on the ward'.[138] Sture admitted that he had been hitting the hair tincture but 'blamed the whole episode on this feeling of anguish'.[139]

A few weeks later, Sture was 'visibly affected by substance/s (probably tabl.). Behaves calmly otherwise'. He confessed that he 'had been offered tabl'.[140] At times, he was off his head to such an extent that he 'was incapable of standing upright. Fell out of bed at night.'[141] The cause turned out to be that he had 'joined tablets & drinks party in the ward. Had purchased 10 tablets Luminal (phenobarbital) in the kiosk at 20 kronor/10 tabl. Refuses to say who he bought from, might be in- or outpatient, he says.'[142] The day after the tablets-and-drinks party the notes read: 'at undressing, patient tries to ingest tablets hidden in his socks'.

After Sture nagged about being allowed out, in June 1974, three months after his attack on Höglund, one of his doctors decided that he would be allowed to leave the hospital for two hours per day on condition that he 'causes no trouble, takes no alcohol or tablets, if such behaviour is discovered all favours cancelled for the rest of the summer'.[143] Sture managed to keep to these conditions for just under two weeks: 'Patient arrives at 20.00, bleeding. Skin at L eyebrow broken. Duty doctor called. Stitches necess. Pat. affected by subst. probably tablets. Patient states that he "fallen over, concussed" hence staggering gait. Stitches to be removed 5–6 days. Permission to leave cancelled.'

Sture socialized with a fellow patient whom I will call Arne Lindroth. Arne was an alcoholic dentist in his forties and the two men would abuse various substances together. Sture remembers Arne as an intelligent man with whom he could have interesting conversations. Something of this comes through in the case notes: 'pat. claims the tabl. taking due to bullying of himself and Arne by others on ward 30 B because of their intellectual interests'.[144]

Sture and Arne enjoyed each other's company. Säter had a common room known as 'the social therapy place' where inmates were supposed to practise their social skills by participating in various group activities. The exercise that Sture and Arne preferred was playing poker. The pot always contained either cash or tablets, and the two friends cheated by blinking when the time was right for the partner to fold.

By the end of July Sture was allowed out on his own. Five weeks later he and Arne ran away to Lund intending 'to party', as the case notes put it. Sture ended up in hospital, utterly wasted on drink and drugs. The police identified him and transported him back to Säter. After a few weeks, his notes remark on his good behaviour on the ward and made special mention of his 'bright, mellow mood'.[145]

A long entry in his notes just a few days later offers an insight into Sture's capacity to lie creatively. Astrid Israelsson, a teacher at the Sami College in Jokkmokk, got in touch with the staff at Säter because Sture had sent her a letter describing 'his life and personal development since his time at the Jokkmokk College'. Sture had told her that his studies in Uppsala were going well and that he commuted between Uppsala and Säter, where he stayed in a flat:

Bergwall also informed A. Israelsson in the letter that he was only too aware of how poor he was at handling money, which is why he had asked for a supervisor and guardian to help him manage his economy while he studied. Since his studies and travelling add up to a great deal and his student loan had not yet been paid out, Bergwall requested a loan from Mrs Israelsson, ideally of 2,000 kronor, which Mrs A. Israelsson was to pay to his appointed guardian. Mrs I could only spare 500 kr which she had sent to the guardian named by Bergwall, namely Arne Lindroth, resident at Säter. As Mrs Israelsson still has had no response from Sture Bergwall, she decided to approach the hospital about Sture's studies, discharge prospects etc.[146]

Astrid Israelsson was a kindly teacher who had been protective of Sture while he was at the college. He had managed to trick her into sending the equivalent of about £50 to 'his guardian' Arne Lindroth. The scam was bound to be exposed but Sture didn't seem to care. His grasp of the future did not go beyond the next few days.

Yet while Sture lied, cheated and got high on whatever was at hand, he also clung to dreams of coming off drugs and being at peace with life. Eventually, he arrived at a solution: he would join a monastery as a lay brother. He had once visited the monks in the Östanbäck monastery in Västmanland County while on leave from the hospital. According to notes from a talk with a doctor, he had been quite overwhelmed:

It had been a v. fine experience to meet the brothers, see and experience someth. of their daily lives. The visit convinced me completely that it was my vocation to be w them, work there and join them in communal prayers. I'm warmly welcomed to go there in the month of Jan. Because I've concluded that a normal job/ life is not for me and that adjusting to normality only causes conflicts that I find hard to endure and cope with, I believe it right that I should be given disability benefit for at least 2 years ahead.[147]

In January 1975, he was given leave to spend a couple of months in the monastery as a guest of the monks. His intention to move in on a permanent basis was based on genuine longing for monastic life. He felt he needed the orderly life and, above all, a drug-free environment. Seven days after moving into Östanbäck, he broke off his stay and returned to Säter. His notes record that the patient was 'Back from leave at 20.30. Slightly exalted mood, seems affctd by tabl. One hour on the ward, then pat. had to be helped into bed. Found 3 tabl. in his trousers.'[148]

Only a few days later, aided by two other inmates, he forged post office cash withdrawal slips and managed to overdraw his empty savings account to the tune of 6,000 kronor. The three of them set out for Säter's kiosk but got distracted, cleared off and went on to party in Helsingborg where Sture experimented with injecting a mixture of morphine and heroin. The police brought him back to Säter four days later.[149] His notes observe, 'Regard. his acc. overdraft, Bergwall believes it will be discovered at end Feb/begin. March. He has no money to repay the sum owed but puts his faith in a lottery ticket.'[150]

Sture's life rolled on but in the middle of the chaos something was changing in his mind. As yet, it did not show but he was getting steadily more fed up with his drug-taking. A decision to put a stop to it began to take shape.

Spring 1975 went by with hardly any misdemeanours and, by the end of May, he had behaved so well for so long that he was discharged on trial to his parents' home in Falun. A local policeman was charged with keeping an eye on him and he was given a prescription for Alepam (25 mg, 2–3 times daily) and Mogadon (1–2 at bedtime).[151] For the next six months or so, Sture seems not to have exceeded his prescribed intake and his overseer's reports were positive throughout. He remarked that Sture 'always seemed content and well adjusted to his new life' and that he 'is hopeful about his situation and settled'.

Sture eked out his disability benefit by writing short columns for the local paper *Dala-Demokraten*. When he went back to Säter to renew his prescription, his doctor noted that he had handed back the old form even though he could still use it to collect more Alepam. But giving up drugs was hard. As he stabilized his intake, Sture had to confront his life head on and it depressed him. He felt that he was a complete failure and could not see a meaningful future ahead of him.

On the Monday 3 November 1975, Sture checked into a room at the Esso motel in Borlänge with 40 Mandrax and 40 Alepam tablets in his luggage.[152] 'I was utterly determined to take my own life,' he told me. 'Just having made the decision was such a relief. I didn't want my Mum and Dad to find my dead body, so it seemed preferable to die in a hotel room.'

He began to swallow the tablets but as he did so he suddenly felt he could not bear to die alone and phoned a psychotherapist he had met as an outpatient and who had treated him in several therapy sessions. Her notes confirm that this was not a 'cry for help' because Sture refused to say where he was. The psychotherapist realized that Sture would die if no one helped him and succeeded in persuading a doctor at Säter to order the phone call to be traced immediately. Sture had not thought of this. It saved his life. When the therapist and the medic made their way into the motel room, Sture was past responding to speech. In the ambulance taking him to the general hospital in Falun he lost consciousness completely. His stomach was pumped and he came round the following day.

'It was the most serious event in my life,' he told me. 'I remember very clearly what I felt when I woke up. Utter despair and grief at my failure. I hadn't even succeeded in killing myself. That's how I felt.'

Sture was re-admitted to Säter. At first, it seemed as if he was going to carry on from where he left off. Only twenty-four hours after his suicide attempt, he was drinking hair tincture and taking smuggled tablets. But he soon showed signs of his exasperation with himself. One of his case notes from the end of November records that he had asked a doctor to have the free pass cancelled because he 'couldn't cope with going outside'. It was very unlike the 'old' Sture.

During the spring of 1976, Sture was fighting a battle against himself and the drug addict often won. He ran away several times and was always brought back intoxicated. Once, when his room was searched, staff discovered a stash of some fifty tablets in his transistor radio.

In February that year, Sture's father, who was sixty-one, had a stroke and was hospitalized at Säter. Father and son became neighbours of a sort and Sture visited his father daily, which seemed to have a calming effect on him. In May 1976, his self-control was so reassuring that he was once again given a conditional discharge. He moved in with his mother in their home in Korsnäs and they visited his father every day. Every second month, he went to the outpatient clinic and renewed his Alepam (3 × 15 mg daily). From spring 1977 onwards, his case notes were becoming briefer. Doctors' notes from occasional home visits stated that Sture had no symptoms of any mental disturbance. The policeman reported that Sture was getting on well and that his mother had expressed 'her satisfaction with him'.[153] In January 1978, close to Sture's twenty-eighth birthday, his prescription was reduced (3 × 10 mg daily). That was a fifth of the dosage he was on in 1973, when he arrived at Säter from Sidsjön. He was truly a changed man.

I asked him how he had managed to stop his excessive drug dependency. 'My suicide attempt was the key,' he explained. 'I couldn't stand the mess and the chaotic lifestyle, all the despair it caused. I knew that keeping off drugs was essential and, besides, the daily Alepam was a help. I knew I must not take more than three a day.'

In May 1977, he was discharged from Säter and, for ten years to come, he took nothing more than the drugs he was prescribed and stayed out of trouble with the police. His father died in September 1977 and now Sture and his mother Tyra remained in the Korsnäs house. He enjoyed taking care of her and meeting up with his siblings, many of whom were his neighbours. He felt part of a community and even got himself a dog and took up cycling, often touring together with his oldest brother Sten-Ove. They cycled 1,000 kilometres in a week in 1981 and went racing in 1982.[154] Sten-Ove writes in his book about this peaceful time:

[Sture] shared a quiet, orderly (enviable?) existence with our mother and saw a lot of his brothers, sisters and their children. He did not yet have a disability pension, so I think he lived on benefits which, added to my mother's pension, worked out very well. He shopped and cleaned, and amused himself with solving crosswords and reading books. Sometimes, he took the bus to town and went to a cafe. And he walked for hours in the forest. [. . .] The whole family would gather to celebrate Christmas and I can't remember any Christmas when Sture wasn't there. He actually took a very active part in our family traditions. [...] As time went by, my mother needed Sture to help her more with the housework, so he went shopping, cleaned the house and generally looked after things. Until the death of my mother, I would come home myself every Christmas and stop on the threshold, always with the same sense of happy anticipation when I saw the decorations and picked up the smells of baking and cooking.

Christmas meant a lot to my mother. It had always been so and my brother knew it. It was the time of year when Mum could most easily see the outcome of her life of hard work: well-nourished children, a table groaning with home cooked fare and gifts that pleased both giver and recipient.

My brother was generous. Whenever he saw something that would be just the right gift for someone in the family, he would buy it even if it meant emptying his pockets. I am totally convinced that there was no calculation behind his giving. Watching the delight at the present made him grin happily. He was especially fond of his nephews and nieces and the children adored him.[155]

Sture now made some money by writing poetic newspaper columns for *Dala-Demokraten* and *Falu Kuriren*:

Tufts of cranberry and blueberry shrubs, stones and tree-stumps, lichen and mosses – yes, the entire forest was flooded with evening sunshine. Upfold, my Scottish deerhound, and I were out on a forest walk. It was in the afternoon, the early rains had drifted away and instead the sky was a strong blue. The air was pleasantly warm and its freshness made breathing it a joy. While Upfold investigated trees and stones, as dogs will, I leaned against a pine tree and stared into the forest. And that's when my tears rose into my eyes. Nature's own work of art, which can never be truly pictured in either word or image, was so lovely that the eyes, recording its beauty, filled with tears. Aloud, I told my dog: 'Look around and see what is given to us!'[156]

In the 1980s Sture had a happy life surrounded by people who cared for him. When, in the autumn of 1983, his mother died, she had enjoyed – as Sten-Ove expresses it in his book – 'settled home finances and grandchildren to love to distraction'. Her troubled son Sture was no longer a hopeless junkie but a local businessman who had started a kiosk together with his brother. Sten-Ove writes that 'my mother's last few years were surely the best in her life'.[157]

11

Margit's second sect

'*It was as if I had come home.*'
Tomas Videgård, a psychotherapist, about his first
therapy session with Margit Norell in 1977

At the point that the happiest period in Sture's life was beginning, Margit was miserable. She had been sacked from the Holistic Institute, and she had lost, in rapid succession, her psychoanalyst and mentor Erich Fromm and the man she loved, David Schecter. Once again, she was alone.

But she remained very much admired as a psychoanalyst and was never short of work. The left-wing radical elite, famous feminists, TV personalities and politicians were among her patients and several psychotherapists sought her out for supervision and therapy. Every morning, she set out from her home in suburban Stockholm and spent her day in the Birkagården practice, listening to an unending stream of people in need of help. She was sixty-three years old and worked six days a week, though if someone called her on a Sunday she would drop everything and return to work.

Many of Margit's patients idolized her in the way small children idolize their parents, but she was still dissatisfied. In the autumn of 1980, the year of David Schecter's suicide, she began to gather around her the nucleus of what was to become a new group of acolytes. This seems to have been something she could not stop herself from doing, only this time the outcome would be disastrous not only for Margit personally but also for the practice of forensic psychiatry in Sweden and the country's self-image as a state governed by just laws. But for Margit and her new group, Sture Bergwall would probably never have been convicted of murder and Sweden's biggest miscarriage of justice this century would never have happened.

The psychotherapist Tomas Videgård was 'one of Margit's'. When I met him, he was sixty-seven years old and still working full-time in his private practice in fashionable Södermalm. It did not take long before Tomas, unprompted, began speaking about the 'Quick scandal'. I had told him I was writing a history of object relations theory but the lie proved unnecessary. Tomas told me that when, in 2008, he watched Sture Bergwall's televised retraction of his confessions, he knew that, one day, someone would come to see him and want to talk about Margit and Sture. He had even considered stepping forward and offering to tell his side of the story but had somehow never found the time. He spent four years wondering when someone like me would contact him.

In the mid-1970s, he had studied psychology with the intention of becoming a psychoanalyst. He had completed the theoretical part of the training, but abandoned the orthodox approach to analysis once he had discovered object relations theory. It had been developed by a scattered group of British psychoanalysts in response to concerns that were similar to those raised by the neo-Freudians. They rejected Freud's theory of drives and believed that psychological development was determined by the quality of the individual's relationships with other people. The word 'object' was used by Freud to signify the person on whom the child focuses drives and desires; the 'object' is a human being and an 'object relation' simply indicates a relationship.[158]

Tomas was attracted to these ideas. He also become interested in Arthur Janov's primal therapy, which Janov raved about in bestselling books, insisting that he had revolutionized psychiatry. According to Janov, almost all mental suffering could be eliminated if people could experience as adults their negative but repressed childhood emotions and scream out their pain.[159] Tomas was treated with primal therapy in the United States but found it disappointing. When he returned to Sweden in the autumn of 1977, he was still distraught by the emotionally brutal treatment he had received. He needed help.

A girlfriend put Tomas in touch with Margit Norell, who had a reputation as an interesting and very skilful psychotherapist whose patients included famous writers, intellectuals and even other psychotherapists. Significantly, she was known to be a left-wing radical. The left had been provoked by the orthodox Freudian analysts, who had internalized mental conflicts with their claim that innate drives were the roots of the trouble. The left believed that a conflicted mind was a result of oppression within the conventional family, or by patriarchal rule and/or the capitalist society. Tomas had liked Margit's politics. Also, the first time he had caught a glimpse of her was when she presented the international star turn Erich Fromm to a packed Citizens' House in 1970.

Tomas began his therapy with Margit in 1977 and formed an immediate bond with her. 'She came downstairs from her practice to meet me,' he recalled. 'I saw her and, despite her full figure, I perceived her as dancing down the stairs. She looked so vital and had such a warm, generous smile. I thought her looks suggested that she was in her mid-forties but early sixties was actually closer to the mark. I can't remember my first session with her, not exactly anyway, but what I can say is that I felt such a strong, immediate understanding. It was as if I had come home.'

For the next thirteen years, Tomas received therapy from Margit and usually saw her twice a week. He told her about his problems and she interpreted his dreams. Much of the therapeutic work focused on his childhood relationships with his parents. Margit rejected many of the usual rules that defined the role of psychoanalyst and was unreservedly supportive. Tomas felt tremendously vindicated and came to see her as more like a mother. During his first few years 'with Margit' he was working on a thesis that was essentially a critique of primal therapy. She was happy to help him in his work and he dedicated the completed thesis to her.

I asked if Tomas thought he had been emotionally dependent on Margit.

'Goodness, yes!' he replied.

I then asked him in what way he had been dependent. 'She was the fixed point in my universe, meaning that when something felt difficult I could always turn to Margit.'

'How would you explain "maternal transference"?' I asked.

'You've just heard me describe it,' he said with a smile. 'It is when a feeling of being safe with your mother takes hold of you. And if you feel overwhelmed by issues that are too big or too difficult to cope with, you can run to Mummy and she will make things better. But I should add that the maternal transference I experienced with Margit was not simply restful. She was exceptionally sharp, often said truly wise things and her authority was huge, intellectually as well as emotionally. Actually, in that sense she was a father as well – she was both a supportive mother and competent, determined father, a truly genuine person.'

'What did it mean to you to have met someone like her just when you did?'

'It was a gift! It was something I had been missing all my life. So, I felt I had arrived at the right place.'

Tomas brought his anxiety under control. He was eventually ready to treat his own patients, who were often referred to him from Margit's long waiting list. By then, Tomas's own sessions with Margit had changed into a mixture of psychotherapy and supervision of his therapeutic work with patients.

In 1980, after three years, Margit offered Tomas the chance to join her new study circle of hand-picked pupils. He was delighted and flattered. There were seven people in the group, most of them about to qualify or already qualified as psychologists. Everyone was either in therapy with or supervised by Margit, or both, and all of them had just as 'special' a relationship with her as Tomas. They would meet in places owned by one of the members, depending on who had the room. They discussed psychoanalytical literature, taking the titles from a reading list compiled by Margit.

During the four first years, Margit rarely joined these meetings because the group was meant to prepare for her eventual arrival by reading up on the theory together. In the autumn of 1984, they had started to discuss whether Margit should attend all the meetings and also initiated minute-taking. The minutes indicate that, although most of the members wanted Margit to join them, some had reservations.

A short note from a meeting in October reads: 'Important alert. Possible consequences of Margit's presence for our group meetings? Worth thinking about. Cf. Margit's dual role as authority and "mother" to all of us.'[160]

In the end, the group decided that Margit would be present at all monthly meetings from January 1985. The study circle agreed that the members would take turns to choose the subject for discussion, for example a book, or a case history presentation. Margit's role was to comment and explain her own views.

At first, the mood of 'the Margit group' was upbeat. She still had the ability to make people feel energized and privileged. 'Each and every one of us felt specially selected,' Tomas said. 'We were the Swedish, possibly the international, elite in our field. We went in more deeply, we were the best. That was our self-image.'

On paper, Margit's therapeutic philosophy looks fairly uncompli-cated: regardless of the patient's mental problems, the cause will always lie in some form of childhood trauma. The patient's ways of thinking, feeling and acting have been adjusted to the expectations of inadequate parents or guardians. Events and relationships that caused the mental conflict in the patient had to be untangled, scrutinized and corrected. The psychotherapist should take the place of the parents and become the good mother or father the patient had lacked. This was to be achieved by supporting and confirming everything the patient con-fessed to during the long therapy sessions. In principle, at least, criticism and doubts were not allowed.

Margit demanded that her pupils follow her lead and put the patients' needs above everyone else's. If a patient wanted to live in the therapist's home, so be it. Former pupils have described patients taking drugs during an ongoing session in the therapist's home. This was con-sidered acceptable because drug dependency was regarded as a form of self-defence that would disappear once the patient felt secure enough with his or her psychotherapist. Generally, Margit had succeeded in persuading her pupils to believe blindly in this treatment model, but, just as before, not every case turned out as well as she had promised. Tomas explained that the group grew restive towards the end of the

1980s, when the failures began to pile up and it became obvious that Margit had no intention of discussing them.

'And that was Margit's huge, really tragic problem,' Tomas said. 'She could not take criticism. Any suggestion that she was wrong made her feel humiliated. She became defensive and a little paranoid. And once that had happened, there was no way to maintain a stable relationship as a patient or as a supervisee.'

'But you didn't notice this until a good deal later?'

'No, we didn't. Partly due to a natural tendency to adjust. What I'm trying to say is that we might well have noticed this long ago but censored it. A kind of self-censorship. One couldn't argue with her, neither in supervision sessions nor in group meetings.'

Some members of the group saw it as their task to protect Margit from any open criticism.

'It became more like a sect,' Tomas said. 'You must not express doubts about the leader, because if you did, it would signify rebellion. And that might well mean exclusion next.'

According to Tomas, the collective wish to idealize and protect Margit was enormously strong. 'Many of us saw her practically every week for therapy and supervision. To most of us, she was our mother. You put your life in her hands and knew that others had done the same. Her position was unique and that in itself was problematic. The group dynamics would have been utterly different if there had been two or three people with roughly equivalent status to her. But that was not the case.'

The psychotherapist Britt Andersson was another member of the group. She was supervised by Margit from 1977 and could confirm everything that Tomas had said. Everyone was afraid of Margit and the slightest criticism could cause big trouble. She recalled a day in the early 1990s when she had come for her hour of supervision. Though she had been in close contact with Margit for fifteen years she had still never before seen the chilly Margit that opened the door. She seemed a different person. Then, imitating Margit's way of speaking, Britt said slowly and emphatically: '"I've heard that you're speaking ill of me." And that was it. She wouldn't explain. Instead, the entire supervision session was spent on making me work out what I had done. I tried to defend myself and persuade her to tell me what she had in mind but she wouldn't say. It was so deeply unpleasant, almost like mental torture. I decided not to come back to her for supervision.'

Later, Britt found out that it had been something she said to one of the most devoted pupils about Margit's unnecessarily harsh attitude to Curt, her husband. The remark had been passed on and Margit took it as a reason to conduct an hour-long interrogation.

Margareta Hedén-Chami had also belonged to the group. She taught for many years as a university teacher in the department of psychology in Uppsala. When I met her she was seventy-nine years old and well into retirement. She told me that she had attended an open lecture given by Margit at Uppsala in 1977. The subject was object relations theory and the importance of early relationships in the development of the personality. Margareta had been gripped by the radical approach and afterwards went up to Margit and asked if she could start psychotherapy sessions with her. 'She was very brusque,' Margareta said. '"I'll think about it", she said, "but I'll require a description of your life." I had young children and was on my own, but as soon as the little ones had fallen asleep, I settled down to write. And went down to the letterbox and posted it at once so I'd have no chance of regretting it. It took a while, but she phoned to say, yes, I'll take you on but I have no time just now.'

Margareta's therapy started the following year and, to begin with, she thought Margit was fantastic. She had been depressed and felt a need to fit in with the expectations of others: 'She pinpointed what I was doing, found out what was genuine about me and what stemmed from my attempts to adjust to others, and then helped me sort it all out. She helped me so incredibly much.'

Margit became something of a new mother to Margareta, who was delighted to be invited to join the group. She felt that it worked well for many years but later, towards the end of the 1980s, the atmosphere seemed to change.

Margareta says: 'It was interesting to watch the group develop. I felt it became more and more like a sect. What I reacted to was the insistence on all of us thinking the same, the lack of freedom of expression and also Margit's tendency to dictate to us. It was all very odd and I felt increasingly ill at ease. Like a captive.'

The breaking point for Margareta came in September 1989, during a group meeting. She had been telling the others about some therapeutic work that she thought was going well but which was not supervised by Margit. After she had finished speaking, Margit tore her work to pieces. Margareta had to endure being mercilessly criticized in front of the entire group for not grasping that she should only ever ask Margit to supervise her. From that meeting onwards Margit began to freeze Margareta out.

'I suddenly saw the schizoid side of Margit. You were either in or out. If you didn't accept her demands, you were out. It was a huge shock for me. I was crying . . . I felt she had taken on a mother's persona. If I didn't do as Mummy told me to, I wasn't any good.'

In the end, Margareta broke with Margit and left the group.

When I met Tulla Brattbakk-Göthberg, she said that she had not understood what she had been part of until after she had left the group and moved to Norway at the end of the 1990s. According to her:

> Margit was unable to connect to her own people, her children or her family. We were her special children, her own creatures. Margit alone decided who would join the group so, in that sense, she chose us as her children. And none of us had started out in life in a good emotional state so it felt wonderful to be chosen. Margit was a celebrity, many wanted to be with her but not everyone was allowed in. So, yes, we felt very special. Of course, now that we had been given a good mother, we mustn't do anything against her will. We had to toe the line.

All in all, I spoke to nine psychotherapists who had been close to Margit for many years. All of them provided evidence of the group's sectarian mentality. Margit was remarkably good at boosting her pupils' self-esteem but could also destroy it at will. This was how she controlled them.

'Things went from bad to worse,' Tomas said. 'I know that NN [one of the most devoted pupils] once said about herself that "I really should start trying to deal with *some* problems on my own." She meant practical problems like "What brand of dishwasher should I buy?", stuff like that. She used to phone Margit. That was the ethos. Margit will know the answer to whatever it was.'

One of Margit's ex-pupils gave me some tape recordings of a few group meetings. Two of the cassettes are dated '26 January 1985', the day Margit made her first appearance at a meeting. In the recording Margit is complaining, in her refined accent, about the Holistic Institute and how little its members had grasped of what really mattered. She called one of them 'an idiot' and her new group mumbled in agreement. She talked about Sigmund Freud, and said that he had betrayed his patients, then read aloud to them from a book about object relations theory written by the British paediatrician Donald Winnicott. I recognized the extract because I had read her correspondence. She read passages very slowly, to give her audience as much time as possible to soak up the wisdom of Winnicott's thoughts. It sounded as if she was reading from a religious tract.

Strikingly often, Margit would speak of other psychotherapists and theoreticians as inept, complaining about their ignorance with resigned, slightly theatrical weariness. The implication was that she had tried and tried for years to instruct these fools but they had been utterly resistant to the light of progress. The group agreed, laughed at the right times and asked ingratiating questions. I remembered Margit's letter to Erich Fromm: '*[M]y standards and expectations for therapeutic work transcend what is the more mediocre standard in institutions and most analytic work here.*'[161]

Margit's self-assurance was still as unshakeable as it had been in Jan Stensson's descriptions of her time at the Holistic Institute. As she enhanced her own status, she also elevated her pupils. Her self-aggrandisement meant that everyone in her group must be superior to all other psychotherapists. In the 1970s, Margit had spat venom at the orthodox Freudians and twelve years later the 'holistics' were declared worthy of nothing but contempt. Her sect-building technique was almost identical every time.

Initially, the group had seven members but on a few occasions another therapist would be invited to join. The first time this happened was in November 1985, less than a year after Margit had started to attend the meetings.

The new recruit was Göran Källberg. He was the medical director at Säter hospital and the secure unit was his special responsibility. It had been used since 1912 to manage violent criminals sentenced to psychiatric care.[162] Källberg took up his post at Säter in 1981. His attitude to psychiatric care was seen as radical. He wanted to modernize time-worn practices and, among other things, offer psychotherapy to the incarcerated criminals. This approach had never been tried before at Säter, where the care provided in the secure unit amounted to keeping the inmates heavily medicated and, mostly, under lock and key.

In the autumn of 1983, a famous patient called Lars-Inge (Lasse) Andersson, better known under the name Svartenbrandt, had been transferred to the secure unit. He was one of the most heavily sentenced criminals in Sweden. His long list of crimes included a large number of armed robberies and he was seen by many as an incurable psychopath. Svartenbrandt faced long-term imprisonment and had spent four years in solitary confinement in a prison facility known as 'the Kumla bunker'. He had become depressed and had asked for permission to serve the rest of his sentence at Säter.[163]

Göran Källberg decided that Svartenbrandt should undergo psychotherapeutic treatment. Källberg was a psychiatrist, a medical man who had specialized in psychiatry, so he had no training in psychotherapy, and hence lacked competence to carry out such treatment on his own. He needed to find a qualified therapist with a good reputation to supervise him. Margit Norell had been well known around Säter since the 1970s, when she had supervised Barbro Sandin and the other psychotherapists working on the 'Säter model' style of schizophrenia treatment. The patients in the secure unit were not included in this treatment but Källberg contacted Margit anyway and she agreed to take on the supervision of Svartenbrandt's psychotherapy.

In 1983, the medical director of Säter hospital began travelling to Stockholm in order to receive both supervision and therapy from Margit. Two years later, Margit invited him to join her exclusive group. The minutes show that he attended for the first time on 9 November 1985 and he was a faithful attendee for many years.

Källberg offered Svartenbrandt therapy that was boundlessly supportive, as Margit had taught him, becoming the good father – the good 'object' – that Svartenbrandt had never had. The treatment proved to be a particularly horrific example of just what Margit's 'supportive' approach meant in practice. Svartenbrandt relentlessly tricked his 'father', lied and betrayed his trust. For instance, Källberg would act as a jobbing driver, ready to take Svartenbrandt wherever he wanted to go when on leave. In 1986 the patient vanished while on leave and was found to have robbed a post office in Uppsala.[164] He was caught, tried and a few more years were added to his existing sentence for attempted murder and aggravated robbery. He was allowed to remain at Säter and his therapy sessions with Källberg continued.

The psychotherapist Greta Thorén, another member of the group said that, in her view, there was no doubt that Svartenbrandt used Göran Källberg as his 'errand boy' but, even so, no one doubted that Margit's method would produce miraculous results in the end. According to Thorén: 'They believed he would get better if only they could truly understand him. It was a seriously insane notion. But, of course, it was applied and applauded by the whole group.'

Margit was convinced that they would cure Svartenbrandt using 'the Säter model'. Källberg was thrilled. In September 1984, he created a post for a psychologist on the secure unit staff. The first person to hold the post was Birgitta Ståhle, a thirty-year-old woman who came to Säter straight from her university course in psychology. She spent a year as a hospital trainee in order to qualify as a clinical psychologist and, in the autumn of 1985, she was given a permanent post although she was not a qualified psychotherapist. Like doctors, clinical psychologists only receive basic instruction in psychotherapy and must continue with formal training, including several years of supervised work with patients, to be allowed to offer therapy. Once the training courses are completed satisfactorily, the social services department will issue a licence to practice.

Birgitta Ståhle was untrained but Källberg solved the problem by allowing Ståhle to be supervised weekly by Margit from January 1988. She also began to receive therapy from Margit, according to a form kept by the social services department.[165] In 1990 Margit invited her to join the group.

Both Göran Källberg and Birgitta Ståhle had star status in the group and both gave much appreciated seminars in which they spoke about their hard work with Säter's cohort of violent criminals. Tomas Videgård remembers the waves of group admiration that washed over these two. 'It was a very special, highly demanding job. You know, going into that hellish place and trying to understand what drove even these appalling killers.'

Källberg felt that Svartenbrandt's therapy had worked out so well that he decided to push ahead with a complete renovation of forensic psychiatric care at Säter and base the reform on Margit's theoretical and clinical models. The local politicians supported the project and, in 1989, a newly built, very costly forensic psychiatric wing opened its doors. At the same time, the old secure unit was shut down. The entire project was aimed at providing the patients with the kind of psychotherapy Margit was teaching Källberg all about.[166] Ståhle was to be the psychologist in the new unit.

As always, Margit's philosophy was founded on the belief that unreserved confirmation would achieve total healing. But one of her other fundamental ideas was that repressed memories of abuse in early childhood were a contributory cause of most serious psychological problems. In 1977 Margit had already taken her patient Hanna Olsson through a 'regression' that meant reliving events which allegedly took place when Hanna was two or three years old. Since then, Hanna Olsson had become a psychotherapist and one of the founder members of the group. During the 1980s, Margit urged more of her pupils to reveal repressed memories, particularly of sexual abuse. As this is a very sensitive subject, none of the ex-members I interviewed would tell me who among their colleagues had proved susceptible to Margit's memory retrieval exercises, but two or three people apparently let themselves be drawn.

Cajsa Lindholm was particularly devout and prepared to obey Margit in every detail. Tulla Brattbakk-Göthberg describes Cajsa as 'the nearest thing to a daughter that Margit ever had – yes, more so than her biological daughter'. Some of the group referred to her as 'Margit's Crown Princess'; one of the other ex-pupils suggested, less grandly, that Cajsa was 'Margit's house slave'. Later on, I was told that Cajsa was present at her bedside when Margit died in January 2005.

In the spring of 2012, I noticed that Cajsa was lecturing on psychodynamic therapy at the Workers' Educational Institute (WEI) in Stockholm. At that stage, I had not worked on the Quick mystery for very long but was aware that Cajsa had dedicated *A Room to Live In* to Sture, as if she knew him. Sture had also hinted that Cajsa had a pupil of her own, a woman I will call Lena Arvidsson. Lena, he said, had played an important role at Säter during the Thomas Quick years. She had admired Margit and received combined therapy and supervision from Cajsa Lindholm. He even emailed me a couple of scanned photographs taken on a day in June 2000. They showed Sture mounted on a horse led by a blonde, bespectacled woman in her forties. I added her name to my list of people I wanted to talk to.

The WEI building where Cajsa Lindholm was lecturing is on Svea Way in Stockholm. The audience of about thirty barely filled half the hall. I sat down in the second row and glanced at the woman next to me. I was startled to see that I had happened to sit down next to Lena Arvidsson.

Cajsa Lindholm's talk dealt with her methods for helping her patients to recover repressed memories of sexual abuse in childhood. She spoke extensively about a particular female patient who had been fifty-seven years old when she first went to see Cajsa. The woman, who had suffered all her life from anxiety attacks, eating disorders and relationship problems, had tried therapy several times but felt that it did not help her. The psychological picture indicated, Cajsa claimed, that the patient had repressed past instances of abuse. It took seven years of analysis, but in the end Cajsa had made the patient see her childhood in a new light: her father had subjected her to sexual violence from infanthood and her mother had been too 'incapable and confused' to deal with it. Cajsa had arrived at this conclusion after much talk with the patient and interpreting 'topics in her dreams', a crucial part of the therapy: 'I regard dreams as an absolutely invaluable source of information about what is going on in the inner world of the patient.'

There was time for questions after the lecture and a woman in the audience asked if, when the patient first saw Cajsa, she truly had had no memory of any of the extensive sexual abuse.

'No, no, no, no, no,' Cajsa replied.

I introduced myself to her after the lecture and explained that I was working on a book about the history of object relations theory in Sweden and wanted to include a pen-portrait of the pioneer Margit Norell. I had read Cajsa's book, *A Room to Live In*, with great interest, I said, and knew how close she had been to Margit. It would be fascinating to find out more about the psychotherapeutic method that Margit had taught and which Cajsa had just described in her lecture. Would she care for copies of my books on psychology? I opened my bag to extract them but first had to remove two volumes I had deliberately put on top. Both were classical works on object relations theory, namely Ronald Fairbairn's *Psychoanalytic Studies of the Personality* (1952) and Donald Winnicott's *The Maturational Processes and the Facilitating Environment* (1965). I discovered at a later date that Margit had brought both books with her when she travelled to Portugal in the summer of 1977 to meet David Schecter and his wife. My little plan worked well beyond expectation. When Cajsa saw me take out these two great texts, her eyes widened. She said it made her almost tearful to see those books.

Thanks to my low cunning, Cajsa accepted me without a trace of suspicion, saying that she was happy to meet me and talk about Margit. Lena Arvidsson stood nearby and I turned to her and asked if she was a psychotherapist, too. Yes, indeed, she had been in combined supervision and therapy with Cajsa for many years and based her therapy on Margit's ideas. I was very welcome to interview her about her psychotherapeutic work.

We said 'goodbye for now' to each other and I walked home through Stockholm in an excited state of mind. I had a chance to gain access to Thomas Quick's third psychotherapist and her supervisor, Margit Norell's most devoted pupil. I would be able to learn more about the therapeutic method that Margit had instructed them in and which had been used for ten years to treat Sture Bergwall at Säter. I couldn't wait. Especially since I had already accumulated a great deal of scientific evidence demonstrating that the therapy Cajsa had lectured on just then was nothing but a set of instructions for the creation of false memories.

12

The myth of repressed memories

'*Through tone of voice, phrasing of questions, and expressions
of belief or disbelief, a therapist can unwittingly encourage a
patient to accept the emerging "memories" as real, thus
reinforcing the patient's delusion or even implanting false
memories in the patient's mind.*'

From *The Myth of Repressed Memory:
False memories and allegations of sexual abuse*
by Elizabeth Loftus and Katherine Ketcham

Sigmund Freud popularized the idea that traumatic memories could
be repressed. In the 1890s he treated women suffering from 'hysteria', a catch-all term that covered a range of conditions, including
anxiety attacks, depression and psychotic states. Psychoanalysis was
beginning to take shape and Freud was experimenting with different methods. During the therapy sessions, he saw that his patients
entered into strange states, making them subject to emotional storms.
His patients seemed to return mentally to childhood and re-experience sexual molestations of which they had no conscious memory –
or so he believed. At the time, Freud's construct of the human psyche
included a mechanism for automatic repression of frightening memories. When these involuntarily rose out of the unconscious, they
caused compulsive thoughts, depression, and other mental disturbances.

Freud's idea that repressed memories of sexual abuse could cause
a whole array of mental disorders is known as his 'seduction

theory'. In 1896, he gave a lecture in Vienna entitled 'The Aetiology of Hysteria' to an audience of psychiatrists and neurologists, about the enigmatic condition of hysteria: 'I therefore put forward the thesis that, at the bottom of every case of hysteria, there are *one or more occurrences of premature sexual experience*, occurrences which belong to the earliest years of childhood but which can be reproduced through the work of psychoanalysis in spite of the intervening decades.'[167]

The reception was lukewarm. His colleagues were far from persuaded that he was anywhere near to solving the enigma of hysteria and dismissed the seduction theory as mere speculation. In a letter to a friend, Freud referred bitterly to one colleague who had called the theory 'a scientific fairy-tale'.[168] He was disappointed but also took note of the criticism. Soon afterwards, he abandoned the seduction theory in its entirety.[169]

Moving away from the assumption that almost all mental problems were caused by early exposure to adult sexuality, he spent the following decades developing his theory of drives and his thinking underwent a complete turnaround. His new position was that psychoanalysts could mostly dismiss real events in their patients' lives, including episodes of childhood abuse, and instead look for evidence of conflicting drives in dreams and fantasies. 'Repression' remained an important concept for Freud but he no longer believed that people repressed memories of real events, but rather that they repressed drive-induced desires that were unacceptable in the eyes of society. An important hypothetical element in the drive theory was the so-called Oedipus complex. It postulated that, at a certain stage of a young child's development, boys desire their mothers, while girls desire their fathers.

Later, when Sigmund Freud was attacked by those who thought his psychoanalytical teachings unscientific, the critics often focused on the Oedipus complex. The 'complex' has now disappeared from psychological research.[170] Freud, however, defended it until his death in 1939. In a 1933 lecture he claimed that he had encountered several female patients who had told him about having sexual intercourse with their fathers. He pointed out that his records began some thirty years earlier, i.e. in the 1890s, and went on to say:

> In the period in which the main interest was directed to discovering
> infantile sexual traumas, almost all my women patients told me that they
> had been seduced by their fathers. I was driven to recognize in the end
> that these reports were untrue and so came to understand that hysterical
> symptoms are derived from fantasies and not from real occurrences. It was
> only later that I was able to recognize in this fantasy of being seduced by
> the father the expression of the typical Oedipus complex in women.[171]

At an early stage in his career, then, Freud believed women's narratives about being subjected to incest. He later dismissed them as fantasies, associated with the Oedipus complex. Among psychoanalysts, this version of how Freud arrived at the drive theory has been regarded as a given truth.[172]

It was not questioned until 1973, when Frank Cioffi, an American philosopher and Freud expert, decided to examine Freud's theory of the Oedipus complex. Cioffi gave a BBC Radio talk entitled *Was Freud a Liar?* in which he revealed that Freud had lied in order to make his much derided Oedipus complex seem a reasonable theory. All Cioffi had done to expose the lie was simply to read Freud's own articles and lecture texts from the 1890s. He found nothing to support Freud's assertion from 1933 about how 'almost all' his women patients had told him that they had been 'seduced by the father'. Frank Cioffi cited one of Freud's early papers where he described inducing a strange state in his patients in which they relived memories of what Freud himself believed to be 'scenes' of early violations. These, however, were not ordinary memories. Here is Freud's account:

> Before they come for analysis, the patients know nothing about these
> scenes. They are indignant, as a rule, if we warn them that such scenes
> are going to emerge. Only the strongest compulsion of the treatment can
> induce them to embark on a reproduction of them. While they are

recalling these infantile experiences to consciousness, they suffer under the most violent sensations of which they are ashamed and which they try to conceal.[173]

In order to make the patient conscious of the 'scenes', Freud used a method that is nowadays known as visualization. He asked the patient to close her eyes, move her mind back in time, and speak about what she saw. Sometimes, he would press his hand lightly against the patient's forehead to help her relax. The hypnotic state that ensued often brought on visions – the patient might twist and turn, gesticulate and scream. Freud argued that this was re-enactment; that is, reliving past events. Freud himself interpreted the content of 'the scenes'. In a way, it was like playing charades, but the patient would act out scenes blindly, without knowing what they were enacting.[174]

When Freud gave his 1896 lecture, he admitted that his patients did not believe that the 'scenes' were memories, and went on to say: '*Even after they have gone through them [the scenes] once more in such a convincing manner, they still attempt to withhold belief from them, by emphasizing the fact that, unlike what happens in the case of other forgotten material, they have no feeling of remembering the scenes.*'[175]

The point Frank Cioffi made was that Freud has no evidence for the Oedipus complex. The theory of repressed memories remained a neglected element in the early history of psychoanalysis until the 1980s, when an unexpected change took place. One crucial event was the publication in the United States of Jeffrey M. Masson's book *The Assault on Truth: Freud's Suppression of the Seduction Theory* (1984). Masson is a psychoanalyst who was for some time the director of the Sigmund Freud Archives (Library of Congress). He was a Freudian and, like most of his colleagues, assumed that Freud had told the truth in 1933, when he referred to all the stories of incestuous violations from women he treated in the 1890s. Masson was inspired to write *The Assault on Truth* when he came across several unpublished letters from Freud to his friend Wilhelm Fliess, written in the aftermath of Freud's much disparaged lecture in 1896. Freud was disappointed about the lack of interest in his seduction theory, and claimed that people were actively plotting against him. Masson concluded that the establishment, reluctant to admit that the sexual abuse of children was relatively common, had conspired to harass and isolate Freud.

The way Masson saw it, Freud was a coward who had abandoned the seduction theory for the sake of his career. He had invented the alternative theory of drives that allowed him to dismiss his patients' accounts of incestuous abuse as mere 'fantasies'. Masson accused Freud of behaving abusively towards these women by disbelieving them, and said that this act of violation had been repeated subsequently by generations of psychoanalysts. Masson ends his book with a call to arms:

> It is high time that we stop looking away from what is in fact one of the great problematic issues in the history of mankind. It is unforgiveable that those who are in emotional pain, who have been subjected to real damage in childhood and are now seeking help, are cared for by people whose blind belief in Freud's betrayal, dictated by fear, in the matter of his seduction theory, means that they continue to subject their patients to the same violence they were exposed to as children.[176]

Actually, this accusation was not new. Feminist critics of psychoanalysis had speculated that Freud's sudden lack of interest in the seduction theory might have been a form of capitulation to patriarchal society's general reluctance to do anything about men's sexual violence against women and children. But it was news – sensational news – that a real insider from the relatively closed world of psychoanalysis voiced this critique.[177]

In the debate that followed the publication of Masson's book it soon became obvious that what Freud had stopped believing in was his own interpretation of patients' narratives – interpretations that even his own patients did not trust.[178] But the idea of Freud's assault on truth took hold among psychotherapists. Worldwide, psychotherapists voiced their conviction that patients with certain signs or symptoms, regardless of what they had to say about childhood violations, would have been exposed to sexual abuse but repressed all memory of it. In other words, there was a strong resurgence of the hypothesis Freud had considered in 1896 and rejected in 1897.

Margit Norell was one of the psychoanalysts who grew enthusiastic about these ideas. As early as in the 1970s, she had helped patients re-experience what she believed to be repressed memories of early trauma. She must have felt that time was finally catching up with her by the mid-eighties. One of her students gave me a copy of Margit's reading list from 1980–1984. It contained several titles by authors such as the object relations theoreticians Donald Winnicott and Ronald Fairbairn, as well as Jeffrey M. Masson's *The Assault on Truth*.

The list also included three works by the Swiss psychologist and psychoanalyst Alice Miller. Her first book was called *The Drama of the Gifted Child: The Search for the True Self* in English (1981). Miller's thesis was that depression is often caused by repressed memories of sexual abuse. Her book became a bestseller in Germany and was translated into many languages. During the 1980s, Miller followed up with more books on the same theme. Janet Malcolm's book *In the Freud Archives* states that there were direct links between Jeffrey Masson and Alice Miller. While Masson was working on *The Assault on Truth*, Miller met him. At that stage, Masson had already been ostracized in the psychoanalytical world and described Alice Miller to Janet Malcolm as his 'only remaining supporter'.[179]

Partly thanks to Masson's and Miller's writings, the belief in repressed memories spread across the world of psychotherapy in the 1980s. The doctrine was expressed in these terms: traumatic experiences can cause the victim to switch on a mental defence mechanism that is variously known as 'repression' or dissociation (dissociative amnesia). The effect is a selective loss of memory causing the frightening experience to be forgotten. Although the memories are beyond reach, 'the body remembers'. Repressed memories generate symptoms like anxiety, insomnia pain, recurring dreams and other mental phenomena. These physical and mental signs can continue throughout adult life without the affected person becoming aware of the root cause.

These psychotherapists believed that hidden memories could be brought back into consciousness using certain techniques.[180] Patients who sought therapeutic help for anxiety, depression and eating disorders would be treated with hypnosis, dream interpretation, guided visualization and other approaches aimed at 'recovering repressed memories'.[181]

The belief in repressed memories became so widespread that patients, assuming that they must have been subjected to abuse, began to ask their therapists to help them retrieve memories they couldn't recall.[182] For many, an important source of inspiration was a book called *The Courage to Heal: A Guide for Women Survivors of Child Sexual Abuse*. It was written by the poet and feminist Ellen Bass and the sometime workshop organizer Laura Davis.[183] Their honourable intention was to help women to recover from the damage caused by sexual abuse but, oddly enough, they chiefly address women who cannot remember being abused.

The book lists violations of children, from forcing them to watch pornography and participate in pornographic acts to subjecting them to rape and ritualistic torture. Bass and Davis go on explain that people who don't remember any childhood abuse might still have been victimised. If so, they tend to exhibit certain symptoms, which are also listed and explained. Indications of past abuse include depression, anxiety and low self-esteem, troubled relationships, eating disorders, perfectionism and being afraid to succeed. Despite being so general, even commonplace, any such symptom is to be taken as a reason for suspecting that one has been abused as a child. Often, the intimation of having been a victim begins with something as minor as an intuition, but the authors argue that this is proof enough and this will inevitably progress from suspicion to confirmation.

The term 'survivor' is consistently used to denote a victim of abuse in childhood. Survivors need not remember any acts of violation. Under the heading 'But I Don't Have Any Memories', Bass and Davis describe a woman of thirty-eight who was sure that her father had molested her, although she had no memory of it. She solved the problem by turning the question on its head and choosing to act as though it had, in fact, happened.[184]

Bass and Davis are in the best of company. Sigmund Freud himself based his theories on self-verifying hypotheses. The Canadian psychologist Keith Stanovich, in a textbook on scientific methods in psychology, has written that Freud has vanished from modern psychological research despite the huge cultural influence of his ideas. He created large, complex theoretical constructs but never carried out any repeatable experiments to test them.[185] Instead, his evidence was drawn from case studies, based on his personal experiences in the therapy room. Today, few psychologists take seriously Freudian propositions such as 'the Oedipus complex', 'the death drive' or 'penis envy'. By taking great liberties with the notion of verifiability, moreover, Freud opened the door to the pseudo-scientific thinking that has infected psychotherapy ever since, and paved the way for publications such as *The Courage to Heal*.[186]

Margit Norell and her circle were part of a community of psychotherapists who accepted Freud's way of defining 'truth', despite the subjective and unscientific way he arrived at his conclusions.

I found the following passage in a Swedish developmental psychology textbook that was very popular in the 1980s and 1990s, entitled *0 to 20 Years from a Psychoanalytical Perspective*:

Initially, Sigmund Freud regarded psychoanalysis as one of the natural sciences but he later came to see it as part of the arts. These two categories of learning are based on different forms of research. The natural sciences require objective observations and data from experimental testing, on the basis of which laws are formulated that attempt to explain the resulting phenomena. In the arts, the testing is subjective and includes dialogue, empathy and interpretation, with outcomes that do not lead to laws and norms but which aim to understand human phenomena either directly or through [further] interpretation. The investigators approach their topics subjectively. The analysts aim to elicit personal responses, gather impressions of their patients and attempt empathy for another's subjective experiences. All this belongs to the arts. Tears can be understood.[187]

It may well sound commendable to reach an understanding of how the human psyche works through focusing on emotions, impressions, and empathy, but it can lead to the idea that the psychoanalyst can claim any kind of perception to be the truth as long as it feels right for the psychoanalyst himself or herself – a dangerous development.

The concept of repressed memories definitely belongs to 'the arts'. No one would deny that the sexual abuse of children is a serious issue. Again, no one would deny that people who have been subjected to traumatic events may well choose not to think about what happened, and that this avoidance can persist for a long time.[188] But to avoid thinking about distressing events does not entail 'repressing' the memory, and placing it beyond normal recall. Despite heroic investigations, research has not produced any convincing proof of the form of 'repression' that Margit and the authors of *The Courage to Heal* believed in. The American psychologist David Holmes carried out a review of all published research into repressed memories from 1930 onwards and published a paper on his results in 1974. At that point he had not been able to find a single piece of scientifically valid proof for the repression mechanism. In 1990, Holmes published another overview in which he arrived at the same conclusion. In other words, Holmes wrote, sixty years of research into memory functions have not turned up any evidence that people 'repress' traumatic memories.[189]

In fact, most investigations showed the opposite to be the case. Memories of frightening, traumatizing events are, generally speaking, more vivid and longer lasting than other memories. For instance, extensive research on soldiers has shown that they remember wartime experiences regardless of the degree of trauma. Two Dutch scientists, Willem Wagenaar and Jop Groeneweg, published a paper in 1990 on what concentration camp prisoners remembered in the mid-1980s compared with interviews conducted in the 1940s. Survivors from the Dutch camp Erika bore witness of torture and appalling violence. Forty years later, a court case was brought against one of the inmates who had terrorized his fellow prisoners on Nazi orders. He was charged with murder and other violent acts. In 1984, the court heard statements made by several camp survivors, of whom fifteen had also been interviewed at the time of their release. It was possible to compare what they remembered. Everyone interviewed remembered well enough what they had endured. Details were forgotten at times, as one might expect after four decades, but there were no signs of repression.[190]

In 2000, Harrison Pope, a Harvard professor of psychiatry, conducted a review of scientific studies on retention of traumatic memories. In total, about 10,000 people were included who had all experienced trauma, ranging from camp imprisonment and warfare to natural disasters. Pope and his team did not find a single case of repressed memory.[191]

It has also been well known for a long time that it is easy to create false memories in susceptible people. One of the outstanding scientists in this field is the American professor of psychology Elizabeth Loftus. The 2002 issue of *Review of General Psychology* (a journal published by the American Psychological Association) ranked Loftus as the most influential female psychologist of the twentieth century.[192] Internationally, she is one of the foremost experts on false memories, and her innovative research has played a crucial role in demonstrating that the 'memory repression' hypothesis is based more on faith than science.[193]

In 1974, Loftus carried out a famous experiment which, more or less by chance, proved how false memories can be created. She and her co-workers were investigating how witnesses of accidents remember the event. A film of a collision between two cars was shown in front of a test group. Afterwards, the subjects were asked how fast they thought the cars had been travelling. It turned out that the speed estimates were higher when the accident was spoken of in terms of 'a smash' rather than in less dramatic terms such as 'a collision' or 'hit'. When the subjects were asked a week later if they could remember any broken glass at the scene, those who initially had been hearing that the cars had 'smashed' were more prone to remember broken glass, even though in fact there was none in the film.[194]

Loftus had proved that leading questions can create false memories. In the 1970s and 1980s, she designed several other experiments, which established that it is surprisingly easy to modify human memory. Contrary to common belief, the mind does not have an archive facility in which memories are kept, like cans of old film. Every time we remember, we are recreating the memory, mixing old and new fragments, as well as the thoughts and feelings at the time of remembering. This reconstruction happens every time we recall the past, and is why our memories can change over time.[195]

Towards the end of the 1980s, American patients who had been exposed to recovered memory therapy started to report to the police that they had been abused ten, twenty, thirty and even forty years earlier. The perpetrators were usually parents, relatives, neighbours and teachers. When the cases reached court, and this happened all over the world, the trial evidence consisted mainly of memories 'retrieved' in therapy.

In 1990, the fifty-one-year-old American George Franklin was convicted of murder. The victim was an eight-year-old girl, a friend of his daughter Eileen, who was also eight at the time. Twenty years later, Eileen claimed to have witnessed the murder, and that she had repressed what she had seen. During her psychotherapy, the memories had slowly resurfaced and became increasingly detailed. Eileen said that she had seen her father attempt a sexual assault on her friend in the back of a van. She was able to describe exactly how her father's voice had sounded when he told the girl to stop fighting him. Her next mental image was of the three of them standing next to the van. Her father held a rock in his raised hand and Eileen could hear herself screaming. Next, she remembered returning to the murder scene and finding her friend covered in blood and with a crushed silver ring on her finger. In the judgement of Eileen's psychotherapist, these memories were true, and some members of Eileen's family also believed her. A prosecutor listened to the narrative, became convinced, and brought the case to court.

Elizabeth Loftus was one of the trial witnesses and gave an account of all the evidence to date of how people in experimental situations can be induced, by means of leading questions, to form false memories. She had to admit, however, that none of the experiments had involved creating traumatic false memories. The jury, convinced by the wealth of detail in Eileen's statement, convicted her father despite the lack of evidence and also despite the absence of proof that a repression/recovery process of the type claimed by his daughter could actually take place.[196]

The Franklin trial meant that many research groups became interested in the question of whether false memories of traumatic events could be created by suggestion and leading questions.

In 1991, the American psychologist Nick Spanos used hypnosis to elicit false memories of childhood abuse from several experimental subjects. In 1993, Elizabeth Loftus published an article in which she described an innovative experimental design: she and her team tricked test subjects into believing that they had become lost in a large shopping mall when they were children.[197,198] Their parents, they were told, verified the story. After they had been given the framework narrative, the experiment investigated the extent to which individual subjects claimed to remember this non-event when asked in interviews. The full report of the shopping mall experiment was published in 1995 and the test design became famous. The results showed that about a quarter of the subjects had created detailed memories. Some of them could describe the clothes worn by the stranger who had helped them and the shops around them. The false memories grew more detailed with repeated interviews. Some of the subjects became so convinced that they refused to accept the researchers' assurance that the story was false and only part of an experiment.[199]

In 1994 Elizabeth Loftus and Steve Ceci published a paper on memory in children: primary school pupils had been persuaded to believe that they had once got a finger stuck in a mouse trap and had been taken to the hospital to have it removed.[200,201]

Yet another American psychologist, Ira Hyman, described how her team, using Loftus's method, tricked a group of students into 'remembering' that, as five-year-olds, they had spent a night in hospital with severe middle-ear inflammation. Once each subject had been told that their parents confirmed this tale, some 20 per cent of them began to develop false memories of their stay in hospital. The research team also conducted an experiment in which seventy-two student subjects were asked to believe that, also at the age of five, they had been to a wedding party given by family friends and that they had managed to topple a bowlful of drink over the bride's parents. The subjects were interviewed three times and around a third of them created more or less detailed memories that they personally thought were real. These 'memories' usually grew more detailed with each new interview. Some subjects who found it difficult to recall the non-event were encouraged to close their eyes and visualize the situation. This process is analogous to how psychotherapists elicit 'repressed' childhood memories but was shown to stimulate these subjects to create more false memories than their peers.[202]

The design of the shopping mall experiment was used in various formats and in a range of studies, which generally showed that about a quarter to a third of all subjects would create false memories of fictitious events, even of truly gruesome narratives. It was possible to make people believe that they had nearly drowned as children, or used their hands to break a window, that they had been seriously injured by other children, or attacked by wild animals.[203, 204, 205,206] One group showed that it is possible to induce a belief in having witnessed demonic possession.[207] In another experiment, the subjects were persuaded that they had been raped in an earlier existence.[208] In other words, the results all pointed the same way: the expectations of others govern a great deal of what people believe they remember – and the false memories feel completely real once formed and established.

All these research results came rather late for George Franklin but after seven years in jail, he was granted a re-examination of his case. The prosecution decided not to retry him 'on a technicality' and he did not have to endure another trial. By then, the legal system in the

United States had taken on board the fact that 'recovered memories' are inherently unreliable.[209]

There were those who still argued that false memories were associated with weaker emotional reactions than true, recovered, memories. Many patients in psychotherapy experience deep anguish and terror during the recovery process, regarded as proof of authenticity by some.[210] That argument, however, was taken apart by Richard McNally, a professor of psychology at Harvard. Through advertisements in newspapers, McNally found test subjects who sincerely believed they had been abducted and abused in various ways by aliens on spaceships. He found that when reminded of these imaginary events, the subjects suffered from stress responses comparable to the reactions of people with post-traumatic stress disorder when recalling genuine trauma.[211] McNally drew this conclusion: 'Physical signs of emotional responses to a memory cannot be used to prove that the memory is authentic.'[212]

Thanks to Elizabeth Loftus, Richard McNally and many others who have researched this phenomenon, we now know that about 30 per cent of the population are capable of creating detailed memories of terrifying events that are entirely fictitious, and that such false memories can create an emotional response equivalent to the response to real trauma. Elizabeth Loftus had so much experience with inducing false memories in her subjects that she was able to write up a set of instructions for how to go about it:

First, the individual gets convinced that the false event is plausible. Even events that start out being rather implausible can be made to seem more plausible by simple suggestion. Next, the individual gets convinced that the false event was personally experienced. Plying the person with false feedback is a particularly effective way to accomplish this. At this point, the individual might merely believe that the event is true but has no sense of recollection. But with guided imagination, with visualization of the stories of others, and with suggestive feedback and other sorts of manipulations, a rich false memory can develop.[213]

The research shows that, at first, false memories are felt to be less reliable than real memories, but that this will change if the subject is made to talk about the false events a sufficient number of times.[214]

Elizabeth Loftus published her book *The Myth of Repressed Memory* in 1994. Among others, she quotes George Ganaway, a psychoanalyst who has said that many psychotherapists unwittingly follow Loftus's instructions when they treat their patients. Ganaway was of the view that poorly trained therapists run the biggest risk of creating false memories in their patients. Such therapists often hold on to, as he put it, 'articles of faith' that are set in stone, such as the mind functioning as an internal video recorder and that the road to the successful resolution of mental distress lies in 'revealing repressed memories'. The outcome is that the psychotherapist – without understanding what is going on – will lead the patient on to create false memories. Loftus writes: 'Through tone of voice, phrasing of questions, and expressions of belief or disbelief, a therapist can unwittingly encourage a patient to accept the emerging "memories" as real, thus reinforcing the patient's delusion or even implanting false memories in the patient's mind.'[215]

As I prepared myself for the interview with Cajsa Lindholm and Lena Arvidsson, I kept thinking about what Cajsa had said about her psychotherapy in the lecture. It sounded as if she had followed the Loftus false memory prescription step by step. When the therapy began, the patient had no memories of any childhood abuse. It was Cajsa who suggested that her patient's distress might have been caused by early abuse, even though trauma research in fact has shown that people subjected to incest have no particular symptoms in common.[216]

Next, Cajsa interpreted the patient's dreams as coded messages about forgotten episodes of abuse, and delivered her analysis with all the authority of her position as psychotherapist. Actually, she might as well have read tea leaves or Tarot cards. The patient, however, trusted Cajsa and went along with the suggestion that she had been abused. All that was left for the therapist to do was convince her patient that these fantasies were memories.

Elizabeth Loftus and many other researchers typically succeeded in creating detailed but false memories of traumatic events in their subjects after two to three weeks. Cajsa, by her own account, had two to three sessions per week with her patient for six consecutive years. I wonder what Elizabeth Loftus could have made her subjects believe if she had had that length of time with them.

13

Cajsa and Lena

'It is like drilling deep down, to extend and increasingly come to closer grips with a believable situation, a situation that feels like the truth. And if it feels true, it probably is. Besides, if you feel better afterwards that will surely mean that it is the real thing.'
Cajsa Lindholm, describing how she helps her patients recover repressed memories of abuse.

Cajsa Lindholm practises in a small ground-floor flat with a view across Krukmakar Street in Stockholm's Södermalm. The single room is sparsely furnished with a couple of armchairs, a bed and a white bookshelf from IKEA.

When we met there, Cajsa's next birthday would be her sixty-sixth but I would never have guessed – she looked much younger. She was friendly but I sensed a hidden tension behind her calm manner, perhaps to be expected, given that she was going to speak to me about her current and daily use of an approach to therapy that has been condemned for more than twenty years.

Cajsa had grown up in a home without a tradition of book learning but, at eighteen, she got a summer job as relief nursing assistant in a psychiatric clinic for children. The life stories of the troubled children moved her and she decided to study to become a psychiatrist or a psychologist. She had personal motives, too. 'It was something that came from inside me,' she said. 'I knew I needed this. And since then, I have found out that I really did have deep-seated issues although I was not in touch with all that at the time. In various ways, I knew what I had had to live through, but so much of it was repressed.'

After completing her first degree at Uppsala University in 1966, Cajsa then trained in group therapy and became a qualified psychologist in 1975. One of her teachers told her about Margit Norell and Barbro Sandin's therapeutic work with schizophrenic patients at Säter. Cajsa felt straightaway that this was for her. She had heard of Margit, who was quite well known among psychologists. 'She was the head of the Holistic Institute and had quite a few establishment people, you know, celebrities, coming to her for therapy,' Cajsa said. 'She was a name.'

Cajsa went north to Dalarna County and looked for jobs in Säter hospital, but there was only one unfilled post and that was in the secure unit. This sounded too hard and she instead joined a psychiatric outpatient clinic in Borlänge, just twenty-five kilometres from Säter. Cajsa contacted Barbro Sandin to ask if she might join the group supervision sessions that Sandin and Margit Norell regularly held with staff associated with the 'Säter model'. She was allowed to sit in, and, for a year, Cajsa commuted between Borlänge and Säter to learn from the supervision given to the young psychotherapists and psychiatric nurses. They usually discussed case histories and Margit would share her impressively sharp analyses, in which she linked the behaviour of psychotic patients to events and relationships that she felt able to trace back to their childhood. Cajsa was impressed. 'I remember thinking "How can she interpret all this in such a fascinating way?"'

One day, she felt brave enough to ask Margit if she would take her on as a patient. She imitated Margit's voice: '"Yes. Currently, the waiting time is three years." She was very much the upper class lady.' That was too long to wait. After another year in Borlänge she got married and the couple moved to Linköping, which broke Cajsa's contact with Säter. But she could not forget Margit and a few years later Cajsa and her husband moved closer to Stockholm: 'My reason was that I wanted to be closer to her.'

In 1979, she called Margit and again asked to be taken on as a patient. There were still no appointment times available but Cajsa, who claims that she was very shy in those days, still insisted: 'You see, I wanted her! So, I asked her, "Isn't it right to try to do what one wants?", a quite banal question but back then, I felt uncertain. And she replied, "Oh yes, one should." And then she offered me an appointment.'

I asked Cajsa what Margit was like as a psychotherapist. She thought for a while, gazing out the window.

'She was calm, friendly, unfussy. Her smile was very warm, she had a sense of humour and knew how to turn a joke. She would sometimes joke about what we talked about to give a new perspective on things. She was an upper class lady, and I was in no way used to people like that. But with her, I felt confident from the start.'

Margit provided Cajsa with the characteristic combination of personal therapy and supervision that was her usual way of dealing with pupils. According to what Cajsa had been taught, mixing therapy and supervision in this way was 'a hanging offence' but she thought it was a good idea. It meant that Margit could help Cajsa manage her own 'deep-seated issues' when they threatened to affect Cajsa's work with her own patients. Margit flew in the face of rules and convention, Cajsa told me admiringly. 'She was brave. She was controversial. When she believed in something she would stand up for it and give one hundred per cent.' Then Cajsa laughed and affectionately imitated Margit's polished accent again, even mimicking the way she would beat the air with her finger for emphasis: "'If I *say* so, it *is* so!'"

When Cajsa had been in therapy for a year, she asked if Margit taught any groups.

'She got up, walked to a corner cupboard and took out a list of names,' Cajsa told me. 'And then she said, "Here's your group, if you phone these people." I saw the name Tomas Videgård among them and phoned him. We talked for a while and then I called all the other names on the list.'

It was actually Cajsa who brought the study group together in 1980. She was very pleased when Margit joined their meetings in 1985. 'We went over the theory again and again. We were always discussing things. It was really great. Absolutely fantastic.'

Cajsa had not trained as a psychotherapist when she came to see Margit, but that was easily fixed. 'I collected all the course units I had taken and then Margit examined me on object relations theory. And of course I was in therapy with her. It was such a privilege.'

'You mean that, as a psychotherapist, you were entirely taught by Margit Norell?' I asked.

'Yes, yes, yes. And that was great. Just imagine that someone would undertake to set an exam for a patient! That's how strong her will to make us learn was. I am so incredibly grateful that I met her. My entire professional identity is built on my contact with her.'

I asked her how she goes about initiating the therapeutic work with a new patient. She then described a method I know that researchers like Elizabeth Loftus call 'guided visualization':

When we start out with the therapy, we map out the issues. We scan emotions and problematic areas. Panic attacks, what do they feel like? What situations do you have them in? And we look around, search for answers, link things up.

I ask questions like, 'Can you link [your feelings] to a particular period [in your life]? Can you see a child? How old do you think you were? What might have happened?' The patient will always remember something [from childhood], so there will be something to hang on to. And we gradually go deeper. It is like drilling deep down, to extend and increasingly come to closer grips with a believable situation, a situation that feels like the truth. And if it feels true, it probably is. Besides, if you feel better afterwards that will surely mean that it is the real thing.

I asked her to explain 'age regression'. 'Regression is when one tries to access the child's experiences,' she replied. 'If you're in therapy with me, in that hour you'd expect to enter a state of mind that summons the child inside you, finding out what the past was like for you. During a session it's possible to control things like that. I might also aim for a few months of reliving things.'

'How are your patients affected by such periods?' I asked.

'The patient finds herself back in touch with what she couldn't bear knowing about before, something that has been in her body. It might have expressed itself in compulsive behaviour, or maybe as if having been non-existent, always submissive. One way or another, she has kept the lid on the past because it has been too hard to go in and confront it. But it can be tremendously liberating to go in.'

Cajsa admitted that it is hard work to 'relive' the past for months on end. 'You become confused, feel cast adrift. You lose your grip on the here and now.'

I had heard this before. On a tape recording of one of the group meetings, Margit spoke about her patients 'queuing up for regression'. She had introduced a queuing system because they became so confused by the 'reliving' that she could not cope with more than one at a time. I remembered that Cajsa, at her WEI lecture, said that one of her patients had to recoup in a psychiatric hospital while in psychotherapy. Cajsa described this as positive proof that the 'regression' had gone really deep. It seemed that there was something very odd, even borderline psychotic, about what Cajsa called 'regression', a state she induced in her patients on Margit's instructions. No wonder that 'memories' rose to the surface under these conditions, I thought.

'How far back in time can you go for the hidden memories?' I asked.

'Just now, I have a person who is working with something that happened when she was one year old,' Cajsa replied. 'What she felt happened to her was oral abuse.'

'Oral? Sexual?'

'Yes. There, she has quite distinct . . . well, what I think is . . .' She stopped to think before continuing. 'Patients of course know themselves. If I ask you, "How old is this child, just try to visualize and what do you see?" then you can tell me yourself "It is a very young child." Because you always know, somewhere inside you. If something has happened to you, the knowledge remains.'

'It remains inside you?'

'It is embedded in you,' Cajsa said. 'But earlier than one year . . .' She paused again. 'I know that at least one of my patients, you know, kind of sensed traumas that were earlier still but they weren't mapped out. Something just strikes you. Something annihilates. More like that.'

160

Cajsa told me that she has memories of lying on scales to be weighed although she was only a few months old at the time. I asked her if she had always remembered that moment.

'No, I haven't.'

'Did it emerge while you were in therapy with Margit?'

'Yes,' she replied.

Modern research into recall of past events suggests that it is much more likely that Cajsa created this memory as an adult.[217] Of course, she did not bother with such details. It would have been surprising if she did, given that Margit, her guru, never cared for whatever the scientists were on about. Margit believed that *she* owned the truth and it was a product of her teaching who sat facing me in the little room on Krukmakar Street.

Cajsa told me that dream interpretation was the foundation of her psychotherapeutic work.

'Dreams show you the way, in my view. Dreams show what is moving around in the patient's mind,' she said.

'So, during the therapy session you talk a lot about dreams?'

'I interpret any number of dreams for my patients, every week,' Cajsa said and smiled. 'You know, in principle, everyone brings their dreams to me. And there is always something in the dreams that points somewhere, that links up. Subconsciously, the patient has understood something.'

I asked her if she and Margit would talk about dreams when Cajsa herself was in therapy.

'Oh, yes! I have any number of notebooks full of my own dreams. Lots and lots.'

'How can you be sure that the interpretation is right in each case?'

'I have worked for such a massively long time and now it's almost like me driving my car – I know what I'm doing.'

Cajsa works full-time as a psychotherapist. I asked her in what proportion of her patients she found repressed memories of sexual abuse in childhood.

'What percentage, do you mean?'

'Yes.'

'Fifty or sixty per cent,' Cajsa told me.

'So, your thinking is along the same lines as Freud's in 1896?' I asked.

'Oh, yes, yes, yes.'

'That it is very common?'

'Yes, I'm absolutely convinced of that,' Cajsa said.

'And how often do these patients say that they can't remember any abuse when they first come to see you?'

'That's what most of them say,' Cajsa replied.

I had also made an appointment to see Lena Arvidsson. She was fifty-two years old when we met. She had finished her psychology course in the early 1990s and spent the summers in 1991 and 1992 working as a psychiatric auxiliary nurse at Säter. In the summer of 1992, she came across Sture and got on well with him, according to her later entries in Sture's case notes. This was before his first murder conviction, and when Sture was on leave they would sometimes meet up. In 1993 and 1994, Lena stood in as psychotherapist at Säter over the summers and took Sture for therapy two to three times a week while his regular therapist was on holiday. Lena got a permanent post as a psychologist at Säter in November 1994, the month when Sture's first murder conviction was announced. From that point, she would take him for therapy sessions every Wednesday between half past ten and midday, while his usual therapist Birgitta Ståhle went to Stockholm for a supervision session with Margit. Between 1995 and 1998, she also acted as Ståhle's holiday replacement.[218]

The woman I was to meet was one of the three psychotherapists who had seen Sture for therapy sessions during the Quick years. It meant that she had privileged access to him. She continued working at Säter well into the 2000s, by which time Sture had stopped both his therapy and his collaboration with the police. Once Lena moved back to Stockholm, she went into private practice as a psychotherapist.

I sent Lena an email before the meeting to ask if she could put me in touch with any patients whose repressed memories had emerged during therapy and who might consider being interviewed by me. She responded that she had a better idea: 'My suggestion is that I tell you about my long period in therapy with Cajsa. The tough journey I have been on might help you to understand what this kind of therapy can do for the person. And I don't mind at all speaking about myself in that way.'[219]

I met Lena on three occasions, the first two in her practice in Södermalm. The third time, I interviewed her in her flat up on Hammarbyhöjden Hill, where she lives alone with her dog.

Lena came to meet me when I arrived at her practice. We settled down to talk and she told me that although she had never been invited to join Margit's group, she had met Margit several times at seminars and lectures, where members of a wider circle of therapists were welcome.

'People put their trust in Margit, I felt it,' Lena said. 'There was a readiness to believe what she said. You felt it was weighty, and powerfully backed up by experience and engagement. You felt that she had done such lot. Just thinking about the situation when she broke with the Psychoanalytical Society and left, only to start the Holistic Institute ... what a development it was, and how much she managed to do! How bravely she took a stand for new ways of working!'

While we chatted about Margit, Lena asked if I had read *The Assault on Truth* by Jeffrey Masson. I said that I hadn't. She immediately wanted to lend me her copy of the book and went to get it from her bookshelf. I leafed through it. On the inside cover, Margit's lovely Ex Libris, a blue tree growing out of her name, caught my eye. Lena explained why the book was so important: 'It is about the entire seduction theory that Freud proposed and then abandoned. It is very interesting.'

She thought it reasonable to compare Margit with Freud at the time when he formulated his first ideas. 'Freud of course has meant so much but times change. His theories have become a little ...' Lena shook her head. 'But there's a difference. Margit's ideas have really stood the test of time.'

I asked her how she came to meet Cajsa and Lena said that she had been a very troubled young woman. In 1982, when she was twenty-one, she still lived at home with her parents. 'Frankly, I felt like shit. Extremely neurotic and kind of "schizoid". Anxious, worried, shy and silent.'

After school, Lena continued her education in a small town college. At the time, Cajsa was working with rootless young people in nearby Södertälje and her husband was a teacher at the college. Cajsa and Lena met so that Lena could talk about her problems.

'At that time, I didn't realize that I had been abused by my father,' Lena told me. 'I was not in contact with that. I simply didn't know.'

Cajsa, however, did not have time to take Lena on for proper psychotherapy.

'She had just given birth to her son and didn't have time for me,' Lena went on. 'That was when she suggested to me that I should read *The Drama of the Gifted Child* by Alice Miller. When I had finished reading it I knew it was all about me. And then I completely broke down. I know I went off to lie down on a bed in the college and wouldn't get up. I regressed totally. That was when Cajsa understood that my therapy had already started. So she had to take me on.'

Lena's therapy sessions with Cajsa began in 1982 but it took years of treatment before she could remember any episodes of abuse. Lena explained that it was 'about three years before I became aware of my first memories', which places the breakthrough in 1985 when memories of her father's actions first emerged. She said that he worked in different military jobs from the age of sixteen and ended up in the air force. She described him as a depressed, self-absorbed and unpleasant person.

'This is what I always remembered, from the beginning. This withdrawn, creepy father, who sat around sulking when he wasn't being nasty and aggressive.'

'Was he violent?' I asked.

'No, not really . . . it was more like he glared at you. He was irritable, kept you at a distance, far away, and came across like a stranger. There was no contact. It was horrible. He hated the prime minister at the time, Olof Palme. And was scared that the Russians would invade.

That was his special fear. So, of course, I veered well left of centre, not only to protest against my family but turning really radical just to be provocative. He had to learn to live with that.'

Lena said that her father was still alive. Her mother had died a few years ago. She had become 'downtrodden and submissive' but Lena had been very fond of her.

'I loved my mother. She was the whole home, somehow. She took an interest in me, made a fuss, cooked and fixed things in general. My mother was a trier but my father never even tried, not really. So, I can't be angry with her. She was a victim, too.'

The therapy with Cajsa took its cue from Lena's fear of the dark. She told me that the prospect of living alone terrified her and that when she was about to go to bed she would always look underneath it first. With Cajsa's guidance, Lena tried to trace the source of her fear back to her early childhood by visualizing herself as a child. The visualization would make her go into a strange state of mind.

'I often had to lie down; it was easier then. And it would come back to me. We knew when it did because I'd become utterly desperate and cry and describe what happened as best I could.'

This is how Lena began to see images of her father.

'I gradually understood . . . What I was frightened of? Well, there is a figure, a dark shape that comes towards me. Then, more and more, it changes into a realization that it's my father who is coming into my room. And I can sense that he is there. That is how close you can come.'

When I met Lena in 2012, thirty years had passed since she started her treatment with Cajsa. She still sees Cajsa every week, but mostly for supervision sessions. While we were talking, however, it became clear that she still goes through regressions and, once in that state, relives the repressed abuse from her childhood. The difference is that now she does it on her own, in her flat.

'I can go through with it myself at home now. There are times when I feel awful and then it all opens up again. It is like stepping into another part of one's self.'

'Is it like time travel?' I asked.

'Yes, that's exactly what it's like. I am really into it. But if anyone should come into the room, whoever it is can talk with me normally. I do get it, I mean that you are you and not dangerous. But I can feel my father's presence in the room and how he does that to me in that way he had and I can somehow feel it in my body. Except I know he isn't there.'

'Do you have other sensations, like noises or smells?'

'I do hear him say things, yes. And as for smells ... well, yes, he might smell of sweat. And he smoked heavily, so, yes, I can smell the smoke. I have problems being with people if there's tobacco on their breath.'

Lena's regressions have been going on for three decades and she still hasn't explored all her repressed memories. Sometimes she needs Cajsa's help to handle her strong emotions. She might phone her therapist, but mostly it is enough to write emails.

'More always comes out when I write,' she said. 'Then I can put down things like "It's happening now, he's in my room and then he does this and I feel that" and the more I write, the more I remember. I can carry on writing for hours, sometimes. But I'm fine with going to work the following day. It isn't gone, but I can cope, can carry it with me. I function, all the time. I have never failed to manage my life in any way.'

Helped by interpretations of her dreams, and regression exercises and intense writing in her diary, Lena has constructed an entirely new childhood for herself. While she was describing the process, I remembered what I had read in *The Myth of Repressed Memory*, how Elizabeth Loftus explains that patients who endlessly go over their fantasies by writing about them between therapy sessions run a greater risk of mixing up fact and fiction.[220]

I asked Lena how old she thinks she was when the abuse began. She became a little evasive.

'It is hard to know when you're that little.'

'But it began before you were a year old?'

'Yes, that's the feeling I have, anyway. It is what Cajsa and I have arrived at. We feel that everything points that way, that it all began when I was still an infant. And then it went on until . . . well, roughly when I began to develop a female shape, at twelve or thirteen, maybe fourteen. Of course he lost interest by then.'

'And how often do you think he abused you?'

'Not just a few times, you know, but regularly, that's how I remember it, I don't know if it was once a week . . . it was really often. That's how I feel.'

Lena told me that she had recently begun to recover memories of her father bringing in other men, his colleagues, allowing them to join in the abuse.

'I woke one night and saw everything so clearly, I, hadn't, you know, really landed in the right time and place but I felt there were two men who took part. Look, I can't be sure but I've got such an overwhelming feeling that's how it was. But I can't be sure exactly, not yet. Because you so easily dissociate that it's hard to see things distinctly.'

'How old do you think you were when the other two men became involved?' I asked and Lena looked thoughtful.

'Look, I must have been . . . my father went to Cyprus for a year, he was in the UN forces and that's a link. They got in touch in the army, you see. It must have been either before he went off to Cyprus, which makes it 1967 or 1968, or else it's just afterwards. I remember that they came back to our house. I remember their names and their looks. And then there's something else . . . there seems to be certain memories that I don't dare to believe in just yet.'

'That would mean you were six or seven years old?'

'That's right.'

'And this is something you had repressed entirely? You can't remember it at all?'

'No. I grasp it because I've started to dream about it. Also, I've sensed more memories will be coming back now.'

By Lena's account, her father had abused her on a regular basis from when she was less than a year old to when she was between twelve and fourteen, and two other men periodically took part. When I saw Cajsa Lindholm again, I cautiously asked her if it seemed reasonable to her that only decades of therapy could help Lena recall all this. Cajsa looked concerned and said she couldn't recall if Lena had been abused for such a long time. Sometime later, Lena emailed me:

Cajsa mentioned to me that, after the most recent interview with me, you wondered about my response to your questions concerning the degree of my exposure to abuse, i.e. with what frequency it happened and at what age it finally stopped. I realize that I was careless, because thinking back, and in the name of honesty, I have no cut and dried answers. During these last few months, I have been in more intense, more profound contact with my memories of past abuse and, at this stage, it is easy to feel that I was exploited more often than was the case. The sensation of vulnerability is overpowering and infinite! I realize that I cannot have been as old as thirteen when the abuse stopped because, if so, I would not have been able to repress the memories. I am so very particular when it comes to analysing and evaluating my patients' memories and should, of course, be equally thorough with myself and my ramblings. So – I write this to get things straight with you. Live well! Lena.[221]

I later discovered that, in the spring of 2013, Lena had appeared in court as an expert witness for the prosecution in a sexual abuse trial. The defendant was a young woman who alleged that her father had used her for sex from the age of two and until she was fifteen years old.[222] She had repressed her memories and only recovered them in psychotherapy sessions. The father was acquitted twice, first in the District Court and then in the Crown Court, but Lena Arvidsson had argued that there was nothing unusual about repressing memories of abuse that had continued until the age of fifteen. Lena and Cajsa must have worried that I would become sceptical about their method; the email was a tactical move.

Lena told me that she had worked at Säter and knew Thomas Quick well but was, of course, prevented by her duty of confidentiality to say anything more about that case.

I asked her: 'What you're telling me just now sounds very much like the therapy Thomas Quick went through, doesn't it?'

'Absolutely, I'd agree,' Lena replied without missing a beat.

So this was Margit's method: allowing her patients to fantasize for years, chewing over their imagined stories until they began to look and feel like memories. I recalled Margit's letter to David Schecter in 1977, telling him about her patient Hanna Olsson who, 'via regression had come into close contact with early experiences and surroundings, including all senses and some specific bodily sensations'.[223] Another description of her treatment approach appears in her last lecture at the Holistic Institute: 'In the course of the therapeutic process, [the patient] reconnects with intense, primary and very early experiences that are recalled complete with the wealth of smells and colours, and with the emotional intensity that surely cannot be greater than in early childhood.'[224]

Lena gave me a document which she thought I would find interesting, a special subject essay that she had written in her last term as a psychology student. This was in the spring of 1994. In the autumn of that year, she became employed as a clinical psychologist at Säter. The title of the essay was 'To treat criminals with convictions of violence at the regional secure unit at Säter hospital: A psychotherapeutic approach based on the British object relations theory.' On the cover of this piece of university course work, the name of Lena's supervisor was given as Hanna Olsson, Margit's patient and one of the group's first seven acolytes. The essay was introduced by a few poems by 'Sture, a patient in the regional psychiatric hospital'. Among others, Lena quoted these lines:

I hid my fear beneath pain,
Hid my weeping behind forgetfulness
I wanted to love and did as I was told
But did not understand the scream caused by my caress
And left my love's longing behind as I was taken away
A captive to forgotten childhood memories, I recalled
    my father's safe terror.

Sture

The essay was based on Lena's interviews with the medical director Dr Göran Källberg and the clinical psychologist Birgitta Ståhle, whom she referred to as 'the doctor' and 'the psychologist'. Margit's influence was unmistakable.

Lena wrote that both Göran Källberg and Birgitta Ståhle were 'supervised by a woman psychoanalyst with several years of practical experience of psychotherapeutic work along the lines proposed by the British object relations theory. She is thoroughly oriented in theory and has worked with severely ill patients for a substantial part of her professional life. The doctor and the psychologist feel that their individual supervision offers them the help and support that they require to carry on with their psychotherapeutic work.'

Lena also explained the aims of the Säter approach to therapy: 'At the regional secure unit, the goal that everyone strives to reach is helping the patients to get in touch with early traumatic episodes. Repressed memory fragments become more clearly recalled and the pieces of the jigsaw fall into place and make a pattern that finally can be seen to form a comprehensible whole . . .'[225]

Ståhle was interviewed by Lena about how the violent convicts responded to the memory recovery therapy. Ståhle explained: 'They might manifest themselves as clear, concrete remembered images in which feelings, and even smells and sounds reach consciousness. They have to be encouraged to approach the early awareness of total vulnerability, the fear and paralysis that they had been protecting themselves against by their violent actions.'

Lena's essay was astonishing. It proved that Margit's psychotherapeutic methods had been turned into the basis for all the therapy conducted at the Säter forensic psychiatric unit.

Later, going through the piles of notes and other material that Sture kept on the shelves in his room, and which he scanned and sent on to me, I found a copy of Lena's essay. On it, she had written in biro:

Thank you, Sture, for everything you have taught me about the pain, the fear and the hatred behind the violence!
Lena

14

Margit's struggle

*'This sense that you'd say anything to be confirmed – that
was a situation one was in with Margit so often.'*
Patricia Tudor-Sandahl, writer and psychotherapist,
speaking of her long period of psychotherapy with
Margit Norell.

Margit was an activist as well as a psychoanalyst, always a combatant
in wars of ideas. Her foes were not only the orthodox Freudians and
their theory of drives, but everyone who thought it valid to apply
genetic and neurological explanations of aspects of human behaviour.
In principle, Margit thought that childhood trauma caused all mental
problems, from psychoses and autism to criminality and aggressiveness. She wanted to change the world, and had a preference for
taking on patients who would join the struggle. She told Erich
Fromm in a letter from 1970 that her patients 'to a large extent are
politically radical people, with positions of influence in our present
day Swedish society'.[226] Two years later, she describes to Fromm an
American doctor and fellow-activist who had just started in therapy
with Margit and who is an example of her ideal patient: *'He has had
a brutal childhood in the midst of the American consumer society and has considerable problems, but also honesty, devotion to tasks he feels are essential and
unusual capacity for working and thinking (IQ 160) and a socialistic orien-
tation. I feel we are working well together and hope we will continue to do
so.'*[227]

Pupils who wanted to curry favour with Margit were expected to
spread the word. Cajsa told me how for years she had worked hard to
preach Margit's message all over the country. 'She really wanted me to

give lectures,' Cajsa said. 'I remember once when I went along and gave a lecture even though I was ill, with a temperature of 39 degrees. In that case I was too soft. After all, I had a husband and children to think about.'

When Hanna Olsson began her analysis in 1977, Margit proudly wrote to David Schecter to say that one of Sweden's best-known feminists was now her patient.[228] Later that year, she described Olsson's regression journeys to childhood and claimed that the therapy had been invaluable to Hanna in her own work:

> From the time when she was two or three years old, Hanna has recovered utterly terrifying experiences with her borderline psychotic father. From time to time she was left alone with him at night in the bedroom when her mother had been too frightened to stay. After long periods of depression, deep anxiety and intense therapeutic work, Hanna now feels free in an unprecedented way – which is important for her work on the task in front of her now as chief secretary to the Commission on Prostitution.[229]

Hanna Olsson headed the secretariat working on a report on prostitution for a government commission appointed in 1977 by the ruling coalition of three right-of-centre parties. During the investigation, several female sex workers were interviewed and their stories of drug abuse, violence and degradation were recounted from a perspective of gender relationships based on power. Margit played an active role in this work. In August 1978, she wrote to David: 'I have lots of work to do and, to help Hanna, I keep reading interviews with prostitutes in my spare time. The reading matter is profoundly involving but also a drain on one's strength.'[230]

In the finished report, which was presented in 1980, Olsson thanks Margit for her time and for her helpful observations on the content, but does not give away that the person she thanks is her own psychoanalyst.[231]

In 1984, Hanna Olsson started a public debate about the murder of Catrine da Costa, a prostitute whose butchered body had been found in Stockholm. Two young doctors, labelled in the media as 'the generalist and the pathologist', were accused of killing her. One strange feature of their trial was that a leading witness for the prosecution was the daughter of one of the accused. She alleged that, when she was eighteen months old, she had been present when her father, assisted by his colleague, carved up Catrine da Costa. At least, this is what her mother claimed after having read about the 'butchered body' in the press. She became convinced that she had heard her child describe a time when her father had let her see a dismembering of a human body during a satanic ritual.

Olsson followed the trial of the two men and believed that they must be guilty but were protected by a patriarchal legal system that condoned male violence against women. Her arguments, presented in a *Dagens Nyheter* article, impressed many. A media crusade was promptly started against the defendants, who were portrayed as monsters. They were eventually acquitted of the murder charges but, even so, the District Court judge clearly had his reservations. He stated that the court had established beyond reasonable doubt that the defendants had been complicit in the dismembering of da Costa's dead body. But because the cutting up per se was by then 'too old' for a case to be brought, they could not be charged with it. In practice, both men had been exposed as human butchers but were unable to appeal because they had been acquitted of the murder. Their lives were ruined.

In 1990, Olsson published her tract *Catrine and Justice*, in which she still insisted that the patriarchal Swedish society had protected the two medics by not convicting them of murder.[232] She claimed that they were guilty of all the charges brought against them and that the child's tale, as told by her mother, was completely trustworthy. The 'butchered body' debate was one of the most enduring public discussions about the individual v. the law that Sweden has conducted in modern times – at least, until the Thomas Quick debate. In 1999, the journalist Per Lindeberg argued persuasively in his book *Death is a Man* that the two men were innocent.[233] He fiercely attacked Hanna Olsson, whom he charged with having turned the 'butchered body' court case into a political show trial about gender issues and set the defendants up as symbols of patriarchal oppression rather than individuals with the right to a fair trial without prejudice.

I was surprised to learn in my interviews with Margit's pupils that it was she who had pressurized Hanna Olsson into taking sides against the doctors. Even the loyal Cajsa Lindholm said she thought that Margit pushed Olsson far too hard: 'She had a tough time, what with the butchered body trial and that book she wrote. And it was Margit who encouraged her all the time. Hanna was made into 'Hanna Olsson' and it cost her a great deal. And the same is true of Birgitta [Ståhle], who has put a lot on the line to be Birgitta. That's Margit for you – the rebel who stands up for honesty and justice.'

'Are you saying that they were both urged on by Margit?' I asked her.

'They were. And compelled by our task, this important thing we had to do.'

The Säter model, the epidemic of repressed memories, the da Costa murder case and the Thomas Quick affair: I was beginning to wonder if there were any major controversies during the 1980s and 1990s in which Margit's influence had not been felt. The shadow she cast was long but, outside of her profession, almost no one knew who she was.

However, Margit's home territory was the therapy room. It was the chief arena for her ideological battle. She would try to change the mind of any pupil who did not accept that he or she had been subjected to sexual abuse and her approach to persuasion was similar to an evangelical preacher's determination to make a non-believer change sides. Tomas Videgård had said that Margit nagged him for years to admit to having been sexually abused in childhood. When he tried to stop his sessions with her in 1990, after thirteen years of treatment, she thought he was making a mistake because he had not yet reached the most important part of his therapy: 'She said things like "You will have been exposed to something like that and that's why we must not stop until you have recovered it",' Tomas told me. And when he asked her to explain on what she based her analysis, she referred to one of his dreams.

Margit also tried to talk Patricia Tudor-Sandahl round. Patricia is a psychotherapist and writer who grew up in an English working-class family but moved to Sweden in 1964. She became a clinical psychologist and psychotherapist and, later, received a PhD in pedagogics. Her first book, published in 1983, was called *About the Child Inside Us* and discusses object relations theory.[234]

When I met Patricia in her lovely flat in Lund, she was seventy-two years old but radiating energy. She has been a full-time writer for many years and has written fifteen books, several of them bestsellers, about psychotherapy and personality development.

It was her first book that caught Margit's eye. 'I was asked to come and see her and of course I was curious enough to say yes. I do remember how she received me. She was rather queenly. I didn't get the impression that she liked my book. Well, she commented that it was quite good but full of Anglicisms. Then our meeting became rather like an exam, because she quizzed me about the theory. I was scared witless that she would think me ignorant.'

At that time, Patricia was doing two jobs, working as a university teacher in social studies and as a psychotherapist. The conversation with Margit ended with Margit offering to supervise Patricia, who jumped at the chance. She had heard people speak of Margit's exceptional ability as a psychotherapist. 'If what I had heard was at all correct, her offer was pure gold! Here was someone who not only knew what she was doing but knew such a lot. So I began to take supervision from Margit and it became more like psychotherapy quite soon, if I remember right.'

Margit's group sometimes held seminars open to a wider circle of people connected to Margit, which Patricia sometimes attended. She had been invited to join the group, but had turned the offer down. She had observed the way Margit's chosen pupils swarmed around their teacher and it made Patricia uncomfortable: '[It was] a very dependent crowd and everyone put Margit on a pedestal, elevating her well above any realistic analysis.'

'What happened at the seminars?' I asked.

'Margit talked, mostly. She interpreted the rights and wrongs for us all the time. I must say, Margit was a devil for that kind of thing. Her manner was something else, so typical ...' Patricia demonstrated Margit's habit of beating the air with an extended index finger while she held forth. 'She hammered her points home, firmly and very distinctly. And then people shut up.'

The fact that Patricia did not want to join the group did not mean that she was any less dependent on Margit than the others.

'Nowadays, I see so clearly that it was a mother–daughter dependency,' she said. 'Perhaps it was mutual since the good daughter confirms her mother who in her turn makes the daughter feel good about herself. It was wonderful to be praised by Margit and that alone was quite addictive. Realizing all this was what made me break away from Margit after many years.'

Patricia broke free in the early 1990s and only then was it becoming obvious to her what had been going on.

'It had grown so much like a sect because it was so very, very comforting to be chosen by Margit. We were all children and Margit was our mother. What can I tell you? It's very strange but that was how it was. I am so glad I got out of it. Eventually, I left the entire field of psychotherapy. And honestly, I pay very little attention to psychotherapy these days.'

Patricia characterizes Margit as having a 'full-blown schizoid' personality, which means someone emotionally cold who tends not to connect with other people. 'Of course, she came across quite differently in the therapy room. She was absolutely focused and concentrated with her entire being on what the patient was telling her. Many of the people I have interviewed described the overwhelming force of her attention, and that it was an important explanation of why people became fixated on her. When Margit turned her intense gaze on you in the therapy room, you felt seen and understood as at no other time in your life.'

However, as time passed, Patricia discovered that this supportive listening was not unconditional. Margit would signal disagreement if she heard something she thought 'wrong'. Her signals were subtle but after years in therapy it was possible to distinguish them, just as children learn to interpret their parents' body language. Patricia showed me Margit's way of almost unnoticeably turning her head away to indicate disapproval. It was possible to see what Margit wished to hear and very difficult not to be affected.

'This sense that you'd say anything to be supported – that was a situation one was in with Margit so often,' Patricia said. 'Just as children are with their parents, of course. It is to say "Do whatever you want, just love me." I believe it to be a fundamental scenario.'

Patricia came to Margit for therapy and supervision twice a week for many years and was firmly pushed towards remembering being sexually abused by her father in her childhood home in England.

'My father was a deeply troubled man,' Patricia told me. 'A young man, caught in the middle of the war . . . A very disturbed, very brutal man. He abused us physically, beat us up. I've written about all that in my [autobiographical] book *What a Bloody Life*. In that sense, growing up was a terrible time for me.' But Patricia had no memories of any sexual assaults. He was violent, frightening and overly tactile. But he was no sexual predator. Still, Margit remained convinced that the truth was different and would not give in.

'Margit could be like a dog with a bone, just keeping at it and not wanting to let go. She grew more so over time, I think. I don't want to suggest it would've been easy to invent something because I've never been tempted to dream up stories. But as for thinking, "But . . . what if I'm not remembering straight? Might what I said actually have been a little bit more than I've admitted?" – it would've been so easy.'

'So you did wonder if you might have repressed memories?'

'Yes, yes, yes,' Patricia said.

She went on to tell me that when she read the media reports about Thomas Quick, she had often thought of Margit's capacity to persuade and that, over the years, these thoughts had worried her a great deal.

'It was so very, very hard to know what was what when one was talking with Margit,' Patricia said.

The concept of recovering repressed memories of sexual abuse grew more and more crucial to Margit's thinking and, towards the end of the 1980s, she decided to write a study of memory recovery as observed in her patients. By then, almost thirty years had passed since Margit had last tried her hand at academic writing. In the early 1960s she had worked on an MSc thesis, which at the time was a requirement for being granted the title of 'Psychologist'. Annie, her daughter, told me that Margit had struggled with the essay for a whole summer. In the end, the university department did not give it a pass mark, which made Margit despair. Jan Stensson was close to her at that time and he told me that he read the essay, and understood why it did not meet the academic standards. Margit had presented a long, detailed case history but it was hard to follow because of the lack of clear distinctions between what the patient had said and what Margit had thought.

'It was very muddled and sort of adrift,' Jan said. He remembered that the 'failed' mark had been very painful for Margit because the case study had been so important to her.

After that experience, Margit managed to avoid committing to any longer pieces of writing for publication. Her unwillingness to appear in print seemed particularly odd while she was the head of the Holistic Institute. The foreign psychoanalysts she met at conferences and corresponded with were all publishing theoretical articles in psychoanalytical journals and would often refer to their work in letters to her. David Schecter's papers were frequently published in the journal *Contemporary Psychoanalysis*, which Margit read with great interest. However, Margit herself – the head of her own psychoanalytical institute and regarded as a remarkably well-informed theoretician – barely had a line in print.

By the end of the 1980s, Margit was finally ready to attempt an academic paper and her subject was the art of recovering repressed memories of sexual abuse. One of her old pupils gave me a copy of the paper, a thirty-page study entitled 'Early Incest. Experiences of the therapeutic process with patients subjected to incestuous abuse'. In it Margit gives an account of the case histories of seven female patients. Her starting point is Freud's betrayal: 'Ever since Freud's complete turn-around with regard to his seduction theory, psychoanalytical literature has said very little about actual experiences of incest and the therapeutic process in that kind of therapy. This is one of the reasons why I wanted to communicate my own experiences.'[235]

It is a strange piece of writing. None of the patients had any memories of abuse when they first arrived in Margit's practice and they all required years of analysis and therapy before any such memories emerged. Margit discovered her patients' concealed traumas through her interpretations of their dreams. She wrote:

> It has struck me how exceptionally good, creative dreamers several of these therapy patients are. Most of them also spontaneously write down so much – their dreams, memories and reflections. Might this not be taken to indicate that the boundary land of dreaming is the best – perhaps the only possible – starting point for contacting 'the other worlds, the land of incomprehensibility'?

Margit refers to forty-seven dreams, all of which point towards past abuse. Here is an example: 'I was standing outside something that could be the Skansen fairground. Two old men (ancient men, especially one of them) were in charge. In there, animals and people live together. A forgetful old man who doesn't look like – but is – my dad. I am going to get new glasses and my dad is, too.'

Another incest dream looked like this: 'A [patient] dreams, after six years of therapy, about a chest of drawers with six drawers. She pulls out five of the upper drawers and finds only stray bits of rubbish in them, but when she pulls out the sixth and bottom drawer, a terrible, black gorilla jumps out and starts chasing her around the room.'

Here is another:

> A patient dreams about a shapeless, doughy trinity that is like a stone sculpture from some ancient Indian culture, which the patient has seen somewhere and had been told was part of human sacrifices. It wants to separate into three parts. My patient does not want to watch it as it splits and does not want to see what comes out when

it does. What comes out is unclean, dark filth and moss that looks as if it would take your weight but in reality is soggy mud, mire in a bottomless pit. The dream is repeated with a similar, tri-partite figure but its splitting apart is less awful. My patient says that she wants to get away from this experience, that she wants to hide from it.

In order to elicit more precise memories of abuse, Margit claims that the patient must be in a certain state of mind: 'When the concrete details of the incest experiences emerge directly in the therapy situation or at home, it often happens first in a different state of consciousness. For some time afterwards, the experiences are often rejected as unreal.'

In the majority of cases, the memories concerned molestations of very young children. For instance, one patient recalled what she thought happened to her at the age of two and a half: 'An episode of anal intercourse, feelings of strangulation and death threats from her father because he feared exposure.' Most of the recovered events were much less distinct. One patient had been made to participate in something that, according to Margit, 'could be determined to have taken place at the age of three, but it remains unclear how long a time it took and how it was done'. Another patient spoke of a memory in which what actually went on was blurred but could still 'be determined to have taken place just after the age of four and at least the most threatening part could be presumed to have happened on two occasions'.

The patients might reject the recovered material as 'unreal' but Margit interpreted such caveats as confirmation that the 'experiences' were real. In a section titled 'Criteria of Truth' she asks, 'How can one be certain that these experiences of incest are true and how can one determine the time at which they occurred?' She answers the question herself: 'Above all, based on what takes place in the therapy room often against the strong resistance exerted by the patient.'

Margit needed no further proof. She adds, though, that occasionally the patients' recollections correlate with what she describes as 'tangible external situations, backed up by others', that demonstrate how the painstakingly extracted 'memories' reflect events in real life. However, the examples of corroboration she presents are eccentric.

Margit quotes as one piece of evidence that both the patient and her mother remember 'the patient's intense thumb-sucking at the age of three' and that her father had 'lost weight' at about the same time. This is the entire 'proof'. Another patient's mother remembered 'an inexplicable hoarseness and loss of voice, with concurrent symptoms of depression, which meant having to take the then four-year-old patient to see the doctor'. In a third case, the reality test was that the patient's mother had been 'speaking about an inexplicable illness with high fever, which the little girl of about five or six had been suffering from one summer'. In a fourth case, the confirmation consisted of the patient's sister's belief that she had been subjected to sexual approaches when she was three and that their mother had started to dress the patient 'in really ugly outfits just when she turned three'. In a fifth case, the evidence of sexual abuse was that the patient had been beaten by her father for 'playing doctors and nurses' with some small boys. Margit's sixth piece of proof was that a woman who had recovered her repressed memories of past abuse had been told by one of her father's former colleagues that he 'used to follow her every time she went to the toilet in a distant part of the house but what he did there she did not know'.

This was what passed for 'evidence'. Margit was convinced and, as time passed, her patients came to share her conviction. In the essay she tells a story about 'patient B' and her dream about having met a snake in the kitchen. Margit understands this to be a strong sign of incestuous violations by B's father and her interpretation results in a vigorous That's it!-experience for B: 'This theme had recurred in several dreams but is only now getting a full explanation, which was followed by an immediate feeling of proof from B.'

The phrase 'feeling of proof' is, of course, a contradiction in terms but effectively captures how Margit construed the concept of truth. Like any true believer, she was simply unable to distinguish between fantasy and reality.

Margit was so pleased with her article that she paid for it to be translated into English. She submitted it to *Contemporary Psychoanalysis*, the journal in which David Schecter had published on average one paper every year between 1961 and 1980, the year of his death. During the last years of his life, Margit had often helped him by reading his work and commenting on it. Now, it was 1989 and, at the age of seventy-five, she had high hopes of seeing her important study of recovered memories published in her beloved David's favourite forum.

Contemporary Psychoanalysis turned the article down and the editors cannot be criticized for this decision. Margit's expectations were crushed and her letters show that she considered the rejection deeply unfair.[236] This was far from her only defeat. Another example is 'the Säter model'. She had been so proud of her contribution to building a Swedish bastion of anti-psychiatry but had fallen out with Barbro Sandin and by 1980 Sandin no longer attended supervision sessions with her. Margit carried on supervising the other therapists working on the Säter model but a few years later Sandin took that task away, too. Margit had been sacked from her own Swedish Chestnut Lodge.

In 1986, the publication of Sandin's book *The Zebra-striped Poodle's Core* was another slap in the face for Margit. Without mentioning Margit Norell once, Sandin described her own approach to treating schizophrenic patients.[237] Many of my interviewees have spoken about how deeply offended Margit was, a reaction that grew bitterer still when Sandin's book received a lot of attention. It came out at the same time as a book written by Elgard Jonsson, Sandin's ex-patient. In his *King of Fools*, Jonsson gave an account of the therapy from the patient's perspective.[238] Both books sold exceptionally well within their genre and both are available in paperback editions in Swedish bookshops today, twenty-five years later. *King of Fools* was even turned into an opera.[239] However, hardly anyone knew that the Säter model probably would not have existed without Margit.

Another hard blow struck in 1988, when the Säter model was driven into exile. The project was greatly respected by many in the media but their enthusiasm was not shared by everyone. Critics pointed out that Barbro Sandin had not been able to produce any scientifically valid evidence in support of her self-proclaimed successes with curing schizophrenics. To those who had not seen the light, the Säter model appeared to be little more than a product of Margit Norell's and Barbro Sandin's charisma and the faith of their respective acolytes. The debate led to reductions in the project funding, which was why Sandin finally lost patience and stormed out of Säter with her therapists in tow. The departure caused a storm of media interest. They set up a private treatment home in nearby Ludvika and their approach was renamed the 'Sandin model' but they never had a convincing record of success and the venture would later close.

Margit watched as her own Chestnut Lodge was wiped off the map. It seemed as if her enemies were about to win the war. However, at the end of the 1980s, she still held some trump cards. Firstly, the medical director at Säter's forensic psychiatry unit, Göran Källberg, was one of her pupils and a powerful ally. Secondly, she was the supervisor of the successful therapeutic management of the hardened criminal Lars-Inge Svartenbrandt, a project that promised to be a spectacular victory for her strategy. Thirdly, Källberg was planning a new structure of forensic psychiatry that was to replace the old secure unit. These plans were based on Margit's theories and her psychotherapeutic methods.

At the same time as the Säter model was driven out of Säter, Källberg demonstrated his firm faith in Svartenbrandt's conversion by writing an appeal against his patient's sentence. In the circumstances, clemency had to be exercised by the government. Svartenbrandt, Källberg stated, was a new man who had learnt his lesson and had shown remorse, guilt and responsibility. He had given up illegal drugs and bank robberies, and preferred to spend his time walking in the forest, reading and meditating.

Svartenbrandt was, however, still serving a prison sentence and his earliest release would be in six years' time, in 1994. Källberg asked the government to convert the sentence to open-ended secure psychiatric care. In practice, this would mean that the decision about when to discharge the patient would be Göran Källberg's alone, which in turn meant that Svartenbrandt would go free just about immediately, as Källberg and Margit considered his treatment completed. He was cured. While the government was mulling over the appeal, Källberg launched his big project, which had been in the pipeline for several years, and had received much input from Margit. It was to be a brand-new psychiatric facility dedicated to offering as many patients as possible the same type of therapy as Svartenbrandt's. The regional authority pumped millions of kronor into the enterprise and funded the construction of the large building that was to house it. The new unit was formally opened in January 1989 and the patients sentenced to psychiatric hospital detention were moved into nice, modern rooms. Svartenbrandt moved in, too, but was regarded as so harmless that he was lodged in ward 37, a holding ward for patients preparing for discharge. Ward 37 was unstaffed and the inmates had key-cards to the doors, so Svartenbrandt came and went as he pleased.

It took almost two years for the Department of Justice to consider the appeal for clemency. The civil servants were impressed by the transformation that Dr Källberg claimed that Svartenbrandt, previously a recidivist criminal, had undergone. Their recommendation was to grant clemency, but the Minister of Justice, the social democrat Leila Freivalds, was still not completely convinced. To make sure, she asked one of the ministry's forensic experts, the criminologist Leif G. W. Persson, to scrutinize the arguments in the appeal. Persson reacted strongly. 'I thought it frightening that we would lose control over the case once Svartenbrandt was placed in a medical secure unit,' he later told a reporter from the influential evening paper *Expressen*. 'That lad is well able to con the medics. I know what he can do from personal experience. [...] It's not a nice thing to say, but Svartenbrandt will always be dangerous.'[240] Persson was so certain he was right that he threatened to resign if clemency was granted. The minister took note and turned the appeal down in December 1989.

Källberg cannot comment on the refusal as he died of a coronary in 2011. A close friend of his told me that, although a timid, quiet man, Källberg had a strong, rather paradoxical desire to show off to the media. It would be reasonable to assume that Källberg had counted on glory for himself and Margit and goodwill for the recently opened secure unit if 'Sweden's most dangerous man' had been officially recognized as cured. It was never to be. Nevertheless, neither he nor Margit had any intention of allowing a hard-nosed criminologist like Persson to stop them from announcing to the Swedish people that Svartenbrandt was a reformed character. Clemency or not, the aim was to swing public opinion behind the new Säter model.

Just a couple of months after the refusal, in February 1990, *Dagens Nyheter* ran a generously spaced series of articles about the revolutionary theory applied to the most dangerous man in Sweden. An interview with Svartenbrandt was given a double-page spread for two days running. The Day 1 Svartenbrandt feature was headlined I WAS A PSYCHOPATH. ONE OF SWEDEN'S MOST DANGEROUS CRIMINALS ON HIS WAY TO JOIN HUMANITY.

Svartenbrandt said that he had been completely cured and that he could not go back to being a criminal even if he wanted to. On Day 2, the paper ran the second interview with Svartenbrandt, who was full of praise for Säter and for its medical director Göran Källberg, who had had the stamina to guide his errant patient back to the traumas of childhood: 'He was with me in Hell, as Virgil accompanied Dante.' The articles were generously illustrated with pictures of the very photogenic ex-psychopath.

On Day 3, *Dagens Nyheter* featured a major interview with the hero of the moment, Dr Källberg, and this time the headline read VIOLENCE AS SHELTER FROM DREAD: GÖRAN KÄLLBERG AT SÄTER HOSPITAL USES TALKING THERAPY WITH VIOLENT CRIME PATIENTS. Källberg explained to the readers that the patients in the forensic psychiatry unit had experienced events in childhood that had created a great fear, a fear that 'must, at whatever cost, be suppressed'. Their acts of violence were coping devices. He also said the therapeutic process could go on for many years but he felt sure that many, if not all, patients sentenced to psychiatric care could be cured, just like Svartenbrandt.

This coverage by Sweden's largest daily paper caused tremendous interest and other media followed suit. The pleasant and soft-spoken Göran Källberg had the potential to become as lovable a public figure as Barbro Sandin. Like Sandin he represented something new and humane, something that inspired hope. In the future criminal psychopaths would be helped and even restored to normal life with talking therapy. Källberg's and Norell's media management had given a great boost to Säter's new drive towards psychotherapy for criminals.

Källberg's victory interview ran on 8 February 1990. Three weeks later, on 2 March, Lars-Inge Svartenbrandt vanished during one of his many periods of leave and robbed a garage near Borlänge.[241] He went on to burgle the home of a colonel where he acquired 'enough firearms and hand grenades to start a minor private war' as an evening paper later put it.[242] He had also captured and locked up a woman in ward 37 at Säter. Nobody had noticed – it was unstaffed.

The media let out a roar of horror. Under the headline INSANE TO LET HIM OUT, a senior public prosecutor raged in several columns of *Aftonbladet*, saying that 'it was wildly out of order' that Svartenbrandt had been wandering in and out of Säter as he pleased. 'Nothing short of pure Monty Python [. . .] It would have been funny if it hadn't been so serious.'[243] Two days later, the same paper ran an interview with Källberg under the emotional headline I WAS LIKE A FATHER TO HIM. The reporter wrote:

> I am seated with Göran Källberg – a kind, decent man and a helpful interviewee – on his sitting-room sofa in his Matsbo villa just outside Hedemora. For six years, Källberg was Svartenbrandt's personal therapist.
>
> 'Didn't you ever sense anything that prepared you for this?' and Källberg replied, 'No, there was never anything that suggested this.'

The article continued:

> Göran Källberg has been seeing Svartenbrandt, who calls himself a psychopath in interviews, for therapy three times a week for several years.
>
> 'I haven't got this right. I shall have to examine where I have gone wrong now. By now, I have been unable to sleep for two nights and had time to think a great deal. This is a total setback. [. . .]'

Källberg spoke with the arrested Svartenbrandt on the phone yesterday.

'A very short call. He asked me a question. When he got the answer, he . . . No, this is too personal.'

Källberg did reveal that the therapy would continue. No hesitation.

'I can't let him down now.'[244]

It was not just Källberg and Säter that were named and shamed. Tomas Videgård recalls the 'awkwardness' that the Svartenbrandt fiasco caused in the Margit group.

Tomas said: 'We had had seminars that discussed the therapeutic treatment of Svartenbrandt and how fantastically well it went. And he was celebrated on the telly and in the press and told how incredibly good it was that a psychopath had been healed. So, when he went back to crime it was a massive disappointment.'

'What did it mean to Margit?' I asked.

'What it did *not* mean was that she was shaken enough to reflect on where she and Källberg had gone wrong,' Tomas replied with a wry smile.

Svartenbrandt's return to crime did not affect Margit's faith in the slightest but had serious consequences for her relationship with Tomas.

'Soon after Svartenbrandt was arrested, I dreamt about Säter and about the therapies at Säter,' Tomas told me. 'And in the dream, I say something like "The problem is that the therapist has listened more to the supervisor than to himself."' He told Margit about the dream at his next therapy session.

She took her time to think about it: 'Her reaction came a few weeks later and it was harsh. "That was pure back-stabbing!" she said. I had criticized her supervision of Göran Källberg! I was baffled at first, then furious. The way I see it, as a patient you have every right to speak about your dreams and expect the therapist to be interested in what they mean to me. All she saw was that I might have been attacking her. And she was above criticism!'

He came back for therapy with Margit a few more times but then went against her wishes and stopped the treatment.

Tomas was one of a handful of pupils who had begun to look critically at Margit, a process of liberation that he shared with Margareta Hedén-Chami and a few others. He said that scepticism had infected the entire group.

'The consequences were destructive mainly because the group split into subgroups,' he continued. 'Some of us began to meet on our own and talk about what we felt didn't work well. Things like Margit's aversion to criticism. Others stayed completely loyal to Margit. The group was dissolving and eventually broke up.'

'Who were the loyalists?'

'The ones closest to her: Cajsa Lindholm, Gillan Liljeström and Birgitta Ståhle.'

Margareta Hedén-Chami also confirms that these three women sided with Margit when the others began to move away: 'Britt [Andersson] and I used to go by train together to and from the Saturday seminars and we were saying things to each other like, "Wonder what will happen to Cajsa, Gillan and Birgitta when Margit dies." They were so tied to her. Completely tied. Dependent.'

Tomas thought that Margit's strongest drive had for a long time been a need for revenge.

'It runs like a red thread through her life,' he said and then counted Margit's defeats for my benefit. They began when she was a member of the Swedish Psychoanalytical Society, where she felt much less appreciated than she deserved. She broke away and set up the Holistic Institute but then it rebelled against her rule. The supervision of Barbro Sandin mattered to her but Sandin left her and did not give due recognition to Margit's contribution to the celebrated Säter model. A new group of pupils gathered around her but Tomas believes that the group's real task was to 'reinstate Margit's lost honour' after the disaster of the Holistic Institute, an attempt which failed, as one member of the group after another turned against her. Added to these defeats were her failures as an academic, the discarded Säter model, the rejection of her 1989 study of recovered memory and the collapse of the Svartenbrandt project in 1990, trumpeted in headlines everywhere.

After all this, Margit's desire for revenge was probably greater than ever.

It was at this stage in her life that Sture Bergwall was admitted to Säter in 1991.

'I feel pretty sure that after all these lows Thomas Quick was meant to be the high-point of Margit's professional life,' Tomas Videgård said.

Margit was seventy-seven in the spring of 1991, so if she were to get her longed-for recognition, there was no time to lose.

PART 3

The World of Thomas Quick

15

The bank robbery

'His own view is that the consequences of his actions should
be closed psych[iatric] care.'
      Quoting Sture Bergwall in the examination of his
                  mental state after the bank robbery.

For Sture, the 1980s started well and ended badly. For almost ten years
he collected his low-dose Alepam prescription from the outpatient
clinic every second week. He never exceeded the prescribed dose; his
medical records show that sometimes he even didn't pick up all the
tablets. For the first time since his late teens, he had his drug-taking
under control. It had opened up new routes for him to return to a
productive life. With his brothers Örjan and Sten-Ove he bought a
newsagent's shop near Falun. Later, when Örjan was interviewed about
this period, he said that Sture had driven the small business venture:
'Sture was the practical one among us, the guy who dealt with external contacts, the authorities and so on. When things got a little tricky,
say, with lottery tickets or newspaper returns and things like that, it was
always Sture who had the answers and knew how to deal with the
issues.'[245]

Sture was thirty-two years old when the three brothers bought the
shop. He sported a neatly trimmed beard and wore glasses with a thin
steel frame. He was a fast thinker and a knowledgeable sort of person.
He had a sense of humour and was a good conversationalist who
charmed the customers. But behind the easy-going chat, he was a very
lonely man. All his life, he had lacked a lasting relationship based on
love.

In the mid-1980s, Sture got to know a woman. I call her Kristina.

She lived just a few hundred yards from the shop with her husband and their son, whom I call Patrik. Sture and Kristina became friends and when the Bergwall brothers closed down the shop in 1986, Sture and Kristina decided to go into business together and bought a kiosk in Grycksbo near Falun. Sture moved into a flat just a stone's throw from the kiosk in 1987.

By then, eighteen years had passed since Sture had been convicted of sexual harassment and he had not been charged with any further offences of that kind. He still liked hanging out with teenage boys though, and as the kiosk quickly became a popular meeting place for young people he had plenty of opportunities. One of Sture's teenage friends was Patrik. The boys liked Sture and used his flat as a place to get together and watch videos. Later, several of them were interviewed by the police and although some of them said they had realized that Sture was gay, they all denied ever having been pestered by him. To them, he was simply an older friend. Sture enjoyed the company of boys and young men, and became popular by sharing their interests and helping to finance their activities, but that was very far from being a rapist or a paedophile. He told me that he had fancied one or two of his young friends but had been content with just socializing.

In 1987, Sture got his driving licence, which made him even more popular because he would cram the car full and drive his friends to rock concerts in Stockholm by bands like Kiss, Twisted Sister, Dio and Alice Cooper.

Kristina's son Patrik came to be closest to Sture. He was fourteen years old when his mother and Sture went into business together and he often did odd jobs in the kiosk. In the police interviews Patrik said that at first he felt that Sture was a kind of stand-by parent he could escape to when he had a fight with his mother or father. Later, they became good friends. He denied that they had had a sexual relationship and insisted that he had always been heterosexual.[246] The police investigation showed that towards the end of the 1980s, Patrik had a girlfriend called Maria. She was interviewed by the police on several occasions and the report states: 'The relationship meant that Sture Bergwall was often part of the group. The three of them met and talked, rented videos and often spent leisure time in the flat belonging to Sture Bergwall on Centrum Way in Grycksbo. [. . .] She saw him as an older but good friend and they have always had a good time together.'[247]

Towards the end of the 1980s, Patrik left home and more or less moved in with Sture. The kiosk was not all that profitable and because Patrik went to school and was short of money, they would deliver newspapers together in the mornings.

Sture has told me that he was in love with Patrik but of course he had to keep it a secret. The hopelessness of it all pained him and he thinks grieving over his unrequited love explains why he turned back to drugs and drink. At some point in late 1988, he started drinking alcohol and increased his tablet consumption at the same time. 'I might have had a beer. And then two,' he said. 'Then, a bit more than that. Afterwards, it would drive me to despair and the hangover didn't help, so I'd take a few extra Alepam tablets. And then I was off again. All so stupid and careless.'

The drug abuse affected his job in the kiosk and Kristina eventually realized that Sture was coming to work intoxicated. 'He tried to keep his drinking secret from me,' she later told the police. It was an unheard-of situation for her. 'To my knowledge, Sture was sticking strictly to soft drinks and milk.'[248] It did not take long before Sture was back on amphetamines and with drugs in his bloodstream he was as out of control and as self-destructive as ever. In one of the interviews, Patrik said that Sture could be 'so sodding high and mighty' when he was under the influence that they sometimes ended up fighting. Sture lost every time.[249]

Sture's amphetamine habit was expensive and money was a never-ending problem, but he thought that his brilliant intellect would make him a successful criminal and seems to have persuaded Patrik that it was true. One night in 1989, Patrik set fire to the kiosk by knowingly leaving a roll of kitchen paper on a switched-on hotplate. The idea was that Sture would trouser the insurance payout. The kiosk was totally wrecked and Sture's time in private enterprise finished. Instead, he returned to his old career as a junkie and petty criminal, putting increasing strain on his friendship with Patrik, a friendship that damaged them both.

Sture managed to land a part-time job as a bingo caller in Falun. He sold bingo cards, called out numbers and chatted nicely with the pensioners, but his wages were too small to finance his drug-taking. His notes show that he applied for unemployment benefit in December 1989 but by then times had grown harder. A rather reckless liberalization of the credit market in 1985 had led to overheated inflation and the politicians tried to cool the economy down with a dose of social austerity. Economic support for the impoverished was no longer a priority and Sture's application was turned down. Not long afterwards, in January 1990, another blow fell when the social services stopped Sture's modest disability benefit, which for a long time had been his basic income. By then he was desperate and in February that year he carried out a heist worthy of a speed freak.

One Saturday, when the bingo hall always pulled in a lot of money, he stayed around after closing and emptied the safe. He stuffed the cash, some 145,000 kronor, into a small rucksack that he kept in the car. Then he called the emergency services to announce that he had been robbed. He was apparently quite inspired when he told the police and the owner of the bingo establishment about a masked man who had pushed his way in through the back door and forced Sture to hand over the day's takings. The owner said that 'Sture was really cut up' about the break-in.[250] Once he had made his statement, he drove to the summer cottage he rented by Lake Valsan west of Falun and shared the loot with Patrik.

Sture was forty years old and once more losing control over his life. His notes show that he twice claimed to the clinic he had lost his Alepam prescription, which he had never done before. The doctor gave him new scripts. He had also told the psychologist that his old attraction to young boys had flared up again and that he found it difficult to control his impulses.[251] It is impossible to know if this was true or just something he said to get prescribed more benzodiazepines, though Sture now says he was after drugs. He knew perfectly well that no doctor would refuse him tablets if he reminded them of his record of sexual misdemeanours from 1969. Whatever the case, his benzo-diazepine intake increased and he sank deeper into drug dependency.

He also descended further into criminality. The spoils from the fictional bingo hall robbery did not last long and he began to plot a new way to steal money. Patrik, who was now eighteen, was to join him this time and, later, Patrik told the police that Sture had promised that the 'plan is idiot-proof'.[252] They were to rob the Gota Bank in Grycksbo and start by taking hostages. After renting a car for the day, they would set out early in the morning and drive to the villa where the bank manager, Bert Löfgren, lived with his wife and son on the outskirts of Falun. Sture and Patrik would enter the Löfgren home and Sture would hold the wife and the son captive. Patrik would blackmail Bert Löfgren into taking him to the bank and opening the vaults. The only problem was that the bank manager knew both Sture and Patrik. The bank was just across the street from the burnt-down kiosk and Sture had even had an appointment to see Löfgren there. If the heist was to work, their disguises had to be first class and so did their acting. Sture decided to play the role of a gangster with a Finno-Swedish accent.

On Friday 14 December 1990, the Löfgren family were woken by the doorbell, far too early in the morning for a normal call. Two masked men stood on the doorstep, one of them (Patrik) wearing a Santa Claus mask. He held a knife in his hand and had a newly bought air pistol stuck under his belt. Sture had a cap pulled down over his face, with two holes cut out for his eyes, and he too was brandishing a knife. They stormed into the house and Sture informed everyone in thick Finno-Swedish that they were going to rob the bank. 'If something goes wrong you'll die,' he shouted and to show he meant business stamped on the floor, slapped a chest of drawers and demonstratively slashed a mattress with his knife. He then took 950 kronor from Bert Löfgren's wallet. Löfgren explained that his colleague Berit kept the keys. 'Fine,' Patrik said through the Santa mask. 'Let's go get her.'

Berit was woken by a phone call from her boss who wanted her to start work early. He would come by in his car to pick her up. Berit followed instructions and, as she jumped into Löfgren's car, she realized too late that an armed man in a Santa Claus mask was hiding in the back seat. Meanwhile Sture was holding his hostages under observation and according to Mrs Löfgren's statement he seemed to calm down once Patrik had left. Then the telephone rang and he panicked. It was a sister-in-law who called for a chat. Sture threatened Mrs Löfgren with his knife and forced her to say that she was not well that morning before ending the call. The atmosphere was tense and he forgot about his Finnish accent.

When they arrived at the bank Patrik forced Bert and Berit to put the till and three cash containers in a post office sack. He then phoned Sture and confirmed that everything had gone according to plan. Sture set out for home in the rented car while Patrik went to pick up his car, which had been left at the airfield in Grycksbo. They met up in Sture's flat. Patrik showered and Sture went to hide the loot. When he returned, they put all the kit in a rubbish sack and dumped it in the River Dal.

The plan, it turned out, had not been completely idiot-proof. Bert Löfgren had recognized Sture and Patrik instantly and at 5.25 p.m. the same day the police arrested both bank robbers at home. Actually, the robbery plan was so imbecilic that both Sture and Patrik had to undergo forensic mental state assessment before being taken to court. Patrik was found mentally sound and given a prison sentence of three and a half years. Sture was found to be mentally disturbed at the time of the robbery and sentenced to closed psychiatric care. However, there are divided opinions about what actually happened during the assessment of Sture's mental state.

I interviewed Sture often and for long periods during the year and a half I have spent working on this book. My assumption throughout has been that I cannot believe a word he says. Sture has lied far too much to be taken at his word in any circumstances and I have not used anything he has said unless confirmed in case notes, psychiatric assessments, police interviews and reports, letters, media interviews or other similar sources. Despite my careful checking I have never caught Sture lying to me, but he has sometimes claimed things I have not been able to verify. One case in point is his version of what happened during the psychiatric examination that led to his admission to Säter.

Sture now insists that he had wanted to avoid prison and that his aim was to be sentenced to forensic psychiatric care. He says that because he had been convicted of sexual crimes, he feared being attacked by other inmates and the prospect of an ordinary prison scared him. On the other hand, ever since his experiences in the 1970s, he felt comfortable with psychiatry. Besides, it was much easier to get hold of drugs in hospital.

The medical records tend to support his story. Sture was first taken to see a consultant psychiatrist called Göran Fransson for what is called a 'paragraph 7 examination' or a mini mental state assessment, which entailed the two of them talking for about half an hour. At the end of the talk, Dr Fransson signed a certificate. It appears that Sture had in fact expressed very specific wishes: 'His own view is that the consequences of his actions should be closed psych[iatric] care.'

This was apparently how Sture argued his case:

Concerning the current crime, he finds it very difficult to give an account of it, especially the timing. He much prefers talking about his relationship with his fellow perpetrator, Patrik, whom he has known for about six years. He states that he has been wholly under Patrik's control. Has been P's slave, quite unable to stand up for himself. His motive has been his fear of losing Patrik. The problem situation would seem to be related to homosexual behaviour. According to Sture, the idea for the crime was Patrik's, and the reason Patrik's insatiable craving for money.[253]

What Sture told Dr Fransson was not confirmed in the police interviews with Patrik and his girlfriend. In their account, everything indicated that Sture had dreamed up the robbery because he needed money for drugs and then tempted Patrik to join him. But Göran Fransson was taken in by Sture and decided that he should be given a full mental health assessment. It was carried out at the forensic psychiatric department at Huddinge Hospital just outside Stockholm. The procedure involved temporarily living in a ward and talking to psychologists and psychiatrists capable of evaluating if he was mentally ill. The evaluation would then be presented as evidence in court.

When I read the report from Huddinge, it strikes me that a lot was made of the fact that twenty-two years earlier Sture was convicted of sexual harassment. He claimed that he had a major problem keeping his hands off young boys. His relationship with Patrik was not just sexual but, he revealed, sadomasochistic. Patrik had subjected him to 'sadistic sexual acts such as beating him with a belt'.[254] The failed robbery was not even 'a real robbery' but a way for him to break out of his destructive relationship with the dominant eighteen-year-old. Seen from this angle, the attempted robbery was not a pathetic failure but a successful cry for help. Sture had intended to be caught all along.

The psychiatrist at Huddinge knew that Patrik categorically denied that there had been anything sexual between himself and Sture. Her report observes that the two perpetrators' stories diverged and that 'Bergwall's reliability is somewhat questionable'. All the same, for reasons best known to herself, she chose to believe Sture, though she did feel that staging a joint bank robbery was a rather odd way to end a relationship: '[F]or an individual with reasonably norm-adapted and well-functioning psychological make-up the alternative would presumably have been an ordinary separation.' Nonetheless, in Sture's case, an ordinary separation process had clearly not been possible: 'The psycho-pathological mechanisms that have made such an alternative course of action a non-option would indicate that the relationship has been, and also has been experienced as, at least for Bergwall, exceptionally pathologically fixated.'

The doctor concluded that the robbery had been planned and executed for motives of a sexual and relationship-orientated nature and not for financial gain. Her only evidence for this conclusion was Sture's own story, so he must have been very convincing. He even managed to make her believe that he had no drug issues. My own reading of his case notes, a volume of some 250 pages, unmistakably shows that he had been on every addictive substance he could lay hands on for most of his adult life. But the report from Huddinge states: 'No substantive problems related to drug dependency appear to be present.' That particular sentence made it much easier for him to get benzodiazepines while he was an inpatient at Huddinge.

The psychiatrist's recommendation to the court was the following: 'Sture Ragnar Bergwall has carried out the act with which he had been charged under the influence of a mental abnormality of such a deep-seated nature that it must be considered on the same basis as mental illness. He unavoidably requires closed psychiatric care.'[255]

In the trial that followed Sture succeeded, against the odds, in his pursuit of a sentence to forensic psychiatric care for a doomed-to-fail bank robbery. On 29 April 1991, he was transferred from Huddinge to the regional psychiatric facility on the shores of Lake Ljustern in Dalarna.

Sture had lied himself into going to Säter.

16

The art of being picked for psychotherapy

*'Pat. has pleaded for psychotherapeutic treatment ever since
he was moved to ward 31, i.e. soon after admission.
Suitability for treatment doubtful, especially given our
currently limited psychother. resources.'*
Case notes, September 1991, referring to Sture's
strenuous attempts to get taken on for psychotherapy.

On Monday 29 April 1991, Sture arrived at Säter. The new regional
psychiatric unit had been open for just over two years. The task of
designing the building had gone to the architects Karl Alexanderson
and Hans Leonard Grau (of the White Arkitekter practice), who had
won the first prize in the regional authority's competition. Göran
Källberg and his adviser Margit participated in the discussions of the
blueprints and the final result was more like an airy, bright hotel in a
mountain resort than a hospital. The common rooms had fine parquet
floors and white-limed open fireplaces. The tables, chairs and armchairs had been ordered from the famous designer Bruno Mathsson,
who worked in classical Swedish style and with natural materials. The
overall rectangular outline of the building enclosed three larger court-
yards, the architects' solution to a request to avoid walls or fencing
around the outdoor exercise areas. The institution was to 'hug' the
patients, like a good parent hugs his or her child, a protective, psychotherapeutic outreach that Margit called 'the Winnicott hug' after
the paediatrician and object relations theoretician Donald Winnicott.
Margit's idea of the right therapeutic approach had literally been built
into the walls of the new psychiatric unit.

The unit had been divided into seven wards, each one with room for only seven patients. They were housed in small but light rooms, each with its own shower and toilet. The ward common room was beautifully furnished as were the other shared facilities: a kitchen, a dining room and a thickly carpeted music room with a stereo music centre. The unit was generously staffed with general and psychiatric nurses. This shiny new edifice stood only a few hundred metres from the old secure unit, now closed down and brooding on memories of darker days of care for the criminally insane. The new building expressed a spirit of humanism and empathy.

Newly admitted patients were placed in ward 30, where they stayed for a short time before moving into a room on one of the wards. Patients due to be discharged were transferred to ward 37, which had no nursing staff. These patients had key cards and, effectively, could come and go as they liked.

A few days after his admission, a room was found for Sture in ward 31. A couple of nurses escorted him when he went to clear out his small flat. His Säter room was only eleven square metres and already kitted out with a narrow bed, a small desk, an armchair and two book-shelves, so his furniture had to go. He packed all 38 volumes of the Nordic Encyclopedia, a Christmas gift from his brother Sten-Ove. This particular edition had been published between 1904 and 1926 and was decorated with pretty gilt imprints of owls. He packed a more up-to-date encyclopedia as well, and a few more boxes full of books.

The regional magistrates' court would decide for how long Sture had to be kept at Säter. The court was in session twice a year and usu-ally went along with the psychiatrists' recommendations. In practice, then, Sture's future would be decided at Säter.

Sture met the medical director, Dr Göran Källberg, three days after his admission. Afterwards, Källberg noted that Sture had taken his incarceration with equanimity: 'He has of course had long experience of psychiatric care.' Källberg also wrote:

We spoke generally about his situation and personal issues. Apparently dependent on his small dose of Alepam that he has been on for many years. He suffers off and on from strong panic attacks, even during our chat he becomes very tense, tearful and has bouts of staccato breathing. Calms down slowly. At other times, offers good, formal interaction during chat. Emotionally, somewhat reserved. No delusions. Not suicidal. Permitted to keep taking 3 × 10 mg Alepam. Also 1 × tabl. Sanoma (carisoprodol) at night, pre-scrbd. for sciatica.[256]

The unit's medical staff under Göran Källberg's leadership included two psychiatric consultants – there were no registrars or juniors. Dr Fransson had carried out Sture's mini mental state assessment and Sture was now on his list, which meant that he had complete responsibility for his patient's care while at Säter, medical as well as psychothera-peutic. Kjell Persson was the other doctor on the unit. Both consultants wore their own clothes at work because the usual white coats were thought to create an unwanted distance to the patients. The norm was casual clothing – no jackets, just shirts worn with corduroy trousers and loafers.

I was naturally keen to interview all three medics about the situa-tion at Säter when Sture was admitted but it was problematic. Dr Källberg had died from a heart attack in the spring of 2011. Dr Persson had changed his surname to Långbergs and consistently refused to utter a single word about Sture in public. Only Dr Fransson remained a pos-sibility. He was now the medical executive at the regional forensic psychiatric department in Sundsvall. When I spoke to him on the phone, he was exceedingly hesitant about talking to me. But when I mentioned that I had collected a great deal of information about Margit Norell, he paused for a few seconds and then said in a new tone of voice that he thought my project sounded important. A little reluc-tantly he agreed to see me.

I was working on a documentary about Margit and Sture for Swedish Television so we had agreed to meet in the SVT lobby. His eyes looked wary as we shook hands, but he seemed friendly enough. He was clearly nervous about the interview ahead of him.

We settled down with our coffee and he began by telling me that, in 1982, he had spent a few months of his clinical foundation years with Barbro Sandin at Säter and that he had felt privileged to work with her. He had eagerly supported her in her faith that it was possible, as he expressed it, 'to reach out to all schizophrenics and release them'. Accepting the Säter model was to rebel against the 'old, hidebound psychiatrists' who believed that schizophrenia was caused by changes in the biological functions of the brain. Göran Fransson admits that these days he himself is convinced that schizophrenia has its roots in the brain's biological functions, and he recognizes that the Säter model had no scientific basis. 'Personal contact is an immensely important factor in the management of schizophrenics because it contributes to a bearable life for them – but it is not a cure.'

In the late 1980s Göran Källberg asked Fransson if he wanted to work in the new forensic psychiatry unit. Fransson was pleased: 'Göran Källberg's reputation was first rate and I was flattered.' He accepted and took up his new post on 1 January 1987. In 1989 he was present at the closure of the old secure unit, 'a hard place of the kind that people nowadays don't even think possible', and the opening of the new one, 'a humanitarian institution. [...] We were enthusiastic. This was the dawn of an enlightened approach. We were going to focus on the human being behind the crimes and find a way to change his personality and hence his behaviour. I was completely gripped by the idea of attempting to change the apparently permanent. By being part of a group of pioneers, if you like.'

The strong sense of conviction emanated from an identifiable source. 'Margit Norell was utterly crucial to everything we did. She supervised Göran Källberg, Birgitta Ståhle and some of the others. They all talked endlessly about Margit and her teaching.'

'What did they say about her?'

'They gave the impression of someone very warm-hearted, a good person who was outstandingly knowledgeable. Going off to be supervised by Margit Norell meant coming back full of warmth and new insights. The whole thing mattered hugely. She was the main anchor of the unit's work, a reassurance.'

'Did this strike you as odd in any way?' I asked.

'Now it would seem odd, but not then.'

'Why not?'

'I had just finished my specialist training. I was young and keen. We were setting out together to change the world. It was a few years after my F2 months with Barbro Sandin, you know. And now I was offered a romantic ideal – to change the world. It seemed a fantastic opportunity to be part of this.'

'What was the relationship between Källberg and Margit?' I asked and he thought for a moment, searching for the right words.

'What comes into my head first is – mother and son.'

Margit never supervised Fransson because he only very rarely treated patients with psychotherapy. All the same, he was convinced that her ideas about repressed memories were correct. He didn't realize that their scientific basis was non-existent until 1995, after he had left Säter. The wake-up call was a lecture by Elizabeth Loftus given in Seattle.

'It became absolutely clear that repressed memories don't exist,' Fransson said. 'We do remember painful events. We may change them and so forth, but there's no way you can kill someone and then forget all about it.'

I pointed out that what Loftus had talked about in 1995 were not new discoveries. A few years earlier, she had published her review article 'The Reality of Repressed Memories', explaining why repression theory should be regarded as highly controversial and in it she referred to, among other findings in this field, research done as early as in the 1980s.[257]

Fransson recalled that Loftus had in fact mentioned Wagenaar and Groeneweg's paper on how well concentration camp inmates remembered, after forty years, the violence they had been subjected to – a report that was published in 1990.[258] I wondered how such knowledge could come as a surprise for him as late as 1995.

His first line of defence was to refer to his clinical work at Säter which had kept him so busy that he didn't have time to keep up with contemporary research. I asked him if staff at Säter and places like it were not obliged to be aware of relevant scientific knowledge.

'That's right, of course,' he replied.

'So, why didn't you?'

He hesitated and then plunged into a confession.

'I can think of only one explanation, which is that a professional mindset developed at Säter which had much in common with a belief system. I shared it. It was like a sect and sects don't encourage you to study critical attacks on its beliefs. You sift out that kind of thing. No need to take on board communications from the outside.'

I wondered aloud if it had been impossible to work at Säter unless you shared Margit's specific attitudes to psychotherapy.

'It was never stated in those terms but it was the case. And I had no problem with that,' he replied and went on to admit that his own faith had been so strong that long after 1995 elements of it had stayed alive. 'It grew into such a shared ethos that I didn't really manage to with-draw from it emotionally until much later, a bit into the 2000s. It isn't easy to detach yourself from cult-like communities of this kind.'

Göran Fransson insisted that he would never repeat his mistake.

'I feel we must all go through some process like it in order to develop into mature adults. It has taken me a long time but today it would be impossible for me to get sucked into uncritical veneration of something. I think. You get more sceptical as you grow older.'

'So the Säter staff are not beyond blame?'

'Of course not. You must accept your individual responsibility for being caught up in some mad process. I absolutely believe that. The Nuremberg trials provided more than enough examples. But anyone can get involved in a cult. What we did might have been stupid, but it wasn't evil. Although you could say that it turned evil. Many have suffered for our beliefs and I have a responsibility to them. There are explanations but no excuses. I shall have to put up with it. And carry on living.'

When we parted company I realized that he felt uneasy about having been so honest.

'No more interviews, not ever,' he said with a wry smile. But he also seemed relieved.

So there it was. The hospital where Sture was to be treated from 29 April 1991 was staffed by members of a sect. The doctors believed in one set of ideas – Margit's – and, as members of a sect will do, blocked outside influences. They shared the expectation that the patients would retrieve repressed memories from childhood and that, once this was achieved, their aggressive and destructive behaviours would cease.

Sture was very keen on therapy. A few weeks after his admission, Dr Kjell Persson referred in Sture's notes to a talk they had had:

> The patient states that he has felt anxious at night, pressure around the chest, slight palpitations, sleep difficulty. Speaks of deep guilt feelings about Patrik, his young partner in the bank robbery. They were apparently in a homosexual relationship. When the patient speaks about his, he shows plenty of behavioural tics, facial twitches, has to fight back tears. He argues that he needs some form of talking or other psychotherapy.[. . .].[259]

When I asked Sture why he was so interested in therapy, he offers three reasons. Firstly, he genuinely wanted to find out why his life had become such a mess. He still felt that being homosexual had a lot to do with it and, like many psychologists and doctors at the time, thought the cause lay within childhood experiences. Secondly, he was also after an increased dose of benzodiazepines and reckoned it would be easier to get if he was in therapy. Thirdly, he needed someone to talk to. The bank robbery had ruined his relationship with Patrik. His siblings were sick of his crazed behaviour and had just about given up on him. He had no friends and his fellow patients were murderers and rapists, most of them clinically depressed and not exactly sympathetic company. Therapy was Sture's one hope of escaping his near-total loneliness.

But for a Säter patient in the spring of 1991, getting therapy was harder than one might imagine. The reason was a shortage of psychologists. Finding trained staff willing to work with those patients and in that cultish atmosphere was a major difficulty. Apart from Birgitta Ståhle, most of the posts were filled with trainees, fresh from university, who tended to take fright and leave as soon as their assignments were completed. According to a set of minutes from a meeting of the Margit group, recorded in the same month as Sture's admission, Birgitta Ståhle even asked the group to help her find two psychologists who were 'suitable for work within the regional psychiatric unit'.[260]

The psychologist shortage meant that before one of the forty-two patients had a chance to be picked for therapy, he had to prove his elegibility and, in Sture's case, that was hard going. His stupid bank robbery bore no comparison to the often very serious acts of violence committed by his fellow patients. He was regarded as a mildly uninteresting case, and unlikely to stay at Säter for very long.

But Sture battled to prove himself worthy. He tells me that he put on the same dramatic performance as he had done before when in contact with psychiatry. He had been suicidal for the entire day before the robbery; Dr Persson recorded in the July pages of the case notes: 'The patient states that he had selected a place to drive his car off the road but when he was to carry it out he caught sight of his dog in the back seat. Now he says he wants confirmation of how bad a person he is, someone who should commit suicide.'[261]

'I must say that was smart,' Sture told me. 'I said I was going to drive off the road or deliberately collide with an on-coming car and I'm just about to do it when I glanced in the rear mirror and there is my dog looking back at me so I couldn't do it. But it's actually not true. I didn't want to kill myself.'

Källberg was impressed by Sture's wish to be honest as well as with his insight: 'He has a sincere wish to sort himself out but feels he can't do it on his own. The patient's discourse is very intellectual. He often uses theoretical terminology but is at the same time aware that this is a way of keeping his distance. Assume that, at present, the pat. needs these defence mechs.'[262]

The summer passed and Sture continued to argue his case. The campaign went his way in the September that year. He was granted a session with Kjell Persson once a week. But, because Persson lacked proper training, he was not, according to social services department rules, allowed to offer psychotherapy. Their sessions were classified as 'talk with doctor'. Persson was impressed by his new patient:

Pat. has pleaded for psychotherapeutic treatment ever since he was moved to ward 31, i.e. soon after admission. Suitability for treatment doubtful, especially given our currently limited psychother. resources. As a temporary soln. I have started contacts with pat, classified as 'talk with doctor'. It turns out that pat shows sincere motivation to think about himself, his actions and his situation. But the talks cause him grave anxiety and muscular tension; pat. pleads for more time.[263]

Two months later, in November 1991, after half a year at Säter, Sture's sincerity had made such a deep impression that he was offered real psychotherapy. He had become so fond of Kjell Persson by then that he didn't to want to change to being seen by Birgitta Ståhle. To preserve a trusting relationship, a solution had to be found. The regulations permitted someone with Kjell Persson's qualifications to carry out psychotherapeutic treatments if competently supervised by a well-qualified professional. Göran Källberg turned to Margit and asked if she would undertake the task; she agreed. Interestingly, Margit's personal take on this arrangement was that Sture became her own patient. In her incomplete manuscript 'The World of Thomas Quick' she writes:

From Nov 1991, the therapy was extended to 2 hours/week and from that month, I undertook the supervision of Sture's treatment, initially with a supervision session with his therapist every second week. During 1992 and 1993, the supervision was further extended, normally to 1 hour/week. Occasionally, the time allocated to therapy was also substantially extended. I undertook the supervision of Sture's therapy on the basis of both my own training in psychoanalysis and my specialization in object relations theory, the premises of which fit with my own experiences from my therapeutic work with patients who are early and severely traumatized. Sture chose Kjell Persson as his therapist and I supported his choice even though Kjell Persson is not a qualified psychotherapist.[264]

From November 1991, Dr Persson started commuting between Säter and Stockholm to be supervised by Margit, just as Dr Källberg and Birgitta Ståhle had done since 1983 and 1988 respectively.

During the therapy sessions, Sture lay on the bed in his room while Persson sat in an armchair at the head of the bed. One of Persson's case notes from April 1992 shows that his approach was identical to Margit's long-established methods: 'Pat. has examined his childhood experiences which seem so far to have been rather kept well out of his awareness but increasingly have come back to him. He has also examined his dreams.'[265]

Sture has said that he wanted to be an interesting patient and to prove himself worthy of having scarce therapy treatment. Sture and his brother Sten-Ove had told each other about their dreams on their forest walks, so discussing dreams was familiar enough. Sture believed that finding links between dreams and childhood events was an integral part of psychoanalysis. He was good at free association and Kjell Persson responded glowingly. Just like Margit's other patients, the therapy was extended by asking Sture to write down his thoughts, dreams and memories between sessions. He gave his notes and other writings, which included poems, to Persson, who handed them on to Margit. She saved up some of this written material to include in her book. Here is one of Sture's emotional pieces of poetry:

> I long so much for death
> And so much fear dying!
> I dread death since my life
> Is one I never got, and never lived.
> So easy then, to slip the noose around my neck
> And know:
> My life was good and I have lived.
> I long so much for death
> But lack a life to die from![266]

Sture was so keen that he was allowed to move to ward 36, a special ward where the Säter authorities housed patients who were thought to be especially receptive to psychotherapy. The nursing staff on ward 36 were picked for their positive attitude to Margit's vision of best practice. Elsewhere in the building, some old school asylum nurses were still around. They viewed the new notions with scepticism and saw their job as more akin to a prison guard's. These old fogies were not welcome in ward 36.

Sture was a model patient on the couch but in other respects his behaviour was less satisfactory. In the winter of 1991–1992, he cheated, lied and got high on drugs, just as he had in the 1970s. His case notes show that he bought amphetamines on site, took drugs in the ward and smuggled pills to a fellow patient. As if to distract attention from his dubious behaviour, he played up his suicidal thoughts.

In December, he and another patient ran away together, rented a car and went to the Åre ski resort. Three days later they returned of their own volition. Sture was on amphetamines when he came back. Just after their flight had been discovered, a nurse had searched Sture's room and found – according to his notes – 'a big bunch of goodbye-letters' which, among other things, contained 'elaborate instructions about what he wished to happen after his death'. He had written that his body would be found 'within an area close to the hospital perimeter'. The staff noted that his suicidal intent had probably not been that serious, since on the day he ran off he had 'gone down to the social services office a couple of times [. . .] and asked for his pension to be paid out [. . .]'. Although Sture was often caught lying and manipulating people and events, his behaviour had hardly any consequences. He was given unaccompanied leave several times a week and, if he misbehaved, the punishment was temporary withdrawal of leave.

One of Sture's fellow patients was Lars-Inge Svartenbrandt, whom the press still gave the epithet 'Sweden's most dangerous criminal'. Sture told me that he often chatted with the handsome Svartenbrandt, whom he found quite an intellectual with views on most things. But their acquaintance was brief because, in the spring of 1992, Säter's biggest celebrity was to be discharged. Two years had passed since Svartenbrandt had seriously damaged Säter's reputation by robbing a garage just as Göran Källberg had declared a victory for therapy in *Dagens Nyheter*.

Ironically, his return to crime had exactly the same effect as the government agreeing to say yes to Källberg's pleas for a change of sentence. Svartenbrandt had been convicted of robbery and sentenced to forensic psychiatric care, meaning that it was now up to forensic psychiatry, as represented by Källberg, to determine when Svartenbrandt was ready to be freed. For the two years since the robbery, Svartenbrandt's therapy had continued under Margit's supervision. By June 1992, Källberg considered the work complete and recommended to the regional magistrate's court that they should authorize Svartenbrandt's discharge. On 24 June 1992 Lars-Inge Svartenbrandt walked out of Säter. The media followed the events with great interest.

Svartenbrandt went straight to Stockholm, where he robbed Handelsbanken's branch on St Erik's Square. Then he bought wine and drank himself into a stupor. He was arrested by two uniformed policemen who happened across him in a shrubbery where he was sleeping off the booze. He had been out of hospital for two days and nights.

The media were in uproar. An article in the evening paper *Aftonbladet* was headlined HOW COULD YOU DISCHARGE HIM? Their interview with Källberg makes painful reading:

A: 'In all these years, you were very close to him. Had you considered the possibility of another robbery?'

GK: 'You can't think like that. When someone is discharged he is well enough with regard to the mental disturbances he suffered from at the time of his previous crime.'

A: 'But you thought that he had had sufficient treatment? That he was well?'

GK: 'Yes. Otherwise he wouldn't have been discharged.'

A: '"Sufficient"? And then he robs a bank after a day or two?'

GK: 'It might sound strange but even people of sound mind commit crimes.'

A: 'In 1990 you said you had failed when he was arrested – now, you say you have been successful.'

GK: 'It is extremely contradictory but the basis for it is that one can commit crimes and be healthy, as I've already said.'

A: 'How do you personally feel today?'

GK: 'I do not bring my heart's desire and pain to market, as the poet Snoilsky said.'

A: 'Is he less dangerous to others today?'

GK: 'I won't comment on that.'[267]

For Säter, this was a catastrophe. The central idea that drove the treatment in the new unit was that all patients would be given the same revolutionary therapy as the psychopath Svartenbrandt and that they would, like him, be cured as a result. Now the lynchpin of their work had held Säter up to ridicule for the second time in two and a half years. The media, the politicians and the public had all watched them fail.

One major concern was what conclusion the politicians might draw. For the municipality of Säter, the fiasco was not just a matter of belief in a method of therapy but a realistic fear that the hospital might be closed down. It would be rather like a bomb going off in a small, vulnerable community. Most people in the town depended directly or indirectly for their income on the large institution in their midst. Failure at Säter threatened everyone's future and it needed to re-establish its good reputation.

Margit's eight years of treating Lars-Inge Svartenbrandt, with Göran Källberg as go-between, was now definitely at an end, but therapy-enthusiast Sture Bergwall was still an inmate in ward 36. No one knew it yet but he was to be seen as the saviour of Säter.

17

The birth of Thomas Quick

*'When the concrete details of the incest experiences emerge
directly in the therapy situation or at home, it often happens
first in a different state of consciousness. For some time
afterwards, the experiences are often rejected as unreal.'*
                    Margit Norell in her unpublished article
            'Early Incest: Experiences of the therapeutic process
                    for patients subjected to incestuous abuse'.

When spring came to Säter in 1992, Sture had been there for a year.
He was quite comfortable. He was given regular doses of Alepam, was
freed from financial concerns and lived in conditions not unlike that
of a hotel guest. He had certain rights of leave and went walking or
jogging daily around the lake. Sometimes he was given twenty-four-
hour leave and would take the train to Stockholm to watch a film.

Kjell Persson came to his room several times a week for their therapy sessions. Sture took real pleasure in being an interesting patient. He
was willing to talk endlessly about his anxiety and suicidal thoughts.
The consultant listened and made his weekly trips to Margit's practice
to report and receive supervision.

Sture often grew very emotional during the therapy sessions and
wept and hyper-ventilated. At times, his anguish was such that he
could no longer speak. He might stutter badly or growl like an animal,
or tense his body until he developed cramps. His whole being seemed
to tremble with anxiety. Sture tells me that he could bring this state on
deliberately if he had taken even a small dose of benzodiazepines. Once
he wound himself up, he could continue on autopilot in a state he
described to me as borderline psychotic. Once in it, he could tell

whatever tale came to mind with tremendous conviction. Words – his 'memories' – came pouring out of him, accompanied by panicky breathing, bellowing, and hysterical weeping. His emotional range made a great impression on almost everyone who was present.

This was nothing new. In the paperwork from Sture's school, I have found references to the ease with which he turned emotional when he spoke about himself – his 'self-dramatization'. After Sture's sentence to forensic psychiatric care in the 1970s, his case notes often speak about anxiety attacks. He explains that conflict situations always scared him and the notes bear him out. He was never involved in fights and rarely even angry. His heartbreaking anguish and anxiety attacks were his way to get what he wanted and he used people's empathy to get out of trouble or make them give him tablets.

Sture's behaviour at Säter in 1991–1992 followed an already established pattern. He played the role of the cooperative patient, and was rewarded with appreciation and drugs. However, all good things must come to an end. Early in the summer of 1992, when he had been a patient at Säter for just over a year, there was talk of preparing him to return to the community outside. His discharge was scheduled for early autumn and social services would help him find a place to stay.

If we are to understand what happened next, we must consider Sture's situation. The psychiatric assessment from Huddinge describes him as 'a forty-year-old man without any post-school training, who has for several years lived on his disability pension'.[268] He was practically alone in the world, friendless and largely rejected by his family. He had registered the new, tough attitude displayed by the social services even before the robbery and realized that he would have to find work after his discharge – an unlikely prospect given his criminal record. Worse, he was back on drugs and knew that he could spiral out of control. All in all, Sture's chances of creating a sustainable life for himself were minimal. I once asked him if he thought he would have survived the 1992 discharge. 'No, I wouldn't,' he said. He believed that drug abuse would have killed him.

On Thursday 25 June the nurses took Sture and a few other patients swimming. The hospital stands on the banks of Lake Ljustern and there are pleasant beaches within easy walking distance. On that trip, he hinted to a young nurse called Therese that he might be guilty of a serious crime that hadn't been discovered and went on to give her a clue: the letters 'mu', something he today says stood for 'murder'. Back at the hospital, Therese spoke to Göran Fransson who recorded the following in the case notes:

> Yesterday, while on the beach, he made a remark to a nurse he really likes. He asked her how we would react if he admitted to a very serious crime and offered the letters m and u as clues. Today, he told me that he of course knows what it's all about but he won't say. [. . .] I told Sture that we're very cautious about riddles. I sense that his thoughts are in disarray just now and he agreed to that. Although he was allowed leave today, he actually turned it down. Now, I had better cancel all leave until we get a grip on what all this is about.[269]

Sture's riddle had no great effect. After ten days, his leave was reinstated and the memory of the mysterious letters faded as the date of his discharge approached. With support, he signed the contract for a single-roomed flat on Nygatan 6B in Hedemora, a small town just quarter of an hour's drive from Säter. Sture worried a great deal about what awaited him 'outside' and was scared of being recognized from the bank robbery, which had been widely reported. On 23 July, two weeks before registering at his new address, he formally changed his surname to his mother's maiden name, Quick. Five days later, he changed his first name to Thomas, which he thought sounded right with Quick. He hoped that the unknown Thomas Quick could live in Hedemora without a lot of tittle-tattle doing the rounds. Still, in his heart of hearts, he knew his new life would end in disaster and began to feel desperate. Säter wanted him out in just a few months so, if he were to stay, now was the time to act. Cryptic word games clearly wouldn't do the trick.

The press came to his rescue: on Sunday 20 September, the evening paper *Expressen* ran a seven-page spread, complete with pictures, which listed 122 unsolved murders and disappearances. Among the missing was eleven-year-old Johan Asplund, who was presented in the newspaper with a large photo and a brief explanatory text: 'Johan disappeared on the morning of 7 November 1980. Presumed murdered. He left home to walk to school, some 500 metres away. 1,000 persons searched the entire residential area where he lived and 900 interviews were conducted but the [Sundsvall] police was never able to clarify what happened to him.'[270]

Sture acted. With dramatic displays of anguish, he began dropping hints during his therapy sessions that memories of a killing were emerging. He had murdered a boy who might well have been the disappeared Johan Asplund.

Kjell Persson did not mention Sture's confession of murder in the case notes until several months later. Though it was his duty as a doctor to break the principle of confidentiality if he learned from a patient anything relevant to a crime with a tariff greater than two years in jail, he could carry on with the therapy without telling the police if he kept the confession out of the case notes. However, we know that Sture began talking about the 'Johan murder' a month after the article in *Expressen* because, in October, he wrote about the murder in a letter to Persson, which Margit saved for her book. Sture had apparently already mentioned Johan's name during therapy sessions without being able to recall any details, but now more precise details emerged:

The image of how Johan was killed has grown clearer during these last few days. I can no longer shut my eyes to them. Everything is horrific, unbearable. I slammed Johan's face into the dashboard, that's how it began. I started the car and drove off. J is unconscious at first, then makes a sound. He tries to say something. I am present at the same time as very far away. A forest track. Trees line the verges. I stop, brake hard. Take Johan's face between my hands and scream at him to shut up. Really scream at him, silence, silence! Then I lean across him, open the passenger door, shove him out. I get out myself, run up to Johan, grab his head and bang it against the ground many times. His face is very badly torn by then. I especially remember the damage to his cheeks, so different now – it was my anger at his 'pretend-innocent' cheeks that made me want to destroy them. I hit them with my fists, then with a stone.

I observe him and realize that he is dying. I want to be inside him before he dies. I strip and throw my clothes into the car. Then I undress Johan, very gently. I caress his body, turn him over, try to push my penis – not quite stiff then – into his behind. It won't work. I fetch a knife from the car. It's easier now. I hold Johan tight (his back against me) and drive the knife into his chest.[271]

In 1980, when Johan Asplund disappeared, Sture was thirty years old. He was confessing on the premise that he had murdered the boy and then repressed all memories of it so completely that, during the intervening twelve years, he had had no idea that he was the killer. This was perfectly in line with how Margit and most of the staff at Säter thought that the human memory functioned.

A week after receiving Sture's letter, Persson drove him 300-odd kilometres to Johan Asplund's home town, Sundsvall. Someone who was close to Margit has told me that she sometimes tried to help her patients remember parental abuse by taking them to visit their old homes. It might well have been her idea to take Sture to the crime scene for an improvised re-enactment. After an eight o'clock start, they arrived in Sundsvall at lunchtime. Their destination was a small residential area, mostly blocks of flats, called Bosvedjan, situated a few kilometres to the north of the city centre. Johan Asplund had disappeared while on his way to the nearby school. This journey was planned, as Persson would say later in an interview, to allow Sture to 'feel his way around, unconditionally'.[272] The doctor had, however, taken the trouble to find out where Johan Asplund had lived and, as he explained in an interview, acted as a guide because Sture got lost.[273]

They agreed to wander around together but 'after only a few metres' Persson says that 'Sture was struck by an anxiety attack so strong we had to return to the car'.[274] They drove back to central Sundsvall. In a case note entry made almost seven months later, Persson wrote: 'We carried on searching at random along the way back and ended up at North City Hill. Sture recognized it as the place where he killed the boy.'[275]

North City Hill is a large park in central Sundsvall. Sture claimed to have taken Johan there between eight o'clock and half past eight on a frosty November morning and, during that half hour, had taken all his clothes off and killed his victim by plunging a knife into his chest while forcing anal intercourse on him. Sture had dreadful attacks of anguish as he searched for the place in the park where he had killed the boy. Once it had been identified, they drove back to Säter.

Sture's imminent discharge was of course called off. He had been an uninteresting patient, on whom it was barely worth wasting precious therapy time, but now he was the most intriguing one of all. Better still, Sture almost immediately confessed to another murder. This time, he had been in his early teens and had been travelling with an older companion to Småland County, where he had murdered fourteen-year-old Thomas Blomgren, someone he had never met before. This was a well-known unsolved murder case: Thomas Blomgren disappeared in Växjö on a spring evening in 1964 after going to a fairground set up in Folkets Park. His body was found the following day in a tool shed situated between the park and his home. The killer was never found. It seemed that Thomas had been Sture Bergwall's first victim: in 1964, Sture was only fourteen years old, the same age as the boy he had killed.

With Margit's help, Säter seemed on the way to solving two well-known murder mysteries. That autumn was very eventful. Kjell and Sture met up three times a week and, every week, the untrained therapist saw Margit for supervision, bringing records of Sture's astonishing recall of dreadful murders.

The psychotherapists at Säter were making history, and the staff were not alone in finding serial killers fascinating. Sture's crimes were trendy. In the spring of 1992, only a few months before his first murder confession, the trial of the Russian serial killer Andrei Chikatilo – the Butcher of Rostov – began in Moscow. Chikatilo was accused of having killed fifty-three women and children between 1978 and 1990. The Swedish media followed the proceedings with great interest and, under headlines such as SATAN TAKEN TO TASK, described how the apparently reticent schoolteacher had raped and tormented his victims, gouged out their eyes, then strangled, knifed and mutilated them.[276] At about this time, Jonathan Demme's film *The Silence of the Lambs*, winner of five Oscars, was on general release in Sweden and large audiences watched as the FBI agent Clarice Starling came to rely on the intellectually sophisticated serial killer Hannibal Lecter to help her find his rather less cultivated colleague Buffalo Bill, who flayed the women he killed and wore suits made from the skins.

American Psycho by Bret Easton Ellis, an international bestseller set in the 1980s, was another sign of the times. Although the novel satirizes the ruthlessness of the American financial elite, there were Swedish commentators who saw it primarily as an attempt to describe the life of a serial killer. Some of them argued that the book should be banned because it contained accounts of grotesque acts of violence.

The protagonist, the stockmarket trader Patrick Bateman, subjects his victims to innovative forms of sexual torture and, when they have finally died, indulges in gruesome acts involving their dead bodies – he eats their brains, rips their bellies open with his bare hands, chews on guts, pushes his face into a disembowelled abdomen and bites the exposed spine, and boils parts of the skeleton down so that he can fill his apartment with mementoes of his killings. Many readers were repulsed but for Sture *American Psycho* was a goldmine. He has said that he read the book when it came out in 1991 and that it became one of his chief sources of inspiration. Among Margit's documentation, I found the first description of how the fourteen-year-old Sture went about killing fourteen-year-old Thomas Blomgren. The story, which should come with a health warning, was told in a letter to Persson and might as easily have been based on *The Silence of the Lambs* as on *American Psycho*:

I tried to pull on Johan's skin and I know I wanted to get inside Thomas in the same way. I know that I looked at his cock and his face and thought 'Soon I'll be inside you, and it will be great!' I know that I wanted to put on Thomas's beauty when I opened him up.

This is getting so hard, Kjell.

How old was I? Fourteen, fifteen, sixteen? I don't know. It can't be possible that someone so young would want to eat another boy's anal sphincter. But I ate Thomas's tight ring of muscle and tore his neck open with my teeth. It was wonderful to see inside him, his death was beautiful, and my orgasm when I strangled him was indescribable, his divine inner being opened like a pearly gate. A wonderful, warm home for <u>all</u> of me.[277]

Margit had always preferred pupils who were interested in psychoanalytical theory. She must have been delighted with Sture, who not only recovered these repressed memories of murder but also formulated his own psychodynamic explanations for his extraordinary behaviour:

Why should I have to do this again? And how did I know the first time that what I longed for was to get inside the boy's belly? There was <u>nothing</u> accidental about it! When I watched Thomas coming towards me, already when I saw him at a distance, I longed with every fibre in my body to be inside his. At first, I tried entering him through his anus. Then through his neck. To be inside that boy would, had it been practically possible, mean my protection against life – by being inside him, I could die without dying! That is how much I long for my own death, which frightens me more than anything else.[278]

Sture was at the same time recovering memories of the violence he had been exposed to as a young child. His inspiration in the memory work was none other than Lena Arvidsson, whom he had first met in the summer of 1992. Once Cajsa Lindholm had helped Lena recover her allegedly repressed memories of sexual abuse from when she was about a year old, Lena decided to study psychology. She started at the University of Stockholm towards the end of the 1980s and arrived in Säter's ward 36 as a temporary psychiatric nurse during the summer of 1992. She met Sture and they got on well. They went for walks around the lake together and talked a great deal.

When Lena went back to her classes in August, they promised to keep in touch. She gave Sture her address and they started corresponding that autumn.

All of Sture's letters to Lena ended up in Margit's possession and many of them are quoted in the draft of 'The World of Thomas Quick'. The letters from Lena to Sture were bundled up and left in his room until he gave them to me in 2012. There are fifteen letters, most of them written by hand. The date on the first one is 27 October 1992, which was the day after Sture's trip to Sundsvall with Kjell Persson. In it Lena says that she had such a good time during the summer at Säter and that she sometimes misses the place. She was working hard at her psychology studies but found the departmental reading list unsatisfactory:

I literally collapse over my books. My brain feels fit to burst with the psychological terminology, and all the thinking, speculation and my own anger. I am angry because all 'the shit' I have to read and all the stupid, lying stuff that my teacher lectures about. Only one of the seven books I'm meant to read seems important and the rest is dull, old-fashioned rubbish (I think). I don't want to learn to accept that people are above all responding to their innate drives and that tiny children are practically born guilty. Most of what a patient tells his or her therapist is to be questioned and re-interpreted – real traumatic events are intellectualized and reshaped to become the patient's internal desires and fantasies.

Lena had been so deeply impressed by *The Assault on Truth* that she almost quotes verbatim from Jeffrey Masson's accusation that psychotherapists are abusing their patients by not believing what they say in therapy sessions: 'In my opinion it's abuse of the patients if you don't take their narratives and feelings seriously [...] It matters to be in touch with reality!!'[279]

Sture absorbed what he read and when he recovered his own memories of childhood abuse, Lena encouraged him and provided him with ideological input. In December 1992, she wrote:

I understand that you have <u>terrible</u> memories because you have been subjected to sexual abuse. It has to be the worst thing that can happen to a child. It's so bloody sick! I am convinced [of that] and have noticed that very many psychiatric patients have been exploited for sex in some way. It's horrible! Just as horrible as all the psychologists who don't see it and won't try to understand, something that's only too common. One might ask oneself what all these psychologists are trying to hide from themselves about their own childhood . . .[280]

By February 1993, Sture had been talking about murders in his therapy sessions for four months but Persson still had not yet written a single line about them in the case notes. Then Persson went on leave and, while he was away, Sture was seen by Birgitta Ståhle – a fact that tells its own story about his new status in the hospital. Usually psychotherapists do not act as each other's locums, but Sture was a special case. Someone had to be ready for him, when his repressed memories burst their banks. Ståhle noted: 'He is undergoing a therapeutic process that is arousing so much material he needs a firm framework to support him.'[281]

By now Göran Fransson, who had overall responsibility for Sture, thought it was time to refer to his patient's confessions of murder in the case notes. He did so after a talk with Sture: 'I explained to him that it would of course have legal consequences and that he must take it up with the police if he is to have any hope of reconciling himself to his deeds. He understands but is understandably very fearful.'[282]

Sture had told me that it was chilling to hear Fransson speaking about calling the police. Somehow he had hoped to lie on his bed for years, telling his therapist about his murder fantasies without any police involvement. All he wanted was to be an interesting Säter inmate, not a murder suspect. He could, of course, get out of the police interrogation by admitting that he had invented the whole saga but that would have meant being despised by Kjell Persson and Göran Fransson. The two doctors were the only people in the world who really cared about him, except for his friend Lena Arvidsson, who would not have been best pleased to hear him suddenly deny all his memories. Retraction of his confessions was the path to abandonment and he would certainly be ejected from the unit without his status as a killer.

To be above board and tell the truth was not an option. Instead, Sture did what he always tried to do when he was in trouble: worm his way out of the situation and hope to avoid anyone getting angry with him. How this went is reflected in a case note entry by Göran Fransson: 'Another talk with pat. today and it seems as if the feelings elicited by his crimes are more distant. Already, he hesitates [...] and [says] what he describes is more like fantasies which he is unsure about the reality of but now he has had the fantasies confirmed by his psychotherapy.'[283]

But Fransson, like Margit, was convinced that Sture was telling the truth: 'I tell him that he has two weeks to go to the police himself and if he doesn't face up to it in that time, I'll go instead.' Sture tried to say that he was unsure about actually having murdered anyone but Fransson countered this firmly:

> I then confront him with his two evasive answers to my direct questions last week when on two occasions I asked if there were any more [murders]. Personally, I think it odd that fifteen years should have passed between these crimes. He tells me that he has fantasies/imaginary visions about another two, linked to the names Peter and Mikael. The order is determined chronologically. He is unsure of whether they were his actual victims or not.

In Fransson's reports, Sture twice refers to his tales of murder as 'fantasies' and twice as 'imaginary visions' and states explicitly that he doesn't know for certain if he had killed anyone. Nonetheless, Fransson was already convinced that Sture was a murderer: '[Sture] is afraid that he won't be able to recall enough factual details for the police interrogations but I advise him to prepare himself by writing things down. Also assure him that our staff will be present.'

Fransson next called the regional police office in Borlänge and asked them to send a skilled investigating officer to interview a patient who might well be a serial killer but had repressed the memories of his crimes and therefore might be a difficult subject to interview.

Sture had not managed to extract himself from the trap he had rigged for himself. Fransson truly believed that one could repress memories of murder and was not even prepared to consider the possibility that Sture might have lied. Besides, to doubt a patient was an abuse of trust and a breach of the unit's belief system. That Sture seemed to doubt himself was regarded as a natural response. In her unpublished article on a psychotherapist's observations on patients who have experienced incest, Margit had established that a criterion for the truth of repressed 'incest events' is 'strong resistance exerted by the patient'.[284]

The further Sture tried to distance himself from his stories, the more he convinced the staff at Säter that what he said was true. Margit's closed, self-confirming system of thought had trapped him. And the police were on their way.

However, Sture did have a plan B. He would deliver a story so absurd that no one would believe it. It would make the officers of the law give up and leave him to his own devices without ruining his comfortable relationship with Säter. Kjell Persson and Göran Fransson seemed to believe anything he said – but the police would not, he was going to make sure of that.

18

The first eight police interviews

*'It disappears or is repressed, or whatever we now should call
it, quite quickly. Err, well, I won't try to tell you about the
state of my feelings, but once I'm back in Falun, when a day
and a night have gone by, it is gone.'*

Sture describing how his memory of the murder
of Johan Asplund was lost from his conscious
recollection soon after the murder.

On 1 March 1993, the police interviewed Sture, in his role of the serial
killer Thomas Quick, for the first time. The last police interview
would take place just over eight years later, on 23 March 2001. He was
listened to about a hundred times in total and, to a large extent, the
records can help to explain the enigma of how Sture came to be convicted of eight murders. The first eight interviews reveal more than
enough.

These were held between the beginning of March and the end of
May. The police in Borlänge sent a constable called Jörgen Persson to
conduct the first interrogation. A temporary interview room had been
set up in ward 36 and Dr Kjell Persson was accompanying Sture. The
case to be examined was the murder of Johan Asplund. No one had
thought of asking a solicitor to attend on the patient's behalf. Sture had
confessed to the Thomas Blomgren murder, too, but since it dated
back to 1964 the Swedish statute of limitation applied and so the case
was of less interest to the police.

According to a transcript of the interview, the police officer started
the tape recorder at 11.20 a.m. and the interview continued until 2.30
p.m. with barely an hour's break for lunch. The officer introduces

himself and says that he understands that Sture has got something to tell the police. This is how it began:

> [Interviewer]: '[If] we start now, what is it you would like to raise here, what would you like to tell me about? Something that's happened that you ...?'
> [Sture]: 'This is really hard for me and you must be prepared if I ... I'll be going to ... that I might go very quiet. And that's that, so we'll have to find a way [...] you know, to tell you. I just want you to know this is going to be very difficult.' [285]

Slowly, the police officer extracted an account of how, in 1980, Sture had borrowed a car from an acquaintance and, in the middle of the night, driven the 300 kilometres from Falun to Sundsvall to hunt for prey. It was morning by the time he arrived and happened to end up a little to the north of the city, in a group of blocks of flats. This is where he caught sight of eleven-year-old Johan Asplund. Sture said he remembered the area but that his memories might have been strengthened because of the journey he had made the previous autumn with Dr Persson. The officer registered surprise at this but Persson interrupted to confirm that he had actually taken the patient to the crime scene.

Sture said he had seen the boy outside one of the blocks and talked him into coming for a ride in the car:

> [Sture]: 'What I told him was that I had run over a cat and probably killed it and that's how I made him come along to the car. And then I opened the passenger door and pulled him inside. It was really quick.'
> [Interviewer]: 'How did you go about pulling him inside?'
> [Sture]: 'I grabbed hold of him by the back of the neck and hauled him into the car and drove off, at the same moment, almost, if you see what I mean.'
> [Interviewer]: 'Where in the car did he end up?'
> [Sture]: 'In the front passenger seat.'
> [Interviewer]: 'How did he react when you captured him?'

[Sture]: 'The whole thing happened so quickly, he was taken by surprise and then, well, you can imagine how he reacted.'

[Interviewer]: 'Aha, yes, of course one can. But what do you remember of his reaction? Can you recall how he was?'

[Sture]: 'The way things happened is hard to order now, it difficult to get the sequence right. The chronological order is muddled but what happens is that, that ... that I bang his head against the dashboard so he's probably knocked out pretty much at once.'

[Interviewer]: 'And which side did you say it was? In the car, I mean, was it in the driver's seat, the passenger ...?'

[Sture]: 'Passenger seat. But did I do that to him as I got him into the car? Or after I have sat down in the driver's seat? I've no idea.'

[Interviewer]: 'No, OK. And then what happens?'

[Sture]: 'We drive out of, or away from, that residential area and I still can't tell where we're going but we come to, we arrive at City Hill in Sundsvall eventually and that's where I park the car. I get Johan out of the car and we walk a goodish bit into the woods there. And that's where the act ... that is, I strangled him there.'

[Interviewer]: 'Aha. And how do you go about strangling him?'

[Sture]: 'I use ... well, I used my hands.'

[Interviewer]: 'Has something happened before you strangle him?'

[Sture]: 'No, nothing special.'

[Interviewer]: 'Where you parked your car at City Hill – can you remember what it looked like there?'

[Sture]: 'I can't remember that. [...]'

[Interviewer]: 'Aha. And how do you get from the car into the woods?'

[Sture]: 'We walked. All right, Johan partly walked and was carried, well, I kind of had to lift him at times.'

[Interviewer]: 'Why?'

[Sture]: 'I don't know.'

Now the officer seemed to remember that Sture had said that Johan fainted when his head was slammed against the dashboard and started to ask about Johan's state when he left the car. At this point, Sture had a severe panic attack, as if the memory was too terrible for him to bear thinking about it. The text does not indicate exactly how the attack manifested itself but after reading hundreds of transcripts, as well as listening to some of the tapes, I know that Sture behaved just as desperately during interviews as he did during therapy – stuttering, hyperventilating, weeping. Persson interrupted and explained to the police officer: 'It's precisely this kind of thing which makes it such a tough deal for us all. What you observe is a severe anxiety attack, these are the signs.'

Sture was given a handkerchief and the interview continued. The interviewer wanted Sture to say why he had taken Johan with him in the car.

[Sture]: 'I was going to force him to have sex with me.'
[Interviewer]: 'Did you, at any time?'
[Sture]: 'Yes.'
[Interviewer]: 'Where did it take place?'
[Sture]: 'There, at City Hill, the place we've just been talking about.'
[Interviewer]: 'Can you describe it in more detail? [...]'
[Sture]: 'Well, I pulled his trousers off.'
[Interviewer]: 'And then, what did you do? By the way, what positions were the two of you in when you took his trousers off?'
[Sture]: 'We were standing.'
[Interviewer]: 'But what about your clothing at the time?'
[Sture]: 'The fly on my trousers was open.'
[Interviewer]: 'So, you got his trousers off. Do you remember what the items of clothing looked like?'
[Sture]: 'No, not really.'
[Interviewer]: 'You know, the material or colour or something like that?'

[Sture]: 'No, I don't think so. I can't remember, I pulled them down, that was it.'

[Interviewer]: 'This was wintertime. Did he wear other trousers underneath?'

[Sture]: 'I couldn't really tell . . . but I pulled down whatever he had on.'

[Interviewer]: 'Right. You're standing there, in the wood. Then what?'

[Sture]: 'It happened quickly, but what I did . . . you see, when I pulled his trousers down, I got close up to him with my penis out. And it's in that moment he died.'

[Interviewer]: 'What did you do with your penis?'

[Sture]: 'I pushed it against him and killed him at the same time.'

[Interviewer]: 'Where on his body did your penis go?'

[Sture]: 'He is standing with his back towards me so you can imagine where.'

[Interviewer]: 'Look, Sture, it's like this – I'm not supposed to work things out myself. There are things I understand and can work out, but I still have to ask you.'

[Sture]: 'So I'm trying to penetrate his arse.'

[Interviewer]: 'Yes. And did you get in?'

[Sture]: 'I don't know.'

[Interviewer]: 'And how does he stand? You've told me that he stood with his back towards you but it's possible to angle one's body in different ways. Is he standing up straight or bending over in some way . . . or . . .?'

The memory seems to make Sture anxious and he starts stuttering:

[Sture]: 'No, I bend . . . bend . . . bend him forward a bit.'

[Interviewer]: 'How does he react? Do you remember?'

[Sture]: 'No, not really, I can't.'

[Interviewer]: 'What about you? What do you do?'

[Sture]: 'It is at this moment that I strangle him.'

Sture claimed to have strangled Johan while simultaneously having at least partial anal intercourse with him, with both of them standing but with the boy bending over, apparently without resisting. It was a different tale to the one Sture had told Persson, and the doctor should have sat up and taken note. In the letter he had received from Sture four months previously, part of the murder sequence had read: 'I strip and throw my clothes into the car. [. . .] I hold Johan tight (his back against me) and drive the knife into his chest.'[286]

In that version Sture had been completely naked and committed a knife murder. In this new version Sture had simply opened his fly, the knifing had become strangulation and the knife had disappeared entirely from the revised narrative. Persson does not seem to have worried in the slightest, presumably because Margit had taught him that repressed memories might be subject to remarkable changes during the course of the therapy because the repression mechanism is active all the time and obscures the actual events.

The officer asked Sture if he had told anyone about Johan's murder. The answer must have given him an insight into the fascinating world of repressed memories:

[Sture]: 'I never knew for sure if it was me.'
[Interviewer]: 'You didn't know?'
[Sture]: 'This is the real difficulty, you see.'
[Interviewer]: '[How] did you feel when you read about the [murder] and learnt something about the details? What did you think then?'
[Sture]: 'I might have thought, you know, this could have been me but it surely wasn't. I sort of pushed it away, or something. I don't know how to explain it.'
[Interviewer]: 'Yes, well, that does happen, I suppose. I think I understand.'
[Sture]: 'Yes, and it has needed a long process between the therapist and myself. The whole thing has grown over time, if I put it like that. And I believe – if I remember rightly – that Johan's name has come up now and then.'

[Persson]: 'Initially, more as part of fantasizing.'
[Sture]: 'Yes, exactly.'

At the end of the interview, Sture was informed that he was now a suspect in the Johan Asplund murder case. Because the kidnapping had taken place in Sundsvall, in the neighbouring county of Västernorrland, a public prosecutor from that area would lead the investigation.

His name was Christer van der Kwast, a man of almost forty-eight, with crew-cut hair and the beginning of a bull's neck. Van der Kwast came from a family of Dutch musicians who had emigrated to Sweden around the turn of the twentieth century. His father played the alto violin at the Royal Opera in Stockholm, and his son also wanted to become a musician. However, his father thought the career was too insecure, so van der Kwast chose to study law instead.[287] By 1986 he had been appointed the chief public prosecutor at the county prosecution service in Härnösand. He intended to specialize in financial crime but cases were thin on the ground so he took on other crimes as and when necessary. He had once tried his hand at a murder investigation but it did not lead to a trial. Now van der Kwast had to find the right policeman to act as the senior investigating officer. He chose constable Seppo Penttinen from Sundsvall, a forty-three-year-old drug squad officer who had worked with van der Kwast on his first, failed murder investigation.

A week after the Borlänge police interview, Seppo Penttinen came to Säter. Since the ward music room had a soundproofing carpet, it was designated as the interview room. The furnishings included the stereo music centre, a low, round table and beautiful Bruno Mathsson armchairs with seats of sand-coloured linen webbing. Penttinen brought along a deputy interviewer called C.G. Carlsson, while Sture was again accompanied by Persson and also by Gunnar Lundgren, a solicitor and a Säter familiar recommended by Göran Fransson. He had acted for Lars-Inge Svartenbrandt and had worked on and off with Källberg for many years. His profound respect for the psychotherapy regime at Säter had not been shaken by the Svartenbrandt fiasco.

The fact seems to be that Gunnar Lundgren believed as strongly in the repressed memory theory as the medics and Margit. In a 2001 interview with him, when Sture had just been convicted of his eighth murder, Lundgren opined that if Sture's therapy was continued, he would eventually be able to lead the way to the body caches. At that stage, the therapy had been going on for ten years without the smallest part of a body being unearthed.[288] Gunnar Lundgren was unquestionably Säter's man.

In preparation for the interview, Sture had been taking benzo-diazepines. Reclining comfortably in an armchair, he was once more taken through the details of the murder. Apparently, new memories had emerged during the past week. After the strangulation on City Hill, he had hidden Johan's clothes, hauled the body into the car and left Sundsvall. After driving northwards for some time, he had turned into a side road on – as he recalled – his right-hand side. Speaking about the place where he finally stopped, he said 'I know precisely what it looked like', and went on to describe 'a very stony area, lots of stones piled up'. The sea might just have been visible from there or, at least one had 'a sense of the sea' being not too far away. The rocks became quite large in one part of the site, 'curving outwards' and then 'curving inwards'. Racked with anxiety, Sture tried to tell them how he had prepared the hiding place:

[Carlsson]: 'By then, had you got the body out of the car? Or ...?'
[Sture]: 'No, but I had opened the car door, the rear door. But I leave him in the car while I do the next thing and it is quite low down, well, at ground level. I drag and manhandle stones into place and I do this for what seems a long time and make a kind of space and so ... [anxiety symptoms] and put him inside it.'
[Carlsson]: 'Do you use your hands for this or do you have some kind of tool to help you drag the stone around?'
[Sture]: 'Well, mostly with my hands but I think I might've used the car jack but I don't know that. I used my hands a lot anyway.'

[Penttinen]: 'These stones, were they of a size that allowed you to lift them?'

[Sture]: 'Yes, I could lift some of them and others I rolled along with, you know, my hands, rolled or sort of hauled. And of course the distance wasn't so great, a matter of tens of centimetres generally.'

[Carlsson]: 'How long did it take?'

[Sture]: 'I don't know, I've no idea.'

[Penttinen]: 'But when you had put him inside this hollow, or space, and covered it all up, was there anything of him that showed?'

[Sture]: 'No, I checked but there was nothing. It showed that I had been doing something, of course, stirred it up, but there was nothing else to see, nothing to see.'

[Penttinen]: 'The ground you were standing on, apart from these stones that you had hauled along, what was it like?'

[Sture]: 'I don't know.'

Sture remembered that when he had got Johan's body out of the car, he had found a pen on the driver's seat. He thought it might have been Johan's so he buried it with the corpse. Penttinen asked if he could describe the pen:

[Sture]: 'Yes, I can. There was yellow, blue and green at the top.'

[Penttinen]: 'You mean it was one of these pens where you can change the colour ...?'

[Sture]: 'Yes, that's right. Yes.'

When Sture had spoken about the pen in such detail, Penttinen wondered if he could describe the victim as well. Sture found this much more difficult:

[Penttinen]: 'You said something about a cap?'

[Sture]: 'Yes.'

[Penttinen]: 'What did it look like?'

[Sture]: 'No ... I don't know. [...]'

[Penttinen]: 'Had he brought anything else with him?'

[Sture]: 'I don't know. I can't remember.'

[Penttinen]: 'So you can't remember if he had something that he would need at school that day, for instance?'

[Sture]: 'No.'

[Penttinen]: 'I'll ask you a leading question in a way and wonder if he had a bag with him?'

[Sture]: 'I don't know.'

[Penttinen]: 'And you have no memory of whether he did or didn't?'

[Sture]: 'No.'

Johan had actually been carrying a red satchel with the Puma logo when he disappeared. Penttinen's deputy was intrigued by memory repression and wanted to know more:

[Carlsson]: 'Have you told anybody else about this?'

[Sture]: (*inaudible*)

[Carlsson]: 'But didn't you talk spontaneously about it ... well, with anyone at all after or in connection with what had taken place?'

[Sture]: 'No, oh no.'

[Carlsson]: 'Instead you repressed it all, it just vanished?'

[Sture]: 'Yes, it had vanished.'

[Carlsson]: 'So, you're saying when you came back to Falun you had no memory of being in Sundsvall? Is that it?'

(*Quite a long pause*)

[Sture]: 'It disappears or is repressed, or whatever we now should call it, quite quickly. Err, well, I won't try to tell you about the state of my feelings, but once I'm back in Falun, when a day and a night have gone by, it is gone.'

[Carlsson]: 'Can you explain to us why you want to tell us about this now, today? Is it what has happened to you during the past year with the doctor here, is that something that drives you to tell us?'

(*Quite a long pause*)

[Sture]: It is above all ... (*pause*) that during the time I have been here, a lot has happened to me. So, for example ... err, I am connecting to a forgotten childhood and I used to believe that I had no memories at all of when I was a child but of course I have, and they are coming up to the surface now. Which is one thing. And these other things, too, have emerged during my time here, so ... err [...] So, I can't any longer keep – to become whole, in order to be a whole human being I must confront all this as well, or else I can't ... (*pause*) well, it's hard to explain.

[Carlsson]: 'Do you have a bad conscience?'

[Sture]: 'There is an enormous sense of guilt and misery in all this.'

Someone leaked the story to the media. The day after Penttinen's interview, a TV news programme ran an item about a mentally ill patient at Säter hospital, a forty-two-year-old man with no previous connection to the unsolved disappearance of Johan Asplund. The investigation had been open for twelve years but this man had only now confessed to murdering the boy. The programme mentioned an interview with the public prosecutor, in which he had said that it would not do 'to dismiss this confession by a psychiatric patient even though it is not unusual for such people to wrongly claim to have committed murder. This man states that he has hidden Johan's body. The police must find the burial place before we can finally confirm whether or not the case of Johan's disappearance is finally solved.'[289]

Christer van der Kwast was also interviewed in *Dala-Demokraten*. His tone was one of cautious optimism: ' ... the most interesting aspect is obviously the matter of the body. Our primary task is to establish if the body can be found. So far, it is impossible to draw any final conclusions. It can't be done before the end of next week – at a guess.'[290]

The interview was illustrated by a large photo of the prosecutor, nonchalantly sitting back in a rather grand office chair with one leg crossed over the other and a telephone receiver pressed to his ear. His cheeks are covered with stubble so thick it is almost a sparse beard. He comes across as a tough guy, an investigator in some American crime flick from the 1980s. So, this was the man who had set out to solve one of Sweden's most notorious mysteries.

All it would take for Christer van der Kwast to become famous was for Sture to succeed in finding the pile of rocks where he had hidden the corpse. But by agreeing to be interviewed, van der Kwast had triggered a troublesome media interest. *Expressen* spread an interview with Johan Asplund's parents across a whole page and press photographers insisted on being in place when the body was found. In order to avoid being chased as they searched the forests, van der Kwast decided that Sture would be driven to Sundsvall in complete secrecy that Saturday, just five days after Penttinen's interview.

A minibus set out from Säter at nine o'clock on the Saturday morning, carrying Sture, his doctor/therapist Kjell Persson, a nurse and Göran Fransson, who would later describe the outing in the case notes. The journey went well 'with the exception of Thomas's few anxiety attacks since he is worried about what lies ahead'. Just before 1 p.m., they arrived at Njurunda, a community south of Sundsvall, where the solicitor Gunnar Lundgren, the prosecutor Christer van der Kwast and three men from the police, Seppo Penttinen, C.G. Carlsson and a forensic technician, joined the crew in the minibus. Penttinen took the wheel and they headed for North City Hill in central Sundsvall. He parked near the path where Sture and Persson had walked when they made their own trip to Sundsvall. Everyone got out and, as Penttinen says in his report: 'After a few moments of concentration, Quick says that he is prepared to show us the place where he killed Johan Asplund. Escorted by his doctors, who support him by holding his arms, Quick walks short stretches along the path. He has visible anxiety attacks intermittently.' The group moved on, but slowly with several stops.

Penttinen continues: 'After walking about 100 metres, he signals with his hand his intention to turn towards the right, where there is a small hill. As he gets closer to it his anxiety increases and one can observe him leaning heavily on the arms of the accompanying doctors.

When they speak to him, he says that he nonetheless wants to carry on but that he needs help.'

The doctors believed that Sture was now shifting his timeframe back to the 1980s and that he was reliving the killing. Fransson wrote that his patient 'lost contact with reality ever so often' and would ask his companions to 'lead him back' to the present, which meant that they 'called out emphatically to state the actual time and place'. Sture's anguish was monumental: 'For the last stretch, he has to be practically carried by Kjell and me holding on to his arms. His intense anxiety makes him hyperventilate.'

In this condition, Sture sat down on a stone at the top of the hillock. As Penttinen wrote, '[he] points with both arms outreached, held at about a forty-five-degree angle from the body, and says that within this area the clothes and footwear that he has told them of in the interviews will be found.' Penttinen uses the word 'footwear' because Sture still couldn't remember if what he removed from his victim was a pair of shoes or boots or wellington boots or whatever.

Penttinen notes that the time travel starts again: 'When Quick still stays sitting on the same stone, he has yet another strong anxiety attack and screams that on that occasion he had urged Johan to be quiet. [...] At 1400 hours, the return to the car begins. The doctors have to intervene also on the walk back since he appears still to be mentally part of the events which took place with Johan.'

The groups drove north to Åvike, an area of mixed grazing and woodland. They drove around on the dirt roads for a while, looking for a rock that was 'curving outwards' as well as 'curving inwards' in a place where one could either see or 'sense' the sea. There had to be a pile of rocks big enough to hide a body. Fransson writes:

Pat. sort of feels his way and is helped by Kjell Persson to interpret his feelings. If he thought he recognized a certain lay of the land, he had a very pronounced anxiety attack accomp. by severe chest pain. By now, he also has a bad headache. He hyperventilated and once again had to breathe into a plastic bag. Given another 5 mg tabl. Stesolid and 2 Co-codamols for his headache.

Sture hyperventilated so vigorously that the carbon dioxide concentration in his blood fell below the normal lower limit. It triggered muscular spasms. The usual trick for handling this situation is to let the patient breathe into a bag. Once the CO_2 content of the blood has increased sufficiently, the spasms cease. Sture was doing this while seated in the car when they spotted a rock at the edge of a meadow and stopped.

Next, something astonishing happened. Penttinen provides a blow-by-blow account:

At 16.15, Quick got out of the car, saying that he recognized the place. While in the car, he had shown strong signs of anxiety and not dared to look right, where a rocky ridge with a visible scattering of stones could be seen. He walked along on the right edge of the grazing meadow, intending to point to the place where he had hidden Johan Asplund's remains. He was accompanied by his doctors and his psychiatric nurse. He found it difficult to look at the rocky ridge.

At 16.17, he looks quickly to the right towards the ridge and states in a loud voice, almost shouting, that this is the right place. He returned to sit in the car together with Dr Kjell Persson.

At 16.20, Persson stated that Quick has just told him that only the head is hidden in this place and not the rest of the body.

Fransson also described how Sture made this terrible discovery in the case notes: '[The patient] was convinced that he had found the place but then it became clear, although he had presumably been unaware of it earlier, that the body was cut up.'

When I interviewed Göran Fransson in 2013, I read this out to him and asked him to explain what he was thinking as he wrote it. The burial that Sture had described in such detail had changed completely in the space of a few minutes despite Sture's prior vivid recall: the building of the stone chamber, the pen with multi-coloured inks, and so on. How could Fransson have possibly believed that Sture was 'presumably unaware' earlier that he had buried only the head?

'I'm not sure I can explain it,' Fransson said. He looked pained. 'It sounds crazy.' He tried to recover by saying that it would have been utterly out of order to question what Persson did with Sture during the therapy sessions. 'After all, he had the best supervisor one could find,' Fransson added with an ironic smile.

In the autumn of 2012, I visited the meadow with the rocky out-crop and saw immediately why Sture had changed his story: there was no pile of stones large enough to hide a body. The only thing that chimed with Sture's interview statements was a small ridge with as many ins and outs as every other rocky ridge in the hilly Åvike area. The sea could neither be seen nor 'sensed'.

In 1993, the disappearance of both the piled-up stones and the body did not trouble the group at all. Van der Kwast and Penttinen both lacked psychiatric competence and relied on the two psychiatric con-sultants, who were deeply committed to their patient. When Sture had been given more tranquillizers, he said that the head was buried some-where near the rocky ridge. Fransson wrote: 'He didn't dare look towards the ridge at first but eventually managed to point out to the policemen the area they should search.'

There was still the matter of finding out where the rest of the body was, but Sture was tired. Van der Kwast tried to persuade the doctors that the whole group should stay the night in Sundsvall and continue the search the following day, but Fransson thought it unlikely that Sture was strong enough and so they set out on their return journey. The doctors and Sture stopped for supper in a restaurant on their way to Säter, and Sture told me that they were all in a party mood. Fransson had ordered three cigars to round off the meal. I did not actually believe this until Fransson himself confirmed it and admitted that he had, on one occasion, thought of Sture as a 'success factor that would help the harshly criticized hospital'. That night, Sture was not back in ward 36 until after 11 p.m.

It stands to reason that van der Kwast was less cheerful than the team from Säter. He had announced on TV that the mysterious Johan Asplund case would be solved within a week. Now he had to return from Sundsvall without anything to show. Two days later, on Monday, the police technicians started to look for Johan's clothes on North City Hill and digging for the head along the rocky outcrop near Åvike. The search continued for a week without uncovering any trace of Johan Asplund.

The third police interview was held three days after the re-enactment trip and, by then, Penttinen had had time to check the issue date of Sture's driving licence. It was a day in 1987, seven years after his alleged drive to Sundsvall and subsequent adventures in a borrowed car. When the police later interviewed Sture's sister Eva, she said that her brother couldn't drive – not even change gears – before 1987.

In the fourth interview, Sture was shown a video that Penttinen had recorded at the rock. The idea was to offer him another chance to show where the head was buried. Sture, wanting to be helpful, drew a sketch, marking the spot with a cross. The sketch was added to the interview transcript. It was and is completely incomprehensible.[291]

In the fifth interview, they discussed how Sture went about severing Johan's head from his body, a topic that troubled Sture greatly. Penttinen tried to help:

> Sture was unable to suggest what might have been used but in connection with the interviewers putting forward various options, he said that neither axe nor knife seemed right. When we mention 'a saw' he has strong anxiety symptoms and does not answer. As his reason for this, he states that in connection with thinking about the tool he has such a powerful mental image of the scene coming into his head that he does not have the strength to utter the word for the tool in question.[292]

During this interview, Penttinen and his assistant managed to persuade Sture to tell them about his new, rather sensational memories of where the body had gone. After hiding the head by the rock, he had put the body in the car and driven to a small mountain about 15 kilometres south of Sundsvall. He had carried the corpse up the mountain, thinking that he would throw it down a cliff face and then jump after it: 'What I was thinking, you see, there I am with Johan, so jump, well, die with him then.' But once he had reached the top and thrown the body down, he had not dared to leap after it and drove off instead. The interview ended with a clarification from Persson:

[Penttinen]: 'I see. Well, the doctor has explained that when Johan was thrown off the cliff it was the body minus the head. Interview interrupted at 14.30.'

The sixth interview was held in the middle of April, four weeks later. Sture had recovered some completely new memories. He had not killed Johan on North City Hill, even though this was something he had insisted on repeatedly, ever since the letter to Persson in the autumn of 1992. All he had done in the park was undress the boy, remove his 'footwear', and hide the clothes. Then he had driven Johan, naked from the waist down, to the Åvike area where he lay down to have sex with his prey – no mention of standing up. Afterwards, he had strangled Johan. Sture was also able to describe the butchery, which, startlingly, was much more extensive than he had been conscious of earlier. He had not only severed the head from the body but also carved up the corpse. At one point, while he was sawing the body up, he had leapt into the car to run over some body parts – he did not specify which and Penttinen did not ask. He had then returned to his handiwork and, once he was done, wrapped the torso in a car rug he had found in the back seat and tied the whole thing up with string. Then he stuffed the other bits and pieces, together with the tools, into a large cardboard box that he had in the boot. Penttinen tried to keep up with all this:

[Penttinen]: 'So, you bundled up the torso and the knife and the saw in the car rug?'
[Sture]: 'Yes ... no.'
[Penttinen]: 'You did say that about the torso, didn't you?'
[Sture]: '*Ye ... es*, that was the part tied up in ...'
[Penttinen]: 'In fabric from the car?'
[Sture]: 'Yes, that's it.'
[Penttinen]: 'With a piece of string?'
[Sture]: 'Yes.'

[Penttinen]: 'What kind of string is it you've got then?'

[Sture]: 'You know, an ordinary kind of string, one of these whitish, coarse . . . do you know what I mean?'

[Penttinen]: 'Like a hemp rope but a thin one, is that right? [. . .]'

[Sture]: 'Yes, but a little thicker.'

[Penttinen]: 'And where did you get hold of it?'

[Sture]: 'It was in the box.'

[Penttinen]: 'And that box, how would you describe it?'

[Sture]: (*inaudible*) ' . . . cardboard box, then. [. . .]'

[Penttinen]: 'Had you got hold of this box [. . .] intending to use it for just this purpose?'

[Sture]: 'I don't know.'

[Penttinen]: 'Can you describe the box in more detail than just saying it was a cardboard box? The size? Or did it have any writing on it, or something? What had it been used for?'

[Sture]: 'I think it said Korsnäs Bakery on it.'

[Penttinen]: 'Korsnäs Bakery?'

[Sture]: 'Yes.'

[Penttinen]: 'Is this your own box? Had you used it for anything before?'

[Sture]: 'Yes, it was my own box.'

[Penttinen]: 'Did you keep it at home in your place?'

[Sture]: 'Umm.'

Sture explained that he had parcelled up the torso and the arms, without hands, in the rug. The knife, the saw and the legs were stacked inside the box with the rug bundle placed on top.

[Penttinen]: 'But, as I see it, the hands aren't accounted for. Where did they go in the end?'

[Sture]: 'They were in the car.'

[Penttinen]: 'In the open, or did you cover them up?'

[Sture]: 'Yes, I wrapped them in the kind of tissue paper you find inside shoeboxes.'

[Penttinen]: 'The paper shoes are wrapped in, inside the boxes?'

[Sture]: 'Yes.'

[Penttinen]: 'Thinner than that?'

[Sture]: 'Yes . . . yes, a bit.'

[Penttinen]: 'Where had you got hold of the paper, then?'

[Sture]: 'It came in (*inaudible*) the box.'

[Penttinen]: 'And that box, where did it end up? Where did it go?'

[Sture]: 'In the boot.'

[Penttinen]: 'In the luggage space. Why didn't you put the hands in there? Why were they to be left lying around inside the body of the car?'

[Sture]: 'Well, that's something I can't comment on now.'

Johan Asplund disappeared in November. Sture claimed that the ground had been covered in snow. Before leaving the place by the rock, he 'drove around for a while to hide the traces of blood'. Then he drove towards the Sandö Bridge. He was now able to reveal that the box also contained stones 'the size of handballs'. He dumped the whole thing into the River Ångerman and drove on. Next to him, on the front passenger seat he had placed the boy's hands, wrapped in tissue paper.[293] No further mention was made of his anguished story from four weeks ago about throwing the body off a cliff.

On 25 May, they were back in the music room for the seventh interview. Penttinen opened the proceedings by explaining that certain features of Sture's account were doubtful and that 'of those who are hesitant about the truth of these statements [and] need more robust evidence, the prosecutor is the most concerned. [. . .] That's why we must try to find as many solid items of evidence as possible.'

Penttinen asked if Sture had 'any clear picture in his memory' of what he had done with Johan Asplund's hands, information 'that he's really holding on to inside himself' but was 'difficult for him to get out'? The way Penttinen formulated this question suggests that he had accepted the Säter explanation for why Sture's story was told in this way. Sture asked for a short break to fetch something he had written, a piece of prose-poetry that he had given to Persson. It spoke of 'a sacred place' where a hand was hidden. He wanted to read it aloud:

'Here, with pen in hand, I'm attempting to reason, but in emotional terms, about my sacred place. I know that these four or five, fist-sized stones mean something – but what? They lie near the stream's central channel and form a low wall behind which Johan's hand is held. His hand, which was to be the boy's last gift.'[294]

This was the first time that Sture had described the ritualistic, 'religious' significance that hiding parts of corpses had for him. He explained that 'the boy's last gift' would be buried by a stream near a village called Ryggen. Penttinen hadn't heard of it but Sture told him that it was less than an hour's drive from Säter Hospital. Penttinen, enthused, wanted them to go there the following day and Sture agreed, saying that he 'had not the slightest doubt' that he would find the hand in its sacred place. Finding the other hand would be much more difficult:

> [Sture]: 'Of course there were two hands at first but I only know roughly where the other one might be, it's probably very hard to find. It is somewhere around Bergvik.'
> [Penttinen]: 'Is it hidden or did you just throw it away?'
> [Sture]: 'It was thrown away.'

Late in the afternoon the following day, Penttinen, Sture, Persson and a uniformed officer set out for Ryggen, a village on the banks of a lake of the same name. They parked a little away from the water's edge, not far from the railway tracks. According to Penttinen's careful report, Sture wanted to begin by walking with the doctor to get his bearings. When they returned to the car after about an hour, 'Quick showed clear signs of anxiety, including spasms' and found walking so difficult he had to be helped into the car. He rested for a while and then said that he was 'prepared to lead the way to where he had hidden Johan's hand'. He took his companions to a stream that ran out of the lake. Penttinen reports: 'Quick states that the hiding place was constructed at water level but that he has the impression that the level has risen since then. He even has a memory of his own hands in the water at some point while he was making the hiding place.'

Sture explained that he had 'taken a few stones from the rail embankment which he had used to cover the place up. In a previous interview, he had stated that the stones were smooth and rounded. He explained that he could not drive all the way there because the road had been closed with a bar across it. When asked if he could walk the last few metres and point more exactly to the place he has in mind, he said that he did not dare.'[295]

Sture had indicated a hiding place somewhere below the waterline, leaving the technicians with an entire stream to search. With that information, the group drove back to Säter.

The eighth and last interview before the holiday period was carried out over the phone. Penttinen wanted to check where the hiding place was meant to be before his men started digging. This is his account of the exchange:

> Quick describes that, in connection with his intention to hide Johan's hand, he dug a hollow at the waterline by the bank of the stream. The depth was said to be about 30 to 40 centimetres. When he had placed the hand in the hollow, he covered it with stones approx. the size of a fist. The wall of stones thus formed would, according to Quick, prevent a strong current from washing the hand away. At least, he claims it is likely that the hand would not be affected by such circumstances and shift from its initial position. He experiences the ground he is digging in as a mixture of soil and stones.[296]

The police technicians went to the stream and dug but found nothing, not a trace of either the hand or the 'hiding place'. By this time it was June and Sture had been interviewed for a total of thirteen hours, but his account could not be matched to verifiable facts or circumstances. Sture had had no idea how the boy had been dressed; the corpse was not where he had said it would be; he was neither licensed or capable of driving a car until seven years after the events and it had turned out that the person Sture claimed to have borrowed the car from had not owned a car of that type at the time. His story changed with every interview and he never referred to the old versions of his narrative. It should have been obvious that he was lying. The investigation should have been closed in May 1993 at the latest; Sture could have carried on fantasizing in the therapy sessions and the 'Quick scandal' would never have happened. But Christer van der Kwast and Seppo Penttinen did not think or act the way a prosecutor and a police officer should.

During my work on this book, I spoke with Christer van der Kwast for many hours. Although he is now retired, he has been hard at work fighting to stop the retrial applications since they began in 2009. He has mostly refused to grant interviews and only agreed to see me because a person who had been close to Margit introduced us. Van der Kwast thought that I intended to defend the treatment that Sture had received at Säter. During one of our conversations, I asked him what he thought about the professionalism shown by the senior staff at Säter in 1993 and he replied:

My impression is that those people are sensible and well qualified. I suppose everyone can misjudge things, one way or the other, but in my view, well, you have to have a theoretical base for what you set out to do. That there was something in this idea about memories of a traumatic nature that might have some validity. And it's surely acceptable when it comes to other kinds of traumatic events that people find it more or less difficult to . . . well, one tries to put unpleasant memories out of one's mind but they might emerge again in the context of therapy and so forth.

I asked him about the first eight interviews with Sture. How did the two doctors explain that Sture should be believed even though he changed his story constantly, remembered nothing about his victim and failed to identify a single place where the body parts had been hidden? Van der Kwast tended to express himself in a curious, rather bureaucratic style. This was his answer:

What was conveyed was, in what you might term a general understanding, that he experienced real difficulties when trying to

248

approach his memories. That he had to circle the real event and get closer to it by giving out information which was incorrect in the precise sense. He crept up on it, if I may use that expression. He didn't dare to approach it immediately. I suppose he wanted to grasp people's reactions to get a sense of how far he could go. This is more or less how I understood the explanation. That he was so deeply anxious he couldn't bear to speak in factual terms straightaway, about what had been the actual case. Instead, he had to make this circling approach.

Van der Kwast did not realize it but he was in fact describing Margit's views of how repressed memories return during the course of therapeutic treatment.

During our talks, van der Kwast referred to Säter's 'explanatory model', which he had assumed had some kind of scientific basis. He felt that he had no choice but to trust Kjell Persson and Göran Fransson:

I mean, look at it the other way. If, as a prosecutor, I had come out with something like 'No, no, this is psychobabble' – that's how lots of people put it, you know, just psychobabble – 'we needn't take any notice of it. Quick is all over the place and never says anything halfway sensible.' What if I had ignored the whole thing and he had turned out to be a serial killer?! I mean, what would the judgement of me have been then? I would have ridden roughshod over the ideas of a well-established profession with many, many years' experience and ignored the psychiatrists' interpretation of the situation. People would have gone straight for my throat, I'd say!

I had to admit he was right. With no expertise in psychology or psychiatry, how could van der Kwast dismiss the passionate conviction of two senior doctors? One wonders how he would have reacted to Sture's murder confessions in the absence of the 'Säter model'. I took the risk of him realizing that I was better informed about the Quick investigations than I had let on, and listed a whole series of contradictory statements and other absurdities from the first eight police interviews. Among other things, I mentioned the change of a knife murder into strangulation. In normal circumstances, I asked, how would he, as a prosecutor, have reacted to such a change? He did not like this much and his answers became a little more heated: 'Goodness, don't ask me. I'm no expert on that kind of thing! It might be the result of a vivid imagination, or wishful thinking and maybe mixing up past events . . . I can't start—'

I interrupted him: 'But, what would have been the simplest explanation, for a prosecutor, or a policeman, if we ignore the psychological models for a moment? Here is a man who had confessed a murder but after a few months knifing is changed to strangling. What is the most straightforward explanation?'

Reluctantly, he admitted that 'our man is lying, of course. No question about it.'

When I interviewed Göran Fransson, I asked him if he thought that van der Kwast had been impressed by his and Persson's strong convictions. Fransson replied, very softly: 'Sure . . . what else could he do?'

In 1994, Göran Fransson was full of admiration for the prosecutor. He even wrote a think piece about Thomas Quick's therapy for *Dagens Nyheter*. Among other arguments, he felt that, given that Quick had confessed to the murder of Johan Asplund, Christer van der Kwast had 'probably had to face the hardest test so far in his career as prosecutor' but that he came through it with flying colours:

Despite the healthy scepticism he showed initially, he soon realized that the basis for this investigation had to be a close collaboration with Quick's therapist, Dr Kjell Persson, the psychiatrist in charge of the patient, i.e. myself, the police and the prosecution service. I am impressed by this prosecutor who made possible a criminal investigation that will be of historic interest and the details of which can only be published at a later stage.[297]

Christer van der Kwast's fateful error was that he trusted the medical expertise at Säter. Instead of cancelling the investigation, he and

Seppo Penttinen accepted, without further reservations, a self-confirming system of thought which meant that Sture was guilty of murder, however contradictory his confessions. They had been converted. However, in May 1993, Christer van der Kwast had come up against a major problem. For two months, he had been hinting in public statements that Sture would soon find Johan Asplund's corpse and now the journalists wanted to know why nothing had been found. He needed to buy time.

A news item on the Säter story was broadcast by SVT on 28 May 1993. The reporter explained that the police, despite intensive efforts to find Johan Asplund, had not identified 'the slightest technical evidence' at the sites identified by the 'Säter man'. The camera cut to van der Kwast at his desk. He was clean-shaven, his hair was crew-cut and he was not wearing his glasses. He looked more like a bureaucrat and less like the cool investigator of the newspaper piece.

'What is your view of the so-called Säter man's story?' the reporter asked. 'In your view, does it hang together?' Van der Kwast leaned back and looked towards the ceiling as he replied: 'Yes, at a superficial level it is plausible in the sense that it is coherent, it is structured and it contains details that suggest he is speaking about events he has experienced personally. Also, his story doesn't contain any contradictory statements of the type that would make you immediately conclude he was lying.'[298]

So said van der Kwast to his Swedish viewers. He was lying but surely believed that he had lied in the service of a greater truth. There was no point in going into detail about the explanatory psychological model; the public just wouldn't get it. It was easier to give them what they needed – the assurance that Sture was believable in a conventional sense. They would surely thank him for it if he caught a killer.

The psychological model remained central for the rest of the 'Quick years'. It would be the basis for every interview, every re-enactment and every court case. Margit must have been pleased. Rational, evidence-based thinking had been abandoned in favour of her 'getting a feel of what's true', not only in the forensic psychiatric unit at Säter but also in the Swedish legal system. She was eighty-one years old and on the road to public vindication.

As for Sture, repressed memories dominated his summer in 1993. When Persson took his holiday, he made sure that his stand-in was one of the faithful. Lena Arvidsson had nearly completed her psychology course and had been offered a temporary post as a psychologist at Säter for the first time. One of her first patients was Sture, her friend, incest survivor and serial killer.

19

Margit's theory

*'To be able to remember is a gift. To be able to help others to
remember is an even greater gift.'*
Lena Arvidsson, letter to Sture Bergwall,
18 August 1993.

The more I learnt about Margit, the more her strange talents fascinated
me. What was it about her that made her pupils give up thinking for
themselves and become, in spirit, her children? The photos in the
family albums offered no clues; all I could see was a little lady with
permed hair. While out jogging I would listen to recordings of her
voice speaking at group meetings. Her tremendous self-assurance was
striking, as was her authoritative manner of addressing her audience,
but I still couldn't get my head around why everyone should have
capitulated to her so abjectly.

Margit's daughter let me have a video of Margit, the only one in
existence as far as I know. It is an interview by Patricia Tudor-Sandahl
from 1991, part of a project meant to document Swedish pioneers of
psychoanalysis. The interview lasts forty-five minutes and was
recorded in what looks like a bleak waiting room. Throughout, Margit
is seated with her legs resting on a low stool while Patricia sits next to
her, trying to ask her prepared questions. She hardly gets a word in
edgewise, because Margit has brought a notebook with her prepared
speech written down. Her voice is full of dignity as she gives an
account of her life. She then goes on to speak about the tensions
between rival schools of thought in psychoanalysis. Clearly Margit
believes that she has all the answers. Her voice becomes somewhat
plaintive when she refers to those who have not seen the light. She

hopes, she says, that the younger generation, her pupils, who share her insights into how 'real therapy' should be conducted, will base their future work on what they have learnt. She never explains exactly how 'real therapy' should be conducted, as if the concept is a mysterious truth which cannot be conveyed in words. Patricia is never less than deeply respectful to her.

I have watched the film several times. I want to understand but have had to give up. What went on in the relationships that Margit forged with her acolytes cannot be experienced from the outside.

To Margit, that Sture was a murderer had never been a primary concern. The therapeutic aim was as much to make him recall memories of childhood abuse as to remember his alleged murders. Fundamentally, Sture was just another patient among the many lined up to recover memories of early incest with Margit's help. As Persson wrote in the case notes in May 1993:

Since the previous entry, the therapy has been exceptionally stormy because the patient has been gripped by strong, painful emotions as he relived terrible situations of childhood fear. A picture of a deeply disturbed family emerged. Pat. was subjected to extremely serious abuse by both parents, situations in which at least one sibling – an older brother – was involved at the same time. [...] furthermore, terrible experiences of fear have also emerged as pat. recalls childhood episodes when his mother came close to killing him. The most serious of these took place during the winter, an attempted drowning in Lake Runn. For pat. the most traumatic events apparently happened at about the age of 3–5, though the sexual abuse continued after this age but with somewhat less intensity.[299]

When Sture's brothers and sisters were interviewed, none of them could recall any abusive behaviour towards Sture or anyone else in the Bergwall home. This was no obstacle to Margit, who doubtless thought that the siblings were either protective of their parents or, like Sture, had repressed their memories.

Margit never developed any theories of her own but collected ideas from many different sources, modified them and incorporated the results into her world view. She combined psychoanalytical concepts taken from Sigmund Freud, Frieda Fromm-Reichmann and Erich Fromm with developmental psychology precepts from British object relations theoreticians such as Winnicott, Fairbairn and Guntrip. Like Freud before 1897, she placed extreme emphasis on 'repressed' sexual abuse in childhood. The outcome was a theoretical patchwork that she erroneously called 'British object relations theory', though none of the originators of that system of thought would have recognized their ideas in Margit's theories or in her clinical practice.

One of the lynchpins of Margit's thinking was actually her own invention. She assumed that Sture's murder or murders were what she called 're-enactments'. In a sense, the patient's symptoms were in a way theatrical performances, symbolic representations of abusive episodes that 'embodied' what had happened to them long ago.

These past events had been repressed and could not be remembered; the need to re-enact would disappear only when the repressed memories had been recovered.

Margit was already formulating this concept when she first worked with Barbro Sandin on what was to become the Säter model. They thought that the strange behaviour exhibited by the schizophrenic patients were unconscious narratives about abuse that they had been subjected to in childhood. Sverker Belin was one of the therapists supervised by Margit at the time, who would later write a book called *Treatments of Schizophrenia* in which he explained the function of representations of the past.[300] He describes the behaviour of a schizophrenic patient who, at the age of three, was chased by other children and accidently drove his tricycle down some basement steps. At Säter, he was often seen wheeling himself along on an office chair that he would crash into the walls again and again. Belin interprets this as the patient's unconscious way of telling the psychotherapist about the trauma on the basement steps. Margit believed that Sture's murders had the same function and were his way of telling the world about what had happened to him when he was a child. In her unpublished book, she analyses Sture as follows:

All that remains for a child with experiences as terrifying as Sture's is complete repression and then re-enacting – in happier circumstances, it can take place in the sandpit during child therapy and, in less happy cases, find expression in perversions. [...] In his murders, Sture has represented what M [*Mum*] and D [*Dad*] did to him. The boys stand in for Sture as he also has exposed them to what Ellington [*a name used for Sture's father during the therapy*] and M had done to him.[301]

Early in his career, Sigmund Freud believed that when his patients behaved emotionally during therapy sessions they were 're-enacting' their repressed sexual experiences as young children.[302] Margit's take on this was to see re-enactments as a kind of symbolic re-telling. This might have been a development of something that the psychologist Alice Miller wrote about in her second book, *For Your Own Good: Hidden cruelty in child-rearing and the roots of violence*.[303] Miller analyses Adolf Hitler's childhood, claiming that, to him, the Second World War was his re-telling of the trauma of growing up under the control of an authoritarian father who beat him with his belt. In the same book, she discusses her interview in prison with the German serial killer Jürgen Bartsch. He had begun his killing spree in 1961, when he was only sixteen years old. He raped, killed and butchered five young boys before he was caught in 1966. According to Alice Miller, Bartsch had been locked up as a child, something he retold symbolically by locking his victims in an old bunker before killing them and carving them up.

For Your Own Good was included in the reading list Margit had drawn up for her pupils in the early 1980s and it seems likely that she might have been influenced by it. But, for her, every single moment in a traumatized person's life was the equivalent of a symbolic tale about specific childhood events. This hypothesis is so outlandish that it can be regarded as her personal contribution to the theory.

Sture had had the re-enactment theory explained to him by his therapists and he was keen to use it in his writing about himself. This, for instance, is a passage from September 1994: 'I have told it in the shape of re-enactments, and am convinced that every detail contained within my killings has its exact equivalent in what M and Dad exposed me to, in every detail and the nuance of every detail!'[304]

This theory generated interesting explanations of why Sture's accounts of his murder were so vague. For example, in a piece of writing from March 1993, intended for Persson, Sture explains why he could not remember what Johan Asplund had been wearing. He felt that the murder represented – symbolically re-told – a terrifying episode from when he was a toddler and Tyra, his mother, had tried to drown him in an ice-hole. He wrote that this was an event he had tried to approach mentally 'for several months':

On Friday night I woke, terror-stricken. I had seen Johan's face in a dream. I sit up, force myself fully awake. Then the memory of the hole in the ice emerges and I feel anguished. [. . .] I don't know if it was in the morning or at night but my M carries me outside and puts me down on a kick-sled. I sit turned towards her. When she kicks off, I feel she does it angrily so I sit very still. I sneak glances at her and see some black, stiff and angry tufts of hair. I think maybe we are going to town but instead we arrive at a place with a big house. The image in my mind is so clear that I now know which house it was and hence the place: it was the Främby promontory. She stops, takes out a knife that in my eyes looks awfully large and says something I can't catch. But I remember her final sentence: 'Sture, I have to kill you.'

Oh, how scared I was. As suddenly as she produced the knife, she drops it on the ground, grabs me, walks out onto the ice and then she says: 'Your dad must have some peace.' There is a gap in the ice and the black water is frightening. M pulls off my mittens and hat, and keeps saying: 'Your dad must have some peace.' He had started to abuse me sexually by then. She leads me towards the ice-hole.

Sture's mother had pushed her child into the ice-cold water, but regretted her decision at the last moment and pulled him out. He couldn't remember what Johan was wearing when he murdered him because he was re-telling the ice-hole event; his mind was in the 1950s and all he saw was what his mother had worn: 'I couldn't describe Johan's clothes, the anguish I felt was too much, and the interview was interrupted. Then, it wasn't Johan's clothes I saw and I still didn't in the '80s. I saw my mother's greyish-black, wet coat.'[305]

The doctors were convinced of the validity of Margit's 're-telling' hypothesis. In May 1993, Persson wrote in the case notes:

> In parallel with the emergence of these bizarre memories [of child-hood abuse] that at times seem very lucid, the memories of the murder of Johan Asplund also become clearer. In therapy, the ini-tial images of this act seemed to be dream-like fantasies but, eventually, they separated out into single, precisely remembered scenes. He has worked on his memories of childhood horrors and of the Asplund murder, until both sets of images have successively become woven together so that the act of killing appear to be a psychological re-enactment of his childhood situation with several aspects open for analysis.[306]

Sture was seen to be vindicating Margit's repressed memory theory and was generously rewarded. As Säter's new star, he was paid bound-less attention and fed increasing quantities of tranquillizers. Benzodiazepines have effects analogous to alcohol, so Sture was in an almost constant state of baseline intoxication and sometimes became seriously affected. He felt that he rather deserved these highs because he was doing so well in his therapy sessions. His status was further established when, in August 1993, he was allowed to move into a rel-atively spacious flat, two rooms and a small kitchen, in the unstaffed ward 37, which had the most relaxed regime of all. Now, like Svartenbrandt before him, he could come and go as he pleased, using his own key card. If he wanted to talk to staff, all he needed to do was knock on the door to ward 36.

Occasionally Sture would travel to Stockholm to have a cup of coffee and watch a film with Lena Arvidsson. Her summer job at Säter had brought them closer and, in August 1993, she wrote to him: 'The days in Säter mattered a lot to me personally but were also important for my future as a psychologist. My views on people and my understanding of them were strengthened, and I feel my road ahead is clear. Oh dear, that sounded religious, but then it is about faith in the good in people and the healing power of the soul.'

Lena had met members of staff at Säter who were not believers:

All of us who work there really want to make a difference but one sometimes sees such a lack of insight and knowledge that people miss out on real understanding of the patients' issues. It frightens me and I feel it's important that I stay strong and stick to my purpose. It's easy to be feeble but my conviction is so terribly strong and really anchored so I will never waver. My ideals are so integrated into me as a person they are part of me. I <u>am</u> my conviction, if you see what I mean.

She had only two terms left of her psychology course before she could set out to help others, a dream she expressed poetically: 'To be able to remember is a gift. To be able to help others to remember is an even greater gift.'

She told Sture about her visit to a Stockholm society of incest survivors, where she had met a woman who had been the group's leader but had not received any help in dealing with her repressed memories:

This girl I met [...] had been given v. bad therapy – hardly any, in fact. She <u>knows</u> she was abused but can't remember, and there has been no help for her. [...] The need [for] good therapists is simply desperate. [...] I'll try to work out what this society can offer people. At least, it represents a patient sector that I could earn a living from. I wouldn't go unemployed any time soon. [...] I'm enclosing some info about it if you're interested. As yet, they don't organize any activities for men (though it is under discussion) but men are welcome to join.[307]

Although Sture was thought to be a serial killer, Lena did not primarily regard him as a criminal and a perpetrator, but as a survivor of incest and a victim. As she construed the world, she and Sture were fighting side by side for the right to remember their past. Sture willingly took on the identity Lena had set up for him. He wrote in a letter to her:

How happy it makes me to know that you exist, Lena, that I can write to you, wait for your letters which let me see your honesty, your unclouded will and your views on therapy and your decisive preparedness to stand up for the patient. You see clearly how important it is to remember and that the memories that emerge during therapy are important and must be taken seriously. I share these views with you 100 per cent. Of course, if you had belonged to the other school of thought it wouldn't have been possible to write to you like this; then I would have felt constrained to adjust my communication with you according to your thinking. [. . .] While I still live, perhaps I can extract something valuable for others from my actions as an adult. I can't reconcile myself to all the evil I have done, as little as I can forgive and forget the evil done by my parents, but I can and will speak out about what my childhood was like, show, as clearly as possible, that my anguish in adulthood and its driving force, its destructive force, is the anguish I felt as a child, the anguish that my parents handed on to their little son.[308]

Sture had told Lena about a collection of poems that he was working on. She was writing her examination essay on the therapy at Säter and offered to ask her departmental supervisor, the Margit acolyte Hanna Olsson, if she would be willing to use her contacts to find the right publisher for Sture's book. Sture thought this was a fantastic suggestion. He had dreamt of being a writer since he was at school and now the dream might come true. Admittedly, the circumstances were a little unusual – his poetry was about his life as a serial killer and his heroic battle to recover his long-lost memories. Whatever, it would be a real book!

Sture has told me that, in the autumn of 1993, he had not grasped that his confession of the murder of Johan Asplund could have serious consequences for him. He saw the move to ward 37 as a voucher for tangible advantages that would follow the advances in his therapy. For a long time, I found this hard to take. How could anyone be so naive? This was why I read a letter to Sture from Lena Arvidsson that autumn with mounting fascination. She was summing up Sture's current situation and concluded that his life was pretty good: 'You are so well fixed now [. . .] living in 37 and feeling very much at home, or so I think. Besides, you hope to buy a dog . . . and I realize just how much a dog can mean.'[309]

I had to read this passage several times. Sture had always been fond of dogs and, in the 1980s, he had owned several. In late 1993, he seems to have been planning to buy another one, which suggests that he regarded his small flat in ward 37 more or less as his permanent residence, the place where he would hole up and write the book that Hanna Olsson would help him publish. When he was not writing or in therapy, he could use his unlimited leave to take his dog walking in the forest. This scenario for the future was, of course, absurd – he had just come out as an insatiable killer and a butcher of corpses. But Lena Arvidsson, judging by what she wrote, thought his vision of the future perfectly realistic. She ought to know, given that she had been working at Säter over the summer. The amazing conclusion must be that Sture had reasons to believe that admitting to murder would propel him into a quality of life that he would not have been able to sustain outside Säter hospital.

There was, however, one fly in the ointment. Even though Christer van der Kwast had stated on TV that the murder confession was believable, the doctors – Sture's only friends but also his masters – were very keen to make him show them where he had hidden Johan's dismembered body. In fact, they insisted. He needed to reduce the pressure but be smart about it, or else he might lose his status and the privileges that went with it. He definitely did not want to be kicked out of Säter. Why, he was going to get himself a dog and become a writer.

One day, he had an idea. It was time to box clever.

20

A hypnotic trip in a time machine

'The patient at Säter is not subjected to actual interrogations and instead enquiries are carried out as part of talking therapy with both medical experts and police interviewer present.'
Christer van der Kwast in a Swedish news agency
interview, 11 November 1993.

Sture had confessed to the murder of the fourteen-year-old Thomas Blomgren, a case that had been unsolved for almost thirty years, soon after claiming to have killed Johan Asplund. The Thomas Blomgren case had been extensively reported but all Sture could remember was the victim's name and that the murder had been committed some-where in Småland. In his 1992 letter to Kjell Persson, he claimed to have torn open Thomas's neck with his teeth and eaten the victim's anal sphincter. A bit steep, perhaps. But, at the time, he had not thought for a moment he would be questioned by the police.

In the first set of interviews the police had asked very little about the Blomgren murder. He had guessed that he killed the boy in Alvesta or Ljunga, two small towns near Växjö. He stated that he was driven the whole 500-odd kilometres by an older friend who had a black Borgward Isabella. The car's owner existed and had driven that kind of car, but Thomas Blomgren had been killed in Växjö. When Sture had not even been able to get the place right, the interviewers had put the Blomgren murder aside and concentrated on the more recent Asplund case.

Sture planned to put the Blomgren murder back on the agenda that autumn. He would do some research and stun everyone by recovering accurate memories. He reckoned he'd be safe enough as, according to the Swedish statute of limitations, the case was closed. Sture could claim to have killed and get the attention he craved without having to risk a trial. Once the investigating team had a reasonably realistic murder confession on their hands they would surely stop going on about that crazy Asplund story.

At the end of August, Sture took a day's leave and went by train to Stockholm to do a little reading in the City Library. He ordered microfilms of newspaper articles and read up on Thomas Blomgren. Like Sture, Thomas had been fourteen in 1964. On the evening of his murder, he had gone to Folkets Park in Växjö to watch a performance on the open-air stage. He had not returned and his body was discovered the following day in a tool shed halfway between the park and his home. He had been strangled. The perpetrator was never identified and the killing had remained a mystery. Sture travelled back to Säter with this new information.[310]

One Thursday night a few weeks later, Dr Persson phoned investigative officer Seppo Penttinen at home. What he had to say could not wait.

The next day, Penttinen wrote a neat report of what he had learnt: Sture had made a sensational breakthrough in his therapy. He had recovered detailed memories of how he had picked up Thomas Blomgren 'in Växjö, near a dance pavilion or something similar' and that the act had taken place 'between hawthorns and lilacs'. Sture also recalled that he had hidden the body 'in some kind of outbuilding, there there were lots of tools in it'. Penttinen noted that these pieces of information 'could be corroborated with the police records and seem correct'. He added that Sture had allegedly worked 'to extract the truth while under an on-going therapeutic regime'. The doctor had been quite impressed: 'Persson also states quite definitively that "if he might previously have had doubts about the veracity of Quick's recollections, these were by now completely dismissed both with regard to the Växjö end of the story and the murder of Johan".'[311]

The atmosphere at Säter was triumphant. Persson wrote almost lyrically about the new result in the case notes:

[Sture] has dived very deeply into times past to retrieve certain events from his childhood and youth. These deep explorations have resulted in a seamless whole insofar as all memory sequences have been accessible and include the actual events, the patient's thoughts at the time, sensory inputs such as smells, recollections of what the patient said and what other people said and so on. The outcome was that pat. has remembered the circumstances when he, at the age of 14, was in Växjö and murdered another 14-year-old boy called Thomas. [. . .] It would appear that pat. can be linked to this crime with certainty, which is a remarkable fact.[312]

Margit must have felt just as deeply satisfied with the way things were turning out. In 1977, she had lectured on regressions in which the patient could 'reconnect to intense, primary and early experiences complete with a wealth of smells and colours'.[313] Now a consultant psychiatrist at Säter, under her supervision, was describing how Sture had regressed to 1964 and relived 'sensory inputs such as smells'. Margit's therapeutic technique, inspired by Sigmund Freud's methodology from the 1890s, had exposed a serial killer. She was getting her own back at last.

Persson was enormously pleased with Sture's efforts: 'His will to get on with the work is intense. He feels very secure in the vicinity of the ward staff and his immediate contacts, while at the same time the relative freedom offered by ward 37 and the option of occasional all-day leave means a lot to him.'[314]

Penttinen's interview with Sture was also pleasing. With a decisiveness that Penttinen hadn't even glimpsed in the earlier interviews, Sture stated that he had, in 1964, gone to Växjö to pick up a boy, that he had spotted Thomas in 'a park setting, but with a dance pavilion and lottery stalls', that he had strangled the boy outside the park and hidden the corpse in an outbuilding which he recalled in some detail (the shed had been pictured in one of the articles he had read in the library). Sture became quite inspired as he elaborated on his story. He said that he and Thomas had hung out for a couple of hours before the murder and had left the park together. Sture's initial idea had been a sexual assault but the man who had driven him to Växjö had stopped him. Instead he strangled the boy and hid the body in the shed before being driven to Falun.

As usual, Persson was seated next to Sture during the interview and became so excited by his success that he started to speak in the middle of the interview about how memories were retrieved in therapy. He addressed Sture as he explained: 'My impression is that [. . .] when all this emerged, these memory fragments [. . .] you were inside these events and that you relive them [. . .] so that it's almost like a hypnotic trip in a time machine. [. . .] I just let it run, right, [. . .] and listen and follow you, connect to your very strong feelings [. . .] and you say things [. . .] speaking as if you were there.'

Penttinen thought that the excitable consultant's words might be relevant to his investigation and asked if Sture could go on a 'hypnotic trip in a time machine' during the police interviews. Sture said that it probably wouldn't work and Persson agreed: 'It can't be done.'[315]

Persson was also able to explain that Sture's deep anxiety could interfere with memory recovery: 'You are struck down with anguish sometimes and then you fight the past.'

Sture had delivered verifiable details and van der Kwast had proof that his decision to trust the doctors' 'explanatory model' had been correct, even wise. As he said to me:

Blomgren cropped up pretty soon and that became a kind of diversion that made us take our eyes off the ball, that is, finding out who killed Johan. I mean, it provided [Sture] with an opportunity to speak up, as it were, a bit more to the point, because this was a victim that had been found so it was a straightforward way to make a statement that could actually be corroborated with what had been recorded at the time [. . .]. And that of course confirmed that he was on the right track concerning factual matters. Which in turn led to my conclusion that the Johan case perhaps shouldn't be shelved after all.

Sture had hoped that his clever plan would shift attention away from the hopeless confession about Johan Asplund. Instead, the opposite happened. By producing verifiable details about the murder, Sture had validated the Säter 'explanatory model'. The outcome was a boost for the belief that he was Johan Asplund's killer.

Penttinen tried to interview Sture about Johan Asplund late the very same day, but the results were disppointing. Previously, Sture's pitch was that Johan's body – less the hands and head but together with large stones – had been placed in a cardboard box and thrown into the river from the Sandö Bridge. Now, Sture changed his story again. Penttinen reported this:

> He stopped the car but when he tried to lift the box the bottom fell out. The cause was that it had been soaked in blood. Sture still threw the box, with the stones and the clothes, over the railing of the bridge. He also threw the saw in the river. Johan's body, that is, his torso, legs and arms, are still in the boot of the car as Sture drives south. He believes he hid these parts near Ryggen, to the east of Falun. This is in other words close to the place which, at a previous re-enactment walk, he identified as the place where one of Johan's hands was hidden.

Neither the hand nor the 'sacred hiding place' had been found anywhere near Ryggen, but now the whole body – less the head and one hand – was supposed to be in the same place. It was preposterous, but the Säter faithful could handle preposterousness with ease.

On Tuesday 2 November 1993, Sture felt like a pizza and walked to the town centre. The newsagents' posters were screaming about the latest on the 'Säter man': he had murdered Thomas Blomgren, according to a leaked story. Sture was so distressed that he phoned the ward and asked to be picked up. Before returning to his rooms, he was given an extra tranquillizer tablet (Xanax) to help him calm down.[316]

A few days later, van der Kwast called a press conference, which was broadcast on TV, to deliver some sensational news. The murder of Thomas Blomgren in Växjö, a thirty-year-old unsolved case, was now solved: 'In a normal situation – that is, if the crime had not been written off under our current statute of limitations and the criminal not been a minor – I would not have hesitated about bringing the case to court on presently available information. I feel justified in drawing this conclusion.'[317]

Lena Arvidsson followed the media coverage carefully and wrote an encouraging letter to Sture:

I have just read in the evening paper about you. It feels so odd and unreal, I realize that there is much going on at your end just now and that you have much to think through. Despite all those hard things you have to cope. I hope you feel hopeful and dare believe in the future. But, what a fucking (sorry) awful, <u>hellish</u> time you must have endured as a child, why, it's a wonder you're still alive!!!!!!!! [. . .] You must be a very strong person who can face up to all that!!!! You will have every support I can give you in this process!![318]

During the next eight years, van der Kwast was to repeat frequently that, in effect, the Blomgren murder case had been solved and that Sture was the murderer. Immediately after the press conference, he told the TT news agency that Sture 'had been proven' to have killed Thomas Blomgren.[319] In June 1994, he stated in *Expressen* that this murder mystery was solved.[320] Half a year later, he said so again to *Dala-Demokraten*,[321] and then again, in March 1996, to *Göteborgs-Posten*.[322] In December 2001, when Sture had been convicted of his eighth murder, *Dala-Demokraten* featured an interview with the prosecutor:

'At the start of the on-going investigation, the investigative team made a thorough examination of the available information in the 1964 murder of Thomas Blomgren in Växjö, an unsolved case that had been closed for some time. As such, this was a very unusual action. It should be regarded as a test run, to see if the case could be solved. At the time, we found so much that I could have prosecuted and expected a judgement for the prosecution, had not the case been closed under the statute of limitation,' van der Kwast says.[323]

However, his 'thorough examination of the available information' was a falsehood. On the day of van der Kwast's press conference, the investigative team questioned Sture's alleged driver in 1964, the acquaintance who had owned a black Borgward Isabella. He was able to prove that he had bought that car a year after Blomgren's murder, so Sture had lied about how he got to Växjö. The interviews with the wrongly accused driver were kept secret for sixteen years, hidden in an off-the-record document box inside Penttinen's office in the Sundsvall police headquarters. He did not admit that the box existed until interviewed by an officer in the team set up to investigate the 2009 retrial application. When he finally handed thirteen folders of documents over, it was found that several of them contained evidence indicating that Sture Bergwall was not guilty of murders of which he had been convicted.[324]

The interviews with the alleged driver were not van der Kwast's only problem. It was even more troubling that Sture had an alibi for the murder. Thomas Blomgren had been killed on the eve of the Whitsun holiday (6 May 1964), the weekend that Sture and his twin sister Gun had been confirmed. Because the Bergwall family was 'chapel', the twins were baptized at their confirmation. It was a major family celebration and the ceremony had continued throughout Saturday and Sunday. Thomas Blomgren had been killed on the Saturday night. It would have taken about six and a half hours to drive from Falun to Växjö. In order to commit the murder, fourteen-year-old Sture would have had to leave his family immediately after his confirmation and baptism proceedings, travelled to Växjö in an unspecified car, committed the first murder in his life at around 11 p.m. and then gone back home to continue with the Sunday church service after a twelve or thirteen hour absence. It was utterly implausible. However, no one seems to have known about the alibi until 2008, when Sture told Hannes Råstam.

In 2008, Hannes interviewed Christer van der Kwast on TV and confronted the prosecutor with evidence that the murder weekend had coincided with Sture's confirmation in 1964. Van der Kwast stubbornly refused to admit that Sture had an alibi. At the time of Hannes's death three years later, van der Kwast was still claiming that the Blomgren murder had been solved.

I was curious about this and wondered if van der Kwast would be prepared to repeat to my face that Sture had murdered Thomas Blomgren. We talked in the autumn of 2012. Hannes had been dead for nine months. I asked van der Kwast if we could meet and invited him over to my place. He agreed and so one day sat in my kitchen where I had laid on coffee and buns. Because of my cover story as a Margit admirer, we spent some time vilifying the retrial process. Then I said that, as a journalist, I wanted to play devil's advocate and ask a few critical questions. Was it true that Sture had been confirmed in Falun during the murder weekend?

'Yes, indeed,' van der Kwast replied. 'But he could have fitted in the return trip to Växjö between Saturday afternoon and Sunday morning.'

Would his family not have noticed that the boy had disappeared, what with it being such a big family celebration – both confirmation and baptism?

'Normally, I would have agreed completely,' he replied. 'But Quick isn't normal and his family seemed far from normal.'

'Rather a long time to be away,' I mused.

'There was quite a long interval,' van der Kwast insisted. 'They finished the first part [of the confirmation] on [Saturday] afternoon and then nothing happened until noon the following day. There's time enough.'

'But how far is it? It is Falun to Växjö . . .'

'It's quite a distance but it can be done. Naturally, we checked that,' van der Kwast said.

'Sure, it can be done. But look, he was fourteen years old! He couldn't drive a car at the time. He must have found someone willing to drive him, in the middle of the confirmation . . .'

I had actually given up but then, suddenly, van der Kwast changed tack completely. Perhaps it was because I mentioned the car, which must have been a sensitive matter. He leaned back in his chair, looked a little pained and said, in a tone of self-criticism that I had never heard before: 'The only unfortunate statement I blame myself for is that I, in a tired moment, claimed that I would have prosecuted if the case had not been formally closed. That was untrue. Well, in the sense that . . . had I been in that position, I would certainly have taken the investigation to quite another stage of completion. So, I really regret having said that. Only a half-truth, and in a tired moment. But it was a stupid thing to say.'

There, in my kitchen, Christer van der Kwast admitted that Hannes Råstam had been right about the Blomgren murder.

I have been thinking hard about what van der Kwast's motive had been when he insisted that Sture was already a killer at fourteen. I don't believe that it was cynicism; rather that the medics' 'explanatory model' had inspired the hope that he would be the one to solve the Asplund murder – and that meant he wanted to keep the murder investigation going at any cost. Once, speaking with him on the phone, he told me that the Asplund case, unsolved after twelve years, had been like an 'infected abscess' – and then Sture had confessed. The doctors had assured him that, sooner or later, Sture would recover the memory of where the boy's body had been buried. Van de Kwast bought time by sticking to what seemed like a 'white lie': that Sture 'had been proven' to have committed an out-of-date murder, a confession that was never actually properly investigated.

What *was* proven was that van der Kwast had lied about the Blomgren murder being solved and that he repeated the lie over the years. His insistence meant that, after the 1993 press conference, it was widely regarded as a self-evident truth that Sture had been a teenage killer. In the eyes of the Swedish people, his guilt was established and he could do nothing about it.

'I was playing all sorts of tricks with Thomas Blomgren and all that,' Sture said to me. 'And then I stumbled over my own trip-wire somehow. I lost control over the trickery.'

There was no way out of the network of lies he had constructed. The monstrous Thomas Quick had sprung into life. 'To avoid becoming totally depressed, I went in for it wholesale,' he said. 'Everything was such a mess anyway. No need to worry about being called "murderer" because I already was, as it were. It sounds weird, but there was a kind of relief to be had in that.'

Sture confessed to more murders. In November, *Dala-Demokraten* published an article headlined IS HE SWEDEN'S FIRST TRUE SERIAL KILLER? A local reporter called Gubb Jan Stigson revealed that the Säter man had already confessed to five murders. Two days later, Christer van der Kwast was again interviewed by the Swedish news agency TT. He was happy to speak about how the new collaboration between the police and the medical staff had been developed at Säter: 'The patient at Säter is not subjected to actual interrogations and instead enquiries are carried out as part of talking therapy with both medical experts and police interviewer present.'[325]

The borderline between therapeutic interactions and formal interviews had been eliminated. All those involved, whether concerned with the therapy or with the interrogation, expected Sture to 'go into regression' and recover repressed memories. When Persson took Sture out for drives to try to hunt down corpse caches without a police presence, it was still part of the interview process. The pair of them wandered through the area around Ryggen looking for Johan's hand, visited the home of Sture's parents in Falun and rooted around for hiding places in another house in town where Sture had once lived.[326] Kjell Persson, Göran Fransson, Christer van der Kwast, Seppo Penttinen and, last but not least, Margit Norell, were all working towards the same goal: Sture should be made to remember.

For him, confessing to murder became a full-time occupation.

'New subjects came up all the time and everything had to be linked to my childhood,' he told me. 'I had no time to miss my brothers and sisters and their children because I had to stick to this task 24/7. I have said that I was stoned night and day. But I was working on this stuff night and day, too. For eight years.'

False confessions that are made voluntarily are sometimes called 'Lindbergh confessions', named after a kidnap drama involving the American pilot Charles Lindbergh's twenty-month-old son. The child vanished in New York in 1932. Lindbergh paid a large sum in ransom but his son was found murdered nonetheless. The deed was a vile infanticide, and yet more than 200 individuals stepped forward to claim they had killed the toddler.[327] The number of Lindbergh confessions tends to be directly proportional to the amount of publicity given to the crime. For instance, the murder of the Swedish Prime Minister Olof Palme has generated 130 false confessions in twenty-five years.[328]

The American Henry Lee Lucas probably holds the all-time record for false confessions. He was charged with illegal possession of arms in 1983 but when interrogated by the police he astonished them by admitting to one murder after another. He did not stop until he was on record as having committed approximately 600 murders. Lucas was convicted of several of them and died a natural death in prison in 2001. By then, he had already been examined by Professor Gísli Guðjónsson, a famous British forensic psychiatrist who subjected him to psychological testing. Guðjónsson, whose aim was to understand more about the urge to confess, presented several interesting explanations in accounts of his research.

Lucas had a personality disorder which enabled him to lie more fluently and credibly than most people. One of his most notable traits was, according to Guðjónsson, 'a total lack of interest in the long-term consequences of his actions' – the corollary was his willingness to say anything that might grant him short-term advantages. Lucas had very low self-esteem. He felt that he had never been respected by anyone. He was eager to impress and was unusually prone to trying to satisfy other people's needs in order to gain their approval. He valued the rewards brought by his confessions, including better living conditions in the institutions where he was held. Lucas 'confabulated' with exceptional ease. The term implies that he was very suggestible and able to make himself believe that he had actually been involved in events that he had dreamed up.

Henry Lee Lucas was sentenced to death but still claimed in interviews that he did not regret his false confessions. Guðjónsson wrote: 'His reasoning for this view is that prior to his arrest in 1983 he was "nobody", that is, he had no friends and nobody listened to him or took an interest in him. Once he began to make false confessions all that changed and he has thoroughly enjoyed his celebrity status and now has many friends.'[329]

When Sture's retrial process was under way, Guðjónsson planned to travel to Sweden and test this new subject just as he had tested Henry Lee Lucas. It did not happen but I can understand his interest. Sture shared many characteristics with Lucas, including a deep, existential loneliness. I found the following passage, written by Sture, in Margit's manuscript: 'I wanted to cry out: <u>Hello, do you know what it's like not to be loved, how indescribably hard it is to be hated?</u> Who loves me? No one. Who hates me? So many, many, many! In what can I take personal pride? Nothing! What respect can I claim at any time, from cradle to the present? None!'[330] (underlined in original)

It is the harsh reality of being a known serial killer that Sture despairs about here, but after I read his own words aloud to him and asked if they were also relevant to his situation when he arrived at Säter, he agreed with me. Sture had failed in most things and was alone in the world. By confessing to murder, he gained more or less the kind of material advantages that had been granted to Lucas. The doctors and the members of the murder investigation team treated him as a fascinating, even a historic, person. He did not need to worry about prison as he was already in forensic psychiatric care. What did one or more sentences for murder matter to him? Why stop confessing?

I have read the interview transcripts as well as the bulk of the other documents that were amassed around Sture's case between 1991 and 2001. It has enabled me to compile what I think is the only complete list of his confessions, tabled in approximately chronological order, based on when the murders were committed, or would have been committed in instances when the alleged victim is still alive or never existed. It reads as follows: Thomas Blomgren (1964); 'Lars, very young' (1965); Alvar Larsson (1967); 'The hospital boy' (1969); Reine Svensson (1971); 'Per' (1972); 'Björn' (1972–1974); 'Martin' (year unknown), 'The boy from Värmland County' (1975–1980); Charles Zelmanovits (1976); Benny Forsgren (1976); 'Michael' (after 1978); Johan Asplund (1980); Trine Jensen (1981); Marianne Rugaas

Knudsen, (1981); Magnus Nork (1981); 'Woman on the roadside' (1982), 'The car boy' (1982–1983); 'The Larvik affair' (1983–1984); Olle Högbom (1983); Marina and Janni Stegehuis (1984); 'Seventeen-year-old in Gävle' (1985); 'Duska' (1985); Magnus Johansson (1985); Gry Storvik (1985); 'Boy from Norway' (1985); 'West coast' (year unknown), Yenon Levi (1988); Therese Johannessen (1988); His brother Torvald's mother-in-law's sister (1989); 'Young boy' (1989); 'Boy from Norway 1' (1989); 'Boy from Norway 2' (1989); 'Tony' (1990); Örjan Sellin (1993); 'The event at Sätra Brunn' (year unknown); 'The Avesta affair' (year unknown) and 'Erik' (year unknown).

Sture confessed to thirty-nine murders. If his drugs had not been taken away from him in 2001 he would surely have added more names to the list.

Why stop?

21

The battle for the serial killer

*'I realize that you have killed six boys but that doesn't
change my feelings for you. I like you just as much as before
and want you to know that.'*
The psychologist Lena Arvidsson in a letter to Sture,
7 January 1994.

When Christer van der Kwast and Seppo Penttinen arrived at Säter,
its two consultants, Kjell Persson and Göran Fransson, ruled the
whole regional forensic psychiatry facility. The hospital's medical
director and founder of the new unit Göran Källberg had become so
depressed by the whole Svartenbrandt saga that he resigned from his
directorship and instead worked for the outpatient service. His departure was sudden and the hospital board did not have time to appoint
a successor. Instead, they asked Kjell Persson to take over as acting
medical director. By spring 1993 he and Dr Fransson ran the entire
unit.

It did not take long before both doctors were at loggerheads with
the board. The root of the trouble was, at least in part, their alarming
generosity with leave for patients in the would-be secure unit. The
media was keeping a close eye on events at Säter, especially after the
most recent Svartenbrandt disaster. The last thing the hospital board
needed was more scandalous headlines. But Persson and Fransson kept
taking risks and by the end of May journalists had another reason to
descend on Säter. The evening tabloid *Expressen* revealed that a patient
who was convicted of raping and nearly killing a twenty-three-year-
old woman, was permitted to go on leave to the very town where she
lived. She told the paper that it made her 'fear for her life'. The

medical director came across as arrogant when he refused to answer the *Expressen* reporter's perfectly reasonable questions.

The hospital board would have liked to see a little more humility but the Säter medics showed no inclination to pay heed to any criticism. Instead, apparently gripped by hubris, they kicked up a fuss about what they felt was Kjell Persson's minimal rise in salary when he took on the directorship. The members of the board thought their only option was to ask Göran Källberg to return as director. He accepted the offer, presumably feeling responsible for the unit he had been instrumental in setting up. Kjell Persson took his demotion to consultant badly and announced crossly that he would leave Säter to take up a new post in Lund. Göran Fransson was also looking for a new job.[331]

Since the Svartenbrandt scandal, Göran Källberg had become much more cautious in his approach to the job. The first thing he did after taking up his post in October 1993 was to inspect the arrangements for patient leave. He soon discovered something interesting.

In his absence the patient Thomas Quick had been found to be a serial killer – and one outcome of this revelation was to move the patient to the unstaffed ward 37, where he was free to come and go as he pleased as long as he returned to the clinic at night. Källberg, who was still seeing Margit for combined therapy and supervision, did not doubt that the patient's confessions were true and he remained an enthusiastic acolyte at group meetings, but the unrestricted leave worried him. He talked to Sture and then wrote the following in the case notes:

His therapy had made it possible for him to begin to remember. Still, some memories remain vague and he says that parts of them are out of touch. He describes this on-going process in a very intellectualizing manner, which is quite understandable in the circumstances. When he does, it is obvious that he is indeed out of touch with what he has done and that he still lacks bridges to the past. This indicates to me that one can't as yet exclude the possibility of an impulse breaking through. True, one valid objection is that the patient is likely to be less dangerous now that he has begun to speak out and will become an even smaller risk with time. But since pieces of the jigsaw are still missing it cannot be excluded that the searches and scrutiny might be too painful, and old behaviour patterns recur.[332]

Källberg raised the matter of risk with Fransson. Their talk coincided with a period in autumn 1993 when Fransson and Persson focused on locating Sture's 'sacred caches for body parts'. They resented any interference with their star patient's privileges. It might, they thought, disturb his positive, collaborative spirit. After the conversation with Fransson, Källberg wrote: 'Göran [Fransson] was very insistent that he and Kjell [Persson] have the situation completely under control.'[333]

But he was not happy, and by January 1994 he had had enough: 'Just learnt from Birgitta [Ståhle] that the patient has confessed to a further 4 murders, i.e. his total by now is 6 murders. Spoke to Kjell [. . .]. Told him I could not support current leave arr. and that I will support neither him nor Frasse [Göran Fransson] if something goes wrong.'

Källberg consulted Margit: 'Yesterday I had asked Margit re her views on patient leave. She told me that she had consistently advised against unrestricted leave for this patient, something she apparently also informed Kjell about. When I asked her, I had already made up my mind to cancel the current leave but I feel my decision has been confirmed.'

Two days after his chat with Margit, Källberg withdrew all leave for Sture. He had pulled rank on Persson and Fransson and it caused a smouldering conflict to flare up. Persson stopped his supervision sessions with Margit in protest, then went on sick leave. Fransson did the same, but Persson already had a plan: he was going to take Sture with him when he took up his new post in Skåne County.

Over the next two months, there was a violent tug-of-war for Sture. Christer van der Kwast entered the fray. Källberg writes in his personal notes that van der Kwast 'highlighted the importance of close contact with Kjell Persson in view of the continued police investigation'.

Penttinen also preferred Sture to move with Persson. Källberg took note: 'Talked to Crime in Sundsvall, Seppo Penttinen, who had phoned on a few occasions [. . .] pleads, as Senior Investigating Officer, that the move should take place.'

As Källberg hesitated about letting go of Sture, Christer van der Kwast started to plot behind the doctor's back. He personally phoned the St Sigfrid forensic psychiatric hospital in Växjö and talked them into looking after the noted serial killer. Every week Kjell Persson would commute between his new base in Lund and the ward in Växjö where he would see Sture for therapy sessions. According to his personal notes, Källberg felt he had been overruled. He was angry with van der Kwast but in the end came round to the proposed change. Källberg now promised the prosecutor that he would 'facilitate the continuing investigation' and accepted that 'a transfer would be justified at least for technical reasons related to the police interviews'.[334] He was concerned that he should not be seen as the person responsible for putting a lid on a groundbreaking run of therapy and an equally unique crime investigation.

In March 1994, Sture was transferred to the St Sigfrid hospital. Birgitta Ståhle was sad to see him leave; just before his departure, she came to his room and urged Sture to come back to Säter if he didn't like Växjö.

In fact, Sture had barely set foot in the new hospital before he wanted to go back. The regime at St Sigfrid did not allow benzodiazepines of any kind. Persson had promised that an exception would be made for Sture but none was granted, not even for a historic serial killer. A few days after his arrival, Sture phoned Ståhle and asked to be allowed to come 'home'. Interestingly enough, he also called Margit, who made the following note in her manuscript on the same day as the call:

Kjell Persson had just moved to take up a new post in Lund. He has arranged for Sture to be transferred to Växjö, expecting to see his patient once a week in the hospital. Sture in Växjö now but, after his first few days there which were very hard, he is aware that he longs to return to Säter, that his contact with staff at Säter simply can't be compared with the situation in Växjö. And so, Sture returns. He had been promised that he would be allowed to if that was what he wanted. On tel. to me, he also wanted to get in touch to find out why my supervision of Kjell's therapy with Sture had ceased, so I told him the reasons.

From now on, Birgitta Ståhle will be Sture's therapist.[335]

It is a pretty extraordinary for a patient to discuss his change of therapist with the supervisor of the therapists, but Margit was no ordinary supervisor. She was Sture's actual psychotherapist and everyone realized that, including Sture himself. Two nurses were dispatched to bring Sture back from Växjö. He was given his first Xanax in the car. When he arrived he moved into ward 36.

Margit had won the battle for the serial killer. There was no risk that Birgitta Ståhle would ever contradict her as Kjell Persson had done. When I interviewed Fransson, he told me that Källberg and Margit had been like 'mother and son' so I went on to ask about Margit and Ståhle's relationship. His answer was: 'As I saw it, the relationship between Birgitta Ståhle and Margit Norell was even stronger.' Ståhle, together with Cajsa Lindholm and one other psychotherapist, made up the devoted core of the group around Margit. None of the people I have spoken to had ever heard Ståhle utter a single critical word about Margit during the Quick years. Margit rewarded her by praising what she called Ståhle's exceptional talents as a psychotherapist.

'In our network, Birgitta was number one. She was thought to be doing a fantastic job,' Tomas Videgård said. I asked him how free Ståhle had been to make independent decisions about Sture's therapy. He replied:

I believe it would have been practically impossible for her. If so, Birgitta Ståhle would have needed some other touchstone outside our system, some place where she could speak freely. But, as far as I know, she had nothing of the sort. Birgitta and two, maybe three other therapists had formed this very tight group. In it, one just praised Margit to the skies. Look, I think it grew into a kind of sick pact – Birgitta colluded with Quick to deliver murders for Margit. The more murders, the better.

When I met the psychotherapist Britt Andersson, another member of the Margit group, she said it was unfair, in her opinion, to portray Ståhle as solely responsible for Sture's treatment: 'If it hadn't been for Margit, Birgitta would have never done what she did, of course.'

Ståhle herself has persistently refused to speak in public about what took place at Säter. Tomas Videgård regrets her silence: 'It's a crying shame. And surely the more mature way to deal with all this is trying to see the pact and the sect for what they are, and to understand how one got involved in it all. There were no evil people around. In this kind of work, such strong forces pull you this way and that. Even sensible people can get dragged in.'

When I spoke with Patricia Tudor-Sandahl, I asked her if she had anything she wanted to say to Ståhle. She replied: 'Come clean, Birgitta! It's not dangerous to speak about what happened. Quite a few of us recognize ourselves in this and we all presumably have something to learn. But to learn, we must talk with each other.'

From the moment that Ståhle became Sture's psychotherapist, Margit's influence at Säter grew even stronger than before. Ståhle was promoted to chief psychologist, a newly minted title. Two clinical psychologists reported to her. One of them was Magnus Brolin, a young man who had arrived at Säter in 1992, straight from the university course. He had begun by completing the trainee year required to qualify as a clinical psychologist but after he had finished his internship he stayed on in a permanent post until 1997. It meant that he was there during most of the Quick years. Today, he runs a psychotherapy-oriented company based in Stockholm. It took weeks of persuasion before he let me interview him. He said he felt loyal to some people at Säter and worried that something he said might do them harm. But when he realized how much I knew about Margit, he agreed to meet me.

We settled in his modern therapy room with a view over the

Skeppsbro quayside and he began to speak about Säter. It had been a great vision, he said. Every aspect of Göran Källberg's project was based on humane principles. Troubled people, who society thought undeserving, even unfit to live, were going to be given respect and help.

Magnus arrived at an impressive, newly built unit with plenty of money and plenty of staff. The rooms were light and airy, a contrast to the bleakness usually associated with forensic psychiatry. The atmosphere in the wards was normally very calm, which was good for the patients.

Göran Källberg and Birgitta Ståhle had interviewed him and he soon realized that they were both seeing Margit. 'She was the spiritual authority, somehow, I understood that quite soon,' he said. He added that members of the Margit group would give lectures to the psychiatric and ordinary nurses: 'The lecture would always begin with a thank-you to Margit Norell for supervision and so forth. And I actually thought that was rather odd. Were they indebted to her in some way? Does one have to say that? But it was just an expression of that authority and respectfulness.'

Before Magnus met me, he had asked his wife what she could remember about the Quick years. She had answered: 'You were totally convinced that Quick was guilty but you did have issues with that sect.' He said that this was quite true. On one hand, he was not keen on the authoritarian atmosphere at Säter that also entailed elevating Margit's ideas to the status of law. On the other hand, he believed in them just as much as anyone. He remembers being disappointed that he was never invited to join Margit's exclusive group, something that pleases him now. Still, just working at Säter made him feel that he belonged to an elite. He told me that he had later asked colleagues from other institutions how they had regarded Säter in the 1990s. A psychologist replied that the psychotherapists there were 'too proud'. 'Not a particularly good thing to hear,' Magnus said. 'But in retrospect I understand what he was referring to. We had this drive, we were passionate about what had to be done and believed no one else understood or could handle it.'

According to Magnus it was the perfect match between Sture's 'memories' and Säter's expectations that made the serial killer such a central figure.

'What went on vindicated our therapeutic vision. It proved, somehow, that we had been right all along. What I'm saying is, it wasn't exactly uncontroversial to carry out therapy like we did. That memories come back after they have been out of one's mind and all that. Far from uncontroversial.'

Magnus backed up what Fransson had said about ignoring research that questioned the repressed memory hypothesis. 'You didn't want to see the criticism, you shied away from it. It was that "too proud" bit again. We *knew*. And we were going to prove it.'

Magnus was not given supervision by Margit and had to be content with her pupil, Cajsa Lindholm. His therapist was another Margit acolyte, Hanna Olsson. I asked him what it was like to have Birgitta Ståhle as his boss, Cajsa as supervisor and Hanna Olsson as psychotherapist, given their close ties to Margit. He said that the strangest thing was that his secrets seemed to be shared around the group:

I didn't know if I was just being paranoid and or if it was really happening. But at times it felt awkward. 'Now, I can talk with you about this, only with you – or am I in conversation with the other two as well, the people you're telling what I say? And when you say something to me, is it what you're thinking or what someone else has thought but says through you?' Yes, it could feel very strange at times. And now, afterwards, I realize that I wasn't being paranoid.

The other psychologist working under the chief psychologist Birgitta Ståhle was Lena Arvidsson. She had completed her psychology course in the spring of 1994 and was employed in November, though she had started working at Säter that summer. Lena had been Sture's stand-in therapist, best friend and pen-pal for a couple of years and felt that she was very close to him, which can be seen in a letter she wrote to him in January 1994. She had just received a letter from her father, denying that he had ever subjected her to sexual abuse. He wanted her to charge him so that he would have a chance to defend himself to the police. When Lena, by then an almost fully trained psychologist, had finished reading her father's letter, she grabbed a pen and wrote to Sture, her serial killer friend:

Sture!

Here's an extra letter because I feel such an acute need to write to you. I must tell you something because I know that you'd truly understand. You know what madness is. I need to let these difficult things out and they make me furious, too. It's about me and my sick, mad father. I wish he were dead and out of my life. Though I know that however dead he is, there will always be some part of him left inside me even though I'm convinced I can have a good life all the same. I had a letter from my father today – yes, sad to say, he is my father and that I'll never get away from. I want to write this just to you because I know you're fearless and dare believe that I'm telling the truth. You are brave and prepared to face up to the existence of madness behind a well-adjusted facade.

Lena said that her father had criticized Cajsa Lindholm's therapeutic approach:

He thinks that Cajsa, my therapist, has given me the wrong treatment and that we together have dreamt up this story. On several occasions Dad had considered the possibility of going to the police and charging me with libel but desisted in the hope that I and Cajsa will 'come back to your senses'. He has also thought that he might submit a complaint about Cajsa to the Council for Responsibility in Health Care but understands that it wouldn't work.

Lena quotes a passage from her father's letter. In order to protect Lena's family all names are changed: 'It is almost four years since you wrote to me and Gunvor and, in summary, presented us with the appalling accusations that I had used you for sex and that Gunvor knew it but had not had the strength or courage to do anything to stop it. That last claim shows just how little you know about your mother, how strong-minded and deeply moral she is.'

Above the quoted words 'how strong-minded and deeply moral she is', Lena scribbled a comment to Sture: 'My mother's morals were fine, what with her abusing me as well.'

When I interviewed Lena in 2012, she said that she had always loved her mother, who had died from cancer a few years earlier without ever believing in Lena's accusations against her father. However, her letter to Sture in 1994 shows that, at least for a few years, she insisted that her mother had joined in the abuse of her daughter.

Lena also told Sture that she was very preoccupied with revelations of new, spectacular memories: 'Dad writes of course that he's innocent and denies everything. At the same time, now, I'm wrestling with the memories of how he did horrible, ritualistic, sadistic and abusive things to me which I barely survived. It is awful for me and very frightening but I don't need to tell you that. It is so sick that it can be hard to get your head around it, that it's the truth.'

Lena was grateful that she had a friend in Sture.

Sture, your experience means a lot to me and it helps me to think that you will understand. I've pulled you into my world and it is also because I want to show you that I understand your struggles and your pain. Well, there you are, we have something in common. I become sad, and feel small and scared at the same time as I feel strong and courageous. Soon I'll be a real psychologist and then I'll fucking well show them.[336]

Five days later, she wrote to Sture again about his repressed memories, which he regularly reported to her in his letters. 'Of course I was shaken by what you wrote but I'm not surprised. Your parents must have been utterly mad because a sicker, more appalling treatment of a child I simply cannot imagine. It's fucking awful that beasts like them are allowed to walk about at liberty and people don't notice a thing. I mean, talk about denial! And not wanting to face up to what's going on.'

Lena realized that Sture re-enacted his own childhood traumas in his murders:

Everything becomes so understandable if one starts out from your account of the miscarriage and how they forced you to eat the foetus at the same time as they also did that. I hope you don't find my straightforward ways too hard to bear. The ritual murder of Johan [Asplund] makes sense and everything fits in. You have recreated what you had to endure yourself, which is of course so totally obvious now! In your acts, you attempted to express something meaningful in the context of your own experiences as a child. Oh, Christ, how obvious and transparent it has all become. Of course it's horrible and really bad to think about but I understand perfectly how it is all connected. And so I'm not so scared. I realize that you have killed six boys but that doesn't change my feelings for you. I like you just as much as before and want you to know that. I remain your friend and you can trust me more a hundred per cent and more! My sympathy for you will <u>never</u> waver!!'[337]

This was written in January 1994 and five months later Birgitta Ståhle took Lena Arvidsson on as Säter's third clinical psychologist. For the next ten years, she would provide therapy to those the Swedish courts had sentenced to forensic psychiatric care. Cajsa Lindholm was her combined psychotherapist and supervisor. On Wednesdays, when Birgitta went to Stockholm to see Margit, *her* combined psychotherapist and supervisor, Lena, continued to act as Sture's reserve psychotherapist.

When Ståhle took over as Sture's therapist, the close collaboration with van der Kwast and Penttinen continued as before. In June that year, Brigitta summed up the work during the spring that had passed:

Work has been intense, a lot of material and active therapeutic processes. During the therapeutic talks, Thomas has often regressed strongly and, through this, come into increased contact with earlier events in his life that he has defended himself against and with which he had not been in conscious contact. The regression entails that the patient comes into contact with on one hand early traumatic events in childhood, and on the other how these events are re-enacted by the patient in his adult life through the abusive act and murder that he is currently telling the police about in their ongoing investigation.[338]

22

The escape

'Helped by regression, Sture remembers events and situations around killing.'
Case note entry by Birgitta Ståhle, August 1994.

When Birgitta Ståhle went on holiday in the summer of 1994, Lena Arvidsson stood in as Sture's therapist. That was when he set in motion a plan that he had been brooding on for several months. He had been very taken with a fellow patient in ward 36, a twenty-year-old called Tobias. Tobias had left on a trial discharge but they had kept in touch. When Tobias told Sture that he had got hold of some amphetamine, he could not resist the temptation. They started planning a break from hospital.

Sture was allowed outside if accompanied by a member of staff so, on Monday 4 July, he phoned Lena and asked if she would like to have lunch with him after the therapy session that morning. He said he fancied going to a restaurant near a golf course within easy reach of the hospital. Lena agreed. Next, Sture called Tobias and told him that today was the day. A few hours later, after his session with Lena, they strolled towards the hospital gates. As they crossed the large car park close to the old, slowly crumbling secure wing, Sture said that he needed a pee and asked Lena to wait while he walked to the back of the empty building. Once out of sight, he ran some 500 metres through the woods behind the hospital to a road where Tobias was waiting in an elderly Volvo. He had recruited a young woman as their driver. A few hours later, driving north-eastwards, they reached the next county, Hälsingland.

Tobias had brought a tent, radio and a small bag of amphetamine

287

powder. They started on the speed straightaway and the atmosphere in the car grew crazily elated. There was shaving foam and a razor for Sture, so he could remove the beard he had worn in all his photos, and Tobias had also brought along a sawn-off shotgun. It did not actually work but they chatted vaguely about a bank robbery to finance being on the run.

This breakout followed the same pattern as Sture's other escapes from assorted institutions but, this time, the consequences were more dramatic than he expected.

The 'Säter man' had been a recurring figure in the media ever since van der Kwast had announced that Sture had murdered Thomas Blomgren. As recently as 17 June, a couple of weeks earlier, *Expressen* had published a full-page story warning the public that Sture 'killed for pleasure' and that the doctors thought him 'exceptionally dangerous'. That last piece of information was a tad baffling, given that he was often out walking, cycling or jogging all over the Säter valley, accompanied by staff who clearly did not regard him as especially dangerous.[339]

But in the wake of that sort of publicity, the media went to work when it became known that the 'Säter man' had escaped. The evening papers printed extra editions and, for the first time, revealed 'in the public interest' that the name of the prowling killer was Thomas Quick. They also displayed unmasked pictures of him on their advertising posters.

The chase was thrilling. The police set out to capture the madman before he killed and butchered someone and pulled out all the stops: helicopters, dog teams and special unit squads in bulletproof waistcoats, armed with machine guns. The driver of the getaway car decided to get away once she realized who was in the back seat. They stopped at a deserted house in Hälsingland and from then on the two friends were on their own.

Then they travelled on two old bicycles they had found near the deserted house. Police cars overtook them from both directions but no one suspected that a serial killer would escape on a bike. Sture and Tobias got within 10 kilometres of Bollnäs and stopped near a small village called Alfta. They erected the tent in a sheltered spot between a wood and a field and settled down to listen to the radio newscasts about the hunt for Thomas Quick. They even watched a police helicopter fly over their campsite.

Sture has told me he soon realized that the escape attempt was hopeless. He told Tobias to set out on his own and try to make his way to Stockholm. Sture would wait for a few hours and then give himself up to the police. Sture dumped the shotgun in a nearby river and spent the night alone in the tent. The following morning, he walked to the Statoil garage in Alfta, where he came face-to-face with himself on posters. He began by calling Säter to try to persuade the staff on ward 36 not to move him to another ward if he turned himself in. The psychiatric nurse said that he didn't have the authority to decide that but he would put in a word for Sture. The next phone call was to the police in Bollnäs. Then Sture sat down outside and waited. When the police arrived, he put his hands up to show he was unarmed. He spent the night in a police cell illuminated by the flashes from the cameras of the press photographers camped outside. The following day Sture was transported to Säter.

Nothing had happened during the escape but for the hospital board it was a nightmare all the same. It brought just the kind of publicity they feared most. On Wednesday, the day Sture was taken into police custody, *Expressen* ran an accusatory rant directed at the entire Swedish system of forensic psychiatry. The headline read THEY LET THE CRIMINALS OUT. Several psychiatrists from the hospitals in Säter, Karsudden and Sidsjön, including Göran Källberg, Kjell Persson and Göran Fransson, were put in the stocks for allegedly having given violent men leave on dubious grounds.

Things got worse when the hospital inspection team was mobilized. The day after Sture's return to the fold, a group of civil servants from the Department of Social Services arrived to conduct an unannounced inspection of Säter. The outcome was a report in which Sture was described as 'the most remarkable patient ever cared for at Säter, according to statements made by experienced members of staff'.[340] It also observed that none of those who provided his psychotherapy treatment had any formal qualification to do so. It concluded that the Säter regime was characterized by 'a surprising degree of gormlessness' and that the board must implement measures to prevent future escapes. Six complaints, all related to Sture's escape, had been lodged with the Justice Ombudsman (JO). The JO set in motion a nationwide examination of how site-restricted and outside leave were handled by all the forensic psychiatric hospitals.[341] It was an election year and the Conservative Minister of Justice, Gun Hellsvik, appeared on TV and promised that, if the right-of-centre coalition won in September, she would see to it that the option of a psychiatric care sentence would be strictly limited.

Sture's escapade had put a huge amount of pressure not only on Säter but also on the practice of forensic psychiatry in general. One might assume that the consequences for Sture would also be uncomfortable but this is to underestimate Säter's self-sustaining system of thought. As soon as Sture was back in the ward, Birgitta Ståhle interrupted her holiday to be ready with a therapy session. Sture used the session to do what he had done so many times before after running away and getting wasted: he wept and said that he had wanted to kill himself, a fairytale which always went down well. Birgitta was profoundly moved: 'Sture experienced his situation as so distressing that he chose to run away, first to see Tobias and then to commit suicide.' She even believed that the escape had given him new, crucial insights because he had managed to resist the impulse to murder Tobias: 'While on the run, Thomas becomes aware of a merging of old traumas in childhood and the then current situation, which frightened him but simultaneously helps him act in such a way as to allow Tobias to get away. [...] He is now eager to find a way back into the therapeutic work and take off from where together we had reached previously.'[342]

Sture knew exactly which buttons to press and was soon reinstated as the star of the unit, but he knew that the media coverage and renewed scrutiny would make things difficult for the regime at Säter. He decided to make a dramatic move. In consultation with Ståhle and Margit, he composed an article for the op-ed pages in Sweden's largest daily newspaper *Dagens Nyheter*, which was published less than a week after his return. This is how it began: 'My name is Thomas Quick.

After my escape last Monday (04/07) and the enormous media uproar that followed immediately afterwards, neither my name nor my appearance is unknown.'[343] He then defended Säter, sometimes in poetic turns of phrase:

> I cannot and will not try to account for my escape from Säter Hospital, but feel that it is essential to speak up for the successful work that has been done and still is being done here; facts that have become completely lost in the furore of the journalistic chase for sensation which makes even those with good intellectual abilities run aground as they try to make themselves heard, not only among the loud-mouthed condemnations but preferably outdoing them. I am aware that within this cacophony my own voice will sound like the susurration of a cicada – but I take comfort in the hope that the sensitive will discern what I have to say.

Sture explained that he was working to recover repressed memories: 'When I arrived at the forensic psychiatric unit in Säter, I had no memories of the first twelve years of my life. The murders to which I have now confessed and which are being investigated by the Sundsvall police were as utterly repressed as those early years.'

He sang the praises of his therapy: 'As I was enabled and encouraged to allow memories of severe traumas from my very earliest years to emerge, so it also became possible for me to approach the sense I had had, but had failed to muster the courage to examine consciously, of having been involved in terrible events during my adult life.'

Sture, showing rhetorical skill, saved discussing his actual breakout for the end:

> So, why did I escape? I did not run away in order to commit new crimes. I ran, because the remembered images of my actions overpowered me – grew utterly unbearable. I ran away to commit suicide. After separating from my friend, I sat for thirteen hours with a sawn-off shotgun directed alternately towards my forehead, my mouth and my chest. But I could not do it. Today I am able to take

responsibility for yesterday and perhaps it was that sense of responsibility that stopped me from killing myself and instead made me phone the police and turn myself in. I would like to think so.

This wowed everyone. It was sensational for a serial killer to express himself with such sophistication. He even used semi-colons! From that day, the Swedes referred to Thomas Quick as highly intelligent and it enriched the aura of mystique that surrounded him. He seemed a very highbrow serial killer, like Hannibal Lecter in Thomas Harris's novels – and apparently shared Lecter's taste for cannibalism.

With an innate sense of how public opinion can be manipulated, Sture followed up the newspaper article with an open letter to the staff in ward 36, in which he came across as a well-mannered boss placing the responsibility for a failure on his colleagues:

After talking with some of you, I have realized that my escape has caused many to speculate and raise questions. In this letter, I will attempt to deal with our concerns – by 'ours' I mean you, the ward staff, and I. It is not my intention to touch on the external consequences to which my escape contributed, such as the Social Services department's investigation, and whatever criticism it may contain, or the threats expressed by other patients etc. To me, the most important aspect is that we can together find our way back to the mutual relationship that existed before my escape. [...] Please believe that what I say is what I sincerely mean – and do not see this letter as an attempt to manipulate you. I could no longer stand myself and perhaps I also felt a little doubtful about you: did you really understand how hard it has been for me?

Sture was willing to give them another chance: 'I also believe that it was very important to take care of all that we have already reached together and hold on to it with firm hands. Storms batter us from time to time but it is after all true that together, with mutual trust, we have delivered good outcomes. It is this part of our joint work that must be allowed to continue. For I cannot manage alone.'[344]

This manipulative homily worked a treat. Sture told me that the atmosphere in the ward improved hugely: 'The escape itself became seen as proof of my trustworthiness – I was burdened by such painful memories that I was forced to try running away from them. And when I chose to return, it was understood as returning to the therapy room and that, in turn, as an enormous vindication of Margit.'

The symbolic meaning of the escape was pondered endlessly. He said: 'The entire breakout episode was interpreted as part of the therapy. My mum grew up in Alfta and it followed that I had run off to confront "mother". It gave me a nice shove in the right direction. The escape had no negative consequences for me whatever.'

After the escape, the drug cupboard was opened wide. Sture was clearly going to need all the medication he claimed to need or else his 'memories' might drive him to kill himself. He was also allowed more medication because a new doctor had replaced Göran Källberg. Källberg gave up and left in the summer of 1994. During the spring of that year, Svartenbrandt had not missed any opportunity to rub salt in his former therapist's wounds. In April, *Expressen* had visited Svartenbrandt in his prison cell and printed the resulting interview as a double-page spread under the eye-catching headline I BLUFFED EVERYONE AT SÄTER. The piece said, among other things:

> Svartenbrandt now admits that throughout all his years of therapy, he systematically bluffed everyone, including Säter's medical director.
>
> 'Sure thing,' he said, sounding very self-confident. 'Sheer cunning. Therapy makes you smarten up. I learnt to handle it, you know, become manipulative and get out of taking responsibility. I underwent eight years of therapy. But I doubt if any fucker more evil than me has ever been discharged from the bin.'[345]

Källberg found a way to leave Säter again and this time he would not be back as medical director until 2001. His successor was Erik Kall, a Danish doctor with the unusual distinction of being over two metres tall. He took charge of Sture's treatment and, from the start, was extremely loyal to the group around Sture, including not only thera-pists but also Christer van der Kwast and Seppo Penttinen. For the rest of the 1990s he willingly prescribed powerful neuro-active medication at abuse-level dosages as and when the group thought that Sture needed something extra to deal with his murder trials as well as the therapy sessions.[346]

Sture was on a fixed dose of 3 × 10 mg Stesolid (diazepam) tablets daily but in addition the schedule had a get-out clause: 'medication as required'. It meant that he could have more when it was considered necessary and, in practice, Sture's drug-taking was directly proportional to the degree of anguish he demonstrated. His 'regressions' became more and more dramatic and, in August, Ståhle wrote:

Helped by regression, Sture remembers events and situations around killing. His own experiences of being exposed as a child to his par-ents' attempts to kill him are tightly bound up with the boys he killed as an adult. His memories are tremendously intense and effort-ful, and so clear to Thomas that he hears sounds, senses smells, experiences and feels himself to be inside the entire situation as it once took place.[347]

His case notes are packed with staff entries about his confused behaviour. This one, from the beginning of August, is typical: 'Anxiety attack at about 17.00. We had to escort him to the music room where he threw himself on the floor and banged his head against it. Can't stand things any more. Given a Xanax tabl. and coffee. We called Birgitta and they had a chat. The worst was over after approx. 1 hour. Dr Kall prescr. 1 extra tabl Xanax as req.'[348]

Three days later, a new entry: 'Walked up & down the ward corri-dor at around 21.00 banging his head against the walls. Given 1 × 1 mg Xanax. Then accomp. staff to the music room where he hyper-ventilated in a plastic bag for about 20 mins. Panic ceased, and he went to bed at around 22.00.'[349]

Even at night, Sture required tranquillizers: 'Thomas woke at 02.15, severe anxiety. Screamed so loudly night staff heard him. He was visited, after a while came out accomp. by nurse. Given 1 × 1 mg Xanax.'[350]

The drugs made Sture manic and feverishly active. He rattled out long, grotesque texts on the word processor he was given to keep in his room for this purpose. Here is an example:

The images of the dead boys always present as visions, emotional memories – for example, I remember how I killed them, how my hands felt, how it sounded e.g. when I sawed off Johan's head. The resistance to the saw, the blood on and in my hands. I remember the smells. Yes, the memory is in the here and now, and it is with me in its full reality, without retouching. Especially present is Johan's torso, bluish and cold, without head and limbs, its sex cut, its buttocks ripped to rags, its nipples torn off. I close my eyes, I carry this torso pressed to my naked chest. I remember Alvar's dismembered body, Charles's, Olle's. I still hide Dustunka's away, but remember with such clarity how Thomas died. Feel him in my hands. How he struggles, all that. I remember, it is so close that today my anguish feels even denser than the anguish that filled me just before I killed. I want to face reality, want to continue the work, the therapy, but I am tempted by the thought of slipping away. I feel the inescapable pain that my connection to reality brings. Charles is dead. Dare I say that Alvar and Johan are dead, that Olle and Dustunka are, too?[351]

This was Sture's mental state when Christer van der Kwast, Seppo Penttinen and Birgitta Ståhle sought for the first time to get him convicted of murder.

23

The memory expert

'He had, of course, this strong need to tell his story. I tried to
capture what he was saying and examine it with my
general . . . well . . . enquiries into how perpetrators act.'
Sven Å Christianson, speaking about his many
years of contact with Quick in a police interview
led by Detective Inspector Kjell-Åke Wendt
during the retrial process.

The tug of war over Sture had forced Christer van der Kwast and
Seppo Penttinen to delay their interviewing for two months. But on
Thursday 14 April 1994, everyone was back in place in the music
room, ready for the eleventh interview in the Asplund case. The latest
episode in the series had emerged in January, when Sture vividly
described how he had carried the boy's torso to Ryggen and, in a
'dreadfully psychotic state', stumbled about clutching his burden in his
arms: 'I'm terribly cold, frozen, all that, but couldn't make myself let
go of it right then . . .'[352]

Apart from Penttinen and Sture, Ståhle and the solicitor Gunnar
Lundgren were there to support Sture. A newcomer had also joined
them, a man called 'Sven-Åke Christiansson' who later changed his
name to the more international 'Sven Å Christianson', which I will
use. Christianson was a reader in psychology at Stockholm University,
and his research focused on the function of human memory. Van der
Kwast had brought him to Säter to conduct tests on Sture's capacity to
remember and, as he was there, invited him to join a real police interview.[353]

Sture began by describing an excursion that he and the two now ex-Säter doctors had made to Lake Ryggen the previous autumn. They had hoped he would feel able to approach the cache with Johan's hand and decided on the trip without telling Penttinen. Sture said that his memory had produced images so precise that he could almost reach the cache. Penttinen had been looking for Sture's sacred hiding place for a year by then and told them that he had actually visited Ryggen the day before the interview. Now he tried to make Sture give him some details but the result was only more evasiveness and anguished panting. After an hour of getting nowhere, Seppo was prepared to give up when Sture suddenly went back to the excursion he had mentioned at the outset. An anxiety attack was mounting as he spoke:

[Sture]: 'But I also think that ... that we found (Sture panics a little) real things ...'
[Penttinen]: 'What was it you found?'
[Sture]: 'Two ... two ... One like this and one like this ...'
[Penttinen]: 'Aha. You are looking at two bits of bone from an index finger. And where are these bits of bone now?'
[Sture]: 'I must go when Birgitta tells me where they are.'

Having said that Sture left the music room. Ståhle had been very concerned by his strong anxiety attack and went to make sure that nurses were ready to meet him in the corridor. Later, when she was alone with Penttinen, Lundgren and the visiting academic, Dr Christianson, she said:

[Ståhle]: 'This is the truly difficult bit. But it is something he has told me about. You see ... now, then ... he has told me that he found pieces of bone, hand bones, by the stream and he showed them to Göran and Kjell but he ate them so they're not available.'
[Penttinen]: 'Really. The interview is interrupted at 16.06.'

Sture had apparently found bone pieces from Johan's hand – and swallowed them. Christianson, a slim man of forty with a laid-back, almost boyish manner, observed the scene as the interview came to its unexpected end. In principle, van der Kwast had made a smart move when he turned to an accredited expert on memory. So far, he had had to rely on the Säter medics and their assurances that the 'explanatory model' was scientifically plausible. Now, by opening the door to Sven Å Christianson, he had invited a real scientist into the closed world of Säter.

Christianson's doctorate had been granted by Umeå University in 1984 and he spent a few years there doing post-doctoral research on memory. His career had taken off when he moved to the United States and he became an assistant to Elizabeth Loftus, the world's foremost specialist on false memories.

In 1987, Loftus and Christianson published a paper with the details of a study of what subjects recall from images of frightening events: on the whole, people have stronger memories of the terrifying central aspects and weaker recollections of more peripheral, less immediately alarming details.[354] Christianson's name was now associated with Loftus's and, with that in his portfolio, he advanced swiftly up the career ladder. On his return to Umeå, the university promoted him to reader. He also kept up a long distance collaboration with Loftus and their joint publication of a series of experimental outcomes confirmed that people remember central aspects of terrifying experiences more strongly than anything else.[355]

Christianson knew that sixty years of research had not provided any convincing evidence for repression of traumatic memories and was aware of the critique against recovered memory therapy.[356] With just a handful of references to current research he could have easily proved to van der Kwast the dubiousness of Säter's psychological ideas and arguments. If he had chosen to do that, it is very likely that Sture would not have been taken to court for the first of his murder trials and the Quick scandal would never have happened.

But Christianson decided not to. Instead, after the interview, he made a strange move. He stepped in to 'coach the police', a phrase he used in a later police interview. Put plainly, he would assist the attempts to push Sture into recovering his repressed memories.[357] With this move, he became a consultant for the prosecution as well as the police, a role he fulfilled up to Sture's eighth conviction for murder in 2001.

The National Police Authority paid Christianson's fees, and he formed a private company with the fitting name Memokonsult Ltd to handle the income. It did not take long before he became even more deeply involved. In addition to being on the National Police Authority's payroll as a consultant, he set out to make Sture 'his personal research contact', as he described the relationship in a police interview. His intention was to study 'modes of remembering and narrating by a persistent perpetrator of violent acts'. This was research carried out as the holder of an academic post at Stockholm University. He also intended to write a book about Sture, well aware that serial killers attracted prurient attention, media interest and a wide readership.

From the summer of 1994, Christianson became a frequent visitor to Säter. He would sit in Sture's small room and listen to stories from the life of a serial killer with the tape recorder running: 'He had, of course, this strong need to tell his story,' Christianson later told the police. 'I tried to capture what he was saying and examine it with my general ... well ... enquiries into how perpetrators act.' Sture has told me that Christianson was looking for answers to questions like why Jeffrey Dahmer was devoted to cannibalism, or what drove Westley Allan Dodd to eat the genitals of his victims. Sture had ready answers and at the same time sucked up the new information. Christianson's interest in real American serial killers and their activities added inspiration to the material he had collected from *American Psycho*.

The book's title was to be *Inside the Mind of a Serial Killer* and, in order to maximize the sales figures, Christianson wanted it to read like popular science. The contract was signed and sealed, and the publishers, Norstedts, had paid Christianson an undisclosed advance. He must have been looking forward to huge success, in Sweden and then internationally.

For starters, van der Kwast and Penttinen wanted Christianson to help them with making Sture recover his repressed memories of the murder of Charles Zelmanovits, a fifteen-year-old boy. Charles's mother was a Swedish nurse and his father a Polish doctor, and as a family they had moved to Piteå, a northern town, in the summer of 1976.[358] One Friday night in November the same year, Charles went to a school dance held in the Pitholmen sports hall, a couple of kilometres from his home. He drank quite a lot that evening. Two girls saw him walking home alone much later, when the dance had ended. It was the last time anyone saw him alive.

The community took his disappearance very seriously. The police launched an intensive effort to find him, the townspeople went out on fingertip searches and the local press publicized the search process, but the case remained a mystery for sixteen years. Then, in September 1993, a hunter found a human skull in an area of forest about three kilometres from the spot where Charles had left his friends and later parts of a skeleton were found close by. It was the remains of Charles Zelmanovits. The police did not suspect foul play. Piteå is in the far north and the night Charles disappeared the temperature was well below zero. Interviews with his family and friends indicated that he had been dressed for the party in low suede shoes, jeans, a shirt and a sweater, a pilot-style brown leather jacket, gloves but no hat. The police, knowing that he had been drunk, considered that the likeliest explanation was that the boy had got lost in the dark forest and frozen to death. His head had ended up separated from the rest of his body through the process of animals dragging away various parts over the years. One thigh bone, one shin bone and the hands below the wrists were never found.

Dagens Nyheter made a short reference to the tragic discovery on 11 December 1993 and, two days later, Sture confessed to the murder in a note that ended up in Margit's manuscript:

The features of the dark boy are growing clearer. I can pick up the sound of his voice, his way of moving, and hardest of all, I remember with such immediacy touching him physically and then what touching led on to. My sexual desire is strong, mixed with the sense of approaching danger, as is the thought of killing the moment I see these images. Today, I know that I killed the dark boy. I can recall

300

distinctly how, and in what surroundings. I sense his first name but can't reach it. I remember, too, the sexual foreplay to the killing, that the dark boy died by strangulation and that afterwards I carried him to a place in the forest where the ground was covered in reindeer lichen and moss.[359]

Reading the transcripts of the Zelmanovits interviews is as weird an experience as reading about the Asplund case. Sture is excruciatingly vague and hides his inability to provide any solid information behind intermittent anxiety attacks. He confabulates away to an accompaniment of heavy breathing, groaning and stuttering.

In 1976, Sture was twenty-six years old and was not to take driving lessons and get his licence for eleven years. He had to be able to explain how he had managed to get all the way to Piteå. He claimed that he had been driven by a friend who was also a sexual partner. They had left Falun, driven to Piteå, killed and gone straight back home, a round-trip of more than 1,500 kilometres. The pair of them had planned to hunt down a boy to carry off and came across Charles quite by chance. When asked to draw a rough map of the area in or near Piteå where they had spotted Charles, Sture picked the northwest of the town.[360] He and his friend had lured the boy into their car and then driven further north, before stopping and killing him. But Charles had been found south-east of the town – diametrically opposite to the area on Sture's map.

The driver was said to have been so shaken by his participation in the murder that he killed himself a few months later. This man had existed and did in fact shoot himself in his garage in Falun, but Sture had been uncertain if his friend had killed himself before or after November 1976. He had phoned Penttinen and asked him to look up the date. Penttinen did as he was asked – an astonishing admission made in one of the early interviews.[361] Before Sture named his partner in crime, he had double-checked that he was not already dead at the time of Charles's disappearance.

Sture had no idea what kind of car his friend had owned and couldn't say how many doors it had, or what colour it was. He did not know when his victim had died and guessed that it was in the late afternoon – the correct answer would have been after midnight. Snow or bare ground? He did not know, but the correct answer was bare ground. He guessed that Charles had been wearing a suit jacket and boots when he had been wearing a leather jacket and low suede shoes. At one point Sture claimed to have dug a hole with a metal shoehorn found in the car and then tried to bury the body. The forensic pathologist's report said that the body had not been buried. Early on Sture said that he had buried the body in one piece but, a few interviews later, he recalled dismembering it by sawing and cutting through the clothes. The record showed that there were no signs of deliberate damage to the clothes and no saw or knife marks on the skeleton.

On it went. The interviews in the Charles Zelmanovits case were bafflingly short of substance. Everything Sture said was wrong.

The prosecutor was delighted when Christianson offered to advise Penttinen on how he could help Quick to remember by using a variant of 'cognitive interviewing'.[362]

This is an interviewing technique that grew very popular in the 1990s and had been developed by two American psychologists called Ronald P. Fisher and R. Edward Geiselman. They had observed that police interviewers often formulate their questions to witnesses and victims of crime in formulaic and insensitive language. Classic police questions such as 'Did the perpetrator have fair or dark hair?' and 'Did he have a gun?' would get answers to precisely what was asked but might prevent the interviewee from remembering important details that the police did not know to ask about. Fisher and Geiselman set out guidelines for police interviews and called the approach a cognitive interview. The main rule was that questions should be more open-ended in order to elicit longer, more detailed answers – not just yes or no. Other suggestions include asking the interviewee to describe a sequence of events from another perspective, or to retell a story in reverse chronological order. Fisher and Geiselman also recommended that victims and witnesses should, if possible, be taken to the crime scene and asked to re-enact events, rather than staying inside an interview room.

The cognitive interview was intended to activate the network of associations that memories consists of, and encourage more details to emerge. However, Christianson was rather reckless when he suggested using the technique with a would-be perpetrator like Sture. The Fisher and Geiselman method was meant to be used with cooperative witnesses and victims, who could be assumed to want to tell the truth, but was considered unsuitable for interrogation of suspected criminals, whose passion for truth would be doubtful.[363] Besides, Fisher and Geiselman strongly advised against using their method as part of therapy: 'Indeed we, as well as others [. . .] have consistently argued against applying the [cognitive interview] as a therapeutic tool in cases such as those involving "recovered memories".'[364]

Christianson ignored these words of warning and, with a measure of ingenuity, constructed his own version of crime scene re-enactment, which he unveiled in May 1994. It was based, he said, on the cognitive interview technique but adjusted especially for Sture. Ordinary crime scene re-enactment usually entails asking a suspect or a witness to demonstrate how the crime was carried out at the site. Christianson recommended that Sture should instead be taken to another place that had sufficient similarities with the actual crime scene so that associative interactions would be triggered without arousing the anguish that locked access to his memory.

The first test of this new approach took place on 25 May 1994, when Christianson and Penttinen escorted Sture into the forest near the Säter institution. The environment was thought to be reminiscent of the forests around Piteå where Charles Zelmanovits was murdered, almost 800 kilometres further north.

Seppo reported what happened: 'The re-enactment took place in a forested area adjacent to the Säter hospital. The intention was that Quick would indicate certain natural features in the forest that are similar to the place where he claims to have left Zelmanovits's body within the Piteå police district.'[365]

This must have semed rather enigmatic to Penttinen, but Christianson was a respected academic who had specialized in how memory worked and surely knew what he was doing. He asked Sture to try to rekindle the feelings he had had in the Piteå forest, and it worked. Penttinen's report states that the memories flowed back: 'The forest area is quite open with tall trees. Quick also says that there is relatively little growing under the mature trees. [...].' He also remembered smells: 'In the Piteå forest there were stronger moorland smells than in the place we are now.' Sture tested digging in the moss and another repressed memory soon surfaced: 'Quick points out that the pit dug in Piteå probably wasn't all that deep, he gets that sense from the patch of ground he is currently digging in.'

Coming up with a generalized description of a forest was easy, but Sture was confounded when asked how far he had carried the body from the road to the place where he butchered it. The question had a verifiable answer so Sture dealt with it accordingly: 'Quick said that the distance from the road to the place where he left Zelmanovits's body is within the range of 50 to 500 metres. He added that his calculation included a certain safety margin for errors.'

By engaging in the memory recovery work, Christianson had been seen to accept the prevailing 'explanatory model' of Sture's flawed narrative – effectively, he provided scientific backup for Margit's personal theories on memory repression. When I interviewed van der Kwast, he pointed out that Persson and Fransson had been the first to initiate him into the 'explanatory model' but not the last:

> Yes, those two were on the spot managing the health care side of things but then there was Christianson, advising on the psychology of witnesses and so forth. I can't remember precisely when he got in on the act but he soon became quite important. He had this cognitive angle on the actual story and a broad knowledge of the problems you are up against with a potential serial killer. So, from our point of view, his presence was complementary.

Several years later, Christianson was questioned about his role in the Quick investigations. He said that he assumed his task to be that of 'a coach' who informed the police about how memory works: 'It's not as if we had a built-in tape recorder. We remember a little differently depending on the clues we are given.'[366]

The key word is 'clues'. Christianson referred to the way we use associations to access memories, a route that has been studied in experimental psychology. This, of course, does not mean that a police interrogator is free to use any kind of 'clue', especially not if there is a risk that the interrogated person might make false confessions or has constructed false memories in (for example) psychotherapy. In such a situation, dropping hints about expected 'right answers' can be as destructive as planting false evidence.

The originators of the cognitive interview technique had alerted interviewers to the risk of asking leading questions to get the desired answer. Already, in 1994, Stephen Lindsay and Don Read, two psychologists with a special interest in cognition, wrote: 'To avoid leading questions is one of the fundamental principles in cognitive interviews', and quoted research showing that the proportion of mistaken statements in police interviews does not increase if the technique is used correctly.[367]

But Christianson seems to have encouraged Penttinen to break with the principle, because once the self-appointed interview coach was in place, Penttinen began to ask Sture any number of leading questions and carried on doing it for seven years until the last trial in 2001. He also tended to repeat questions to which Sture had given the 'wrong' answer, and ignored the mistakes. By allowing Sture to keep guessing, he often arrived at the 'right' answer by means of exclusion.

I have read all the interviews and it is clear to me that Penttinen did not set out to cheat. If he had wanted to, it would have been simpler to tell Sture what to say with the tape recorder switched off. Penttinen genuinely seemed to think that he was helping a confused man in his struggles to retrieve long-buried memories. It is obvious that Christianson, with his aura of scientific respectability, legitimized the use of leading questions and clue-dropping.

There are many examples of Penttinen helping Sture out during the Zelmanovits investigation. In one interview he asked about the ground in the forest when Sture was carrying the dead body over it. Sture replied: 'I think that it looks like . . . there is quite a lot of snow [*inaudible*] . . . just as we leave the car and walk into the forest.'

Seppo knew that there had been no snow on the ground in and around Piteå, so offered Sture a hint, which he must have thought would hook the right memory: 'If I ask the question in very straight-forward way – what do you think, are you absolutely convinced that you saw snow? Is it impossible to say the ground was bare?'

Sture changed his mind: 'No, that's not impossible. In fact, there was no snow where we stopped.'[368]

Here is Sture, in the same interview, answering a question about how Charles had been dressed: 'I would be able to say that-that Charles had . . . (*short pause*) he wore jeans and boots and a dark sweater and on top he had a . . . I-I-I think I remember it was a suit jacket but then I think it might be wrong as well. Err . . . I think there's a m-m-mix-up somewhere.'

If Charles had been wearing a jacket, Penttinen would almost certainly not have asked again. But the answer was not quite right:

[Penttinen]: 'Aha. What mix-up might that be? I mean, if the other option is not a suit jacket what might it be? Any association or something like that . . . to something else?'
[Sture]: 'Ye-es.'
[Penttinen]: 'Like what?'
(*longish pause*)
[Penttinen]: 'If you just associate?'
[Sture]: 'Well, then it's perhaps . . .'
[Penttinen]: 'Aha?'
[Sture]: 'A jacket . . . is a little associated with [*inaudible*].'
[Penttinen]: 'Aha, yes. If it's not like a suit jacket then a sort of outdoor jacket? Any idea of the colour?'

Over time, Sture's story of what he did with the corpse became more and more complicated. At first, he said he had undressed it, but then he must have picked up on the fact that the zip on Charles's jacket had been pulled right up. He next launched into a messy account of how he had undressed the body, carved it up and then put the jacket back on. The process of dismembering also changed. He had initially forced the joints to break with his hands but in later versions he had used a knife and a hacksaw.[369]

The hacksaw triggered many intriguing exchanges. The police had actually found an orange bow saw that someone had forgotten in the forest. The spot where it was found was some 100 metres from the corpse. Later, when the National Forensic Science labs tested the saw, no traces of blood were found. But the day of the saw discovery, Penttinen had been keen to help Sture get at the memory:

[Penttinen]: 'This saw we've been talking about, what kind of saw was it?'
[Sture]: 'It was a hacksaw, like I said earlier.'
[Penttinen]: 'Now, you have said hacksaw ... but are you sure you meant hacksaw?'
[Sture]: 'Yes, I did say that before, too.'
[Penttinen]: 'I thought I heard you say bow saw?'
[Sture]: 'I'm not the one who said that.'

Sture was quite right. He had never said anything except hacksaw in the previous interviews. But Penttinen did not give in:

[Penttinen]: 'A hacksaw is something one uses to saw metals like iron, to cut pipe and so on, but very thin. A bow saw is what you use to saw logs ...'
[Sture]: 'I see, isn't there anything in between then ...?'

Sture must have gestured to show the saw's size, because now the solicitor, Gunnar Lundgren, joined the discussion:

[Lundgren]: 'Yes, I see, that's a smallish bow saw you're showing us.'
[Sture]: 'Yes, yes, not one of these big ones ...'
[Lundgren]: 'No, but it has quite coarse teeth, hasn't it?'
[Sture]: 'No ... oo.'

[Penttinen]: 'What was the saw used for normally, do you know?'

[Sture]: 'No, I don't know but I can imagine one could use it to cut down a tree.'

[Lundgren]: 'Branches, maybe, to prune it.'

[Sture]: 'Yes.'

[Penttinen]: 'So is it really a smaller type of bow saw?'

[Sture]: 'Yes.'[370]

Many years later, Bengt Landahl, a chief prosecutor who had been working on Sture's retrial process, said this about the interaction between interviewer and interviewee:

> Bergwall seems to have tested the ground as he delivered his story and quite smoothly adjusted it to the lead interviewer's often tendentious questions. Bergwall's answers are often formulated in a guarded manner. [...] The questions have rarely or never seemed to imply any doubt of Bergwall or put any pressure on him. When Bergwall has made obviously unreasonable statements, these have been ignored if more appropriate answers were delivered later.
>
> Nonetheless, Bergwall has made statements throughout the investigation which still remain to be incisively questioned. One such is Bergwall's claim to have carried the body of a recently murdered man into the forest in the Piteå neighbourhood during a dark, cold night and then set about dismembering the body.[371]

Sture was taken to Piteå on 21 August for a demonstration of how he went about the murder. The re-enactment began outside Piteå police station. The unmarked police car carried Sture and Penttinen, accompanied by Ståhle, Christianson, a forensic doctor called Anders Eriksson, and a nurse from Säter who was there to supply Sture with Xanax 'as required'. Van der Kwast was there, too, but in his own car. Sture was to show them the way to the crime scene but, as Penttinen explains in a later report, it didn't happen: 'Quick refers to his interview statement to the effect that his sense of direction is poor. Hence, we set out to the area in Piteå of immediate police interest.'[372]

Sture was driven to the right place. Once out of the car, he was faced with the task of leading the way to where the body was found, a site a few hundred metres into the forest. He had a cunning plan, though. Penttinen wrote that Sture had asked for help to walk on the rough ground since 'he hasn't got the strength to reach this place. Quick displays signs of anxiety, needs support and finds moving difficult.' As a result, Penttinen and the nurse half-dragged Sture in the right direction and throughout this strange country walk Penttinen closely observed Sture's anxiety level: 'The closer we get to the relevant site, the slower our rate of progress. Quick's anxiety increases. [. . .] At about 20 metres from the site, Quick wants us to stop and let him rest. From this vantage point one can also see, with some difficulty, the area of ground that was disturbed by the site investigation.'

The officers had been digging for parts of the skeleton and had removed 15–20 centimetres of moss cover over a wide area around a large stone near to where the remains of Charles Zelmanovits had been found. Once Sture could see where the digging had been done, there was no need to drag him for the last few metres.

Sture's therapy was thought to bring out his psychotic traits and so, in preparation for his journey, the medical director Dr Kall had topped up his excessive dose of benzodiazepines with Clopixol, a typical antipsychotic, and Nozinan, a strong hypnotic with antipsychotic properties. This formidable drug cocktail did its work on him. In response to Christianson's suggestion that he should try to return mentally to the night of the murder in 1976 Sture erupted. Penttinen reported: 'After a short while, Quick sat down on the stone, closed his eyes and tried to recall the event. [. . .] Concurrently, his anxiety seems to grow and he again and again emits various inarticulate noises.'

Sture had been handed an adult-sized doll to demonstrate what he had done to the body. He was bellowing as if he had been turned into a large animal – and then the 'memories' bubbled up. Penttinen reports, adding explanatory comments in brackets:

The first thing I did was to bite off the nipple, then I stand up with the 'doll' on the ground and break one of its legs upwards, like this (puts his foot on the thigh just above the knee). Then I sit down again. And take the doll in my arms and bite its penis at the same time as I . . . or just afterwards . . . then I cut here (shows with a stick on the groin, then turns doll over and shows the cut on its backside).

Sture had no problem with remembering details that could not be proven, for instance, that his partner had been in tears as he watched, or that the body had bled a lot less than he had thought it would. This kind of uncheckable stuff poured out of him, with much weeping and bellowing. He was much less fluent when asked where he had left the body. After having demonstrated that he was unable to indicate the right place, Penttinen and Christianson had to help Sture out. The 'clue' was simply to put the doll down in the right place:

[Christanson]: 'Let's try to put it down in this direction, too, so he can feel if it fits?'
[Penttinen]: 'Can you do this again so we get it on the video?'
[Sture]: 'No, you do it.'
[Christianson]: 'We could put it down the other way round as well, so you get feel of that.'
[Penttinen]: 'Is this the alternative you're after?' (Doll moved about 1 metre back from its original position near the stone, along its rounded side.) 'Look, I'm not sure this will be on the video but Thomas is nodding eagerly.'
[Sture]: 'And it . . . perhaps somehow . . . err, it's more credible like that.' (*Quick weeps*)

With the doll in the right place and positioned correctly, Penttinen tried to make Sture tell him which body parts he had removed from the site but got nowhere. Sture was far too anguished to be able to remember anything. This is how the police re-enactment ended:

[Penttinen]: 'Did something happen with the hands?'
[Sture]: 'No . . . I can't take any more.'

[Penttinen]: 'Is that supposed to mean both or either?'
[Sture]: . . .

The site visit was disrupted because Sture needed more medication to calm down. He panicked, wept and trembled.

The re-enactment report is twenty-one pages long but does not contain any suggestion that Sture knew more about the death of Charles Zelmanovits than he could have gleaned from newspapers. Under normal circumstances, this particular police investigation should have been stopped after the Piteå site visit. But the circumstances were not normal. Three days later, a pleased van der Kwast told the TT news agency that he was going to prosecute Sture for the murder. The mystery of the young man's death had been solved thanks to a new method of therapy: 'The therapy model for his treatment is unique to Säter hospital and has received international attention. Small wards, with doctors, therapists and nursing staff close at hand are factors contributing to mutual trust, so that patients feel that they can open up and speak about experiences and actions that may have been repressed for a long time.'[373]

24

The trial in Piteå

*'His screaming was like an animal's, deep as if echoing from
the abyss. He was tormented, the psychologists told us. This
was the sound of his anguish. The rest of us wondered:
What kind of creature is this?'*
Report from the Charles Zelmanovits murder trial in
Expressen, 2 November 1994.

The autumn of 1994 had arrived and Sture was waiting for his first
murder trial to begin. His medication regime was based on large doses
of Halcion (triazolam), Xanax (alprazolam) and Stesolid (diazepam),
all benzodiazepines. The World Health Organization (WHO) warns
that this class of tranquillizer has side effects including confusion,
euphoria, hallucinations, restlessness, depression, rebound insomnia,
anxiety and suicidal behaviour.[374] Unsurprisingly, given Sture's high
intake, his case notes record all of these. However, at Säter it was generally believed that his symptoms were side effects of his successful
memory work under therapy. The possibility of overdosing was not
even mentioned in the case notes. Instead, attempts were made to
control the side effects by administering more drugs. This is an example from the case notes: 'Severe anxiety during the day. At 09.30, 10
mg rectal tube Stesolid. At 17.00, severe anxiety. Lack of coordination,
sensory loss, communication difficulties. Given 1 × 1 mg tabl Xanax
at 17.00 and at 18.00. Helps so that Thomas can at least himself insert
a rectal tube 10 mg Stesolid at 18.30. Relatively less anxious after
19.00.'[375]

The case note entry lists only the medication given 'as required'.
The two Xanax tablets in the evening were 'extras' to calm Sture down

enough to self-administer the Stesolid. All this was on top of the mixture of tranquillizers and painkillers that he received on a regular schedule during the day.

Sture, now something of a celebrity, was occasionally interviewed in the evening papers. *Expressen* came to see him at Säter and published a large feature under the headline I AM AN EVIL MAN.[376] He was described as 'a melancholic and rather pathetic figure waiting for us in the visitors' room at Säter Hospital'. He tried to 'explain why his life turned out the way it did'. Sture may well have made a bleak impression but when it came to feeding the press one-liners he was as skilled as any spin doctor: 'Thomas Quick (44) says "I was created an evil man. I wish I had never been born." He said that experiences during his childhood had made him a serial killer and that the Simon event was the most significant.' The article continues:

> 'My father exploited me for sex from the age of four and until I was thirteen ... When I was four and my father was all over me, my mother came into the room. She got terribly upset and then right there in front of me, she had a miscarriage. His name would have been Simon. The pregnancy was in the seventh month. I remember everything in detail. What the foetus looked like, how the blood was everywhere. My father got hold of a knife and cut the cord. I thought my mum had burst from sheer anger! She blamed me for what had happened, because my father had been with me. I promised Simon that I would "save him" when I was a grown-up. He is an illusion. He has always existed inside me.'
>
> Thomas Quick says that he continued to be brutally abused by his father throughout childhood. Sometimes, his mother would also join in.

Sture also took the opportunity to explain the psychological theory of re-enactment: 'It is difficult, painful. Almost unbearable. But in some way I have wanted to retell my own experiences of the murders. All the time, there are parallels between what happened to me once and what I have later done as an adult.'

The news agency TT distributed a summary of the feature to all Swedish media, which meant that Sture's accusation against his parents was widely published.[377] His brothers and sisters read it and were at a loss about what to do. His brother Torvald's wife, Åsa, phoned Dr Kall and told him that she would lodge an official complaint against the hospital if Sture, who was obviously very sick, was not prevented from coming out with accusations against innocent people. The medical director replied that if Sture's siblings were so cut up they, too, might benefit from therapy at Säter.

One of Lena Arvidsson's letters contained a passage about Sture's siblings:

> Your brothers and sisters come across as so scared by what you said in the interview. Presumably 'those old things' are threatening to be aroused inside them. All that has been sealed in and stowed away ever since childhood. Do you know if they remember when Simon was born? Don't they remember anything about all the abuse (of different kinds) that went on in the family? Presumably, they don't. It is so typical that scared people go all defensive and threaten to complain about whatever comes to mind. My father tried to complain about Cajsa to the Council for Responsibility in Health Care. So rotten of him, so weak and silly! [...] Just imagine, if ordinary people could understand the ideas behind re-enactment and repressed memories.[378]

Throughout the Quick years, the Bergwall siblings were repeatedly questioned and they all consistently answered that Sture's stories about his childhood were pure invention. But nobody believed them – Sture was the only member of the family who was trusted. The family interview transcripts were left to gather dust in the secret document boxes kept in Penttinen's office. They were never referred to during any of the trials and the very fact of their existence was not acknowledged until many years later when the retrial process was under way.[379]

On 1 November 1994 the first Quick trial began. It was out of the ordinary for a local District Court case to become a nationwide concern, but with Thomas Quick as the defendant, national media organizations dispatched journalists to Piteå. I asked Sture what he felt as his first day in court approached and he replied that ever since he had confessed to the murder of Thomas Blomgren he had thought of himself as a convicted murderer. His first court case as a murder suspect meant much less to him than one might have expected. When I had read what was written about him at the time, I saw what he meant. Van der Kwast's campaign to have Sture tied to the Blomgren murder had been so successful that, even before his case was heard, the press unhesitatingly presented Sture as a serial killer. The trial was mostly seen as a formality.[380]

In Sweden, criminal court cases are governed by the so-called 'immediacy principle', which means that the court's final decision is based on what is presented orally during the proceedings. The bench – in criminal cases usually consisting of one member of the judiciary and three locally elected lay judges – is under no obligation to inform itself about the prosecutor-led investigation and the documentation it has generated. It is up to the prosecution and the defendant's representative to explain all relevant evidence to the court. Witnesses, lay or expert, are heard by the bench if they have something pertinent to say in the police interviews, and all the technical evidence must be presented in the courtroom. A few weeks after the judgement, the sentence is announced, backed by what is termed 'reasoning of the court'. The latter is an explanation of how the court reached its verdict. It includes a clarification of how any existing guidelines were applied and which witness statements or pieces of evidence were considered especially important.

The 'immediacy principle' defines court proceedings as one-off theatrical events. Once the trial has ended, it cannot be repeated, what has been said is not recorded and no transcript is added to the records. The sentence, with its account of the reasoning of the court, is all that remains. The trial in Piteå went on for two days but the documents covering the process only run to eighteen pages, excluding a handful of written expert statements and, of course, the media coverage by the journalists. Finding out what happened when Sture was found guilty of the Charles Zelmanovits murder is a difficult task.

It's safe to say that the trial was out of the ordinary. For one thing, the prosecution and the defence did not take each other's arguments apart, as one would expect. The prosecutor, Christer van der Kwast, and the solicitor acting for the defendant, Gunnar Lundgren, competed over who was the most convinced of Sture's guilt. In the spring of 1993, Lundgren had criticized van der Kwast for not taking Sture to court in the Asplund case,[381] and now he was at it again, announcing to the evening paper *Aftonbladet*: 'Quick has actually confessed to five murders but the police are not yet convinced that everything he says is true. Unlike me.'[382]

The big draw of the trial was of course Sture, who appeared in public for the first time. Kall had been generous with medication and doped his patient with everything from Xanax and Stesolid to Clopixol and Nozinan. It was a very subdued Sture who acted as remorseful serial killer and *Aftonbladet* noted his falsely meek manner: 'Of course it would have been satisfying to see his monstrous character on show in some not too excessive way, but that is a meaningless thought. In fact, he is a pale, balding and unremarkable-looking chap wearing jeans. Now and then he wrings his hands.'[383]

But the crime was remarkable enough. TT reported that the judges 'tried to keep their expressions neutral' but that unprepared people in the courtroom 'became deeply uneasy' as van der Kwast proceeded with his 'factual but detailed'[384] account of the deed:

Mid-morning on 12 November 1976, Sture and a friend who had since died (van der Kwast named him) left Falun together in the friend's two-door Opel and arrived late at night in Piteå. They had a shared interest in young boys and were looking for someone to use for sex. On the south-eastern side of the town, they spotted Charles. Applying the brakes in a way that made the boot fly open, a move they had planned, they started to talk to the boy about the mishap with the boot. Charles had seemed dejected about something and they offered him a lift back home. Sture remembered in particular that the boy had worn gloves. The fifteen-year-old climbed into the car willingly and 'a degree of trust developed' between him and Sture, resulting – according to van der Kwast – in them 'masturbating each other'. The driver parked the car outside a timber storage yard and the subsequent violence was due to a mental shift that made Sture 'psychotic'.

After having asked Charles if he would masturbate the driver as well, which he agreed to do, Quick experienced a moment of psychotic confusion. He thought that Charles had said 'Alvar is alive' and this triggered fury and aggressiveness in him. They were standing outside the car and he grabbed Charles's neck from the front in a powerful stranglehold and kept squeezing until the boy had died.[385]

'Alvar' was a reference to Alvar Larsson, a boy who had disappeared in 1967 and allegedly was Sture's second victim. While van der Kwast set out his case, the room was completely silent but for Mrs Zelmanovits, Charles's mother, who was sobbing. Sture, with Birgitta Ståhle at his side and surrounded by six psychiatric nurses from Säter and the national police force, also became very moved but, as *Expressen* said: 'He burst into tears – but no one felt sorry for him. [. . .] Truth, reality, anguish – all had caught up with him. He rested his head on his clasped hands. The nurses administered tranquillizers. When the prosecutor produced the saw Bergwall had used to dismember his victim, he looked the other way [. . .].'[386]

Then van der Kwast showed the court the video recording from the re-enactment and horror peaked at the sequence showing Sture seated on a stone in the forest, bellowing as he described how he butchered the dead body. The scene had the effect of a bomb blast. *Expressen* was shaken: 'The tape was horrible. No uncensored film could have been worse.'

Aftonbladet's man was just as upset:

When Thomas Quick weeps the sound is inhuman, a deep, senseless wailing. A kind of yawling. As if from a tortured animal. The sound of human horror. [. . .] There is something about that sound of his. I twist and turn on my seat in the courtroom, full of disgust and a kind of rage. Will it never end? [. . .] Having heard the sound he made, I can no longer doubt [him]. The words are ejected as if by deep convulsions, as if vomiting. Yes, this must be true.'[387]

When the video started up, Sture fled from the room, accompanied by Ståhle and the nurses. *Expressen* wrote: 'His screaming was like an animal's, deep as if echoing from the abyss. He was tormented, the psychologists told us. This was the sound of his anguish. The rest of us wondered: What kind of creature is this?' [388]

When Sture gave his own account of his dreadful crime to the court, the courtroom was cleared. His legal representative had asked for a hearing behind closed doors, a request that was granted. *Aftonbladet* explained why: 'He is fragile. The police and the psychologists are worried that he will stop telling his story. Or possibly retract everything he had said, in which case the murders of other boys (at least another three) will not come to trial.'[389]

It took Sture two hours to get through his story, bit by bit. According to *Expressen*'s reporter, who had talked to someone who had been allowed to stay, 'Throughout, he wept off and on, and had to be given more medicine.'

The trial documents refer to what he had to say about carving up the body. He had revealed that, on the way back to Falun, he and his mate had had 'a fight' about the 'body parts he brought along' and also that they 'had a wash at some garage'. He was unable to 'give an account of what had happened to the body parts'.[390]

The police witness, Seppo Penttinen, stated that 'what Quick indicated on site substantially agreed with what he had said in previous interviews' and that 'the place located by Quick as the spot where he left the body is exactly the same as where the remains of Charles Zelmanovits were found'.

That all this was untrue would have become obvious to the court if they had read the interview transcripts. But they had not, so Penttinen could say what he liked. He lied, but almost certainly because he was totally convinced that Sture was the killer and felt he was assisting the cause of justice.

It was probably the statement by the expert witness Dr Sven Å Christianson that more than anything else persuaded the court of Sture's guilt. Christianson had made two written submissions to the court and also took the stand in person. One of his submissions was the memory test that had been Christianson's initial reason for visiting Sture at Säter. The result simply showed that Sture's memory was slightly above average.[391] However, the other submission was truly interesting. Entitled 'Psychological Conditions Affecting the Statement by Thomas Quick', Christianson's document explains, on the basis of 'current scientific findings and clinical experience', the extent to which 'a perpetrator might be expected to grasp, remember and recount a violent crime that he has committed'.[392] I found the following familiar ideas on page 4, under the heading 'The Murder as a Narrative': 'Murders can be narratives that reflect events, [often] traumatic ones, which they [the murderers] have experienced. These memories create primitive beliefs which the perpetrator is unable to consciously articulate. Instead, murdering becomes the language in which various past events are expressed.'[393]

Christianson is presenting his version of Margit's re-enactment theory. When I read this for the first time, it was unclear why this personal hypothesis should turn up in an expert statement supposedly based on 'current scientific findings and clinical experience'. No source was given. It was all very strange.

It became no less strange when, a little further along in the document, Christianson says things that could have been lifted from one of Margit's lectures in the 1970s:

This type of perpetrator feels bereft of something, that something has been stolen from him and he must take it back by whatever means. To talk about the loss hurts too much (it leads to depression), and, instead, cravings for revenge and restitution develop. His acts are symptoms that can be understood as strategies for survival. In this sense, his murders become rebirths into a better life. Rapes and killings have symbolic dimensions, enabling the taking of his own life while at the same time conceiving his self – that is, he can be reborn. (Such acts can also be understood as raping his mother, whom he wants to humiliate.)

The members of the bench must have been utterly baffled. Murder as 'restitution'? Rape and murder 'enabl[ing]' the criminal to 'take his own life while at the same time conceiving his self'? What was he on about?

Later in his statement, Christianson refers to the curious fact that Sture had been unable to show the police where he had hidden the body parts that he claimed to have carried off: 'To relinquish parts of the dead body would have taken from the perpetrator the illusion of existing through the boys.'

What did this mean? Few members of the court were likely to follow Christianson's line of thought. However, the document submitted by the expert from the University of Stockholm had all the authority of science. Christianson went further. In the witness box, he actually stated that Sture's confession was *not* false. This is how the judges referred to the expert's submission in the 'reasoning of the court':

> Quick has confessed to the act, which is relatively unusual. However, confessions can be falsehoods. There are, for instance, confessions made under duress and confessions made in situations in which the suspect cannot remember but accepts evidence as is presented to him. Neither pertains in the case of Quick's confession. There are also voluntary false confessions, made by those who want media recognition or who feel a sense of shared guilt. In many instances of false confessions, the person admitting guilt is unable to distinguish between fantasy and reality. It does not pertain in the Quick case.

Interestingly, this passage proves that Christianson was aware of some of the different types of false confessions that had been discussed by experimental psychologists since the mid-1980s.[394] He claimed to know that Sture's confessions did not fall into any known category of false confession, although his grounds for this certainty are not clarified. The District Court had no option but to take Christianson's expert witness statement as a declaration that Sture was telling the truth.

Sture was duly convicted of the murder of Charles Zelmanovits.

The main emphasis in the 'reasoning of the court' was on the importance of Christianson's statement: 'The evidence provided by Dr Christianson concerning the function of Quick's memory and his understanding, based on experience, of memory functions, heavily tips the balance towards accepting the truth of Quick's statements to the court.'

Van der Kwast badly needed Christianson's help, because the prosecution's case was full of holes. When the chief prosecutor, Bengt Landahl, applied for retrial of Sture's conviction in the Zelmanovits case, he had no time for van der Kwast's efforts:

> The prosecutor in this trial claimed that the police investigation supported the decision to believe Bergwall's confession. The standard of the technical evidence alone is such that it is highly questionable if there is a basis for stating that a crime has taken place. The police investigation of a missing person, set in motion on 13 November 1976, and the interviews with Charles Zelmanovits's friends that were carried out in that context, speak strongly in favour of the conclusion that Charles Zelmanovits froze to death while in the same place where his remains were found seventeen years later.

Nevertheless, it is easy to understand why the court was impressed by Christianson. He 'argued strongly' for Sture's guilt and the court naturally assumed that this was an expert with the backing of science. Christianson added to his impact by giving media interviews at the time of the trial in which he sold, with complete conviction, Sture's trustworthiness and the role of the murders as 'narratives'.

TT wrote: 'According to Christianson, Quick is not fantasizing when he confesses to having murdered one boy after another. The crimes are recapitulations of his own feelings and experiences in childhood.'[395]

Aftonbladet reported:

> He sees the murders as part of a narrative that is meaningful to Quick, that has a kind of 'inner logic'. At the age of four, Quick was

raped by his father. His childhood was 'stolen' from him. [. . .] His delusion is that he can recreate his own life when he destroys another's. But the solace is short-lived. He must kill again. It becomes a ritual. He feels that he owns his victims. He needs to possess their bodies. Only then, at the site of the murder of a boy, Christianson tells us, is the killer able to relive not only the act itself but the abuse he himself suffered as the boy he once was.[396]

What was Christianson up to? I ploughed through his articles and book in search of an explanation. In the end, I found something interesting. In March 1997, roughly three and a half years after the trial in Piteå, Oxford University Press published a collection of essays by international memory researchers called *Recovered Memories and False Memories*. The editor had asked his contributors to present their views on an old and controversial issue: did they or did they not agree with the founder of psychoanalysis, Sigmund Freud, when early in his career he claimed that people repress memories of terrifying events? Sven Å Christianson from Sweden was one of the contributors and his paper, written with a PhD student, presented a case history in support of the hypothesis that some murderers are unaware of the violent crimes they have committed. The case history was that of an unnamed Swedish serial killer:

> *A man is receiving therapeutic treatment at a psychiatric ward. After some time, he begins to tell about one murder after the other that he has committed. Murders committed during a time span of 25 years, and which he had been very reluctant to consciously access before going into therapy.*
>
> *Not until this serial killer was sentenced to psychiatric treatment for a series of minor crimes and found himself in the relatively safe environment surrounding therapeutic treatment, did he begin to slowly recover memories for the sexual-sadistic murders that he had committed on young boys. Memories of the killings caused overwhelming anxiety, due to the fact that they were in part a re-enactment of the sexual-sadistic abuse that the serial killer himself had been subjected to as a child. It was therefore*

difficult for him to tell about the murders during interrogations by the police.[397]

Christianson was writing about Sture. He added that he had personally assisted the police in clearing up a problematic investigation, clearly referring to the crime scene re-enactment in the forest near Piteå:

During the murder investigation, the reinstatement of internal and external context information was found to be surprisingly effective for retrieval, for example at a site where he had dissected a boy 14 years [in fact 17 years] earlier. Before specific questions were asked about the killing, the senior author [i.e. Christianson] assisted in reinstating both the internal and external context that he had experienced at the time. A method similar to the cognitive interview technique (see Fisher and Geiselman, 1992) was used, in which memories of smells, body positions, various sounds and emotions were triggered. After this reinstatement of his internal context, he showed strong emotions and could describe vivid memories of the killing. He was able to give specific details, which he had not had access to in previous interrogations.[398]

Christianson used Sture as proof that a murderer could repress the memories of his or her killings and as proof of the validity of re-enactment theory. This means that the reference to 'current scientific findings' made by Christianson in the Piteå court was his own research on Sture's mental state, work that was incomplete and unpublished at the time. Christianson was trying to turn the Säter ideas and hypotheses into science and to do so he used the conclusions published in 1997 to advise a guilty verdict in 1994. The outcome – that Sture was officially a murderer – was a necessary condition for using the Quick case in the way Christianson did in 1997.

Just thinking about it is rather like making a hypnotic trip in a time machine.

How could a respected academic researcher act in this way? Why was Christianson so keen to turn Säter's weird hypotheses into science?

His contribution to the OUP volume might as well have been written by Margit Norell herself.

The motives of the memory expert were adding up to the trickiest enigma of all in the entire Quick affair, and I wanted to find the solution.

25

The world of Thomas Quick

'Once more, I want to emphasize that it required a
continuing therapeutic process for Sture to become aware both
of his early experiences and the murders of which he is guilty.'
Margit Norell, in her unpublished book manuscript
'The World of Thomas Quick'.

Now Sture was officially a convicted murderer, but his life hardly changed at all, because he was sentenced to continued forensic psychiatric care. At least two days every week, he was in therapy with Birgitta Ståhle and, on Wednesdays, he was offered therapy treatment with Lena Arvidsson. Between sessions, he spoke to Ståhle and Penttinen on the phone. He wrote a lot and his writing mostly took the form of long, emotional poems about the murders he had committed, the abuse he had suffered and the hard battle he was fighting with his memory.

For Margit, the Zelmanovits sentence was very important. In her book manuscript she writes:

So, how can we be certain that what Sture says is true? [...] Of course we will never be able to issue complete guarantees but the therapeutic process, in its totality, seems to me to confirm the meaning of what it has been about. It is also worth repeating that Sture has not been suspected of any of the murders to which he has recently admitted guilt but that it all came from him and once aware, he has contacted the police and told them of what has emerged from his memory. The police confirmed what Sture had said.[399]

Margit's sense of confirmation was based on van der Kwast's and Penttinen's wholehearted acceptance of her own absolute but groundless faith in Sture's grasp of the truth. The confirmations were mutually interdependent – biting each other's tails.

Margit was obsessed with Sture and talked about him all the time, with everyone. Patricia Tudor-Sandahl told me that her therapy and supervision sessions often started with Margit reporting the latest stomach-churning items from Sture's therapy sessions. I interviewed a well-known writer who had seen Margit twice a week for twenty-three years, and he said that Margit had been 'full of Thomas Quick' and would indeed talk about him to her patients. Annie Norell Beach said that her mother even talked about Sture's revolting stories when she came over for supper. It was hard to take, especially for Annie's children. She recalls once practically ordering Margit either to stop going on about Sture or leave.

The day after the sentence had been announced in the Zelmanovits case, Margit wrote to Sture in response to a letter from him mentioning that he wanted to find a publisher for his collection of poetry. She clearly believed that she and Sture were fighting the same ideological battle and now she wanted to give him a little maternal advice:

Dear Sture. Thank you for your letter and the long prose-poem you had enclosed.

I have of course read it and given it much thought. What I would like to share with You is this: I feel it would be better not to present Your weighty material in poetic form but rather as a coherent prose account in which what You write follows the spontaneous time sequence of your therapeutic discoveries. No matter if it leads to repetitions, which would mean more details and more contexts, and thus, in consequence, make it easier to follow the therapeutic process as a whole. This should – or so I believe – contribute greatly to You being understood by as many as possible and also influencing both therapists and others as strongly as possible. Those are, naturally, goals that both You and I wish could be reached.

I am very aware of how hard it must be for you to wait and first go through with most of the trials and then with all those difficult things that emerge as You and Brigitta work together. I can only hope that You can cope with the strain, and that You feel that I want to support You as much as I can during this process.

Margit also took the opportunity to provide Sture with an analysis of the Simon event, which to her was crucial. Her analysis started from the poem Sture had sent her:

As you write yourself –
'It can feel possible to reach tomorrow if I believe that my story, the entire story of my life, is important and should be told.'
I am also certain of this, Sture, with regard to Your mention of 'the entire story of my life'. Of course, as a 4 or 5-year-old, You did not have the strength to truly see what your eyes were seeing and instead you turned into Simon and You thought of Simon's shut eyes and so You wanted to help Simon – if you did not, what had happened to Simon might also befall you. Naturally, these were Your thoughts as a 4-year-old from inside Your terrible loneliness and because You had been blamed for Simon's death. So, it is not until now, during the long and troubling therapeutic process, that you can take into Your mind what Your eyes saw then and hence no longer need Simon for seeing it. Would that You could feel much less alone as You were then, Sture, and that You do not need to hide
'behind the shut eyes of the foetus with my soul-less body,
   My empty shell.'
You are no soulless body, Sture, and no empty shell but a living human being who, inter alia, can tell of
'what it is like to live with guilt so heavy and true that by itself
   It motivates my survival!'
You have after all already found, and outstandingly so, in all You have written

'the language that helps the listener to understand and the reader to grasp.'

The great and uphill task is to continue on that road, Sture. I can only hope and wish that You will be able to complete it.

She ended her letter with a handsome offer:

I read what you have written about your therapeutic work and the approach of the therapists, and I like it very much. I would like your piece, with an introduction by Birgitta, to become part of the anthology about therapeutic work that is now being planned by our working group on Object-relations therapy. It will be the editorial board that make the final decision, probably at the meeting on 5 Dec.

With warmest regards!

Margit

The letter had been typed by her secretary and signed by Margit with the same kind of blue pen that she used for her many letters to David Schecter. Margit was offering Sture the chance to contribute to *A Room to Live In*, the anthology her pupils were preparing in her honour. Only members of her group were invited to contribute; Margit essentially viewed Sture as another pupil and as concerned as she was with the task of enlightening the masses. Sture joined in happily, as he told me:

It matters to me that no one should forget how much of an outsider I was when Säter took me in – because of my previous history, including the bank robbery – and that my isolation became total after my first murder conviction. I had nothing to lose by being 110 percent loyal to Säter, Birgitta and Margit. It was among these people in that place where I felt I belonged and it also allowed me to live inside a fog of drugs – 24/7. We – the ward and I, Birgitta and I, Seppo and I, Sven-Åke and I – we all stuck together, a tightly linked gang, and we felt we could take on the world.

That sense of unity also comes through in these lines, written in one of Sture's daily notes in May 1995:

I have one deeply felt wish (to fulfil it we'd have to forget about the rules and regulations) and it is that Birgitta, Margit, Sven-Åke and I could meet and just talk. Then we can (because I feel good in their company) talk and exchange ideas. As of now, such a meeting matters very much to me and I think it would have an important function. In such conversations, there would be no need for secretiveness. I would be able to speak freely about my experiences, air them in public, as it were. This note ends with a plea that such conversations would be set up. What do you think?[400]

Sture would never write anything for *A Room to Live In*. Margit had had a brainwave: she had been collecting material for her book on Sture for a couple of years already and, in 1995, she asked him to contribute to it. It would contain not only her own material and Ståhle's therapy notes, but also Sture's work, in the form of his poems and daily notes. He even had a say in the book's title. In the summer of 1995, he wrote to Ståhle: 'It gives me real satisfaction to think that some of my texts will be included in the book. Overall, I have no problem with the concept "The World of Thomas Quick".'[401]

Margit started writing in earnest in the autumn of 1995. It seems to have triggered a major outbreak of explanatory theorizing around Sture's unique persona, an activity in which he participated vigorously. His speculations, never mind how absurd, went straight into Margit's manuscript. One example: while under the influence of assorted tablets, it suddenly came to him why Thomas Quick hid certain of his victims' body parts – the reason was that he literally wanted to recreate Simon, his chopped-up baby brother:

The image of how I build him up step by step, making a whole boy take shape, an entire Simon body, by collecting elements of that body from other boys, how I re-enact my traumas but at the same time make sure to keep my promise to Simon: One day, I will make you whole again.

The foundation stone was Alvar's heart and when my memory reminds me of how I longed to swallow Simon to make him safe and to transform my loneliness into togetherness – when I killed Alvar, that memory has stayed with me as I open his chest and take out his heart. [...] I do not dare, not now when I'm alone and all this is so new, recall the boy I killed after Charles, but somehow know that I cut off his right leg and ate some of his stomach. When I cut up Charles, I take his left thigh bone and so, when I kill again, there is no need for it.

Still, there was something else that Sture wondered about:

When I commit each murder I remove certain different body parts in line with my wish to recreate a whole Simon. What I can't quite understand is why, just about every time, I bite off and swallow either one or both nipples, and the anal sphincter – except from when I killed Thomas [Blomgren]. These acts are common denominators in my murders, apart from the sex act, and I cannot find inside me their emotional meaning, whether symbolically or in real terms.[402]

Odd, indeed. Obviously a subject for the next therapy session. These ruminations were also added to Margit's manuscript.

In September 1995, Ståhle reported to Margit that Sture had come across a new memory fragment: 'As a teenager he had used to mix flesh from his victims' bodies into the mix of meat and offal made ready for sausage making in M's massive meat grinder.' This became a subject for discussion during therapy, and after one such session Sture put forward this analysis: 'It is so awfully dreadful to observe, feel, etc. what we were talking about today. I have a vision of the repetitive pattern and can trace its origin, but I also sense the lust for revenge it represents. When M made the *pölsa* sausage mix, I knew that at least someone in my family would share in my macabre action.'

Margit completed the picture by adding her own analytical note to Sture's retelling: 'The origin must be the episode when M forces Sture to eat parts of Simon's body.'[403]

Sture was a dream patient. Just after the New Year in 1996, he consolidated his elite status by having another article published on the op-ed pages in *Dagens Nyheter*.

The social democratic party had won the election and Sture's escape during the summer meant that the new Minister for Social Services, Ingela Thalén, had to make good on her promise to scrutinize the provision of forensic psychiatry. Now, Sture launched a wholehearted defence of Säter. He praised the therapy that had brought back the first twelve years of life in memories that 'his thoughts had not recognized'. There would have been readers who knew enough about the history of psychoanalysis to observe how the serial killer closed ranks with theoreticians like Judith Herman, Jeffrey Masson and Alice Miller when Sture made this subtly pointed remark directed at the treacherous Freud and his theory of drives: 'The therapists took up that which my body had remembered with such seriousness and so vividly, [and] did not dismiss as fantasies what I was at last able to articulate in words, nor [did they fit] it into a closed theoretical structure.'[404]

In April, Sture granted an interview to *Dagens Nyheter*. The paper splashed the piece over two pages, just as it had the fateful write-up of the therapy that had allegedly turned Lars-Inge Svartenbrandt into a model citizen. A journalist called Kerstin Vinterhed wrote up her interview and chose to portray Sture as a hero – practically a martyr – in painful pursuit of the truth. In the largest newspaper in the country, Vinterhed established that Sture, 'from a very early age had been subjected to anal sex by his father, a practice that increased in intensity after his mother had given birth to a stillborn boy at home', and that after the miscarriage, 'his mother also joined in the abuse of the little boy [...]'. Vinterhed took the view that the murders were 'reenactments' and that Sture should not be blamed for committing them: 'The restaging of the abusive acts that he had been subjected to as a child is driven by an inner force outside his control, beyond or apart from words.'

Vinterhed's description of Sture's battle has a poetic vibrato not unlike Sture's own: 'In Säter, he is taught to speak. There, as if inside a womb and protected against all dangers, he dares to slowly approach the core of his own fate, dares to remember and put past events into words. In his inner darkness, he moves as if blind but is now guided by the therapist Birgitta Ståhle [. . .].'

In the interview Sture explained his altruistic motives for fighting this battle with himself: 'To take responsibility, I must first remember, which is the one and only way open to me. I do it for the sake of my victims.'

Kerstin Vinterhed felt sure that the future of forensic psychiatry depended on whether he succeeded: 'By now, Thomas Quick's life story has become a test case, an evaluation of all of forensic psychiatry and the issues that have been debated with regard to its effectiveness. He has so far confessed to two murders while under therapy. If there are more, it will be a victory for Säter [. . .].'[405]

The piece is illustrated with a photo of Sture, lying on the bed in his room. Ståhle is posed on an armchair next to him, apparently deep in conversation with him. The caption reads: 'The therapist Birgitta Ståhle pulls threads from the tangle that is Thomas Quick's perverted sexuality and past violence. Undergoing therapy, he is allowed to be a child again.'

Interestingly, *Dagens Nyheter* ran a short interview with the child psychologist Anita Cederström on the same page. Cederström denied that 'repressed memories' could suddenly re-emerge in adulthood and referred to contemporary research on memory function. 'This is not how the brain works,' she stated, and added that there were 'examples of false narratives told to satisfy the therapist'. That the paper decided to introduce this caveat into its coverage of the Quick story shows how controversial what was happening at Säter was in 1995.

Sture did not stop at stating his belief in the hypotheses about repression of traumatic memories and symbolic re-enactments, but also backed up the dubious diagnosis of 'multiple personality syndrome' aka 'dissociative identity disorder' (DID), a more recent term. People suffering from this mental condition are thought have at least two separate personalities, each with its own feelings, memories and behaviours. In the 1990s, the existence of people with 'multiple personalities' was as tantalizing and intriguing a possibility as that of serial killers. DID had recently been included in the American Psychiatric Association's diagnostic manual of mental disorders and it only took a few more years for it to go from being a rarity to one of the best known – and most contentious – psychiatric conditions.

The questions raised about the disorder mostly concerned the function of 'split personality'. Was it a way to repress childhood abuse or was it an outcome of therapists encouraging role play? In popular culture and in clinical settings such as Säter, the trauma theory won the argument.

Meanwhile, research by experimental psychologists increasingly supported the idea that DID was one by-product of certain approaches to therapy. In 1994, the American professor of psychology Nicholas P. Spanos published an influential paper in which he presented evidence supporting the hypothesis that 'multiple personality disorder' is the outcome of patients attempting, more or less consciously, to satisfy the expectations of the doctor or therapist.[406] Many other sceptical voices in the profession agreed.[407] The notion of dissociated identities was, in their view, a social construct – a form of role playing rather than an actual disorder.

The consequences of the 'disorder' could, in some cases, become very serious for patients. The case of Nadean Cool, an American assistant nurse, was much talked about in the 1990s and confirmed the suspicions of the sceptics. Cool went into therapy in 1986, to treat her bulimia and moderate depression. During the five years of therapy that followed, her therapist convinced her that she had been subject to abuse in childhood. She uncovered terrible memories of ritualistic torture and some 130 different personalities within her, a varied collection that included children, angels and even a duck. The psychiatrist used questionable methods, including hypnosis and suggestive regression. Cool later sued the psychiatrist for malpractice and in March 1997, after five weeks' trial, her case was settled out of court for $2.4 million. The 'treatment' had made her believe in fantasies and destroyed five years of her life.[408]

Margit was convinced that dissociated identities were outcomes of particularly dreadful experiences in childhood, meaning that she practically expected to see Sture suffering from DID as well. Sure enough, the first signs emerged during therapy. Sometimes, he spoke with an unusually rough voice. In August 1994, Ståhle wrote to Margit:

> Enclosing some of Sture's recent writings. He is under such pressure now, but bears up. We had to strap him to his bed for a while when he became Ellington, i.e. the father who killed Simon. As you can see, what he writes shows how much contact he now has at many different levels. We progress cautiously and respectfully to let him meet his father and see what the man did. I promise you, I saw him transformed to Satan, fully personified, sort of literally, and then [I witnessed] Sture's response to [the transformation]. He bares his throat – and then comes the denial in the words, 'No, this is not Dad, it is a gramophone record that has jumped out of him and says this.' What Satan has told him is – you shall taste death.[409]

Sture's new identity as the evil Ellington caused much excitement. Margit was so intrigued by the concept that she reserved a special section of her book solely for this phenomenon. It was established that Sture had turned into his evil father as a child, in order to survive spiritually the appalling abuse, and that he, as an adult, had committed all his murders in the Ellington persona.

On Monday 13 March 1995, Sture allowed evil Ellington to make his first appearance outside the therapy room. In her report to Margit, Ståhle said she had been woken in the middle of the night by a phone call – 'I woke up when my husband said "There's a madman on the phone who wants to talk to you, he says his name is Ellington."'

In the account, Ståhle's comments to Margit are in italics.

[Ståhle]: 'Sture, this is Birgitta.'
[Ellington]: (*laughs for quite a while*) 'This is Ellington. I want to speak to the therapist.'
[Birgitta]: 'Sture.'

[Ellington]: 'Sture is in bed. He's anxious (*laughs*). They believe him, his anxiety and his stories. He is manipulating everyone.'

[Ståhle]: 'Who are you?'

[Ellington]: 'I am Ellington. We've met a few times (*laughs*).'

He lets me know that he despises Sture who is always anxious, who is weak, and also tells me that he despises the therapy, as he calls me 'the therapist'.

[Ellington]: 'I will tell you about the trip to Norway.'

Now I know for sure that it is Sture in the Ellington persona, and decide to listen to him and work to get through to Sture himself.

[Ellington]: 'It was Patrik and me. We are driving to Oslo. Nearby, just before – (*now he starts laughing again*) – I try to manipulate Patrik and succeed (*sounds triumphant at his power and ability*) to make him leave the car (*laughs again*). He goes along and kills the boy. It's he who killed the boy. He wanted it, you see. And it was I who made him want it.'

Now, the man starts weeping quietly. Then I hear Sture's voice whisper 'Birgitta'. Realize straightaway that I must connect with Sture, make him see all this clearly, become strong, strong in his relationship with Ellington. Ellington's voice sort of growls in the background but Sture starts talking to me and I believe he has found the way back to himself.[410]

Later the same night, Sture made a note about this episode which ended up in Margit's document collection. He wrote that he had just gone to bed when something strange happened to him:

[I] switched the light off. A few minutes passed and then – a very powerful wave of anxiety flowed through me, I had strong spasms making all my joints twitch, a sensation of fighting for air (I'm sure I didn't breathe). I was about to press the alarm but couldn't. And then, a transformation – as the cliché has it, like a bolt from the blue.

Ellington got out of bed, mobile, strong. He had 'left Sture behind'. He went off to phone Birgitta. I don't know what they were talking about but after a while I hear, faintly, Birgitta's voice and the tension and spasms are back. Gunnar and Lena [*nurses*] help me and soon (with Xanax and Stesolid) I feel calmer. I am back in bed. It was the first time Ellington controlled me, apart from his appearances during therapy. I am very keen and interested to talk to Birgitta about this – what Ellington said, what it all meant etc.[411]

This piece of theatre was received so enthusiastically that Sture added to his repertoire of alter egos with a woman known as 'Nana', a stand-in for his allegedly mean and nasty mother, and with the English-speaking 'Cliff', an incarnation of his eldest brother Sten-Ove. The more drugs Sture was given, the more uninhibited his perform- ances; and the more frequently he performed, the more drugs were administered. It took some time before his identity-shifts began to appear in his case notes, but in July 1995 it was officially recognized that he possibly suffered from multiple personality disorder (as they called it then): 'The patient has a superficial ability to function well, he demonstrates verbal skills and is logical. But his personality has deep cracks and unfavourable circumstances trigger such desperate reaction patterns that psychosis seems likely. MPD is another option.'[412]

Intriguingly, Ellington often claimed that Sture was lying and that the therapy was only a game, as in this exchange in another night-time phone call:

[Ståhle]: 'I want to talk to Sture.'
[Ellington]: 'You can't. Only Ellington here.'
[Ståhle]: 'Can you help me?'
[Ellington]: 'What? Do I get to join one of your therapy
    games?'[413]

Another example, from October 1995, in a hand-written letter from Ellington to Sture: 'Sture is a mythomaniac. And a fucking pig. He hasn't got a chance against me! I am Ellington and tonight I'll trick him into hanging himself. Watching him do it will please me, please me a lot. I know the truth, not Sture!!'[414]

On one occasion, Sture came out into the ward at 21.40 with a shallow cut on his throat. He had inflicted it himself with a broken bottle of shaving lotion. He said that he was Nana and that 'Sture should hang'. The ward staff reported: 'Runs around on the ward, breaks a wall clock. Strapped down, given medication and can then be left alone.'[415]

Sture has told me that his performances were attempts to make himself as interesting a patient as possible. He was disinhibited and confused by his benzodiazepine consumption and now claims that by now the liberal drug regime was beginning to turn him into a psychotic. He was apparently out of his mind most evenings because of all the tablets he had taken during the day. Then, he might phone Penttinen or Ståhle at home and admit things he could hardly remember the following day. There is proof of this in his case notes, where I found the following entry on 19 September:

At 17.15, Thomas becomes restless, starts walking up and down in the ward. At 17.30, given 2 × 1 mg tabl. Xanax as req. and we go with him to the music room because he wants some peace. Anxiety increasing all the time, he lies down on the floor, crawls about, moans. Anxiety persists. Says he is somewhere but can't remember what he has done. Can later be led back to his room, given 1 × 10 mg rectal tube Stesolid which was made available to Thomas at 18.35. Feels better after a while. Wants to phone the investigative officer re his murders, talks to him for a long time, about 1 hour.[416]

Penttinen wrote a report about the call, so we know what troubled Sture that evening. He said that he was in a low state mentally and wanted to tell Penttinen about certain things he was anxious about.

What followed was a long list of confessions and statements. Sture said that on one of the site visits to Lake Ryggen, he had been within 50–75 metres of the Asplund hiding place. He said that a 'Norwegian boy' he had murdered was buried in a sports ground in Lindesberg. He went on to speak about Olle Högbom, an eighteen-year-old from Sundsvall who disappeared without trace after a friend's party in 1983: 'He was in tears as he said that Olle was still alive at least at the point in time of his entering the car that Quick was driving. Quick's intention was to hide the body in the same area where he had previously buried Charles Zelmanovits.'

Sture also said that he had kidnapped an Israeli called Yenon Levi in Uppsala and could provide details. Next, he confessed to a brand-new murder: 'Quick also speaks of a person he calls "Martin" whom he hid beneath a pile of moss in the area of Sätrabrunn. The name Martin is not necessarily the person's actual name. The person is 18–19 years old. Quick was on his own when he killed this person.'

To bring the conversation to an end, Sture confessed to another two murders.[417] This wealth of information could have kept Penttinen busy for months and, later on, there was indeed much fruitless digging in the Lindesberg sports ground.

The case notes record how Sture spent his evening once he had finished talking with Penttinen: 'Later in the evening he spoke on the phone with his therapist for about 45 minutes. Minor anxiety attack around midnight, dealt with by 1×1 mg tabl. Xanax. Fell asleep later. Talked in his sleep occas. saying that he wants to die or to kill.'[418]

In this hyped-up state, Sture's mind was a cornucopia of information, all of which was of legal interest. Once the first murder conviction had established his status as a murderer, the Quick investigation was effectively granted unlimited resources. The national crime squad set up a dedicated Quick commission chaired by Christer van der Kwast. Its brief was to organize the investigations of Sture's long list of murder confessions that had to be constantly updated. During the spring of 1995 police records nationwide were picked over for unsolved murder cases and missing persons.

Soon, several murder investigations were running in parallel. In April, Penttinen conducted another interview about Johan Asplund in which Sture tested his patience by claiming that his brother Sten-Ove had driven him to Sundsvall in 1980 and stood by, masturbating, while Sture butchered Johan. Sven-Ove had then brought the boy's head with him to Uppsala and Sture had lost track of what happened to it.[419]

He made this statement just after the publication of Sven-Ove's book *My Brother Thomas Quick*. It was written after the trial, and Sven-Ove accepted that Sture was a killer and probably a serial killer, since he was suspected of other murders. He insisted, however, that Sture's allegations of childhood abuse were all lies. The family had lived in crowded circumstances and, if only for that reason, it would have been impossible for their father to rape and torture Sture without anybody noticing. Sven-Ove defended his parents' characters and dismissed Sture as a fantasist. This was like a red rag to Margit and Ståhle – and, of course, to Sture. He might well have fingered his brother as an accomplice as a reprisal for writing that scurrilous book. After that interview, van der Kwast put the Asplund case on ice for three years.

As luck would have it, there were other options that looked promising. One day, when Penttinen visited Säter, Sture, without warning, confessed to two new murders. One of the victims was supposed to have been a boy who had spoken hardly any Swedish at all, with black hair and Mediterranean features. His name sounded Slavic – something like 'Dusjunka'. Sture had come across him cycling on a man's bike that was too big for him, a few years before being taken to Säter. However, no boy of that description had been reported missing in Sweden at any time.

The other confession was of a double murder. Sture told Penttinen that an *Aftonbladet* journalist had interviewed him a few months earlier and, among other things, asked if he happened to be involved in the investigations of a double murder in the mountainous region of northern Sweden. Sture had said no at the time, but it got him thinking. As Penttinen put it in his report, 'Quick has started to wonder if he should not be interrogated about this incident. He claims to have been present at one time within the area in question.'[420]

This was the start of an investigation that would lead to Sture being convicted of two more murders just over a year later, in January 1996.

26

The double murder at Lake Appojaure

*'Do you have information somewhere inside you that you
know about but don't have the strength to bring out?'*
Seppo Penttinen, interview with Sture about
the Appojaure murders.

Marinus (39) and Janny (34) Stegehuis lived in Almelo in an eastern
part of The Netherlands. The couple had no children. In 1984, they
took their green Toyota Corolla on a long-planned camping tour of
Scandinavia. They drove through Sweden, stopping in Ödeshög near
Lake Vättern where they stayed with relatives for a couple of days,
before carrying on to Finland. After a detour to visit some friends, they
drove up through northern Finland to reach the North Cape, arguably
the northernmost point in Europe. From there, they turned south-east,
which meant driving back into Sweden via the village of Karesuando,
near the Finnish border.

The long journey had taken its toll on the car. It had to be fixed in
a Kiruna workshop and they camped for two days before starting off
southwards again. On 12 July, they took a road running west along the
northern bank of the wide river known as Stora (large) Lulevatten.
They had magnificent views of the mountains and were able to admire
nature in the Stora Sjöfallet National Park, where they photographed
the reindeer. In the afternoon, they turned back east and picked a place
off the road running along the shore of Lake Appojaure. They took the
gravelled track leading to the water's edge. There, in an open area near
the forest, they parked and erected their silver-coloured tent.

Their evening meal of sausages and green beans was cooked on their
camping gas stove. They ate it in front of the tent and then got ready

for bed. Janny wrote in her diary about the visit to the national park, how beautiful it had been and how they had seen a stoat crossing the road. She added: 'Put tent up at 16.30 on a bit of clear ground. Mosquitoes are still tormenting us. Constant drizzle until 150 kms from Kiruna. Then the weather brightened up. Now it is raining.'[421]

Eventually, Marinus and Janny Stegehuis fell asleep.

Late in the evening the following day, some Swedish tourists stopped near the lake to look for a camping site. They saw a parked car and then, a little closer to the forest, a tent that had collapsed. Beneath the canvas, the contour of at least one body was visible. They called the police and the Gällivare force sent a detective inspector and a uniformed officer, who found that the occupants of the tent had been knifed to death by someone wildly stabbing at them through the tent fabric.

The two policemen carefully pulled the canvas up and pushed the poles into position. Both zips, in the outer canvas and the inner mosquito net, had stayed fully closed. No one had got in that way. Inside, they observed two people in their sleeping bags, on separate inflated mattresses. The tent could easily have held three people, so there was space between them. Marinus's body lay to the left of the tent entrance. His vest was red with blood from a large number of wounds. The forensic pathologist counted twenty-five stab wounds. Some of these had been made through the left hand side of the tent while it was still upright. The fabric had sprung back with each slash, preventing it from getting soaked in blood. The rest of the cuts had been inflicted from above when the tent had sagged and the blood soaked the canvas. Marinus's right arm and part of his left hand – the web between thumb and fingers – were injured, indicating that he tried to defend himself before becoming unconscious. Many of his injuries penetrated so deeply that any one of them could have killed him.

His wife Janny had fallen asleep wearing a long-sleeved nightdress on a mattress to the right of the tent entrance. She had been stabbed twenty times, both from in front and from the back. Many of them had gone straight through the sleeping bag and the flower-patterned liner sheet. During the attack, Janny had rolled off her mattress towards

Marinus and bent her upper body at a 90-degree angle. She died on her right side with her head close to Marinus's hip.

Marinus must have been struck first because he had only had time to raise his hands in defence. Janny was attacked later, which gave her time to move a little more before she died. The weapon, a long-bladed filleting knife, belonged to the murdered couple and had probably been left among the cookery things outside the tent. Its thin blade had broken during the murderous frenzy and ended up inside the tent, next to Janny's body.

At the head end, the tent contained a small storage space. The knife had been used to cut the wall open, a long, vertical slash. It seemed reasonable to suppose that the killer had turned up while the couple slept and cut the tent to try to steal what he could. Marinus might have woken up, perhaps said something, which made the thief attack his side of the tent with violent force. The tent fell when the killer went on to stab Janny to death. That the orgy of violence had started as a burglary seemed likely since the murderer had extracted quite a few objects through the gap in the storage compartment wall. Among other things, he had stolen a stereo cassette player, a smallish, black leather suitcase and a brown handbag with Janny's diary. Both bags were found later, dumped on the verge of the road towards Gällivare. The handbag still contained the diary. The cassette player was also found on the roadside, this time along the road going north of Gällivare.

This was a crime of nightmares. In the middle of the almost unpopulated high hills in northern Sweden, two people had been taken unawares as they slept in the light summer night. The murder investigation was the largest in Nordic history and a large number of people were interviewed. One suspect was a twenty-eight-year-old drug addict, nicknamed 'The Bodybuilder' by the locals. He had been in the area fishing with a friend who provided a credible alibi. The police had been interested in a German citizen but that trail, too, led nowhere. The investigation continued and the case was still open when, eleven years later, Sture referred to the Appojaure murder in his talk with Penttinen.

Two days after Sture's intimation that he should be 'interrogated' about the Appojaure case, he was interviewed about it for the first time. Anyone who had eavesdropped on the interview without knowing about repressed memory theory would have been utterly bewildered. Penttinen's report begins like this: 'Quick says that he does not want to confess to the murders of the Dutch couple in Appojaure. Instead, his story is more of an attempt to clarify if he has had anything to do with the killings or if his unease is caused by fantasies and associations.'[422]

It was a rather unusual opening to a police interview. Most officers in charge of interviewing someone who had confessed to a murder would probably be incredulous if the person warned that his replies might be nothing but 'fantasies and associations'. Not so Penttinen, who would have been more baffled if his chief suspect had made a definite statement of guilt. Penttinen was simply convinced that Sture had repressed all his memories.

It seemed that quite a few memories had emerged in the therapy sessions. Penttinen had studied the police files and knew, more or less, the details of the murder. He asked Sture to describe everything he could remember from that summer's evening.

On 11 July 1984, Sture had taken the train to Jokkmokk, a place he knew quite well from his time at the local college (1971 to 1972). He had walked from the station to the Co-op and bought food. As he passed the Sami museum, he spotted a three-geared men's bicycle, stole it on an impulse and set off northwards. Along the way, he met a small group of foreign tourists and chatted to them in rusty English for a while before cycling on. His tour grew so long that he had to spend the night under the stars. Sleeping outdoors was hard, though, because he was 'in ordinary street clothes [. . .] and not equipped for the wilds. For one thing, I had no rainwear.' Although, luckily, 'the weather was fine', Sture only slept for a few hours that night.

At ten o'clock the following day, he reached Lake Appojaure. Penttinen pulled out a map and asked Sture to point to the lake. He indicated an area about 50 kilometres south-east of Gällivare, rather than the lake's true location to the south-west. In Sture's mind,

Appojaure was not a lake but more like a 'pool' and the place where the Dutch couple had put up their tent was between 500 metres and a kilometre from the road. The actual Lake Appojaure is roughly one by two kilometres in area and the campsite just 100 metres from the road, which runs very close to the long side of the lake. Sture thought the tent had been greyish yellow. He said he had read it in one of the many newspaper articles published on the murders. Published or not, the information was wrong. He clearly recalled, he said, that the tent had some kind of rain-cover in different colour. That was wrong, too, as was his recollection that there had been a clothes line stretched between trees nearby.

Penttinen asked Sture to draw an outline map of the positions of the car and the tent in relation to the lake. His map was included in the interview transcript. He had marked the 'pool' with a small circle on the right side of the sheet of paper, placed the tent next to the water's edge and the car further inland, near a forest, pointing towards the tent. The whole scene was wrong. The real lake is far, far bigger than his small pool, the car stood closest to the water and the tent further away. The car had been parked with its long side parallel with the tent.

Next, Sture described how he crept toward the tent with a knife in his hand. It was big, a weapon he had bought a few years earlier from the arms depot in Falun. He stabbed three times through the long, right-hand side of the tent. The man was lying there and he died instantly, without having a chance to defend himself, though, in fact, Marinus had been on the left and was the only one to show self-defence wounds. Sture had killed the man when he saw the woman crawling through the tent opening. He clearly remembered her long, dark hair and her naked torso. He knifed her in her left shoulder and then in her belly, then he pushed her into the tent so that she fell onto her mattress to the left of the opening. As he did this, Sture noticed the rucksacks standing on the left side of the tent. He walked round the tent, stabbing with the knife through the canvas a total of ten to twelve times, mostly on the right side.

Sture was getting every single detail wrong. Janny's hair was not long and dark, but cut short and clearly greying. She had worn a long-sleeved nightdress so the upper part of her body was not bare. She could not have crawled out of the tent because both zips were closed. When, in 2012, chief prosecutor Kristian Augustsson, after considering the evidence in the Appojaure case, took the decision to apply for a retrial – an unusual decision for a prosecutor – he wrote in the application:

> If Bergwall's initial account had been correct, the woman, after sustaining the first wounds, would have put her nightdress back on and returned to her sleeping bag, or else it would be impossible to explain how she received the wounds in the upper part of her body with the knife cutting through both her nightdress and her sleeping bag. It is unlikely that an attacked person would react in this way.[423]

That he had inflicted ten to twelve wounds was also a poor guess at the real number, which was forty-five. Later, Sture claimed to have cycled back to Jokkmokk and taken a train to Falun the following day. He had not taken anything from the tent.

It took Sture two and a half hours to tell his story but he got only one thing right – two people had been killed in a knife attack while sleeping in a tent near Lake Appojaure. He had proven beyond doubt that he had not killed the Dutch couple. The interview should have led to Sture being dropped as a suspect and he could have returned to his quiet, drug-fogged existence in ward 36. But Penttinen did not think like other policemen.

During the next ten months or so, Penttinen conducted another ten interviews with Sture, lasting a total of thirty-two hours. The transcripts added up to a volume of 570 pages and each one made for reading as unreal as any of the interview records in the Asplund and Zelmanovits cases. Penttinen asks leading questions and when he gets the wrong answer, he asks it again and again. For instance, Sture said that he had struck at the victims through the walls of the tent, but did not mention that he had cut open the canvas at the back. Suddenly Penttinen asked: 'What was your intention when you cut the canvas open?' Afterwards, Penttinen pretended that Sture *had* said he had cut the tent and referred to it: 'So, you tell me that you used the knife to cut through the canvas.' Sture smoothly adjusted his story to fit with what Penttinen had suggested.

I cannot find anything to suggest that Penttinen was cheating deliberately. It is obvious that the poor ex-drug squad officer thought he was helping a suffering fellow man to recapture his evasive memories by dropping 'clues'. Sometimes, he sounds like a psychotherapist: 'Do you have information somewhere inside you that you know about but don't have the strength to bring out?' Or: 'Do you think it's at all possible for you to retrieve what all this is about?'[424]

When Sture made obvious errors, Seppo often responded by simply changing the subject.

In some of the interviews it comes across clearly that Sture is high on drugs. The following conversation, which included Birgitta Ståhle, took place in December 1994:

[Sture]: 'I'm dozing off now.'
[Ståhle]: 'It's nothing bad, is it?'
[Sture]: 'No.'
[Penttinen]: 'You're dozing off in (inaudible).'
[Sture]: 'Err . . . no, in my face.'
[Ståhle]: 'In his face.'

Something similar happens in the fourth interview:

[Penttinen]: 'What about it, Thomas shall we take a lunch break now . . .?'
[Sture]: 'Yes.'
[Penttinen]: ' . . . I can see that you've, well, it looks like you've taken some medicine so you can't really follow this . . . or aren't you feeling all right?'
[Sture]: 'I'm not all that well.'
[Penttinen]: 'How's that?'
[Sture]: 'No problem with the medicine.'
[Penttinen]: 'Right, we're breaking for lunch at 11.55.'[425]

346

One of the most eccentric features of Penttinen's Appojaure investigation is the story about Sture's alleged partner in crime 'Jonny Larsson'. In the first interview Sture took care not to mention any driver, as he had in previous confessions. He might well have thought that managing discussions about an accomplice was too much like hard work. However, without some such figure, he faced a transport problem because, in 1984, he still could not drive a car. He chose to say that he had cycled the full 80 kilometres from Jokkmokk to Appojaure, carried out a double murder and cycled all the way back. The trouble was that, even at the first interview, Penttinen had an accomplice up his sleeve, one Jonny Farebrink whom the national criminal police vaguely suspected of the Appojaure murders. Farebrink was a drug addict with a history of violence and a long criminal record, who in 1995 was held in the high-security prison Hall. His links to the double murder were so weak that he had not even been questioned about it – but he had grown up in Jokkmokk and the police had information that one of Farebrink's fences had tried to flog camera equipment belonging to the Stegehuis couple. The national force had told van der Kwast about their suspicions when he informed them that Sture had started to talk about the Appojaure incident. Van der Kwast made the astonishing decision that Sture should be asked if he knew a Jonny Farebrink, also giving Jonny's surname before he changed it in 1968: Larsson-Auna.

When Sture had finished with his grossly erroneous version of the campsite killings, Penttinen asked if he had ever heard of anyone called Jonny Larsson-Auna or Jonny Farebrink. Sture jumped at the bait: 'Quick's reaction was one of strong anxiety. His speech grew disturbed and his chin started to tremble. After a while he asked to have the name repeated and immediately stated that he recognized it. However, he cannot connect the name to any specific event.' In later interviews Sture said that Jonny Larsson-Auna had been involved in the Appojaure case but that he had never heard the name Farebrink.

Sture had failed to dodge a tricky accomplice situation and was soon up to his neck in trouble. Since he could not have brought Jonny to Lake Appojaure on his bike he had to rethink his story. In the second interview he claimed to have run into Jonny by chance when he

347

cycled past Gästis Inn in Jokkmokk. His new friend had driven both of them to the lake in his VW pickup truck, a vehicle the police could not prove existed. Of course, this cancelled out the earlier, richly detailed account of a long cycle tour and a night spent in the open air.

In the ordinary run of the Quick interviews, all he would have to do was stop talking about something like the cycle trip for it to be forgotten. This time, it was not quite so straightforward. The police had found out that a woman's bike had been reported stolen in Jokkmokk at around the crucial time. Penttinen asked Sture about it, and he instantly thought that he had probably stolen a woman's bike. After this breakthrough, it became obvious that Penttinen would prefer Sture not to eliminate the bike from the picture, so it stayed despite its lack of a function. When Sture and Jonny drove off toward Lake Appojaure, the bike had been loaded onto the back of the truck. To satisfy Penttinen and van der Kwast, the bike remained part of the narrative right up to the trial and was lost only when the retrial investigation established that it had not been stolen until after the campsite killings.

In October 1995, Sture was taken to meet with Jonny Farebrink face-to-face and it became clear that he didn't know a thing about him – not even his name, which Sture had consistently claimed was Jonny Larsson. In fact, Larsson changed his name to Farebrink long before their alleged meeting and, besides, Farebrink had an alibi for the day of the murder. The confrontation was humiliating for the prosecutor, who closed the investigation on Jonny Farebrink for the stated reason that nothing connected him to the scene of the murder 'neither in the company of Quick or on his own'.[426] Sture kept Jonny in his murder narrative right up to the trial.

In between the Appojaure interviews, Sture was on his therapy couch and going into regression to relive the double murder. He frequently turned into Ellington, his persona when he had killed the Dutch couple. Ellington even materialized during an interview. Sture said he needed a pee, got up and left the music room. Next, there was uproar in the corridor and Ståhle ran out to see what was going on. She came back with Sture after a while, they sat down and Penttinen asked what happened.

'I can explain. Just outside, Thomas . . . err, well, he underwent the same change that happened up there [in Appojaure], like I explained earlier, when the change takes place he becomes another person, he becomes "Ellington" and as "Ellington" he gets in touch with an utterly wild rage. When the change came over him here he ran head first into a door and that was the crash we heard just outside.'[427]

Margit, Ståhle and Sture had their work cut out explaining why he had suddenly killed a pair of adults, so unlike his usual habit of targeting boys. They cracked it just in time for the fifth and sixth interview. Sture said that he had spotted a boy in Jokkmokk and made up his mind to kill him, but lost track of his intended victim and was cheated of a murder. That evening, he had met the Stegehuis couple on their campsite and wrongly assumed that the boy he had been after was their son. When they told him that they did not have a son, what he understood as a denial of their son enraged him.[428] The consequence of his anger was that, in the night, he turned into Ellington and killed them – with a degree of support from Jonny Larsson. Now, the campsite killing fitted into the re-enactment theory version of events, because the killing-spree signified a response to Sture's parents denying him.

Sture's inability to describe the crime scene correctly, despite many attempts, was a major obstacle. Over and over again, in one interview after another, he was asked to illustrate what he remembered and he persistently misplaced the tent and the car as well as Marinus's and Janny's places inside the tent. Finally Christianson solved the problem. He organized a crime scene re-enactment at Lake Appojaure to help Sture reach his true memories.

The entire Quick team took a flight to Gällivare. Christianson told everyone that he was applying the techniques of 'cognitive interviewing' and made the police recreate the 1984 site in its exact details. A car should be parked and a tent put up where the Stegehuis car and tent had stood, and a camping stove and cooking utensils set out in front of the tent. Furthermore, the victims should be represented by a man and a women lying down in the right places. According to Christianson's instructions all Sture's errors would be cleared up once

349

he saw the reconstruction. Faced with such an exact replica, he couldn't fail to 'remember' what it had been like in 1984.

Thure Nässén was in the investigation team and present at the reconstruction. He eventually grew certain that Sture was innocent and left the team. He wrote a letter to Penttinen in 2002 in order to explain his reservations:

> My first doubt 'turned up' in connection with the Appojaure investigation when I was present at the so-called 're-enactment', or rather reconstruction, as is perhaps more appropriate. I had never before been at a re-enactment or reconstruction in which the suspect arrived at, as it were, 'a set table', as happened in this case. Under the usual rules, the suspected perpetrator should be arranging things such as, in this case, the tent and the car because only he knows exactly what it looked like before he started to 'do in' that poor couple. [...] I ended up with the impression that it was the psychologists who 'fixed it' in this reconstruction and not, as is the usual practice, the leader of the investigation and the police.[429]

Sture was heavily drugged when he climbed into the minibus to visit the crime scene. He was joined in the bus by Birgitta Ståhle, Sven Å Christianson, Seppo Penttinen, DI Thure Nässén, the charge nurse on ward 36, Bengt Eklund, and another nurse from the ward. As they came close to the lake, Penttinen noted that Sture's anxiety became so overwhelming that they had to stop the car: 'He climbs outside and tries to vomit. Birgitta Ståhle has to intervene personally to restore Quick's balance before the journey to Appojaure can continue. He says that he recognizes the stretch of road and this causes his anxiety to increase further. He weeps and moans at the same time as he keeps mumbling "This mustn't be true."'[430]

Sture was given another Xanax. Then they arrived at the scene of the murder: 'At 15.00, Quick steps onto the open area where the deed was done. The place had been arranged as to be in almost the same state as in 1984. This was possible by using photographs and other investigative data.'

Quick is given an opportunity to walk around to orient himself: '[Sture]: We will walk a bit ... I must not look, not straightaway. (Quick circles the place and avoids looking at the tent.) Umm ... umm ... I'll soon ... soon turn round. (*sighs*).'

Nässén was watching from a little way away and later said in an interview: 'He was completely lost. It was clear for all to see that he hadn't been there before. I pointed that out at the time but it was not recorded in the investigation files.'[431]

After an hour of wandering around, Penttinen must have thought a regression was on the horizon, because he made this note while taking a break for coffee: 'During the break, he pulls off his knitted sweater since he thinks it's too warm in comparison to the weather and temp. at the time of the deed.'

He clearly thought that Sture was on a mental trip to 1984 and had to adjust what he was wearing to the weather back then. Next, the video cameras started recording, because Sture was going to demonstrate how he went about the double murder. He swung his fake knife at the left side of the tent and showed the Jonny Larsson stand-in what to do. Then he pulled down both zips and leapt at the two people on the mattresses. One of them was Penttinen's assistant, Sergeant Anna Wikström, who screamed with distress. At that point, van der Kwast interrupted the exercise. The cameras were turned off and Sture crawled back outside. Penttinen reported:

> During Quick's acting out of the crime, the [video] tape recorder developed a technical fault. The interruption lasted about one minute. During this break, he said that he had not entered the tent through the proper entrance but through a slit made in the canvas. He had no memory of having clambered over the people inside the tent. He seemed in despair about having acted in a way that was wrong in terms of the reconstruction. He repeated: 'It's not right, it's not right.'

The time coding of the videos show that the break actually lasted for the best part of an hour, a fact observed by prosecutor Jörgen

Lindgren much later. Lindgren thought it strange that the 'technical fault' had occurred, given that 'it is on record that two fixed and one mobile camera had been delivered to film the event and that sound recording was done separately'.

At the time, DCI Jan Olsson was head of the group specializing in perpetrator profiling in the national police force.[432] He was a member of the Quick commission but with time became very critical of the ongoing investigation and finally refused to participate for ethical reasons.

Jan Olsson told me about an analysis he had carried out of how the murderer moved around the tent and stabbed the victims. The information Sture had given in his first, interrupted, demonstration did not fit the analysis at any point. During the hour when the cameras had shut down, Penttinen had a talk with Sture and when the cameras were running again, every blow he struck fitted the analysis. This exactitude baffled Jan Olsson. 'Normally, an analysis won't fit the actual event 100 per cent,' he said. 'But Sture's second go was just that exact. I must say, it made me wonder.'

Chief prosecutor Kristian Augustsson referred on several occasions to Jan Olsson's account of Penttinen's talk with Sture. He hints at the possibility that Penttinen instructed Sture. This upset Penttinen, who wrote in a submission to the retrial application process:

This requires an explanation of what actually passed during the break that took place. [Bergwall] had been wrestled down by me when the first run had to be interrupted. He explained soon after-wards, when in a less anxious state, that he wished to try again in a retake of the re-enactment. He indicated that he had had a bad attack of anxiety when he saw an exact copy of the tent. [Sture] was cared for by the hospital staff and taken to the bus that had been employed. He talked inside the bus with the nurses, Birgitta Ståhle and Sven-Åke Christianson. [...] SÅC came out to speak to me a little later and advised me as to the rest of the reconstruction from a memory-expert's perspective. This was SÅC's role in this situation. Later, there was a short talk with [Sture] just before Part 2 of the reconstruction was begun. I asked him to shut his eyes and try to feel what he had felt at the time in connection with the murders. I asked him to try to remember the weather, if it was sunny or cloudy, raining or dry, windy or not, and how the world of his emotions felt at the time. That any guidance as to the details of the crime should have been divulged is **out of the question**.'[433] [Emphasis in original]

It seems that just pondering over the weather was sufficient to make Sture regress enough to strike the tent as exactly as if he had known Jan Olsson's analysis.

Seppo had read Olsson's analysis, of course. When I asked Sture what Penttinen had told him in the break, Sture said that he had been reminded of things he stated in the interviews. Penttinen had made remarks like 'You remember, don't you, that you said that you folded back the canvas?' and so on. He had simply given Sture the clues that Christianson had recommended.

Ståhle later wrote lyrically in the case notes about what she had experienced on the shores of Lake Appojaure. Sture's initial failure had actually been a journey into regression of the kind he would usually do during therapy: 'Thomas is able to carry through with a reconstruction in the most convincing way. Through an initial regression he gets in touch with the entire episode and is enabled to present a clear memory. Just as in therapy, he regresses in order to establish contact with past situations and emotions. It is possible to use the process also in this context.'[434]

The reconstruction continued the following day but by then Sture was in such anguish that he tried to kill himself by leaping in front of a car. Despite this, everyone else was pleased with the exercise and the group flew back home in a chartered plane.

The trip to Appojaure was a success. Only two more interviews to go and then the charge would be made. The trial was to take place in Gällivare District Court in January 1996.

27

The trial in Gällivare

'*We counted the victims, Birgitta and I, and got to 12. 12
living lives, which I silenced, 12 living lives who in their lived
days made so many other lives meaningful. 12 lives who in the
movements of their living had hopes for themselves and for
others. And if I count to 12 by 12, if I limit my social
multiplication to these numbers, it grows to 144. The outcome of
my struggle to survive is 12 dead and 132 damaged people!*'[435]

From Sture's daily note, on 18 September 1995,
in Margit's unpublished manuscript 'The World
of Thomas Quick'.

Before the trial, Sture wanted a new lawyer. By now he was a celebrity
and felt that Gunnar Lundgren was not glamorous enough to repre-
sent him. He was aware that the journalist who had written that
glowing article about him in *Dagens Nyheter*, Kerstin Vinterhed, had
a younger brother who was the well-known defence advocate Claes
Borgström. Sture called Borgström and asked if he was willing to act
for him, adding that Lundgren was too passive. During the reconstruction in Piteå, he had spent most of the time grilling hot dogs
down by the lakeside.

Claes Borgström rose to fame in 1981, when he represented fourteen children who had sued the Greater Stockholm city council for
allowing heavy traffic outside the Birkagården day and leisure centre,
the same Birkagården that Margit's husband Curt Norell had taken
over as manager when he and Margit had left Ådalen in 1946. Curt
stayed on as manager until 1976 and as a member of the society's board
for another nineteen years. Borgström had placed his children in the

nursery and was elected to the board of the society in 1977. During the years that followed, he and Curt got to know each other. Borgström also met Margit, whose practice was in the Birkagården building. In the 1981 civil case against the city council, he spoke for the children in the environmentally symbolic trial, which was widely covered in the media. The children lost their case but Borgström was seen as something of a left-wing hero.

Claes Borgström had always been interested in psychology, partly for family reasons. His brother had suffered from schizophrenia and, before his death, spent a major part of his life in psychiatric institutions. Borgström's take on psychiatry was radical, anti-authoritarian and psychodynamic. He had read up on anti-psychiatry and the R. D. Laing approach and might have been specially designed to be Thomas Quick's new lawyer.

Borgström met van der Kwast, took stock of the situation and then they jointly recommended to Gällivare District Court that the court should appoint Sven Å Christianson as its expert witness in the trial. The court accepted and asked Christianson to submit a report. He agreed but was so keen to appear in person that he wrote to the senior judge: 'I will undertake this task on the understanding that I will be heard in court, so that I can develop in speech the points made in my written reports concerning the psychological analysis of the conditions affecting Quick's plea.'[436]

While waiting for the trial, Sture continued his strange life at Säter. He was given tranquillizers as and when he wanted. High as a kite, he rumbled about in the ward as 'Ellington' or 'Nana'. Ståhle's therapy sessions took him through dramatic regressions in which he alternated between roles, playing his raped four-year-old self, or 'Simon' being cut up, or either of his monstrous parents abusing him. Lying on the bed in his room, he wept and wailed, and would often go on to make half-hearted suicide attempts.

This is a typical case note entry:

Thomas pulled the blanket over his head and refused to speak. Also refused to drink, stating that he intends to starve to death.

355

Alerted psychologist B Ståhle, who promised to try to break through his current state. Strong anxiety attack prior to her arrival. Stopped by staff from running head first into the stone wall around the leisure area. Tries to suffocate himself in a plastic bag, places his belt around his neck. After Birgitta Ståhle's visit, Thomas is once more contactable, eats and drinks. Out on ward. Watch still on.[437]

I read entries about attempts by a clearly drugged Sture trying to 'drive a screwdriver into his chest' or 'strangle himself'. At other times he 'crawls around on the floor, moaning' and 'throws himself against the wall, head first'.[438] A lot of notes record that he is generally anxious and restless, with the almost invariable result of getting more tranquillizers.

During the retrial application process Dr Anna Dåderman went through Sture's case notes and came to the conclusion that his behaviour was directly related to overdosing on medications, notably benzodiazepines. But at Säter, the patient's mental instability was seen as proof of the effectiveness of the therapy. In one case note entry, Birgitta writes that Sture had become 'in better contact with reality', meaning improved contact with previously repressed memories of childhood trauma and murder. This view was shared by everyone in this unit of the hospital. In September, the medical director himself, Erik Kall, wrote that Sture had suicidal thoughts but that these should be taken as one 'natural aspect' of the patient's 'new access to previous traumatic experiences which require further work to allow him to move on'.[439]

When I discussed this period with Sture, he said that the medication routine was destructive but he was an addict and took whatever was on offer.

A great deal of his anxiety stemmed from being in two minds about his deepening involvement in murder investigations. He could not stop playing this bizarre game. The thought that Ståhle and the ward staff would realize that he had been lying all along was unbearable, but in moments of clarity he saw his predicament, understood that his life was ruined and that he would die in the hospital. When depression set in, he might attempt suicide or simply stay in bed, not eating or drinking. There are many such entries in his case notes. This one was made just over a month after the visit to the Appojaure crime scene:

Has refused food and liquids for 48 hrs. without saying why. Pat. has been looking quite weak and worn out recently. Lying down, covered by bedspread but feels quite calm, clear-headed in this state. Not as if he was dreaming or about to fade out. Pat. has just been up, walked about. Seemed unaffected, but a little melancholic and weakened. When you meet him, he spreads his arms in a gesture of hopelessness.[440]

There was a certain ambivalence in Sture's attitude to his situation. One week, he would try to kill himself when thoughts of the trap he was caught in drove him to it – only for the conman inside him to spring back to life the next week. In the autumn of 1995 he demanded a fee of 50,000 kronor from the Norwegian tabloid *Verdens Gang* for an interview package including a murder confession.[441] The interview was done and Sture stated that he had killed two boys who, as the reporter had already told him, disappeared in the late 1980s from an Oslo camp for asylum seekers.

During the autumn of 1995, the police and the unit worked together to help Sture prepare for the demands of the court hearing. I found a note among his papers about a film showing arranged at Säter on 16 October. The film was the Appojaure reconstruction and the gang had met up to keep Sture company on the TV-sofa – Penttinen, Ståhle, Lena Arvidsson, ward charge nurse Bengt Eklund and a woman psychiatric nurse. Every time I read Ståhle's assurances to the Social Services Ministry about strict boundaries between the psychotherapy and police work, a vision of that line-up comes back to me.

The trial began in Gällivare District Court on 9 January 1996. Two relatives of the murdered Janny Stegehuis had travelled to Gällivare to see the man who had killed Janny and Marinus. In the Zelmanovits trial, concern about Sture's 'mental health' had led to him taking the stand behind locked doors, but this time he was heard by the court in the presence of both press and public. *Dagens Nyheter* wrote approvingly that his answers 'were well expressed and delivered clearly and distinctly'. The news agency TT described the support he received from 'his legal representative, Claes Borgström and eight other persons, some of whom came from the hospital in Säter and [ensured] that there were sufficient breaks for rest and recuperation'.

Ståhle and Borgström were seated on either side of Sture and looked after him while he told the court about travelling to Jokkmokk to hunt for a boy to murder for sexual gratification. He stole a three-geared bicycle and was 'cycling around' when he met a group of foreign youths.[442] He picked one of the boys in the group as his victim and went off to the Domus store to buy a clothes line for the killing. He then met Jonny – already ditched from the murder investigation by van der Kwast – and was given a lift in his 'pale-grey Volkswagen pick-up truck' to Appojaure. He got talking to the Dutch couple and asked them when their son was due back. *Dagens Nyheter* takes up the tale:

> When the defence lawyer, Claes Borgström, asked directly what had triggered his aversion towards the Dutch woman, Thomas Quick replied clearly and unhesitatingly:
> – It was her denial. It immediately identified her to me as M, whom she also resembled physically.
> M is Thomas Quick's term for his mother.[443]

When the couple had gone to sleep, Sture and Jonny walked around the tent and stabbed at it with their knives. The man had died immediately. Sture crawled into the tent through the slit cut in the canvas and knifed the woman to death.

According to the court's reasoning, Quick had wanted to 'put what had happened out of his mind' and he had therefore avoided 'informing himself of the media coverage of the events'. What he told the court was based on clearly remembered episodes, although certain discrepancies in factual detail might have occurred.[444]

The same newspaper report also quoted Penttinen's statement about how Sture had come to access more and more memories:

Quick's approach to telling us what had happened turned out to be the same as in previous cases. He would give an account of certain memory fragments but as the interrogation continued, the sequence of events 'opened up'. In the beginning, the story was quite incoherent. He stated that he felt deeply anxious and had to protect his conscious mind by inventing elements of his story that came close to the truth. At the next interview he might already be prepared to correct a previous piece of information.

This is how Penttinen had described the final outcome of eleven interviews: 'In Penttinen's view, there are remembered episodes in Quick's narrative which are clear and distinct with regard to central elements in a particular set of events. On the other hand, more peripheral aspects, such as the modes of travel from place to place, remain more diffuse.'

This was unmistakably something that Penttinen had been fed by Christianson. The observations are based on findings by Christianson and Loftus in the studies of how people remember traumatic events. In fact, Sture's story did not agree with what Christianson and Loftus had described at all.

Penttinen also told the court that as early as the first interview Sture had provided 'information as well as a detailed drawing of the campsite and the road that leads to it' – which was true enough, but Penttinen did not mention that everything Sture had said and drawn was completely wrong. At the end of his statement, Penttinen delivered an even grosser lie: '[Quick] also provided a description of the couple's appearance and their positions inside the tent. This information was produced without prompting. Penttinen stated that there were no discrepancies between Quick's final account during the investigation and his later statement during the main proceedings.'

Still, Christianson stood out as the brightest star of the trial. His written submission began with a declaration: 'The information presented below is based on current international scientific findings and clinical experience.' Christianson went on to explain that the human mind is equipped with 'two mechanisms that oppose each other' and which 'are activated when people are exposed to and later attempt to remember events with strong emotional connotations'. On one hand, he argued, we are prone to remember terrible things in order to 'quickly identify and recognize threatening situations'. Without this ability, mankind 'would surely not have been able to survive and develop into what we are today'.

So far, so good. Christianson's arguments are logical and easy to follow. However, in the next instant, he leaves logic behind. In the report of his presentation to the court, he is said to have claimed that 'an opposing mechanism has been found':

> It is important to be able to forget but this does not imply that the information disappears from our brain. We tend to keep unpleasant events out of mind and that makes us isolate such events so that they have few connections to other events or things we experience in our daily lives. In other words, there are few routes that enable us to access such memories. One potential way of recreating access is to reconstruct the external circumstances. [...] The person can then perceive clues in the environment and, as it were, adjust to recollect the original situation.

What the court did not know was that the theory of the two 'opposing memory mechanisms' was Christianson's own idea. It appears in the book *Recovered Memories and False Memories*, which was not published until 20 March 1997, a year and three months after the trial in Gällivare. He was repeating his trick from the Zelmanovits trial, referring to his own research on Sture's memory in support of his supposedly objective expert opinion that Sture was a murderer.

In *Recovered Memories and False Memories*, Christianson and his doctoral student wrote:

[W]e suggest that there are two opposing mechanisms at work when we are exposed to and try to remember emotional events. From the workings of the first mechanism we can infer that it is important to identify and recognize threatening situations. We doubt that mankind would have survived and developed in the way it has without this memory function. From the workings of the second mechanism we can infer that it is important to 'forget' unpleasant experiences. Life would be unbearable if we were forced always to carry unpleasant memories with us in our conscious awareness. Thus, to the same extent that we need mechanisms to identify and recognize unpleasant events, we also need mechanisms to 'forget' unpleasant experiences.[445]

To provide proof for the hypothesis of 'opposing mechanisms', Christianson gave an account of the case of Thomas Quick. At the time of publication of his book, Christianson had contributed to getting Quick convicted of three murders by surreptitiously referring to his own, unpublished hypotheses.

There are several other amazing features of Christianson's written submission in the Appojaure trial. Under the heading 'Murder as Narrative' he revived the re-enactment theory from the Zelmanovits trial but with some interesting new twists: 'The murders/events become the unconscious language (a body language) in which the experiences can be expressed although the murderer is not aware of his own narrative since it is concealed. Once a murder has been committed it too becomes a mental trauma that later must be retold. Subsequent murders in other words tell of past murders as well as previous traumatic experiences.'

Sture had murdered for the first time in response to a subconscious urge to 'narrate' the story of his repressed childhood traumas and then repressed the memory of the murder because it too was traumatic. Christianson had worked out that his combined trauma would make him commit a new murder and this time, the 'narrative' was about both the bad childhood events and the first murder. Once more, the repression mechanism was activated, the new murder was pushed out of mind and soon Sture had to murder again ... The memory expert outlined the workings of a vicious circle of narration and repression of which Sture was never aware. All this was declared proven by international front-line research.

Some of Christianson's assertions could have been scripted by Margit Norell. His explanation of why Sture killed the man by swift stabs through the canvas roof, but crawled through the slit in the tent to murder the woman, was as follows:

> He wished to degrade the seductive woman or 'mother' who had failed to meet the child's needs – it is worth observing at this point that a serial killer should be regarded as a child with a child's needs and responses inside the body of a grown man. Given a situation in which he is about to commit murder, his hatred will focus on the woman rather than the man who will be swiftly killed while the woman is subjected to a symbolic, ritualistic murder that potentially includes fantasies and sensations of sexual lust.

Christianson rounded off his presentation, as he had in the first trial, by insisting that Sture was entirely believable: 'Finally, Christianson stated that, in his opinion, no evidence whatsoever has emerged in the present case to support the assumption that Quick might have made a false confession.'

Barely two weeks later, Sture was convicted of the double murder at Lake Appojaure.

In 2012, chief prosecutor Kristian Augustsson applied for a retrial and his application was examined by deputy prosecutor Jörgen Lindberg, who decided to cancel the new investigation. This, in effect, meant that Sture was declared not guilty. Despite Jörgen Lindberg's dry, legal language, one senses his outrage at what he discovered about the joint efforts of Penttinen and van der Kwast:

> All available documentation in the investigation has been examined and relevant data analysed. It has been established that, in general, SB [Sture Bergwall] made vague and unclear statements about what has happened and also often changed his statements, although none

of these features have been sufficiently brought to his attention at the time. In addition, the interviews were characterized, to far too great an extent, by SB adapting and consequently changing his answer, or requesting a pause in order to come back with an answer, or apparently having a break-down when unable to answer a question or when his answer evidently did not fit with what the interviewer knew, or believed he knew, leading to SB being questioned further. The discrete, precise information that the lead interviewer referred to in his witness statement to the court is in my view completely lacking. After having examined the murder investigations, I have also concluded that, over time, a certain unsatisfactory symbiosis had developed between SB and the lead interviewer, which has come to obscure the objectivity that is usually typical of the thorough and critical police work underlying, for instance, a murder investigation. Such facts and observations which strongly contradict the veracity of SB's statements have hence not been scrutinized or foregrounded.

After having read a hundred interviews, some of them several times, I felt I understood why Penttinen acted as he did, and had come to know Margit and her spiritual daughter Birgitta Ståhle rather well, too. They were the true believers and their capacity for rational thought had been put aside. But I could not work out where Christianson was coming from. What drove him to act as an ambassador for Säter's groundless theories? After all, he made his statements under oath.

Sture could not explain Christianson but has long since become certain that everyone was under Margit's control. He suggested that Christianson might have been supervised by Margit, which made no sense to me. Christianson was an academic researcher with no patients to treat, so he surely would not need supervision from an elderly psychoanalyst. Sture added that for all he knew Seppo Penttinen had been to see Margit and maybe received some kind of supervision, but I dismissed that out of hand.

When I interviewed Margit's pupils, I asked them about Christianson. Some of them knew about his involvement in the Quick investigations, but he had never been a member of the Margit group and hardly anyone remembered seeing him around at all. It was so frustrating. Here was a man who had given scientific legitimacy to Säter's 'explanatory model' and, by doing this, had supported a number of wrongful convictions that allowed the real murderers to stop worrying about being apprehended. He carried a heavy responsibility.

What if Sture was right? What if Christianson had some kind of relationship with Margit? I decided to make one last attempt to sort out what drove the memory expert.

Without any real expectations, I emailed him at the address I had found on the home page of Stockholm University. I said that I was a journalist who specialized in psychology, offered to send him my books and explained that I was currently working on a book about the introduction of object relations theory to Sweden. One of the leading figures was the psychoanalyst Margit Norell, who I claimed was 'the first one in our country to grasp the importance of object relations theory'. I could not very well tell him of Sture's suspicion and instead listed some of the people I had been interviewing over the last few months. Then I tried a long shot:

Many of those interviewees told me that I had missed talking to the best known of the Swedes who were close to Margit: Sven Å Christianson! It is this mistake I now hope to make good by asking you if you can find the time and energy to allow me to interview you. I am curious about your own history, how you came to know Margit, your memories of her and the role she played in your life, both personally and professionally. And, that goes without saying, your views on the contemporary psychological focus on relationships. I know that my book would gain greatly from your contribution so I hope for the best . . .

Three days went by without an answer but I had not really expected one. Christianson had been lying low ever since the retrial processes got underway. If he had known Margit, he almost certainly would not want to talk to me about her. If he had not known her, he might have thought that I sent the email to the wrong person.

His reply arrived on the fifth day: 'Hi Dan and thank you for your email. My reply is late because I am just back from Berlin. Yes, I was close to Margit – she was probably the adult who meant most to me in my whole life.'

28

The memory expert's secret

'She had this incredible ability to create a relationship out of an encounter.'
Sven Å Christianson speaking about Margit Norell.

Sven Å Christianson asked me to send my books and said that, later on, we could meet for my interview with him. Presumably he wanted to check my credentials. He followed up the interview proposal and suggested that I meet him in the Department of Psychology in a few weeks' time. I used the time to read up background material.

With the Appojaure trial out of the way, Christianson took a more than year-long break from his role as the Quick team's memory expert. Meanwhile, van der Kwast and Penttinen investigated the murder of the Israeli Yenon Levi and, in May 1996, Sture was duly convicted of that murder, too. Christianson then returned to the group and became deeply involved in all the murder investigations until the eighth conviction in 2001. Afterwards, Sture fell silent.

During the Quick years, Christianson published frequently, both articles and books. Since the 1990s his reputation in Sweden was to a large extent built on his deep involvement in the Quick case. He lectured extensively on the topic all around Sweden and his book *Inside the Mind of a Serial Killer* (only published in Sweden) came out as recently as 2010. The title seemed to reflect the fact that Christianson had only ever met one serial killer, i.e. Sture. It must have caused his publisher a headache, since the retrial process had started by then. They solved the problem by placing much of what Sture had said in the mouths of anonymous killers, creating an illusion of multiple sources. However, Sture's way of expressing himself is very much his own and

I found it easy to work out which of the quotes came from him. The book contains a special section on Sture where it is established that he is not simply a serial killer but a 'serial killer personality' – an invention of Christianson's own which seems to have been a version of psychopathy subject to environmental factors that can trigger murderous and obsessive behaviours.[446] *Inside the Mind of a Serial Killer* was on the reading list for the students studying forensic psychology, one of Christianson's own university courses, until very recently.

The Department of Psychology is a handsome stone building situated a little to the south-west of Stockholm University. I waited for only a few minutes before Christianson came down to greet me. He was fifty-eight years old and his hair had gone grey but he otherwise looked just like the man in the videos of the re-enactments from the 1990s.

Our footsteps echoed in the high stairways and corridors as I followed him to his room. As we walked, he told me that we were inside one of the largest psychology departments in Europe. His office was furnished with five bookcases packed with books and folders, a desk, a low, round table and several armchairs. I settled down, feeling uneasy. It is not nice to approach people under false pretences and, after hours of snooping on true believers like Cajsa Lindholm and Lena Arvidsson, I was beginning to feel fed up. I realized that my small talk sounded strenuously jolly and felt that, at any moment, he might suss me out. But he did not. He sat down opposite me and began to speak about Margit.

In 1994, Christianson had been contacted by van der Kwast. He needed advice on how to go about extracting the truth from a man called Thomas Quick. Christianson had already helped the police in other crime investigations by meeting perpetrators for 'psychological conversations' (his own term), which encouraged them to speak about their crimes. He agreed to join the Quick investigation and started seeing Sture at Säter later in 1994.

However, the unending task of chatting to murderers and rapists wearied him. Some of the insights into the criminal mind were so ghastly that he had to soak in the bath for several hours in order to 'wash them away'. He started to look for someone to see for counselling. There was also 'the truly crucial factor of my private life', as he put it. Sven had 'a bad record when it comes to personal relationships' and his history included a few car-crash marriages. In 1994, he was once more involved in divorce proceedings. 'I felt rather like you did once, that I had to find someone to help sort me out,' he said, nodding towards one of my books. (In its foreword, I had written about my own problems with getting relationships to last and the help I had sought from a cognitive psychotherapist for half a year.) Sven said he had recognized himself in my story. 'One gets so totally into one's career, it's all work, work, work. Successful, yes. But it collides with so much in one's private life, previous children and so forth.'

He needed someone to help him with both professional and personal issues and, in the spring of 1994, Birgitta Ståhle made a suggestion. 'You see, I had specifically told her that I wanted someone with plenty of experience of working with people who had had a rough past,' he told me. 'And who knew about troubled relationships, too. Well, she put me in contact with Margit. And it was life-changing.'

He visited Margit's practice for the first time in September 1994. I asked him if he had any memories of the first encounter.

'No, not really,' he said. 'Or, at least, all I remember was that the contact was . . .' He fell silent and eyed the ceiling as he searched for the right words. When he started speaking again, he emphasized his words, as if to make sure that I would understand.

'You see, she had this *incredible* ability to create a relationship out of an encounter. But it was of course also true that . . . I wanted an older person to avoid any of the transference and counter-transference between women or men of similar ages . . . and so forth. And it was absolutely perfect, the relationship we developed.'

Sven began by seeing her once a week and continued to do so for more than ten years. I asked what Margit did in the therapy room that was so exceptional.

'One felt so incredibly secure and sustained in every way,' he said. 'And, off the record, I can tell you that she actually became the mother I've never had. That's not necessarily unprofessional. One can have different roles. Anyway, that's what it grew into. There is no way one can regain one's childhood, of course, but much can be repaired by seeing and being part of a real relationship and that was something I had never had. Not with an adult. But she proved able to create just that. By then I was in my forties but, you know, it was a true experience of a true relationship. And that's of course a necessary condition for being able to develop other relationships, in every sphere of life.'

Sven really was in a bad way when he first started seeing Margit: 'For the first four years, our encounters focused very much on me, on creating the possibility of a self. An experience of an "I" resilient enough to last through my continued contacts with clients and patients and so forth.'

I asked him if he could expand on his 'true experience of a true relationship' and he replied that he felt that Margit 'unconditionally supported him' but also offered him something more: 'Our relationship had a mutual quality. I felt that I meant something to her. I believe that.'

That last observation – that Sven himself mattered to Margit – he returned to later in the interview. He thought that he had not only related to Margit as his mother but that her feelings for him were of the same kind. 'I experienced another bond, too. Perhaps like that between a mother and her son.' He was very serious when he said this. Margit had been dead for seven years but it was clearly still important to him to feel that she had seen him as her son, as if he drew some comfort from that vision.

I pondered the wider significance of what Sven had told me. In the middle of November 1994, he stated in Piteå District Court that Sture's story about how he killed Zelmanovits was not a false confession. At that time he had already entered into his life-changing relationship with Margit, experiencing the same kind of powerful mother-transference that practically all Margit's pupils had described to me, from Monica von Sydow and Jan Stensson to Patricia Tudor-Sandahl, Tomas Videgård and Cajsa Lindholm. They had all grown so dependent on Margit that they were prepared to do just about anything to earn her love.

Something Patricia Tudor-Sandahl had said came to mind: 'This sense that you'd say anything to be confirmed, that was a situation one was in with Margit so often. Just as children are with their parents, of course. It is to say "Do whatever you want, just love me." I believe it to be a fundamental scenario.'

I also recalled the things her pupils had said about Margit's remarkable skill in making other people work for her. She had made Hanna Olsson take on the fight about who killed Catrine da Costa, even though the personal price Olsson had to pay was so high. One pupil had said that Cajsa Lindholm became Margit's 'slave', and it was an analogy that Cajsa herself seemed to agree with, at least partly.

Every week, Sven Christianson sat back in the leather armchair and looked at Margit, his new mother, with the same wide-open eyes as Hanna Olsson had, back in 1976. Strong psychological forces were at work in him, so strong that he seemed nowhere near to freeing himself even now, seven years after her death.

This would have been all well and good if their relationship had stayed within the confines of the therapy room. But Sven threw his authority as an expert witness behind Margit's theories, assuring the courts that her ideas in general, and as they applied to Sture in particular, were in line with current scientific thinking. He even claimed in his written submission in the Appojaure case that Sture in all probability had not lied. The last sentence read: 'No false confessions in the range of known variants fit the contingencies of Thomas Quick's confession and narrative concerning the Appojaure murders.'[447] Actually, every single indication pointed to falsehood, but the expert witness did not say so and Gällivare District Court did not know that Sven was Margit's 'son'.

I talked with Sven for two and a half hours. He praised Margit more warmly than I ever remembered hearing, even from her most devoted acolytes. Even Cajsa Lindholm had the odd critical comment to make about her deceased 'mother'. But in Sven's eyes, Margit was beyond criticism. 'She was enormously creative and enormously receptive,' he said. 'The most accomplished psychologist I have ever met, even at a distance. That, of course, had a lot to do with her unrivalled experience, but she had this quite remarkable ability to synthesize information from many sources. [. . .] She was never conventional or under anyone's control.' He said that, over the year, he had helped the police understand how violent criminals functioned 'as part of perhaps a hundred investigations of violent and sexual crime'. Throughout this work, Margit gave him 'incredibly valuable guidance'. Margit 'created this incredibly structured knowledge', he explained. It had helped him to understand in depth how murderers functioned. 'You know, one of them said to me "Sven, you've killed people! You have, haven't you?" I had reached so far into him that he somehow couldn't work out . . . where is the shrink getting all this stuff from? But of course, it was thanks to Margit!'

Sven thought that Margit had helped him to see through the perpetrators and into what he called 'their system'. As I sat there listening to the enthusiastic professor celebrating his mother, I finally understood why, in one court case after another, he had dared to insist that Sture was telling the truth. He must have believed that Margit, with her unique insight, simply *knew* what Sture was thinking at any one time, and her insights had been passed on to him. With Margit's transferred skills, he felt he was entrusted with unique knowledge, not only about Sture but many violent criminals. He *knew* and it did not trouble his conscience to establish Sture's guilt.

Sven apparently did not realize that Margit had been just as masterful throughout her professional life. She always felt she knew everything about her patients. In 1973 she pronounced on the cause and treatment of schizophrenia with perfect confidence. She could interpret dreams and sense that many of her patients had been subjected to abuse when they were infants. Her aura of omniscience had helped her to seduce her pupils since the early 1960s. Many of her acolytes were later forced to recognize that much of what Margit 'saw' was inside her own head, but Sven did not reach that particular insight before his new mother had passed on.

Our talk was only supposed to be about Margit and I could not think of a way to introduce the topic of Sture. I did not want to give myself away because I hoped that Sven would be my ticket to meet van der Kwast and Penttinen – which he was, later on. But, spontaneously, he began to speak about Sture. He said that he had interviewed Sture at Säter for about 200 hours between the summer of 1994 and the spring of 2002. The contact was arranged because he hoped that he would find a way of 'optimizing' Sture's opportunities to speak about the murders. But their meetings had meant more than that: 'Our contact grew deeper in many ways and all the time. For instance, we spoke about other perpetrators. Without me giving any details, of course, except what was already in the press. And how well he could elaborate on these themes! That was such important knowledge that he had. So useful for other investigations.'

Sven called his prize client Sture, not Thomas Quick. When I asked him why, he said that Quick was just a name for the outside world and the media, whereas to Sven he had always been Sture and that was significant: 'I think it shows that we had a real relationship,' he said. As if to prove how close he had been to Sture, he got up and took a book down from one of his shelves. 'This is a book Sture gave me,' he said. I saw that it was *What Remains*, a collection of poems and psychotherapeutic diary notes that Sture had persuaded the obscure publisher Kaos Press to publish in 1998. I did not admit that I had read it. Sven opened it and read out Sture's dedication: *To Sven-Åke. Fondly, Sture.* He handed me the book and told me that, in it, Sture claims that since his first murder in 1964 he had lived behind a facade that made it practically impossible for anyone to realize he was a serial killer. Sven thinks that Sture is still hiding: 'We never know, of course, when he tells the truth and it has never been my role in the investigations to state whether he does or not.'

'So you were never asked to determine if he lied or not?' I asked.

'No, not at all. Not even when the cases came up in court. My witness statements have always been concerned with how serial killers behave, generally speaking. Oh, I tested his memory once, all very practical, using word lists and that kind of thing. But, no, I would never have pronounced on whether he ... I formed my own opinions, naturally.'

I glanced at the dedication in *What Remains* and found that Sture had written something that Sven had not read out. I did, aloud:

Those who have no memory of the past are doomed to repeat it.

Cautiously, I said that I believed Margit had been very interested in the idea of repressed memories. Had he ever discussed the theory with her? He stiffened. As a professor of psychology, he knew perfectly well that the ideas he had presented during the various Quick proceedings were already controversial in the 1990s and trying to defend them now would be insane. But could he bear denying Margit? Well, yes. It was the only way open to him. He looked pained and admitted that there were 'certain topics' on which he and Margit disagreed: 'And in that category I guess I must place Thomas Quick and his assorted child-hood memories. We did have different views about it. Not that we fought each other, no, she had her opinions and I, mine. I focused on what she knew that chimed in with the knowledge I had acquired independently.'

He explained that he had known that Sture could not have had the detailed memories from the ages of three to four, as he claimed to have. On that point, Sven and Margit agreed to differ.

But Sven was not telling the truth. In a book that he co-wrote in 1996 with the freelance journalist Görel Wentz, *Crime and Memory: Narratives of severe crimes from emotional and memory perspectives*, the blurb informs us that it is primarily intended for 'social workers, the police, the legal profession and health care staff as well as all others who wish to widen their insight into reactions and behaviours connected to crimes which, to most people, seem utterly alien'.

In the introduction, Sven Christianson wrote this about Sture:

When Thomas Quick confesses his acts of violence, he is far from emotionally frigid. He endures the greatest pain and effort as he confronts his action and his memories. The difficulties do not just lie in recalling all the crimes he has committed but also in becom-ing aware of what has driven him, about the sexual abuse he was subjected to as a child [. . .] It is the fact that Thomas Quick has been unable to talk about these things and then work on the childhood trauma at an early stage that is one of the reasons why he, as an adult, had developed such an extreme behaviour pattern.[448]

The final lines might have been lifted from Jeffrey Masson's *The Assault on Truth*: 'Not to be believed is in itself a traumatic experience.' But here I was, a witness as the professor of psychology humiliated himself by denying his mentor as he claimed he had never believed in Sture's childhood traumas. It was very sad.

I asked him about the re-enactment idea and he backed away from that, too. He did not 'belong to that school of thought', nor could he explain where the idea came from. He could not bring himself to admit that it was based on Margit's theory of 'murder as a narrative', which he had claimed in court to be scientifically proven.

Towards the end of the interview, Sven seemed to want to clear the air. Perhaps he instinctively wanted to avoid having to end the interview with a betrayal of his spiritual mother.

Instead, he spoke about her ' . . . incredible ability, she made me see and understand, and supported me in an atmosphere of incredible warmth. She was . . . well, except for my children, the most important person in my life. Strong words, I know. But that's it.'

I thanked Sven for his time and took a long walk back to central Stockholm.

29

Seppo's tears

*'Thomas Quick has a need to tell what happened, which is
in direct conflict with his wish to keep things bottled up.'*
Seppo Penttinen explains Quick's difficulty with
giving correct information in interviews.

After Sture's conviction for the Appojaure murders in January 1996, the
Quick investigations continued for another five years. In May 1997,
Sture was convicted of the murder of the twenty-four-year-old Israeli
tourist Yenon Levi, who had been found battered to death in 1988 on
a deserted forest road near Rörshyttan in Dalarna County. The site was
only about 20 kilometres from Säter. By chance, Sture had watched a
report about the murder in the TV3 crime-watch programme *Wanted*
on 17 May 1995.[449] He first mentioned the murder in July, during a
conversation with Christianson at the crime-scene reconstruction at
Lake Appojaure. He made cryptic references to the 'Shalom event'.
This was, however, the only contribution Christianson made to the
forthcoming Levi investigation, before taking a break from the Quick
investigation in the spring of 1996. Sture was found guilty of the Levi
murder in May 1997 and during the trial Christer van der Kwast didn't
replace Christianson with another memory expert, instead making do
with an expert testimony from Birgitta Ståhle. Not long after the trial
Christianson returned. He began by intervening to bring about another
murder conviction for Sture. The presumed victim was Therese
Johannessen, a Norwegian girl who had disappeared. Sture had read a
brief item about her in the Norwegian daily *Verdens Gang*, sent to him
by a Norwegian journalist. He then confessed to having killed her. In
the summer of 1997 Christianson masterminded the big re-enactment

375

in Örje Forest, primarily to hunt for body parts. This was when he issued a written instruction to the police, to allow Sture a private moment with the relics once the cache had been opened.

By then, Christianson had been promoted to professor. He spoke at the trial in May 1998 and explained to the court why Sture had made so many mistakes in the interviews. For instance, Sture had spoken of the girl's 'blonde, shoulder-length hair, her hair flows around her as she runs' but Therese's dark hair was short. He had described her home in Drammen as a small village with only gravel roads and maybe a hundred small houses, while in reality it was a concrete suburb with tall blocks of flats.[450] Sture had also been unable to find any trace of the body, despite trying for more than a year and two re-enactments in Örje Forest. Christianson declared that such oddities were quite in order: 'Normally, planned and traumatic events are generally well preserved in one's memory,' he said, but there are also 'protective mechanisms in operation that subconsciously act to suppress the remembered scenes'.[451]

Christianson was once more staking his integrity as an academic on the claim that a murderer might plausibly 'suppress the remembered scenes' from his murders. He also used his usual tactic of presenting the court with such creative analyses of Sture's psychological make-up that members of the bench must have felt pretty lost: 'Sven-Åke Christianson further stated that, for Thomas Quick, the events have a strong symbolic content – not just random acts of violence – which also has the effect of pushing the memories into the future. This will entail, according to Sven-Åke Christianson, Thomas Quick repeatedly trying to reach them [. . .].'

He never got round to explaining exactly how the 'symbolic content' of a murder had the effect of 'pushing the memories into the future'.

After aiding and abetting van der Kwast's prosecution of Sture for the murder of Therese Johannessen, Christianson lent his expertise to a couple of other Norwegian cases under investigation. The first one concerned seventeen-year-old Trine Jensen. In August 1981, after visiting the shop in central Oslo where her mother worked,

Trine vanished. She had arranged to meet a friend at a tram stop that afternoon but did not turn up. Her dead body was found a couple of months later, in a wooded area about 15 kilometres south of Oslo. She had been strangled and the lower part of her body had been stripped naked. The police never found her killer.

In August 1996, when Sture was in Norway to demonstrate how and where he had killed Therese Johannessen, he read about the Trine Jensen murder in the leading Norwegian newspaper *Dagbladet*. There was an article about Quick and the paper commented that it might be time to question him. The prediction became reality as soon as Sture had finished reading. That autumn, he began talking about the new killing in his therapy sessions and, in October, he confessed to Penttinen during an interview.

The other Norwegian murder investigation that Christianson got involved in concerned twenty-four-year-old Gry Storvik, a prostitute with a heroin habit who disappeared in Oslo at some point during the night between 24 and 25 June 1985. At about one o'clock in the morning, she had been seen eating a salad in a fast-food joint in the town centre and, half an hour later, a friend saw her at the street corner where her heroin dealer usually hung out. Soon afterwards, the same witness saw Gry climb into the passenger seat of a car that drove off. At half past four in the afternoon the following day, she was found dead in a car park just off route 152, only a few kilometres from the wood-land where Trine Jensen had been discovered four years earlier. Gry was naked and all her belongings were missing. The post-mortem showed that she had been suffocated, probably because someone had applied pressure to her neck or to her mouth and nose, although suf-focation through stomach contents entering the lungs could not be excluded. The police launched a large-scale investigation but failed to find the killer.

Sture heard about the murder from a Norwegian journalist who interviewed him at Säter. Sture told him that one of his victims had vomited over him and the interviewer asked if that could have been Gry Storvik – he could not remember the facts exactly and thought she had vomited. In fact, there had been no trace of stomach contents outside the body, only lodged in the lungs. The journalist wrote several articles about Quick and reported that the serial killer had confessed to the Gry Storvik murder. In September 1998, the local reporter Gubb Jan Stigson wrote in *Dala-Demokraten* that Sture was now suspected of the Storvik murder. Stigson helpfully described just where in the Oslo region the car park was situated.

There were no connections between the murder of Trine Jensen and Gry Storvik other than the facts that they were both Norwegian women and that Sture claimed he had killed them. The methods had been different and several years had passed between the murders. Nevertheless, van der Kwast decided that the two cases should be prosecuted in the same trial. It must have seemed a good idea at the time.

Christianson was a busy contributor to the re-enactments and, as usual, played a leading role in the court proceedings. He appeared in person and submitted a new scientific study that provided circumstantial evidence: Sture knew far more about both murders than ten control subjects who had read Norwegian newspapers. On 22 June 2000, Sture was convicted of the murders of Gry Storvik and Trine Jensen.

In preparation for the retrial application in 2011, Sture's lawyer asked an expert to go through the design of Christianson's knowledge test. Unsurprisingly, it was afflicted with major methodological flaws. The ten control subjects had been told to read cuttings from Norwegian newspapers about the murders and had then been individually examined in Christianson's own psychology department. The 'test' consisted of fifty-six questions about facts concerning the murders and, afterwards, the control group's answers were compared to Sture's. The sentence states that Sture's knowledge had been proven to be unique: 'The results [of the test] support the conclusion that Thomas Quick had access to considerably more factual information than was published in the press.'[452]

But Sture had never answered the questions; the investigation team did it for him. Besides, some of the questions were unanswerable unless one had been to murder sites. Sture had, of course, been taken along more than once for re-enactments. Another absurd flaw was that the test included questions such as 'How did the perpetrator contact her?', 'When did the perpetrator contact her?' and 'Can you describe the vehicle that the perpetrator drove?' The only available answers to these questions were the statements made by Sture and none of them could be verified. Still, his account was regarded as a given truth. The expert who scrutinized Christianson's test filled twelve pages with catastrophic methodological problems of this type and ended his report by dismissing the exercise as worthless.[453]

In 2012, when the senior prosecutor Bo Ericsson acquitted Sture of the 'Norwegian' murders, he concluded that the court had been misled: 'TQ's confession was devoid of credibility. Had the court been given access to the many varying and contradictory statements, this would have become obvious.'[454]

When the sentence for the Gry Storvik and Trine Jensen murders had been pronounced in 2000, Christianson and the rest of the group were already in the run-up to what was to become the last triumph of the Quick investigation team: they had decided to get Sture convicted for the murder of Johan Asplund. They succeeded on 21 June 2001.

At times, the interview scripts underpinning Sture's eight murder convictions read like the darkest of black comedy and the craziness of it all makes me laugh out loud. But, more often, I am gripped by a sense of unreality that is deeply unsettling. Penttinen seemed not to hear what Sture says and not to see what Sture does. True, Sture was a good liar. He knew that details add verisimilitude and seemed to take some pride in these grace notes to his wobbly accounts. Penttinen must have interpreted the details as proof that it was all drawn from the storyteller's own experience. It probably did not occur to him that most fiction is full of invented but apparently realistic observations.

This example is taken from near the end of the sixth interview in the Appojaure case and begins with Sture's answer when Penttinen asked if he had anything to add before ending the interview:

[Sture]: 'Well, there is something, it's totally irrelevant overall but
    it is that when everything is over, the injuring and the killing,

379

there is a scent still around – it's completely apart from all
that – and it smells like a deodorant, like perfume. That sort of
scent and it's one I can't place properly, as it were. But it's
there, in the final stages, just before leaving the tent, before
one leaves the tent it's suddenly there.'

[Penttinen]: 'Are you inside the tent at the time?'

[Sture]: 'I don't know, don't know for sure but it's very close to
the tent.'[455]

It is not hard to see why this kind of literary touch would impress
Penttinen – but only for as long as the wealth of detail agreed with the
known facts. The trouble was, Sture lied and embroidered as fluently
when he said things that Penttinen knew could not be true. In
October 1999, Sture described stabbing Gry Storvik in the side, just
below the ribcage. He was tormented by anxiety and spoke in bursts
as he recalled the disgusting scene:

It's made up of ... err ... how it feels, somehow ... err ... to slash
through the skin ... how it feels when the knife blade slips inside
upwards and ... I sense it is going in and it's ... directed well
enough, aimed or how I should put it ... that it doesn't puncture the
lung, umm, and there is [inaudible] a memory of the intention not
to puncture ... that she should stay alive, umm ... the actual knifing ... the bodily harm ... but all the same the knife does serious
damage of course ... err ... that the knife causes ...[456]

Penttinen listened, knowing that Gry Storvik's murderer had not
used a knife. She had been suffocated and had not even the slightest
knife cut on her body. Sture's sensing of the knife as it sliced through
the skin, the upward thrust, remembering his decision not to puncture
the lung, the care he took – it was all sheer invention. It is when I read
this kind of thing that the sense of unreality sweeps over me. How
could Penttinen have believed so strongly in the Säter 'explanatory
model' that he did not pack up and leave whenever Sture started weav-
ing another tissue of lies?

Penttinen himself tried his hand at writing an explanation for the annual volume of *Annals of Nordic Crime* in 2002, in response to the critics who said that Sture knew nothing about the murders he had confessed to and hence it was reasonable to think that his confessions were false. Penttinen tried to explain Sture's psychological make-up:

> Thomas Quick has a need to tell what happened, which is in direct conflict with his wish to keep things bottled up. As a case begins, he describes only fragments of the deed and seems incoherent. He becomes very anxious and this prevents him from telling the story in full. He says that, at this stage, he has to 'make deliberate diversions' in order to cope with the strain of carrying on. In his view, these misstatements are not lies but a sort of protective measure taken to prevent him from falling apart in the ongoing interview situation. Eventually, he will himself correct the 'diversions' and link the fragments up into a coherent narrative. This process will keep pace with his anxiety coming under control.[457]

Penttinen wrote that he could understand if 'this way of recounting' was 'bewildering to many' outsiders, but insisted that the criticism was unscientific: 'The underlying, deeper psychological mechanisms have been discussed by expertise present at the trials.' The 'expertise' he referred to was of course Sven Å Christianson.

Another interesting insight into how Penttinen thought comes in a letter to the Norwegian police, written in March 1996. Penttinen was writing with information on what Sture had said about murders he had committed in Norway, which had not yet been properly investigated, including the alleged murder of Therese Johannessen. Before Penttinen gave an account of what Sture had said in the interviews, he provided the Norwegians with a brief introduction to Sture's unusual psychology:

> The information presented below are the facts according to Quick's interview statements. It is important to regard these as part of a stage in his story of the events in question and among the items of information that he provided there will be some of a type Quick

describes as 'deliberate diversions'. His explanation is that, due to the anxiety he feels, it may at times be impossible for him to recount exactly what has passed and that he instead will make a reply that touches on the real situation, or else is erroneous. Some of his statements may be associated with the real situation and, within these, Quick will have consciously left a 'clue'. These presentations of the real events are his way of telling the officers in charge of the investigation that he actually is the perpetrator. It is important that you are aware of these factors when you read the interview transcripts.[458]

After this introduction, various statements followed including Sture's vision of Therese, with her 'blonde, shoulder-length hair, her hair flows around her as she runs', which did not match the girl's short, dark hair. Still, someone must have taken note of Penttinen's explanation because the murder investigation was set in motion with full support from the Norwegian police. Penttinen helped Sture to get his story right and he was convicted in 1998.

One consequence of Penttinen's take on Sture's mental condition was that he became ever more convinced of Sture's guilt the more errors his account contained. He thought that the errors or the 'deliberate diversions' were symptoms of anxiety and that being anxious indicated guilt. Penttinen's system of thought was closed because it permitted no conclusion other than 'Sture is a serial killer'. He had bought in to Margit's circuitous logic as it had been applied to alleged victims of childhood incest.

Penttinen has almost always refused to be interviewed and there is very little personal information about him. He is often seen at Sture's side in photographs taken at crime re-enactments but I have not found any other pictures of him. I wanted to meet him and, as luck would have it, my ingratiating interview with Christianson made it possible. Christianson provided the connection to Christer van der Kwast and he, in his turn, thought I should talk to Seppo Penttinen.

I knew that in the 1990s he had been giving lectures on how to go about interviewing Thomas Quick and sent him an email to ask him about it. He replied that he had indeed lectured on the interviews in the Gry Storvik case to the advanced Interview Leadership course at the police college:

I usually describe the interviews with the phrase 'Venetian blind effect'. S B begins his account by twitching a little, opening up a few slats. It exposes some of the core of the crime which makes his story of interest to the police. But at the same time as he allows you to peep through the slats, he displays completely mistaken facts. He calls it 'deliberate diversions'. [...] S B said in his first statement that he had stabbed Gry's lower chest with a knife. [...] That's how he controlled his anxiety. He allows himself to make wrong answers. My view of his way to deal with facts is that he climbs one step at a time.

It was the familiar explanatory model, yet again. But what he said next was more interesting: 'In my opinion, spoken or written words are "marginal" manifestations of a language. When you sit in an interview room, you make note of breathing, gestures, changes of tone, pauses, facial expressions and other such clues to what is going on. In the case of S B, such non-verbal clues sent clear signals about what he really said and meant.'

The words Sture spoke and which are preserved in the thousands of pages of interview transcripts – all that amounted to no more than 'a marginal manifestation' of the truth. Penttinen was not listening to what Sture said. Hour after hour, he kept interpreting what he called 'signals' in order to understand what Sture 'really' meant, i.e. things that Penttinen already knew about the murders and that he felt Sture was communicating with 'breathing, gestures, changes of tone, pauses, facial expressions etc'. This explained why the knife cutting into Gry Storvik's flesh did not disturb Penttinen in the slightest. He felt that he perceived Sture's real account of a quite different event. No wonder Sture could say whatever came to mind without facing any real interrogation.

Penttinen suggested that I come with him to Sundsvall to see a few key places in the Johan Asplund case, the spots where Sture had murdered the boy and where he had dismembered the body. I told him I was keen and a few weeks later I was shaking hands with Penttinen outside my Sundsvall hotel.

Seppo Penttinen, a tall, nearly bald man with a round face, was casually dressed in chinos and a sweater. His eyes were a little sad, he seemed gentle and ponderous, the opposite of a hard-bitten policeman. Under the calm surface I sensed a huge frustration. He still thought that Sture was guilty and was engaged in an ever-more desperate struggle with his uncomprehending countrymen. I responded sympathetically to his predicament – it must have been hellish. He had been the lead interviewer in all the cases involving Sture, and the outcome was the century's biggest miscarriage of justice. He would go down in history as Sweden's most incompetent policeman of modern times, just as Christer van der Kwast would be remembered as the worst screwball of a prosecutor in the history of the Swedish legal system. Naturally, they fought like trapped tigers.

Seppo drove us northwards from Sundsvall and towards Bosvedjan, where Johan Asplund had lived in 1980. I asked him to give me an idea of what van der Kwast was like to work with: 'He's got a good head on him, really brilliant,' Seppo said. 'Over the years, I've come across quite a few prosecutors but never one so hands-on. No long discussions with him, no dithering. You can't work with a scatty prosecutor, it means trouble. He must be able to take in the whole situation and be ready to make up his mind once and for all.'

He turned off the main road and drove to the small Bosvedjan estate. He pointed out where Sture had left the car, next to the narrow road which served as both entrance and exit route, leaving the door open as he did when hunting for a boy. The kidnapping took place at around eight o'clock on an ordinary morning when the whole area must be crowded with people on their way to work and school. Seppo showed me how Sture had walked some 10 to 20 metres between the three-storey blocks, attracted Johan's attention and got him into the car.

'Wasn't that a very risky thing to do?' I asked.

'Yes,' Seppo replied. 'But it can be part of the whole sick fantasy that he has to have an element of tension in it as well. It's the kind of thing one might speculate about.'

We went back to the car and Seppo drove north-east of Bosvedjan to the forests, fields and meadows of the Åvike area. After 20 kilometres he turned into a narrow road and then stopped at a junction. He explained that this was where Sture had told them to stop at the first re-enactment in 1993: 'He really was stressed out of his head and when we got to this place, it was "stop!". He went completely wild in the car and the doctors had to take over. They made him breathe into a bag, you know. I remember Göran Fransson saying "Is his heart really up to all this?" They were scared he would die.'

I glanced at Seppo. He looked quite convinced of the significance of Sture's panic attack on this forest road in 1993. But I had read the police investigation of the Asplund case from beginning to end and could find no rational arguments to support the notion that Sture had been to Åvike at any time other than that re-enactment. Seppo seemed to be blind to this – his eyes positively shone with faith.

He drove me to the meadow with the rock where Sture was supposed to have cut up the body and we inspected the place. Seppo said that it matched everything in Sture's interview description without mentioning the crucial difference: the pile of stones supposed to have covered the remains was never found. He spoke volubly about Sture's anxiety – 'You know, Sture actually threw up when he saw the rock' – as if this added verisimilitude.

We returned to the car and began to drive toward a place where Sture claimed to have taken Johan's head. I took note of this leap forward in time. In 1993, Sture had said he had buried the head near the rock, but Seppo did not mention that to me. The place we were driving towards had only surfaced seven years later, on 9 September 2000, when Sture, escorted by Seppo and Christianson, was taken for a *fourth* re-enactment in Åvike.

They were, as usual, chasing some remnant of Johan's body and had wandered out of a clear-felled stretch in the forest. Sture noticed a hillock and insisted on climbing it. Standing on the top, he told the others that he had carried the head there in 1980 and had flung it out among the tree stumps. He then drove away, leaving the head where it had landed. Seppo said that, afterwards, they had taken a cadaver dog to search the area. The head had gone but the dog marked twice below the hillock and in a straight line from the place where Sture had stood when he threw the head. Seppo glanced meaningfully at me but I didn't quite get it so I asked what his conclusion had been. He explained that the first spot might have been where the head had hit the ground, before bouncing and landing on the second place the dog had marked. Later, some wild animal must have carried the head away.

This theory is a little unconvincing, because cadaver dogs mark dead animals as well as dead people, so marking in a forest means nothing until the police find the remains they are looking for. Seppo trusted that the dog had found the right scent, but there was another problem with his story. When I was back from the Sundsvall visit, I looked up the dog handler's report among the documents. The search using a cadaver dog took place nine days after the re-enactment. This is what the report says:

In connection with interviews and crime scene re-enactments, T Q had indicated a place north of Sundsvall where he allegedly threw the victim's head away. The throw was made in the north-west direction from the top of a mossy hillock. Dog handler John Sjöberg with the dog Sampo searched the area. Sampo marked two places below the hillock. The marked places were 11 metres apart.[459]

If Seppo's version was to be accepted, the head must have bounced eleven metres from the spot where it landed. One had to imagine the head bouncing over the roughly shorn forest floor like a well-pumped football. It was both fascinating and sad that Seppo had taken me into the forest to tell me this story.

As we drove back to Sundsvall, I asked him about the search for Sture's special hiding places. He replied that Sture had sought out many of his old caches and emptied them, which was why they had never found any remains of Therese Johannessen and Johan Asplund. Sture had gradually assembled his collection of relics in one large space. Extensive police resources had been devoted to finding it and Seppo's eyes still had a dreamy look as he spoke about this, the mother of all caches. He told me that there had been a lot of digging but the search had to end when the funding ran out.

I asked if he ever felt like having a go himself. 'Sometimes I've been itching to,' he admitted.

After the Åvike visit, we went to have lunch at a skating rink. As we ate, I asked Seppo if he had ever met Margit. Oh yes, he had been supervised by her at one point after the Therese investigation. He had needed to talk to someone who could help him deal with all the terrible things Sture was telling him. 'What he told me could be so grotesque that I needed to make sure my own thinking was sound,' he said. 'You stay as neutral as possible during the interviews, but of course the images stick in your mind.' Seppo had been offered an appointment with Margit and spent an hour in her armchair. I asked him what his impression of her had been. He said that she came across as a wise person and that she was a very good listener.

Sture had said that he was pretty sure Seppo had been to see Margit but I had not believed him. Even so, I was not surprised to hear Seppo speak of consulting her. Nothing in the strange case of Thomas Quick could surprise me any more.

I kept thinking about Seppo on the way back to Stockholm. Sture had told me about the time an upset Seppo had phoned him during the investigation of the murder of Yenon Levi to say that he had cried on the train on the way back from Sundsvall. When I interviewed Jan Olsson, the former detective chief inspector, he mentioned that Seppo had been in tears because van der Kwast had considered Sture's account of the Levi murder so shaky that he wanted to cancel the preliminary investigation. In Margit's manuscript she quotes a letter from Sture to Ståhle on 26 October 1996. In it, Sture mentions that Seppo had just phoned him to say that the Levi investigation had been closed and that it had made him weep all the way from Sundsvall. Sture was disappointed because Ståhle had not been in touch all day – if closing the case had been so painful to Seppo, how did she think he, Sture, felt?

I thought for a long time about Seppo shedding tears. He believed so strongly in Sture's guilt that he could not bear the investigation not leading to a prosecution, then he rang the alleged serial killer to say how sad he felt. Policemen do not normally behave like this, I was certain of that.

Seppo had worked in the drug squad before being seconded to the Quick case. His experience of murder investigations was minimal and he had no knowledge of psychology and psychotherapy. Everything he thought he knew about Sture's mental functions he had learnt from others, beginning with Kjell Persson and Göran Fransson. After the ten-month period between March 1993 and January 1994, Christianson instructed him for eight years (1994–2002). Margit was looming behind every one of Seppo's teachers and he had neither knowledge nor experience enough to resist her influence. In practice, Seppo became one of her pupils and still was when I saw him in Sundsvall. I felt sorry for him. He was led astray by others, who had been misled in their turn.

Still, Seppo is responsible for the consequences of his blind faith, and especially because he chose to be dishonest about what he told the District Courts.

I found an instructive example of how he approached his role as a police witness in the 1997 Levi murder trial. The Hedemora District Court knew that Sture had changed his story during the course of the investigation but the bench had not read the interview transcripts. Instead, the senior investigating officer was heard under oath. The court wanted to know if Sture had needed any help to arrive at the recorded answers and the sentence includes the following passage about Seppo's statement: 'Thomas Quick has changed his account between interviews but these changes were made spontaneously. There have been no attempts to influence him. Hence, Thomas Quick's attention has not been drawn to any "errors" by many repetitions of the same question or by being asked if he was sure of what he had just said.'[460]

Seppo was guilty of perjury. The interview transcripts contain evidence of the real situation. For instance, one of Sture's early statements that he later changed 'spontaneously' concerned his first encounter with Yenon Levi, which he initially described as occurring in a side street near the railway station in Uppsala. Arriving from the north, as Sture would have, the station lies on the road south to Stockholm.[461]

Sture and a partner, who was never charged, threatened Levi with a knife to make him climb into the car. They then drove north towards Rörshyttan and killed him there.

The problem was that witnesses had seen Levi in Stockholm Central Station before he disappeared. The murder investigation could not find anything that linked him to Uppsala and there was no reason for him to be there. It was more probable that someone had induced him to come north from Stockholm to Dalarna, where he was later found dead.

For five months, Sture insisted that they had met in Uppsala but by the time the sentence was pronounced, he had changed his story to say he had picked up Levi in Stockholm Central Station. He stated this in a music room interview conducted by Seppo and Anna Wikström, Seppo's assistant, on 23 February 1996. This is what was said:

[Penttinen]: 'Are you 100 per cent sure that you met Yenon Levi in Uppsala?'
[Sture]: 'Yes.'
[Penttinen]: 'No doubt about it?'
[Sture]: 'No.'
[Penttinen]: 'You know, I felt you reacted in a way I recognize. If I ask the question this way, I sense that there was some hesitation when you gave the answer. Your face gives that away.'
[Sture]: 'Umm.'
[Penttinen]: 'This is a crucial question. You've insisted for a long time that you met Mr Levi in Uppsala but now you hint that you're not so sure. What was the thought that struck you at the time when I put the question to you? Any other memories linked to ...'
[Sture]: 'There are other memories that are about ... well, let's leave that for now.'
[Penttinen]: 'But will we reach the right conclusion in the end unless you get the account right of when this first meeting happened, and where?'
[Sture]: 'I suppose ...'

[Penttinen]: 'What makes you unable to tell us in a straightforward way about this meeting?'

[Sture]: 'I've stated, already given information about . . . how we met . . . and . . . yes, well. I won't carry on twisting and turning. Let's leave this be for now.'

[Penttinen]: 'When you say leave it for now I get the impression that this is information you might change, that there's something you haven't told us . . .'

[Sture]: 'Doubt that.'

[Penttinen]: 'I understand you to say that your story isn't quite right.'

Soon afterwards, Constable Anna Wikström took over:

[Wikström]: Just a minor point . . . It's true of course that there was quite a big effort by the police at the time and . . .

[Sture]: 'Ye-es.'

[Wikström]: 'As we've been saying before, there's a lot of information available in this case.'

[Sture]: 'Ye-es.'

[Wikström]: 'And that means there are little traps waiting all the time while we're talking to you.'

[Sture]: 'Ye-es.'

[Wikström]: 'And that's why we ask you again to please tell us if anything feels wrong and try to give us what seems to be most right.'

After Wikström's plea that Sture should change his mind, Seppo worked on Sture until he finally caved in:

[Sture]: 'Well, it could be that we took a commuter train to Stockholm and then back again.'

[Penttinen]: 'So, you say that's how it might have been, you took a commuter train to Stockholm. Did you do that journey?'

[Sture]: 'Yes, we did.'[462]

Barely three months later, the District Court in Hedemora heard a detailed account of Sture and his partner catching sight of Levi in Stockholm Central Station, picking him up and persuading him to come with them to Uppsala where they had parked the car. Then they drove northwards.

When the prosecutors who examined the evidence in the applications for retrial discovered that this was how the Quick interviews were conducted, all van der Kwast's cases collapsed like so many houses of cards. But the courts that convicted Sture had had no idea he was stage-managed. All they heard was a police officer stating, under oath, that Sture changed his accounts without prompting – 'spontaneously'.

I think it is unfair to blame Seppo Penttinen for his fervent commitment to the 'faith'. He was in a very difficult situation and lacked the mental equipment needed to resist the fanatically strong faith preached at Säter. However, he alone is responsible for the decision to perjure himself, whether or not he did so in the service of a 'higher truth'.

30

Sture's faith

'Quick has only had the occasional private visitor during the
ten years he has spent in this hospital.'
Charge Nurse Bengt Eklund in the final Quick trial.

Everyone around Sture was of the faith and Christer van der Kwast
weeded out the few who saw through the 'serial killer'. During the
investigation of the murder of Yenon Levi, the experienced detective
chief inspector in the violent crimes unit, Jan Olsson, became convinced that Sture was lying. He had had his reservations ever since the
Appojaure case, but certain aspects of the Levi investigation confirmed his earlier suspicions. On 31 January 1997, barely four months
before the court pronounced Sture guilty of the murder, Olsson compiled a list of features of the case indicating that the confession had
been false. He sent a copy to van der Kwast and was bawled out for
his trouble. As a result, he left the investigation. Detective Inspector
Thure Nässén was another doubter who left in protest. In a 2002
letter to Penttinen, he set out his reasons for not believing in Sture's
confessions. Some of his examples – as we have already seen – are
drawn from the strange re-enactment at the Appojaure crime scene.
He also referred to Sture's behaviour when the team were out searching for body parts in Örje Forest and at a failed reconstruction of the
Levi murder, both in 1996:

> Concerning the murders of Therese and of that poor Israeli, I must
> admit that I found it disquieting to see and listen to this man. I had the
> impression that he was inventing everything he said as he went along.
> As soon as he was asked a tricky question, he staged a breakdown

and started to shout and scream, run around and 'make an ass of himself'. Personally, I thought it was embarrassing to watch him as he played the fool and/or made us look foolish.[463]

Clearly it was possible to point a finger to Sture's play-acting but the rest of the group around him were utterly united in their faith and unable to read the cues as Jan Olsson and Thure Nässén had done. The psychologist Magnus Brolin described the situation in Säter as 'like a sect'. 'We *knew*. And we were going to prove it.' Was Sture himself in any sense a believer? In 2008, when he officially retracted all his confessions, he was unequivocal – he had known all along that his stories were lies. Dr Anna Dåderman, one of the experts scrutinizing Sture's medication in the retrial applications, thinks that the answer is not quite so straightforward. She says that, at the outset, Sture had probably been able to distinguish between fantasy and reality, but in the long run his heavy drug usage and his immersion in the exceptionally suggestive psychotherapeutic treatment would have made it practically impossible to remain in touch with the truth. As I read the case notes, the interview transcripts and the rest of the documentation, I came to believe that Dåderman might be right, especially after 1997. The steady trickle of drugs had become a deluge and Sture was surrounded by people who believed in his confessions with near-religious intensity. How could he keep track of what was plausible or implausible, true or false, healthy or sick?

When I spoke to Sture about this, he told me that there are great gaps in his memory for the period of 1997–2001. This is supported by something Hannes Råstam said while doing a TV interview with Göran Källberg. In an unbroadcast section of the programme, Hannes wonders about Sture's claim to selective memory loss and said that his own research had shown that even events which would have backed up Sture's not-guilty plea had slipped from Sture's memory. This had convinced Hannes that the partial amnesia claim was valid.

Defective memory is a likely effect of overdosing on benzodiazepines. WHO's register of side-effects of medicines rate amnesiac effects as common for drugs like Xanax and Halcion, both prescribed in large doses for Sture throughout his ten-year stay in Säter.[464]

In my research, I repeatedly returned to the question of what Sture actually believed when he acted as Thomas Quick. He grew more and more uncertain as we talked. At one point, he admitted that he believed he had been a victim of incestuous abuse – or at least believed it when he went into the state that Ståhle called regression. He was supposed to 'recover' forgotten events and had felt like he was dreaming while awake. The 'dreams' could be very vivid. In between therapy sessions he knew that what he had experienced was fantasy.

On another occasion, he suddenly said that there had been times when he truly thought he had killed people; for example, he felt certain he remembered stabbing Gry Storvik. What he says about himself is contradictory and I can't exclude the possibility that he adapts his answers to my repeated questions rather as he had to Penttinen's. Regardless, he probably only has a tenuous grasp of what was happening to his mind during the most chaotic years.

The picture became a little clearer after I had talked with a fifty-year-old woman I will call Stina, herself a therapist who had undergone more or less the same kind of therapy as Sture, although in less dramatic circumstances. One of Margit's former pupils put me in touch with her.

Stina had begun as a social worker in the early 1990s and took a foundation course in psychotherapy. In 1994, Cajsa Lindholm gave a lecture about object relations theory to the students. Stina, who was rather unhappy at the time, asked afterwards if Cajsa could take her on for therapy. Cajsa agreed. At the time, her practice was outside central Stockholm and Stina started going there once a week. She said that the first three years went well and that it had been a relief to have someone to talk to, though Cajsa's insistence on linking her problems to childhood problems troubled Stina because, as she put it: 'It felt as if I hadn't had a life since then.' But in the beginning Cajsa was not too insistent.

After a few years in therapy Stina was allowed to meet Margit. It made her feel quite special. She describes Margit as 'a queen', celebrated by Cajsa as 'the best of the best in the whole world'. Other pupils were present at the meeting and the atmosphere was so deferential that Stina automatically curtsied when she was introduced to Margit. Stina found the great lady arrogant. 'She stared straight through me as she shook my hand. Cajsa, Gillan and Lena hovered around her like servants. At one point I asked if she would like a glass of water but she didn't reply.'

Stina's father was an alcoholic who beat both her and her mother. She needed to talk about this and Cajsa had been interested at first, but after three years she grew more demanding. Stina felt that her memories of domestic violence somehow were not enough. Cajsa began to help Stina recover repressed memories of sexual abuse that she had previously had no idea about. I asked her to explain how it was done, and it was obvious she had rarely spoken about it to anyone.

'Christ, yes . . . how was it done?' she said and shook her head.

Then: 'It's so hard to explain. Some kind of suggestive interaction took place between Cajsa and me. We talked together for two hours every week. All about interpretations of things, all the time. And with the tacit agreement that Cajsa's were the right ones, that what she said was true.'

Cajsa interpreted Stina's dreams and the longer the therapy continued the more fruitful it became: 'I've never had such weird dreams, before or since.'

She did not just deal in the meanings of dreams. Memory retrieval as re-enactment was fundamental to Cajsa's approach to psychotherapeutic treatment and she thought that all Stina's actions could be understood as symbolic retellings of the sexual abuse she had experienced. Stina told me about the time she was in financial trouble and worried about her unpaid bills and intractable creditors. When she tried to speak about it, Cajsa explained that these problems were re-enactments of her father's sexual demands.

'It became impossible to speak about anything that happened in reality, in the present,' Stina said. 'Everything centred on my relationship with my father and his abusive behaviour. One day, when I was cycling to the therapy session, the draught of a passing bus sucked me in and I fell off the bike. Once I had said that, the therapy sessions were all about how Dad had used violence to "suck me in". Do you see just how sick all this was?'

Stina had quite a few positive memories from her childhood. One of the warmest was of the time she helped her father clean his fishing nets. He hugged her afterwards and told her what a good girl she had been. Cajsa instructed her patient that this had been yet another act of sexual abuse that Stina had prettied up to avoid the truth.

She was so affected that she began to feel physical intimations of the alleged abuse and responded strongly if someone touched her. The therapy, which continued for many years, became an essential part of her life. Throughout, she accepted as a fact that her father had subjected her to sexual, sadistic abuse in her childhood, starting when she was a year old.

In the late 1990s Stina joined the circle around Margit, at a time when Margit's worst fears were coming true – her pupils were turning away from her. Tomas Videgård and Margareta Hedén-Chami left as early as 1994, and they were followed by Patricia Tudor-Sandahl, Britt Andersson and several others. Almost all these separations led to irreconcilable conflicts with Margit, who could be extremely hostile to those who distanced themselves from her. It was barely possible to end a course of therapy or a series of supervision meetings without a complete breakdown of the relationship. Sometimes, when Margit felt she had been betrayed, she was capable of gross, personal attacks on the culprit. One example is the letter Margit wrote to Patricia Tudor-Sandahl after she had made up her mind to leave. In it Patricia was told, in effect, that she was a bad person and that her life would become a worse mess from now on. I have heard many others say that this was how Margit operated. The outcome was that, by the mid-1990s, Margit had lost contact with most of the people who had been close to her since the end of the 1970s. She was left with a retinue of loyal pupils that consisted of Birgitta Ståhle, Cajsa Lindholm, Gillan Liljeström and a few others. This was the group that Cajsa invited Stina to join.

Stina felt more valued and important than ever before, now that she was allowed to be together with select people around Margit. Everyone praised the 'therapeutic work' she was carrying out as courageous and morally commendable. Stina described it to me as 'being part of a narcissistic system' and added that it was an addictive experience. Before starting her therapy, she had been dismissing herself as useless. She had needed to matter to others and that was precisely what Cajsa and the others offered her. Stina said:

> The more memories one retrieved the more one was singled out as special and cheered on. I guess I had reached a stage in my life when I fought to become someone and I was easy prey. My parents were alive and I resented them both. My dad had hit me and hurt me badly. Still, he did not cross *that* particular boundary. Today, I am prepared to swear he didn't. But being made to feel special had a fatal attraction. It's tragic. When Dad died in 1999, I was utterly shut off from him. Hated him. I couldn't go to him. I couldn't grieve.

But in the early 2000s, it began to dawn on Stina that the sexual abuse she had spent thousands of hours speaking about during therapy was nothing but fantasies originating in Cajsa's expectations. However, Cajsa would not under any circumstances let her end the 'treatment'. She accused Stina of 'entering into an alliance' with her evil father, of sinking back into a state of denial. By then, Stina was herself working as a psychotherapist and Cajsa had passed some patients on to her. Now, Cajsa made it very clear that if Stina stopped coming for therapy, there would be no more support forthcoming, not from Cajsa or anyone else in the Margit group. Stina fought to free herself from her mental dependence and in the end achieved it. Her last session with Cajsa was in 2008.

'I'm leaving now, and I won't be back,' Stina had said as she walked out of the practice.

I asked Stina the same question as I had asked Sture so many times: 'At the time, did you believe in your "memories"?'

'Yes, I did,' she said. 'But it's also true that, all the time, a small voice inside me insisted that none of it was true. That I was submitting, that

I was forced somehow to say that these things were true and really believe it. If someone had questioned the therapy, I would have defended it.'

Stina said that Sture had been a big topic of discussion among the members of the group. 'I understand Sture. When I was young, I acted up as well. Drugs, stuff like that. And then, suddenly, all this attention ... Sture was absurdly highly regarded. If I had been more like him when I came to Cajsa in the beginning, I mean, if I had had fewer friends and been a little less competent, I could so easily have started to invent more stories about myself. Just a few years earlier and I would've been easy meat.'

'And what do you think must be missing from one's life to make one prepared to adapt in such an extreme way?' I asked.

'Space to reflect on one's own,' Stina replied. 'And someone to talk to, toss life and death questions to and get ideas back. And some kind of basic moral steeliness. An awareness of what's right and wrong. Ethics. If you're wavering in that department you will soon fall victim.'

Just before I left, Stina said: 'I am so pleased you're doing this. That the truth will come out. They are still out there, working with patients. People spend twenty, thirty years in therapy with these people. They're draining their patients of money and time and life. What they do is not therapeutic. Therapy is meant to help people understand the world and how relationships work.'

I was deeply moved by Stina's story of how she needed to be acknowledged, to become somebody and so turned herself into Cajsa's favourite patient. I understood that it is possible to feel that one must believe in something because it opens a door to a sense of togetherness and respect that one has never previously experienced.

During my research, I had collected a list of observations and quotes that I gave the working title *Sture-as-Christ*. It was made up of celebratory statements about Sture that I came across here and there in the documentation of the Quick years. He had not only been rewarded with drugs but also with something else that is, as Stina had reminded me, as addictive: Respect. Admiration. Love.

In fact, his elevation coincided with the moment in November

1991 when Margit undertook the supervision of his therapy. Margit was already a much-admired, leading figure at Säter and before long the multi-addicted Sture Bergwall, a lonely outcast and petty criminal, had become her most significant patient. I think he must have adored his new status. All his life Sture had wanted to be important but failed and failed again. He had wanted to become a writer and cherished the memory of what his senior schoolteacher had once said about his talent. He was what he was – an addict, a criminal and a homosexual, and despised himself for all of it. He longed for love but had been incapable of building a functioning relationship. He had no friends who knew him well. His attempt to cut drugs had failed and the embarrassing bank robbery proved that he couldn't even carry off a crime. Understandably, his brothers and sisters had turned their backs on him. When he arrived at Säter he was isolated and run-down. The only thing he was any good at was pretending he was something he was not. He had had life-long practice. Margit expected him to remember bad things so he pretended that he did and, just like Stina, he received the respect, admiration and love that he had always craved. He was bewitched and in thrall to the narcissistic system Stina had spoken about.

No one had ever planned the murder convictions until his con-man instincts led to him being picked out as Thomas Blomgren's murderer. After that, he was branded. He knew that the brand would mark him for ever and all he could do was carry on as he had before. It probably was not a very difficult decision, because it made everyone love him. Kjell Persson loved him because Sture made him feel that he was a brilliant therapist and gained him oodles of respect from Margit. Göran Fransson loved Sture because he vindicated the Säter theories and looked likely to become the trump card for the beleaguered hospital. Christer van der Kwast and Seppo Penttinen loved Sture because he would help them to solve dozens of old unsolved murder cases and make them both into heroes. Birgitta and Sven Å Christianson loved Sture because he held the key to Mummy Margit's heart. Margit loved Sture because he was living proof of her theory's validity and a promise of the retaliation she had spent twenty years longing for.

And ex-junkie, ex-pervert Sture Bergwall was swirling around in this whirlpool of neediness and longing, becoming seen as the rescuer, the man who brought salvation. If only he would continue to remember things, he would eventually rise high above his old loveless, useless, shameful self. They told him that his special insights would help to catch serial killers, even stop them in good time. Useless Sture would become a life-saver, for far into the future. For years, he sat at his computer elaborating on Margit's theories. After explaining repression and re-enactment, he went on to invent new mechanisms at work in the mind of a serial killer. He drew diagrams of the killer's mentality, illustrations that Sture himself can no longer make head or tail of. At the time, everything he did along these lines was regarded as profound. Dr Christianson greedily acquired the theories for his great work *Inside the Mind of a Serial Killer*, which no doubt would make him world famous. Birgitta, too, collected Sture's writings and hurried them off to Margit, who earnestly added them to her manuscript 'The World of Thomas Quick'.

Sture was told that he had become an icon of moral behaviour. On the wall in his room, he had put up a picture of the serial killer Westley Allan Dodd in his orange prison jumpsuit as he was led into a courtroom. Dodd was executed by hanging in the Walla Walla Penitentiary in Washington State on 5 January 1993. That was barely two months before Sture's first police interview in Säter. Margit and Birgitta said that Dodd was a coward who had escaped into death without accepting his responsibility to tell everyone about the childhood abuse that had made him become a serial killer. Sture, on the other hand, was not a coward. Unlike Dodd he had accepted his moral responsibility and carried out his brave memory work. He displayed the photo of Dodd to remind himself of his duty. In the eyes of the faithful in Säter, Sture was a kind of inverted martyr whose courage was shown by his refusal to die despite a grim awareness of guilt that could have made death seem the right way out. Unselfishly, he took on the pain of staying alive in order to assist science and the victims' loved ones. How he was celebrated for his sacrifice! Lena Arvidsson, soon to become employed as a psychologist at Säter, wrote to Sture:

Your courage gives me courage, your strength gives me hope and your eagerness to find out the truth inspires my own search. You are a confirmation of all I believe in and fight for. What your friendship has taught me will stay with me for ever. Your narrative helps me to resist what I don't believe in, all that which I have learnt during my training, and you show me the way to what is important and meaningful. Your narrative expresses and offers images of what I had already understood but defined it and makes it more comprehensible. Your struggle is so important! You make possible what many think impossible, you open your eyes to what others turn their backs on. I see, understand, am touched and amazed at your immense capacity for good and which we all share. [...] Your narrative reminds me of my own vulnerability, helps me to remember and to be more willing to endure a painful past.[465]

Long after he had left his job in the unit, Dr Persson also sent fan mail to Sture. He wrote this in the autumn of 1995:

It is self-evident that your crimes are grotesque. On the other hand, your magnificent work in attempting to square up to the past will never fade from my mind. It is another reason why I wish desperately that you should stay alive so that a wider circle of colleagues can benefit from your experiences and your willpower. Settling the fight against evil may sound a little too theatrical and idealistic but it is truly what is happening.[466]

Sture felt pumped up by his own greatness. In September 1994, he wrote: 'Our life-stories contain knowledge which – and this is my belief and my motive for survival – tomorrow, or later on, will help to free the tormented child of its pain or prevent handed down mental disturbances from spreading.'[467]

He began to identify with Jesus, as for instance in this therapy note from March 1996: 'I am thinking about Christ on the Cross. Surely he would not become good, not after the abandonment and the pain he endured. One feels a need to strike back, to revenge oneself.'[468]

A few months later Birgitta made this note during a therapy session: 'Initially, Sture has been very withdrawn and distant. Paraphrasing the quotation "My God, why have You abandoned me?"'[469]

When Kerstin Vinterhed wrote up her interview with Sture for *Dagens Nyheter* in the spring of 1996, she presented him as a suffering martyr. Later Vinterhed invited him to contribute to *The Book of Jesus*, an anthology based on her collection of famous people's 'personal images of Christ'. The short essays had been written by philosophers, poets, theologians, musicians, psychologists, members of the clergy and of the Swedish Academy – and by Thomas Quick, serial killer. As his image of Christ, Sture had chosen *The Veil of Veronica* by Francisco de Zurbarán and explained why: 'Christ exists in me and outside me. I glimpse his distorted face on the veil of Veronica. His suffering is my own but also belongs to those I have made to suffer.'[470]

Kerstin Vinterhed's younger brother, the lawyer Claes Borgström, shared his sister's respect for Sture's struggle. In his final plea in the 1996 Appojaure trial, he emphasized his client's noble motives: 'Today, Thomas Quick is taking the only action open to him which is to clarify the sequence of past events. He has many motives. Justice for the victims' loved ones. Knowledge that will be important to future generations. Awareness of the vulnerability of children and their need of help when traumatic things happen to them.' And, finally: 'Never before has the perpetrator's role as victim been so clearly shown to us.'[471]

In 2000, at Sture's trial for the murders of Gry Storvik and Trine Jensen, Borgström delivered a fiery plea in which he listed the circumstances he thought demonstrated Sture's guilt beyond doubt and then ended with praising his man's high moral tone:

I, as Thomas Quick's defence advocate, want to state just how much respect I feel he should be given for telling us what he knows. [...] It requires a high degree of moral rectitude to confess to the most immoral thing anyone can do, that is, to murder a fellow human being in order to satisfy a personal craving. Thomas Quick *is* a highly moral man. Thomas Quick is also a tragic man. He takes responsibility through telling his story. It would be tragic indeed if those who listen chose not to believe him.[472]

In the same trial, Birgitta Ståhle took the witness stand and said that Sture had three reasons for undergoing his therapy treatment with her:

> He decided to use psychotherapeutic work to try to understand how he became the man he is and to retrieve the repressed memories of his childhood years and of the murders. [...] I do truly believe Thomas Quick possesses an unusual ability to formulate and describe the relevant psychological mechanisms. His insights will contribute to both the psychology of perpetrators and to the theory of trauma.[473]

Throughout his ten years of life as Thomas Quick, Sture was constantly given accolades of this kind. Being praised was now an expected part of his life.

Sture was also helpful to the forces committed to spreading the belief in repressed memories. He was used as an ideological battering ram. The sex crime investigator Monica Dahlström-Lannes was very well known in Sweden and when she argued with her critics she claimed that Sture's recovered memories proved her right.[474] She, too, penned adoring letters to him, like this one from the summer of 2000: 'Once more, I must let you know how praiseworthy I feel you are, and so is the enormously great and courageous work you – and your therapist – carry out. Work of which you can be very proud.'[475]

In his trial for the murder of Yenon Levi in 1997, Sture stood up to speak and managed to move himself to tears as he addressed the court:

> It is only after the greatest hesitation that I chose to say a few words here. But I will speak, taking as my theme the concept of human worth. Can it really be that someone like me, someone who has, as I have, degraded and denied human worth, himself has some value as a human being? I struggle to find in myself, inside me, this human worth. Should my task, the work which I do now and of which this

trial forms part, contribute to making it easier in the future to identify tomorrow's serial killers before they kill – yes, if so, my being
here today may also count towards that which is human worth.

Now, when you are here and listen to me, but at the same time
remember the terrible crimes I have committed, you will instantly
realize that the story of my life must be seen from a perspective that
allows for complex, diverse sequences of events if there are to be any
circumstances in which it becomes possible to have an understanding of, or to arrive at an explanation of, the acts of which I am
guilty.

Human worth.

Worthy to be human. Worthy to be allowed to be human.

Without being granted the right to be human, at least as the
person I am, together with and facing up to those with whom I
share my life from day to day, my courage to attempt to contribute
an explanation would be non-existent. Perhaps I still dare to say that
I do have human worth? Perhaps I must say it and at the same time
feel it is in order, today, to take responsibility for the murder which
this trial has been conducted to examine and judge?

Help me, today, to glimpse my human worth or, rather, help me
to confirm the rightness of my striving. Do so, by using the human
worth that you have and that I do much need.[476]

Sture was very keen to keep his saint's halo intact. People who
accused him of lying frightened him and also filled him with self-right-
eous indignation. In the summer of 1998, when several commentators
said that Sture seemed to be either a mythomaniac or someone with
therapy-induced false memories, he let it be known that the criticism
caused him great pain. His lawyer, Claes Borgström, leapt to his
defence and wrote an article for the op-ed section in *Dagens Nyheter*,
targeting in particular the psychologist Astrid Holgersson and the
reader in forensic psychology Nils Wiklund. Both had expressed their
concern over the possibility that Quick's psychotherapy might have
created false memories.

Borgström was indignant: 'During the years that I have been

Thomas Quick's legal adviser, I have never felt that he needed some-one to act in his defence as much as I do now' and put it to Astrid Holgersson that she had 'vilified not only Thomas Quick, which pre-sumably is of no concern to her, but also the victims' families and friends'. He had found that 'both Wiklund and Holgersson have failed to meet even the most minimal demands that we are justified to make on those who purport to be scientists. Their frivolity is astonishing.'[477]

He made short work of his colleague Kerstin Korti, who had 'won the lemon prize for gross irrationality' when she predicted in a TV interview that the Quick trial would, one day, turn out to be one of the twentieth-century's biggest miscarriages of justice. Borgström wanted to destroy Korti's good name: 'I feel nothing but contempt for her immoral attitude to these profoundly complex issues which, above all, also reflect on the personal tragedies that are central to the Quick trials.'

He let off a similar barrage in another leading paper, *Svenska Dagbladet*.[478] His obvious intention was to scare all critics off the sub-ject and it seems likely that he was quite successful.

Sture himself wrote articles to reassure everyone that he was a real serial killer. He also attacked the sceptics, as in this piece from 1999, where he used hurt irony as his weapon:

> I had come believe after a while that what I was doing was right, that I should be supported and encouraged. At least, I hoped that some people would understand the personal courage it takes to take responsibility for such unspeakable acts, tell the police about them and, at the same time, survive. Of course, it has not happened. So, I have deliberately – oh, terrible thought – conned a large number of policemen and women, and nursing staff as well as members of the judiciary, a couple of lawyers, one chief prosecutor, several psy-chologists and forensic psychiatrists, etc. For this, I am sincerely sorry.[479]

Within the Quick team, Sture would occasionally rage at the lack of powerful enough attacks on the critics. On 18 June 1996 he tore a strip off detective inspector Stellan Söderman, a member of the national police commission set up to deal with the Quick case. After a stormy telephone call, Sture went to his computer and wrote a furious letter to Söderman:

Don't be so awkward when confronting all the derogatory messages in the media. Among other examples, I'm thinking about the massive attack in TV4's *News and Reports* yesterday – in addition to the articles you just referred to.

On no account allow yourself to be gagged.

Step up, ready to be emphatic and make it clear to all that you and the team handling the investigation have <u>the facts and the knowledge</u> as well as an <u>outstandingly</u> good overview of what I say in the interviews.

<u>State the facts</u>: describe the technical evidence, as, for instance, in the Appojaure case. Point out that the information I provided about that incident was <u>a part</u> of the overall evidence. [...] Return to, for instance, the Thomas Blomgren investigation and display it! Don't leave it in some desk drawer gathering dust and don't speak of it as some mystical fairy-tale file that no one ever opens.

<u>Show, with clarity, what we have achieved to date!</u>

Take the stage – do not rely on anonymous press releases – and speak up about the facts. Don't be so bloody passive and submissive!

Finally, Sture threatened to stop cooperating with the police if the critics were not stopped:

Do not abandon me to stand alone – the consequences will be that I can no longer sustain the pressure and then you will be on your own with the investigations – in any case, you would miss my active participation.

I had prepared myself for an active autumn, full of work, side by side with you – but the persons who do not know about the investigation and whose judgements are never contradicted could cause my frustration to interfere with my ambitions.

406

The responsibility will be yours. It is utterly necessary that you take it on!
Thomas[480] [emphasis in original]

Perhaps wondering whether Sture did or did not believe in the 'memories' of incest and murder is to put the wrong question. If Stina had chosen to believe that her memories were true, despite that small voice in her head mumbling that it was all fantasies – why not Sture? He became valued to a much greater extent than Stina. Having started as nobody, a human being regarded as worthless even by himself, he was elevated into the saviour of Swedish citizenry from future serial killers. He became a prominent person, a celebrity. The group around him spoke of him as a martyr worthy of profound admiration. And he got all the drugs he craved, too.

It could well be that this bargain offer was so appealing that, just like Stina, he simply decided to believe.

Being placed on a pedestal that reached all the way to heaven mattered hugely to Sture, there is no question about it. But at times it was not enough and then he wanted to jump off the murder investigation roundabout. He felt this most strongly during the moments of clarity when he realized that the Säter drug regime could kill him. His case notes demonstrate how right he was to worry. One example is a harrowing description of the twenty-four hours between 27 and 28 January 1997. All the drugs that were administered in the quoted entry are supplied 'as required', i.e. in addition to the potent mixture of benzodiazepines and painkillers Sture was treated with at set times:

Thomas regressed during the morning therapy session and had strong anxiety attacks and spasms. Staff had to hold him and give 2 × 10 mg rectal tubes Stesolid. Some improvement after approx. 1 hour. Frequent checks. Slept approx. 1 hour after lunch. Got up at about 14.00 and quickly deteriorated. Strong despair and anxiety. Was given 1 × 1 mg tabl. Xanax, somewhat improved after approx. 45 min, but limp and tired. At about 16.00 Dr Kall prescribed 1 × 300 mg

407

capsule Heminevrin plus 3 × capsules at night, also watch since Thomas had been actively thinking about death. He was affected by medication in the evening but able to pull himself together. Listened to music and chatted normally with staff. Had a further breakdown around 18.00, violent tears and despair. Was given a further 2 × I mg tabl. Xanax, and staff helped him get back to reality. Took 3 × 300 mg caps. Heminevrin at kl 20.50. Slept until approx. 01.00 when he woke up with a headache. Took 2 × tabl. Panodil and 1 × 50 mg suppository Diclofenac, then 1 × 1 mg tabl. Xanax, after about 1 hour. Fell asleep around 03.00 and woke up at 07.00. Difficulties with walking, moving about after the morning therapy session. His body did not obey him. Given 2 × 1 mg tabl. Xanax. After about 1 hour he felt better, rested on his bed. The round decided that the watch should continue until further notice. [...] Thomas has further therapy talks in the afternoon. At about 16.00, he came running full tilt through the common room and towards the telephone booth, ran head first into the wall. Staff had to wrestle him down and hold him.

The case notes make clear that Ståhle was always happy with the treatment results. As she wrote in February:

The psychological defence mechanisms that during a relatively long time have been gradually weakened still place Thomas under severe strain. However, it is emphasized that this process is a component of the therapy that should entail greater contact with reality. [...] Recently, [...] he experienced a serious and very deep crisis. It began when he told me of difficult recovered memories from some of his actions that are currently subject to police investigation. This was followed by associations to personal exposure to abuse during his early years.[481]

The over-dosage grew steadily worse and, in the spring of 1997, Sture had good reason to fear that his life was on the line. I have read about how he was wandering up and down the hospital corridor and 'wanted to die'. On 10 April, he had a severe anxiety attack and felt that 'he was precipitated into a multiple personality state'. Three days later, he was so restless that he was given a massive dose of Stesolid by intravenous injection, topped up with Heminevrin and Rohypnol. This was a knockout combination and he slept for an hour and a half. At about 8.00 a.m., he was heard to shout in his room. He had 'gone rigid in a sitting position', was 'practically catatonic' and found it 'hard to speak'. He was injected with a powerful dose of Stesolid and then, by 9.30 that morning, given another injection.

And so it went on for another few weeks. At the beginning of May, the Yenon Levi murder case opened. The man who confessed to the court was a junkie stoned out of his mind.

Sture feared for his life after that trial and wanted to drop out of the whole relentless process. He wrote this letter to Seppo on Saturday 31 May 1997:

Decision:
 After much hard thinking that has included consideration, analyses of consequences and arguments for and against, I have made the following decision:
 I can see no further possibility of participating in the police investigations which are currently focused on my person. I will say no to all proposals that I should participate actively. My reason is that any such participation is/entails a threat to my life. My choice is, in other words, conditioned from a purely selfish perspective; the moral aspects of this I will allow others to form their own opinions about.
 My decision is firm and unshakeable. It must be, in order to enable me to hold on to what I have now: A life, my life (even though my decision will not liberate me from anguish and suffering). [...]
 My decision to cease all active participation in the investigations is founded on my decision to continue to live. And, in its turn, this is evidence of the strength of the decision mentioned above.
 Respectfully,
 Thomas Quick[482]

However, Sture wrote his letter influenced by one of the sudden flare-ups of decisiveness that are typical of addicts and usually subside as quickly. Even if he had been able to sustain his new mood, the enthusiastic Quick team would never have let him drop out. Even as he was composing his letter, the preparations for the big re-enactment in the Örje Forest were under way. Helped by Christianson's re-enactment instructions, he was finally to show the way to the cache containing Therese Johannessen's body or body parts. With just over a week to go, the whole crime scene visit had been carefully planned and the Norwegian police were working away at it. Sture could not possibly be allowed to leave the stage.

Their solution was to subject him to reinforced peer pressure. In a tearing hurry, a so-called 'motivational re-enactment' was arranged in a forest near Säter. When they set out on the excursion, only two days had passed since Sture's letter of resignation. The usual crew came along: Penttinen, Christianson and Ståhle were joined by the lawyer Claes Borgström, constable Anna Wikström, nursing staff from Säter and a group of police dog handlers who were to scare curious members of the public off the site.

Penttinen outlined the intention behind this exercise in his report: 'The reconstruction was planned in order to allow Quick to indicate the ground features corresponding to the actual situation in the area of forest where he has stated that he hid the remains of Therese Johannessen in Örje, Norway.'[483]

They set out at 4.30 p.m. and drove to the forest which was about 10 kilometres south of Säter. They were some 350 kilometres away from the crime scene where Quick had allegedly hidden Therese's remains but Penttinen had brought a camera all the same. He took photos of the places Sture seemed interested in and Sture, who seemed to have forgotten the letter from just two days ago, participated vigorously. Penttinen carefully wrote down absolutely everything Sture said and did in his report:

During the walk, he makes his way towards a couple of largish stones and, as he walks around them, he probes with his hand

410

underneath the stones. He also thoroughly investigates the root systems of several tree stumps. The stone he found particularly interesting is pictured in PHOTO 3. [...] At this stage, Quick says that it is important to remember that he might in his thoughts be in two different places in the Norwegian forest and that he now can point to and remember such circumstances that fit these places.

And:

As he traverses an area with dry branches and twigs, he stamps on them. Then, he turns round and says "Yes!" He has at this point a very clear reaction as he would appear to recall the sensation/sounds of the dry twigs.

And:

Stops at a larger tree stump where there is a large stone nearby. Cf. PHOTOS 8 & 9. Here, Quick has a stronger emotional reaction and begins to pull out stones scattered around the stump/ big stone. He lifts one of the larger of these stones and creates noises by banging it against other stones. As the noises are made, he glances in a worried manner towards the road. His gaze travels towards the right and then downwards but not in the direction of the parked car. Our car is below and to the left.

Penttinen's report is eleven pages long. Reading it, I kept wondering if he was quite clear that they were not already in Norway.

Penttinen tells us that Sture had climbed up on a tree stump: 'After a few seconds, Quick's legs are affected by strong cramps, he crouches down and is unable to straighten up. He appears to be in a state of some kind of psychological collapse. While standing on the stump and before the cramps began, Quick pointed and described that, from where he stood, he could spy "the secret".'

Back home again, Ståhle wrote a note to Margit: 'Yesterday afternoon, a preparation was carried out to prepare for next week's journey to Norway. The intention was to find a place which resembled the Norwegian location as much as possible. This led to a regression to 1988. A few memories previously unconscious now were actualized.'[484]

I asked Sture about that exercise. He could not remember it. But when I described the black and white photos included in Penttinen's report, Sture had an idea. He searched out a small bundle of photographs taken outside in a natural setting that he had never been able to recognize. He gave them to me on one of my later visits to Säter. They were the pictures from the motivational re-enactment. Now, Sture recalled that Seppo Penttinen and Sven Å Christianson had advised him to take his time and study at home in preparation for the hunt for body caches in Norway.

They are sharp, precise. Seppo had taken a photograph of a torn-up root-plate of a fallen tree. A bush. A clearing with some trees. A dirt road. I leafed through the bundle again and again. They were all photos of a forest some 350 kilometres from the place where Therese Johannessen's remains were allegedly hidden.

I thought, these images are the outcome of collective madness.

And Sture was not allowed to stop.

31

The search for Quick's 'universal cafe'

'We were so close, so close to Johan's cache when the fear of death – as another word for it I might use the idea of the look in Ellington's eyes – came over me so strongly, was so much within me, that with deep emotion I felt, well, I knew, that to reveal where I had hidden his body would mean the end of my own existence . . .'

Sture, quoted in a note by Birgitta Ståhle.

Margit did not want to bring her great work on Thomas Quick's world to completion until at least one of his caches had been found. Sven Å Christianson explained this to me at our meeting in the psychology department. Her view had been that Sture was still in his 'state as perpetrator', for as long as he avoided showing his collection of hidden body parts so it followed that his psychotherapeutic treatment had to continue. She would not publish until it was over. 'She was very determined,' Sven said.

Gillan Liljeström is another acolyte who knows a lot about how Margit regarded the caches. She was sixty-three years old when I met her in 2012 at her home in Stockholm. Gillan said she had become Margit's patient in 1978, when Gillan was twenty-nine years old. She needed support to cope with her grief after a tragic death in her family. The therapy that followed grew intense and she was helped to recover hitherto unknown traumas from her childhood. Margit was so delighted with Gillan that she passed patients on to her for treatment, even though Gillan had never cared to train as a psychotherapist. She had studied sociology but later came to accept the career Margit felt she was suited for and took the course in psychotherapy. She made the grade, then passed the strictest of tests: she was asked to join Margit's group. According to several people who knew her, she became one of the most devoted pupils, along with Cajsa Lindholm and Birgitta Ståhle. Gillan and Cajsa were both with Margit in hospital on the day she died.

For many years Gillan has been treating patients at home, still following in Margit's footsteps. She estimates that some 40 per cent of those who come to her for help have repressed their memories of past abuse. I happened to get in contact with a former patient of Gillan's, a woman who told me that she had had to end her therapy after five years because Gillan simply would not stop trying to persuade her that she had been abused by her father, even though the patient knew that it had never happened.

Gillan said that she and Cajsa were charged with assisting the elderly Margit with the completion of 'The World of Thomas Quick' but that the work stagnated because Sture failed to find a single cache. It was his inability to get out of the denial stage that made him keep failing for a decade, or so Gillan thought. She recognized the phenomenon in her own patients: 'It can happen in the therapy room that someone persists in evading reality. The patients will talk about the abuse, all their dreams point the same way and all their remembered scenes focus around something in the past – but there's something unreal about it all.'

In this phase of the treatment, her patients would speak about 'memories' but experience them as fantasies. According to Gillan, this kind of thing can go on for a long time but, sooner or later, the breakthrough will come.

'Suddenly, from deep inside, the mind becomes aware that "this has happened. It's *me* who has been subjected to this. It's for real. It is true." At that moment, you perceive the world differently, shapes and colours change. And then you feel these very, very strong emotions. I believe Birgitta and Margit interpreted finding the caches in these terms. You know, "finding one will be the moment everything becomes real for Thomas".'

'Was Margit disappointed that he never showed anyone a cache?' I asked.

'Well, she saw it as an expression of his aggressiveness. And yes, it made her sad and disappointed that he wouldn't display the proof of the reality of what he said.'

Against the background of Gillan's story, it is easier to understand why Ståhle and Christianson were so deeply engaged in attempts to make Sture show them a cache. Margit's book project had stalled. The last of Sture's pieces of writing that she had added to the manuscript was dated November 1999. After that, she did not want to collect any more material until he had retrieved some objects from a cache. The entire project – and Margit's dream of triumph – depended on Ståhle and Christianson succeeding in helping Sture. Just how eager Christianson was can be seen in his notorious 1997 instructions for the hunt for body-part caches in Örje Forest: 'It is essential to remove all potential complications which might disrupt TQ's concentration and mental focusing on the place where Therese is buried. Police concerns about the incident and developments at the time of the murder must be shelved for another opportunity. The top priority for 11 June is to find the hiding place.'[485]

The hunt for hiding places had started directly after the first interview in 1993, but because Christer van der Kwast later homed in on getting convictions for the four cases where bodies had already been found – the murders of Charles Zelmanovits, the Stegehuis couple and Yenon Levi – there was no legal incentive for chasing caches until 1996, when the first intense effort was made to find Therese Johannessen in Norway. Penttinen's assistant Anna Wikström wrote about the outcome of that Örje Forest re-enactment in an internal report: 'The re-enactment led to tremendous efforts by the Norwegian police including the unforgettable search in the Ringen pool during 8 weeks in the summer of 1996. The cost rose to about three million, according to usually well informed sources, [. . .].'[486]

Their Swedish colleagues were digging for buried corpses in places like Lindesberg and in Salbo Moor near Sala – unsuccessfully, of course. Wikström provides this insight into the Quick team's excuses:

We have discussed theories and consider some of them to be credible with respect to TQ. Could it be that he had initially buried his victims in various sites only to return later to dig them up and transport them to some final 'place of sacrifice'. (?) TQ has later confirmed the correctness of this theory, e.g. for the burial of body parts in Lindesberg sports ground etc. In his macabre world, be it fantasy or reality, he says he wanted only 'clean' bones for his, as it were, 'final' place of sacrifice.[487]

Penttinen speculated along the same lines in an internal memo: 'TQ has also stated in an interview that he had to let body parts rot in order to get at the actual bone material.'[488]

Already in the spring of 1996, the chase for caches received a boost. The police investigators had become interested in the flats at 4C Bruk Street in Falun. Sture had lived in the building from the age of six until after his thirty-fourth birthday, except for when he was away at college, studying at Uppsala or locked up at Sidsjön and Säter. They suspected he had hidden human remains in his old home and, in April, he was taken there for a reconstruction. The whole team went with him, including Christianson. During the following eight weeks, forensic technicians took the place apart. They pulled up floorboards and bashed holes in ceilings and walls. The headline in *Expressen* read QUICK'S HOME DEMOLISHED IN HUNT FOR EVIDENCE.[489] Sture and several of his siblings had taken turns staying in a certain attic room and, in the wardrobe, right at the back, they found a matchbox, a cigarette packet and a cardboard box for cigarette filters, all empty except for tufts of pubic hair.

The Norwegian tabloid *Verdens Gang* followed the 'excavations' with interest. The new development was written up as 'the police finally discover parts of Quick's victims'. This story was re-run by the Swedish media, leading to relatives of missing persons getting in touch with van der Kwast, anxious to learn if the remains of a lost child had been found.[490]

In August, Sture was asked about these mementoes and he admitted straightaway that they were from his victims. He added that he had read about the pubic hairs in the press. The news reports were not entirely correct, so when Penttinen asked Sture to describe the finds, he claimed he had hidden two matchboxes full of hairs 'high up, under the ceiling in a hollow or cavity'. Not so good (the relics had been found on a shelf), but what really ruined it was the technicians finding that the cigarette packet had not been manufactured until 1989. In 1984, a year after the death of Tyra, Sture's mother, Sture cancelled the rental contract and left Bruk Street for good. The hair must have been deposited at least five years later, when new tenants had taken over the attic room. This saga was added to the series of irritating errors that the Quick team wrote off as 'deliberate discrepancies' and never spoke about again. Ten years later, in December 2006, a man came forward in *Aftonbladet* to say that he had responded to the reports about boxes full of pubic hairs already, back in 1996, because he knew it was a friend of his who had hidden the boxes when he lived in the house. The hairs had belonged to his mate's girlfriend.[491]

In the spring of 1997, the chase for sacred caches stalled. Instead, the team concentrated on getting Sture convicted for the murder of Yenon Levi, whose body had been found in one piece. But in the summer, they were back in Örje Forest, electrified by Christianson's instructions. Still no finds, though.

By May 1998, there was a qualified success in the form of Sture's conviction for the murder of Therese Johannessen, despite the lack of a body. Van der Kwast and Penttinen were still keen to see Sture declared guilty of the Johan Asplund murder, but they were probably uncertain that they could pull off another no-body murder conviction. They were also busy looking for several other missing persons, all supposedly Sture's victims: Alvar Larsson, Reine Svensson, Benny Forsgren, Marianne Rugaas Knudsen, Olle Högbom, Magnus Johansson and Örjan Sellin. There was also a list of names of people not known to the police but whose corpses Sture claimed to have tampered with and removed parts of: 'the 17-year-old from Gävle', 'the boys from Norway', as well as a list of first names that Sture admitted were not necessarily the right ones, like 'Tony', 'Duska', 'Martin' and 'Erik'. On top of that, his hidey-holes were said to contain skeletal parts of Charles Zelmanovits, including the left thigh bone, right shin bone and possibly a few bones from his hand. No one could explain how Sture had managed to control his strong urge to carry off body parts from Thomas Blomgren, Yenon Levi, Marinus and Janny Stegehuis, Gry Storvik and Trine Jensen.

With Margit's support Sture and Ståhle had created a pretty detailed mythology, according to which Sture's body-part fixation was an outcome of the so-called Simon event in 1954, when his parents cut up his prematurely born brother Simon. After the butchery and the acts of cannibalism, his father had wrapped what was left of Simon in newspaper, got on his bike and took the parcel to a place called the Främby promontory, taking little Sture with him. Främby is a beautiful place, just east of central Falun and only a couple of kilometres from the family home. Sture had been told by his father that the parcel contained 'fish innards'. It was buried in a hole in the ground. Sture had known that it was Simon being buried and silently promised himself that one day he would 'make Simon whole again'. He felt that he was the cause of his brother's death.

In the mind of the child, Simon's grave was a sacred place and Sture often visited it. But when he was six years old his family moved to the flat on Bruk Street, which meant that Främby was much further away and, after a while, Sture could no longer find the grave. This was one of the reasons why he eventually started to murder people. He started to kill in 1964, when he was fourteen. From the age of seventeen, Sture also removed parts from most of his victims. He put the pieces in carefully constructed hiding places in forested areas near where he lived. The hiding places functioned as substitutes for Simon's lost grave and, like it, they became sacred. The body parts were to be used to rebuild Simon and fulfil the vow he had made as a four-year-old.

Finding the hiding places was, however, far harder than talking about them. In 1998 alone, forensic technicians, aided by sniffer dogs, carried out twenty-one searches. Several sites in and around Falun were excavated and the digging was later extended to other areas in Dalarna County. Typically, Sture was taken along to places he had indicated for a site reconstruction. He would make cryptic, sweeping suggestions about where caches might be found and the technicians would start digging.

The reconstruction exercise on 8 June 1998 is a typical example of such an excursion. As often happened, the entire team joined the trip: Penttinen, Ståhle, Christianson, Borgström and van der Kwast. No one wanted to risk being left behind on the day Sture opened the first cache. The outing was filmed and Sture had a small microphone pinned to his jacket so that every word he said could be recorded. A transcript of the tape was kept, as was an hour-long video recorded in the woodland around Lake Ryggen. Looking like a group of ramblers the Quick team plodded on among the trees. Sture wore black jeans, a navy sweater, trainers and a black cap on his head. Penttinen was casual in tracksuit bottoms with contrasting seams and a light red anorak. Borgström had chosen jeans, a matching jacket and wellies, and Christianson a grey fleece jacket. Ståhle, in a short raincoat and jeans, appears to have had her blonde hair permed recently. She carried a small notebook into which she made occasional brief entries. Van der Kwast must have been behind the camera because he was nowhere to be seen. Sture and Penttinen were in the lead and the rest of the group followed along the path, now and then making detours into the forest.

They walked in respectful silence. Whenever Sture stopped and turned to Penttinen to point out likely landmarks, the others gathered around him as if to sustain their hero's courage with their physical presence. They regarded him as a man fighting a heroic battle against his innate repression mechanisms. Watching the video, I saw a man doing solo improvisations in front of a bunch of people who had switched off all capacity for critical thinking.

As ever, Penttinen wrote up the excursion in a detailed report that is of interest because it allows us to see Sture through his eyes. This was the fifth year he had followed Sture across the countryside but his faith was still undented. He seemed to expect that at any second the hiding place would be found behind the next bush. His dedication to hunting for clues meant that he painstakingly recorded Sture's body language and anxiety levels. Not even the most obvious absurdities in Sture's haranguing of his audience made Penttinen stop and think:

When Quick reaches the top of the slope/ the ridge he spots a lon-gitudinal runnel/ditch. He suddenly turns right round. Here, Quick displays obvious difficulties with making himself look down and along the ditch. At this place, he provides a description of how he returned to the body and with the saw removed a part of the hip bone on the right side. He says that 'the gully is like a long grave . . . talk about landmarks . . . let's hurry back!'. In response to a direct question about where the part of the hip bone ended up, Quick replies: 'In the long grave.' Due to a certain roughness in the sound recording, he might afterwards have added 'in this gully' but this last remark is included here with strong reservation as it might be a mis-interpretation. Quick says that 'the gully or ditch would be both a landmark and . . .' As we walk back down, Quick says in a whisper, not audible to the others in the group but registered by the micro-phone, 'here is the gully'.

After the Ryggen visit, they drove to Grycksbo, the small town to the north of Falun where Sture ran a kiosk and stayed in a flat between 1987 and 1989. Penttinen wrote: 'As we pass a very distinctive, pointed stone on the right hand side, he says with much force behind his words: "film upwards" and points to the right side of the road. Immediately after passing the stone, he stops abruptly and has an anx-iety attack, then continues slowly up the slope.'

The blow-by-blow account continues:

A fir tree grows in this place. There are 2 largish stones a little fur-ther away from the road. He bends and quickly picks up a fairly small stone splinter and hides it in his hand. He has a pronounced anxiety attack. A short dialogue ensues and I draw Quick's attention to the fact that he had collected a small stone. Quick then returns to the same place. Clearly emotional, he arranges moss, smaller stones, breaks off a good-looking fir twig and finally pulls a small, dry fir tree across the site, all of which he later states are the type of actions that can be relevant in connection with the composition of a cache.

Sture had demonstrated how to build a cache. I stopped the video-tape at a frame that showed Sture's lawyer, Claes Borgström, in profile. He is observing Sture and Penttinen. Borgström's faith was just as strong as everyone else's. He confirmed this when I interviewed him in his Stockholm office. Not long before my visit, an evening paper had exposed Borgström as a secret supporter of a campaign, orchestrated by (among others) van der Kwast and Penttinen, aimed at presenting Sture as a probable serial killer even though the appeal process had already quashed several of the murder cases brought against him.

Ensconced behind his desk, Borgström looked sad. He realized, he said, that there were those who called him an idiot, and others who accused him of chasing big legal fees and of knowingly having done his best to get an innocent man convicted of murder again and again. His voice cracked a little and his eyes glistened with tears as he admitted: 'Honestly, I don't feel so good.'

He continued: 'The past few years of being put through the mill have toughened me up. But they've targeted my good name. Questioned my legal ethics. And not just questioned, but shot to kill.' Borgström swore that he believed Sture and that it was the whole truth. 'There were excellent reasons for trusting him,' he insisted. 'And this is at the heart of the problem for the people who are pursuing the case now. They weren't there!'

I asked him about these excellent reasons and he gave examples, but was clearly ill-informed. All the 'reasons' he produced had, without exception, been ground to dust during the retrial process. I ended up thinking that Claes Borgström was still a believer who felt he did not need, or couldn't find the strength, to study the retrial documentation.

In 1998, when the cache-finders had given up on Grycksbo, they boarded the minibus and drove on to Lake Valsan west of Falun. Sture had owned a cottage near the lake for two years (1986–1988), which made the whole area of interest to the investigating team.

Penttinen continued, in his inimitable style, to record Sture's every move: 'We follow a tractor route. Quick walks at a variable pace and puts his feet down in a distinctive manner. Occasionally, he applies a cautiously hovering mode of walking and sometimes hurries up inclines.'

They wander down into a small valley: 'In this dip in the ground there is a larger stone assembly. Quick puts his feet down very circumspectly. He suddenly turns on his heels and walks back. In response to a direct question whether he, in connection with his reaction, had observed something that instantly caused it, he answers firmly "yes!". With his next breath, he states that he will deny this later.'

Before they set out for home, Penttinen outlines the Lake Valsan situation:

In connection with our arrival at the parked vehicles at 18.55, Quick gives an account in the presence of his legal representative Claes Borgström and acting chief prosecutor Christer van der Kwast, that the area above the summer cottage is relevant to a victim, that the said victim was 'dealt with' in the period of time during which he owned the cottage, that the remains were not burned, that it is a matter of body parts and not clothing, and that the parts are likely to be found in the area. He cannot presently convey who the victim was.[492]

Throughout June 1998 the technical crew searched every area that Sture had indicated. No finds were made. The general frustration this caused was presumably not diminished by a bombardment of critical articles about the Quick investigation in *Dagens Nyheter* and *Svenska Dagbladet* during May and June. The writers included two fathers of missing boys: Björn Asplund, father of Johan Asplund; and Ruben Högbom, father of Olle Högbom. Other contributors were the journalist Dan Larsson, the reader in forensic psychology Nils Wiklund and the psychologist Astrid Holgersson.[493] Worse still, in July, Dan Larsson's self-published his book *The Mythomaniac Thomas Quick*.

Borgström went for the throat when he made character attacks on the critics and Sture was so alarmed he called while a TV4 morning show was on the air because Dan Larsson was talking about his book. The producer let Sture deliver a powerful plea for himself as a real serial killer, but everyone knew that the doubters would not be silenced until van der Kwast could display human remains at a press conference.[494]

The team formed a tight pact against the hostile world outside. As if to find a way to deal with the absence of tangible proof, Ståhle and Sture elaborated on the mythology around the hiding places. One new idea was that every time Sture moved house, he had to get his relics out of their old caches, because he needed them close by. The reason for that was because, it was suggested, he masturbated over his mementoes.

Sture had moved seven times between 1973 and 1991 and was thought to have built several caches near each home. The Dalarna landscape should have been pockmarked with emptied stashes, especially the area around Falun. Because nothing was ever found, they developed the idea that Sture had collected the body parts into fewer and fewer places and, in the end, constructed one grand, final hiding place where parts of many victims were stored together. Van der Kwast had hinted at a possible super-cache at an early stage, as emerged from an article by the crime reporter Gubb Jan Stigson, published in *Dala-Demokraten* on September 1997:

> The theory currently adopted by the investigators is that Quick stored parts of the bodies of several of his victims, collected in one or possibly several places. It would be like a mausoleum or an altar. [...]
>
> 'In my view, Quick is perfectly aware of where his victims are buried. He knows what he can present to us by way of concrete evidence. I believe there is one principal hiding place somewhere around Falun,' chief prosecutor Christer van der Kwast says to D–D.[495]

The super-cache had many names. In the interviews, it was often called the 'final hiding place' or, rather poetically, the 'hiding place of the many'. I found what I thought was the most inspirational of the names in a handwritten note by Anna Wikström, who had heard Sture speak of 'my universal cafe'. Among Sture's notes I found an undated poem about this very strange 'cafe':

My universal cafe
Is a meeting place
And though I haven't made that journey
I am there. [. . .]
Thomas's neck, his throat gape wide open
And my sperm is [on] his lips,
My semen
That I left with him before
He became the first guest in my cafe.

In the rest of the poem, Sture describes a number of other victims as 'fellow guests', all in a similarly grotesque style.

In September 1998, the team took Sture on a new, grand re-enactment excursion, which was also recorded on sound and video tape. Sture's initial announcement made the point that although all caches had been cleared out, small pieces might well be left inside some of them. They climbed the Jungfru Hill north of Falun, the city where Sture, then in his mid-thirties, had lived between 1984 and 1986. The team then travelled on to Sågmyra, to the north-west of Gryckbo, where Sture had stayed for a year (1989–1990). Here, raising everyone's hopes, he pointed at a small stream and said that 'in the bed of this stream there's a cache with a wrist-bone in it'.

A little later, he said that 'the hiding place of the many' was nearby and that he would show them the way. Penttinen became excited and tried to help Sture to break through the barrier set up by repression: 'Carry on, Thomas, don't stop now, keep going. Just go in the direction you feel drawn to. [. . .] Just go on, don't try to think it out, just carry on.'

Sture was becoming very anxious but managed to continue, step by step, with Penttinen urging him on:

Don't give up now, Thomas, you're getting close. It shows in your face. You're shying away from something. All the time. Try to find a way to get there. Just a little bit at the time. Look down on the ground, just move on, you will find it in the end. [. . .] Take one small step at a time so you get up there and can see and point to show us where the most interesting place is. You've come this far and fought so hard and well, let's do this last thing together. You can move another little bit just so you get up enough to see what's what. We're all here with you, at your side, Birgitta is here, and Claes, too.

When Sture finally says that the cache is 'somewhere over there, behind van der Kwast', it is something of an anticlimax. A little later, Penttinen tries to persuade Sture to explain his bodily signals. The conversation offers us new insights into how Seppo construes things:

[Penttinen]: ' ... when we climbed up this hill, you responded
    with ... to something by shutting your eyes and turning your
    head. What did these, you know, sequences mean, when you
    had your eyes open and then shut them? Did you look ...?'
[Sture]: 'Yes, I had a look around.'
[Penttinen]: 'A look around. And when you shut your eyes, what
    did that mean? While you twisted your neck like that?'
[Sture]: 'No ... o, I looked around.'
[Penttinen]: 'Can we interpret it any way we think then?'
[Sture]: 'Well now ...'
[Penttinen]: 'Did you notice that you had shut your eyes?'
[Sture]: 'No.'
[Penttinen]: 'Fine. Right.'[496]

Sture was interviewed about his caches for five hours a couple of weeks later and was asked to use a white marker pen to show their positions on colour photographs that the police had taken during the re-enactment. The digging started again, but this time it was not just police officers wielding shovels. Van der Kwast had made up his mind to go all out to succeed.

On 16 September, *Expressen* revealed that 'today' the police and a crowd of assorted experts 'are beginning one of the largest attempts to unearth evidence of murder in the Swedish history of crime detection' in the expectation that 'about ten murders' would be solved.

According to prosecutor Christer van der Kwast, Quick has indicated that certain areas are 'very interesting' and especially concerned are Stensjö, Valsan and Sågmyra. The police hope to find remains of several of the serial killer's victims.

'The information provided by Quick himself is supported by other developments in the investigation,' van der Kwast told this paper.[497]

The journalist Gubb Jan Stigson, at *Dala-Demokraten*, had an excellent relationship with Penttinen and van der Kwast, and managed to write about 300 enthusiastic articles about the Quick murder investigations. He reported on the planned dig: 'Here, in the forests around Lake Valsan, the most extensive search for murder victims in Swedish forensic history will shortly start. The chase is on to find the remains of an as yet unknown number of murdered people. Police technicians and archaeologists will carry out the excavations, protected by military tents inside the extensive police cordon.'[498]

The digging continued throughout the autumn of 1998. The police cordoned off one area of forest after another while the experts laboured at the soil sieves. Huge quantities of soil were transported to a military compound in Falun to be analysed for traces of dead bodies using, among other tests, DNA determinations.

Van der Kwast masterminded an operation that amounted to a full-scale, land-based version of the emptying of the Ringen forest lake in 1996. Meanwhile, Sture was constantly taken to new re-enactments. Before being transferred to Säter in 1991, he had stayed in a flat in a residential area called Kvarn Hill just outside central Falun, near to Främby promontory – the alleged site of Simon's burial in 1954. The team speculated that Sture might well have set up his universal cafe at Främby. It would have meant a closing of the circle: the cache for the elements that would help him rebuild Simon would be close to Simon's grave.

On 13 November 1998, the team brought Sture to the Främby promontory and, during the re-enactment, he revealed that his very last victim had met his end there – 'I call him Tony.' Among Sture's papers, I found a note that Ståhle had scribbled with a biro during the re-enactment. It has a strangely poetic flavour:

Martin's rib and spine are in Ölsta.
   Martin's, Tony's and Duska's pelvises are in Sågmyra.
   Tony's and Duska's heads are kept separately
   (here, somewhere – S makes a sweeping movement towards Främby).[499]

The technicians kept digging. In January 1999, Sture was once again taken to the Främby area. This coincided with the time when the police faced up to the hard fact that 'the most extensive search for murder victims in Swedish forensic history' was a hopeless failure. On 10 February, Sture was called to an interview in the music room and told that nothing had been unearthed. For once, Penttinen was down-hearted:

[Penttinen]: 'Which conditions must be met in order to make
   you advance far enough to show us one of your caches?'
[Sture]: 'Well, you know, a straight answer would be when . . .
   when I personally can find the courage to do it. That's a very
   simplified way of saying it.'[500]

In March, Sture phoned Penttinen to say that he wanted to be inter-viewed and that he would like Ståhle to be present. It turned out that Ståhle had prepared a short speech. She explained that, since Christmas, the two of them had done 'an enormous amount of very extensive and thorough therapeutic work' and that advances had been made which meant they now had 'increased differentiation, finding distinctions between the different murders, the background, [includ-ing] the emotional background to the murders and the distinctive meanings of the different murders'.[501]

It was obvious that the intention was to stimulate van der Kwast and Penttinen into searching for more hiding places, but the crisis-laden atmosphere did not lighten up. Sture's inability to find his caches paralysed the entire police investigation just as it had Margit's book project. Hardly any interviews were set up during April and May 1999.

A note in Sture's calendar shows that Margit travelled in person to Säter on 14 May to meet with him. He told me that when he looked out through a window and saw her being helped out of Ståhle's car in the hospital car park, it had struck him how physically small she was. When she was escorted in, the ward apparently filled with a 'worshipful' reverence. However, he remembers hardly anything of what was said while they spoke together, except that she emphasized how important it was for him to trust Ståhle. He recalled that she kept using his first name and imitated her authoritative, upper-class manner of speaking, just as I have heard her acolytes do: 'You must put your trust in Birgitta, Sture. It's important, Sture. Birgitta feels her way into this, Sture.'

Margit did not succeed in getting Sture to reveal a cache. Instead, the crisis was solved by van der Kwast moving on to investigate the murders of Gry Storvik and Trine Jensen, whose intact corpses had been identified. This at least eliminated the need for more searches. Ståhle appeared as a witness in the trial held in May 2000. She spoke about the Simon event and struck an almost religious note: 'To Thomas Quick, his brother Simon became a saint, the only one who saw and understood his desperate vulnerability as a child. He actually went back to the cache containing Simon's remains on several occasions, just to seek comfort and sense a glimmer of light in his otherwise so very dark life.'[502]

After Sture had been convicted of murders six and seven, everyone took a hard-earned summer holiday. In September 2000, the hunt for hiding places began again with renewed vigour. It was high time to take the Asplund murder case to court, so something like a body had to be found. The team set out on a big re-enactment in Sundsvall. Accompanied by Penttinen, Ståhle, Borgström and Christianson, Sture demonstrated how he went about disposing of the body parts, including throwing Johan's head off the hill, as Seppo had shown me in 2012.[503]

Sture mentioned in particular a cache where he had put parts of Johan Asplund as well as other murdered persons:

[Penttinen]: 'How many are we talking about [. . .]?'

[Sture]: (*long pause*) 'I will answer that question but can't answer the one that you'll ask next about who those victims are. There are five of them. [. . .]'

[Penttinen]: 'Are there more parts of Johan in caches other than the one you're after now?'

[Sture]: 'Oh yes! That's why I had a discussion with myself about where I should go.'

[Penttinen]: 'And the remains of the five victims, are they the same kind? Bones?'

[Sture]: 'That's right. To me, they're identifiable. So, I can tell you . . . say, we find a neck of femur, then I can tell you it comes from Johan.'

[Penttinen]: 'How can you do that? What makes you sure you can separate . . . distinguish between bones like that?'

[Sture]: 'They are stored in my memory . . . yes, I can . . .'

[Penttinen]: 'What's the difference, if we stick to the neck of femur?'

[Sture]: 'Umm.'

[Penttinen]: 'I mean, you've stored necks of femur from five different victims?'

[Sture]: 'Umm . . . size-wise . . . and appearances, too, there really are differences.'

[Penttinen]: 'This specific cache [. . .] what is its holding capacity [. . .]?'

[Sture]: 'No . . . o, that's . . . I don't know how to calculate . . .'

[Penttinen]: 'Could you compare the volume with something we've got in this room?'

[Sture]: 'Then it'd be like . . . volume-wise, this large.'

[Penttinen]: 'Twenty by twenty centimetres . . . half this loudspeaker.'

[Sture]: 'Yes, thereabouts, or a bit more.'

Penttinen asked once again – as he had, so often, over the last seven years – what he could do to help Sture find a hiding place. Sture told him that one way would be to keep repeating the excursions to Främby promontory. Sooner or later, he would no longer 'have the strength to resist pointing it out' and then 'suddenly I'll show it to you'.

At the end of the interview, Penttinen managed to extract unusually detailed information about how the caches were constructed. Unfortunately, the tape recorder broke down while Sture was going into the essentials and Penttinen had to report what he remembered: 'The caches are constructed from stones and "other materials". They are ventilated and placed so that they are accessible in winter as well as summer. However, he has not visited them or handled the remains during the winter because of the risk that the contents might become damp or damaged in connection with this.'

The Quick team took Sture to Främby again and again, hoping that he suddenly would not have 'the strength to resist pointing it out'. It is difficult to keep one's reactions to the tapes from these re-enactments under control, even if one is aware of the mental states of the Quick team members. For example, this is how Penttinen reports a walkabout on Främby promontory on 27 September 2000:

When T Quick passes by the place, he spots 2 larger stones about 20 metres to the left and his body twitches and he then walks along the path that turns sharply to the left. His level of anxiety goes up more and more as he walks and he finds it difficult to continue. The reporter asks the staff following immediately behind, i.e. qualified psychologist B Ståhle and ward charge nurse Bengt Eklund, to move forward and look after T Quick. T Quick however continues to stagger along the path, even though, at this point in time, BS had gripped his arm. The reporter understands that Quick wishes to reach an intersection with another path that, together with a few stones, is visible some 20 metres further on.

When he has arrived, he wants to be helped up to sit on top of a stone and is lifted up to sit on the 0.5 metre high stone. He complains of severe pain in his chest and then collapses, apparently unconscious. He recovers after a while. However, he is in a bad way, with severe cramps in his arms, hands and legs. After 7–8 minutes, he is able to stand and slowly move towards the car for a return to Säter. During this journey, T Quick states that he has made eye contact with the hiding place and that the walk has enabled him to 'ring in the area where the cache is located'.[504]

Penttinen added an A4-sized map to his report. He had marked the map with a cross using a red marker pen and written next to it 'T Q faints'.

Three weeks later, the team is back again to let Sture 'make some further and more precise indications of the cache': 'On site at Främby promontory, Thomas Quick made the following comments after having waded out into the water near the bank and with his hands dug out a few minor stones from under an unusual pine root that in part overhangs the surface of the water:

That the body part should be found in this location consists of a piece of an arm bone, 4.3 centimetres long.

That he is able to state the length to a tenth of a centimetre is due to psychological need for control.

That, in the water, close by a striking-looking stone, one lumbar vertebra is placed in the water. He cannot be more precise as to its location.[505]

Despite having initiated cache searches in vain since 1994, van der Kwast made the astonishing decision to root out the 4.3 centimetre-long fragment from the lakeside and dispatched four forensic technicians equipped with waders, spades and sieves.

But deep inside, van der Kwast must have felt more ambivalent than he let on, because he changed his mind the following day, by which time the digging was well under way. Penttinen called Sture and asked to see him at Säter for an extra interview. Van der Kwast came along and Ståhle sat at Sture's side. Penttinen began by explaining that the lakeside at Främby promontory was made up of stones and compacted soil, which made digging very difficult. The crew had to dig while standing in ice-cold water. They had sieved what they had dug up but found nothing.

Penttinen reluctantly admitted: ' . . . our expectation is that you'd be able to assist further since we feel that it is in your own interest to succeed with this . . .'

'Mmm,' Sture said.

' . . . which is why we wanted to come here for another talk with you . . .'

'Mmm,' Sture said again.

' . . . that's all for this time. The question is, what to do next?'[506]

It was a cry for help. Penttinen explained that he wanted to take Sture with him to Främby again but Sture refused. Penttinen tried to persuade him: 'You know, we have another pair of rubber boots, so you would be able to step into the water and wade.'

Sture said he was too tired. Actually, this seems quite reasonable given the amount of medication he was taking. The list for that day included a rectal shot of Stesolid, administered just forty minutes before the interview. He was woozy. Why should he be forced to stomp about in cold water in a spare pair of boots?

'So you don't accept that you might be helpful to us on site?' Penttinen asked again.

'No,' Sture said.

Van der Kwast interrupted at this point. He asked if there was no *alternative* place where some part of Johan Asplund was hidden, other than under water, and, if so, could Sture not point it out to them? Not really, there was no such place, Sture told him. Penttinen said he thought Sture's tone was hesitant and couldn't it be taken to mean that there was another cache after all? Sture was having none of this. The 4.3 centimetre-long piece of arm bone was in the lakeside cache and that was that.

Now came what Penttinen must have known was coming, something which he had tried to avoid to the last. Christer van der Kwast spoke:

[Kwast]: ' . . . from my point of view, the problem with the
  Asplund murder is that there are few other features that could
  be a basis for taking the case to court so, the simple conclusion
  is . . .'
[Sture]: 'Umm.'
[Kwast]: ' . . . that we really haven't got anything in your narrative
  [. . .]'

This exchange took place on Wednesday 18 October 2000.
Penttinen stopped the interview at 5.30 p.m. Killing Johan Asplund
had been the first murder Sture confessed to and the investigation had
been ongoing since 1 March 1993 – seven and a half years. Now, van
der Kwast was ready to close the case. Sture would never be charged
with the Asplund murder.

Or so you might have thought.

Less than seven months later, the trial opened in Sundsvall District
Court and in June 2001 the court declared its unanimous decision that,
beyond all reasonable doubt, Sture had murdered Johan Asplund.

Had the universal cafe suddenly been found? Not at all. It was not
the forensic crew with their spades and sieves who saved van der
Kwast. It was Birgitta Ståhle.

In one of Sture's lined writing pads, I came across a brief note he
made at the time of that fateful interview on 18 October 2000 when
van der Kwast said he was going to close the case:

18/10/00. 16.55
  Kwast starts chatting with Birgitta S. Asks to 'have a word' without me being present.

After that, only four other words apparently scribbled down during
Penttinen's heartbreaking description of the harsh digging conditions
at the lakeside near Främby:

Lakeside
Technicians

The rest of the page is blank.

We do not know what van der Kwast said to Ståhle during that private chat but we can make an informed guess: he presumably told the psychologist that Sture had better remember where he hid Asplund or else the case would be closed.

Certainly, Ståhle went on to do her very best to make Sture recover more memories of the murder. The very next day, she interrupted a therapy session to phone Penttinen to tell him that Sture had something else to say. She handed the receiver to Sture, who said – or so Penttinen reports – that Johan Asplund had lacked a molar tooth. Ståhle then added that, as Sture left the room, he had pointed to his left cheek.

Johan had not lost a molar tooth. Sture had chanced things like this before. He had claimed that he associated 'Johan' and 'diabetes' and that the boy had a recent, slightly inflamed surgical scar below his navel. But Johan had not suffered from diabetes and had not had any surgery.

Ståhle carried on with the regression therapy regardless. Sture was pumped full of tranquillizers, reclined on his bed, closed his eyes and retrieved a vision of the blocks of flats in Bosvedjan. He had visited the place with Kjell Persson in 1992, and later studied it on maps and aerial photographs. Memories rose to the surface and Ståhle wrote steadily in her notebook.

On the Sunday, four days after van der Kwast's alarming threat, Sture asked his lawyer to come and see him. The Social Democratic government had recently appointed Claes Borgström to the post of Equality Ombudsman and Borgström had passed the job of acting for Sture on to another lawyer, solicitor Sten-Åke Larsson. Borgström explained that Larsson was one of his best friends.

Sten-Åke Larsson travelled to Säter and met Sture early on Monday morning. At 10.40 Larsson sent a fax to Penttinen consisting of two A4 sheets. It was a list of all the new memories Sture had recovered entitled 'Observations in Connection with the Kidnapping of Johan Asplund'. Sture had retrieved a memory of seeing a twelve-year-old he called the 'Dark Boy' near the Asplund home. The boy had worn a striped sweater and carried a rucksack of the brand Fjällräven. Furthermore, Sture had seen 'an office lady' in her fifties, wearing a pale-brown coat, who crossed the square in Bosvedjan's small central shopping area. Another woman had called out after her, perhaps 'Lisa or Elisabeth', and she had stopped in her tracks and waited. The two women then walked away side by side. While standing around near the school in Bosvedjan, Sture had heard a noise he describes as 'rather a diesel generator' and other details had become clear, like seeing a lorry in a car park and a largish vehicle he 'associated with [septic tank] sludge cleansing' near a bungalow.

The fax triggered an outburst of frantic activity. Penttinen and van der Kwast had to fit Sture's 'memory fragments' into the observed reality, like a 3D jigsaw. They did find a boy with dark hair who had lived in Bosvedjan and had owned a striped sweater in 1980. True, it was different from the sketch Sture drew in a later interview and it was uncertain if the boy had worn it on the relevant day. And Sture did not get the photo identification right. Anyhow, the sweater *was* striped.[507]

The investigators combed Bosvedjan for the 'office lady' in her fifties 'named Lisa or Elizabeth' and found Liisa Liljedahl, who had worked in the local supermarket in November 1980. True, she had not been fifty years old, but twenty-four, and in the seventh month of pregnancy. As it happened, it was possible to change Sture's recollection to an older woman, maybe in her fifties, calling to a younger woman and this became the version presented to the court.

As for the rumbling diesel generator, that was problematic. Since they could not find one, it seemed likely that Sture had heard the school's noisy ventilation system. To ensure a successful outcome to the trial, they also asked Sture a large number of leading questions which converted Johan Asplund's abdominal surgery scar into a faintly brownish birthmark on his back. The boy's mother had described this birthmark to Penttinen.

In this way van der Kwast's case moved from 'we really haven't got anything' to 'we've got it all' in just a few months. The trial began on 14 May 2001 in Stockholm. The prosecutor called Professor Christianson as an expert witness. He stated under oath that there were reasons why Sture had been unable to say where the body was:

> Perpetrators who have committed the type of crime which the defendant is accused of feel a need to make public the narrative of their deed but, simultaneously, a need to resist interference. Furthermore, the perpetrator often feels compelled to preserve body parts. The compulsions respectively to narrate and to hide parts of the corpse create conflict within the mind of the perpetrator.[508]

On 21 June 2001, the District Court announced its conclusion. The proceedings had established beyond all reasonable doubt that Sture Bergwall had murdered Johan Asplund. This was his eighth murder conviction.

32

The rebellion against the mother

'I believe truth alone can set us free'
Margit Norell, in a letter to David Schecter (1978).

After the first court sentence had been announced in 1994, Christer van der Kwast said that it would become 'part of a new chain of evidence'.[509] The chain grew longer and longer with each murder conviction. By the time Sture had been convicted of the Johan Asplund murder, the chief prosecutor had eight murder connections forming strong links in his 'chain of evidence'. He seemed able to get Sture declared guilty of practically anything without having to bother with finding a body, or produce technical evidence or even logical arguments. All that was needed, given Sture's record, was a new, adjusted 'narrative' and an expert witness statement from Professor Christianson.

The media critics could squabble to their hearts' content. No external threat could shift the Quick team off course in their progress towards what they reckoned would be murder convictions nine, ten and eleven. The investigations were well under way. But, quite unexpectedly, a new and worrying situation had arisen inside Säter hospital in 2001. Göran Källberg, the founder of the unit, was back in charge and turned out to be a threat.

In 1994, he had left the medical directorship of the hospital and moved to a post at a psychiatric outpatient clinic in Hedemora. Over the years the hospital board had become displeased with his successor Erik Kall and so persuaded Källberg to return after seven years in the wilderness. On 1 March 2001, Kall was demoted to consultant and Göran Källberg reinstated as medical director.

He had been away for many years but knew quite a lot about the treatment Sture had been receiving. He had occasionally worked as a locum duty doctor in the secure unit and had also offered advice over the phone to less experienced colleagues when Sture had had a breakdown outside normal working hours. He also kept in touch with the unit through his wife, Viola Källberg, who had stayed on in ward 36 as a psychiatric nurse and saw Sture every day. As the years went by, Viola had become more and more worried about Kall's excessive medication regime, and she had come to suspect that the murder confessions might be false. The Källbergs had talked these issues over and, in spring 2001, when Göran Källberg was back in harness, his first action was to examine the pharmacological aspects of Sture's treatment.[510]

Three weeks before the Asplund murder trial, Källberg and Sture had a conversation that was quite unlike any other talk referred to in Sture's large volume of case notes. The topic of discussion was medication and Sture seems to have been ready to confess things he had not previously admitted. Källberg made this entry in the case notes afterwards: 'The patient is aware of being addicted to his medication. When I put it to Quick that he obviously takes medicines in order to "get a high" he did not deny it.'[511]

Years later, when the retrial applications were being submitted, Källberg outlined Sture's drug consumption in a police interview: 'His intake of medicines was far too much. He was also prescribed totally inappropriate combinations of benzodiazepines and painkillers. I must say that he normally didn't seem that hugely affected and I was never witness to any of his drama-queen displays, or his anxiety attacks for that matter. However, his drug regime was way out of order [...].'[512]

When Källberg and Sture had reached the end of their talk, the doctor decided that his patient would no longer be offered anything on top of the already high doses given at fixed hours three times a day. There would be no extra Xanax tablet with the mid-morning coffee, no rectal Stesolid during therapy and no codeine-laced painkillers. The chief psychologist Birgitta Ståhle and the psychiatric consultant Erik Kall both disapproved. They felt pretty sure that Sture would not cope with the Asplund trial unless pepped up with tablets and Sture agreed with them. Kall was persuaded to break with the prescription routine determined by his superior. Just before the trial, he made an entry in Sture's case notes saying that it was 'essential' for the 'orderly conduct of the trial to institute a temporary change' so that the 'as required' medication could be administered: 'If pat. feels severe anxiety such that the conduct of the trial might be compromised, he is to be given 1 × 1 mg tabl. Xanax as req. Also, should a strong tension headache affect the conduct of the trial, pat. to be given 2 × tabl. Anadin with codeine as req.'[513]

Thanks to this intervention, Sture munched tablets as usual during the five days of the trial but, once the court had risen, he was in for a shock. Källberg had asked Viola, his wife, to keep an eye on 'extra medication' lists and soon found out what had been going on. Several people have told me that Källberg could become exceedingly angry. He was angry now. In orders issued to all members of staff, including Erik Kall, he made it clear that it was forbidden, under any circumstances, to let Sture have any additional medication without his own authorization.[514] If Sture had an acute anxiety attack, he was to be isolated and placed under observation or taken to the admissions unit which was equipped to manage unstable patients, but not given as much as a single extra headache tablet.[515]

Källberg did not stop at this but also made an explicit entry in Sture's notes on 5 June. He stated that the patient's medication had taken on 'a clearly addictive pattern' and that administration of certain drugs in the past possibly had been a direct cause of increased anxiety. Sture was to be on a detoxification regime.

Källberg informed Sture about his decision. An exchange of views followed:

Pat himself argues that in his unique situation the medicines have provided a sense of security and that this has allowed him to dare to confront his memories and to cope with the police interviews. I then made it clear to pat. that I am not under any circumstances prepared to accept ongoing substance abuse just to enable him to deal

439

with the police. It is of course up to him how he wants to handle the situation but these are not premises on the basis of which it becomes medically acceptable to permit drug abuse. During this talk, he chiefly used such arguments as blackmail. Pat. generally conforms to an addictive behaviour pattern.[516]

Sture did everything to make Källberg change his mind. He said that the abstinence would be unendurable. If not allowed 'drugs as required', he threatened to 'withdraw from the therapy and also from further police investigations'. Nothing he said had any effect on Källberg. In a case note entry, he observed that during one talk Sture had displayed 'some twitching and shaking of his right hand' but that these signs had vanished once he realized that 'nothing would stop continued tapering of his intake'.

Something had obviously happened to Göran Källberg. After starting his mixed therapy and supervision sessions with Margit in 1983, he rapidly became a very devoted pupil. It was at his initiative that the new unit was built in 1989 to incorporate her ideas about treatment, expressed in her successful – as it was seen at the time – transformation of the incurable Lars-Inge Svartenbrandt. When Källberg stepped in as medical director in 1994, he was still loyal to Margit. He had even consulted her before he cancelled Sture's leave.

Now, seven years later, he was insisting on a detox programme that could lead to Sture stopping his psychotherapy treatment. Apparently Källberg was indifferent to the risk of depriving Margit of the most important patient in her life as a therapist. What had changed? I could not ask Källberg himself as he had a fatal heart attack in 2011, but I got in touch with Viola Källberg and asked her if she would talk to me about Göran and Margit. Very kindly, she said that I was welcome to visit her at Säter, where she still worked.

Viola invited me to coffee and sandwiches. She was sixty-three, dressed in casual trousers and top, and wore her dark hair long. She said that losing her husband had been hard, not only because of the shock and the grief but also for purely practical reasons. For example, it had been Göran who dealt with the bills so, in the middle of her crisis, she had to learn about household finances. She spoke unsentimentally about her loss and gave me the impression of being a strong character.

She and Göran and their three children had moved into a house in Hedemora in 1982. Their youngest had been two years old at the time. Göran had already started in his post as medical director and, a year later, he initiated the treatment of Lars-Inge Svartenbrandt and started going to Margit every Tuesday for combined therapy and supervision sessions, leaving Viola to look after the family almost single-handed. From 1985, he also became a member of Margit's group, which meant that he was away for weekends from time to time. Viola sometimes felt that Göran seemed to prefer Margit and her circle to his family and it made her jealous, but she tolerated the situation because, she said, it was obvious how much Margit meant to him. Viola had met Margit and her husband Curt on a few occasions and remembered Margit as pleasant but a little forbidding.

For as long as the children were young, Viola stayed at home, but in 1988 she started working full-time as a nurse at Säter. She was there when the new regional unit was opened in 1989 and during the 'Quick years' she was a nurse in ward 36. One of her tales from that time was about the occasion when Margit came to have a talk with Sture – it had been rather like 'a visit from a head of state'.

When Göran left the post of medical director in 1994, he stayed in close touch with Margit. Viola thought that his attitude to his mentor started to change gradually towards the end of the 1990s but she was uncertain about what had caused the schism. She had grown somewhat fed up with Margit and her group and avoided discussing them with her husband. Göran, who realized how she felt, respected the truce by not airing these topics unless he had to. When Viola was telling me about this, she added that she should have talked more with him.

We speculated, as we sat at her kitchen table, about what might have happened between Göran and Margit. I knew that as late as Saturday 28 September 1996 he was still an acolyte. It was the date of the last meeting of the Margit group and Ståhle entered Göran's name under 'present' in the minutes.[517]

Some of Margit's pupils had already broken away from her by then and the process of disintegration upset the loyalists. The group was torn apart by internal conflicts. Margit herself had not attended that last meeting. The minutes record that she had instead sent a message via Hanna Olsson to say that she, Margit, felt 'no personal need' for a group and that she would have to consider whether she would be 'present at the meeting of any newly constituted group, should that come about'.

The meeting included a convocation in which each one of its nine members expressed his or her opinion about its future role. Cajsa, Gillan and Ståhle voted for dissolution because they had already formed a new group in support of Margit. The others were less certain. One voice called the situation part of 'a process of separation', someone else spoke of her 'grief' and Tulla Brattbakk-Göthberg is quoted as saying that she regarded the group as 'a family in decline'. Källberg said that he did not want the group to dissolve but hoped that, in the future, 'the expression of personal views would become a little freer'. The outcome was dissolution.

It seems likely that Källberg would have tried to join the small, devout group that now formed around Margit. After all, it included his former colleague Birgitta Ståhle and many of the people I interviewed have said that she and Göran were close. However, at some point after 1996, his view of Margit had changed radically and we will probably never find out what his reasons were. It might have been that he had found freedom of expression even more limited in the new group than in the old. Perhaps Margit had snubbed him just as she once humiliated Tomas Videgård, Patricia Tudor-Sandahl and others who distanced themselves from her. The fact remains that Källberg finally went his own way. Viola said that it had been a major step for him: 'It's fair to say that he once was something like Margit's crown prince.'

Sture's constitution had become so dependent on constant, large doses of medication that Källberg was forced to reduce the drug intake gradually over nine months to make sure that his patient did not die during the withdrawal process. Sture tried every trick in the book to keep his drugs coming. I found this draft letter to Källberg in one of Sture's notebooks:

I have dared to allow the most dreadful memories to emerge, secure in the awareness that my anguish would be tempered by medication. I am sure that there are many reasons in support of scaling down these substances but there is <u>one</u> reason for not doing this which should be weighed against all the others: that I cannot contain within me the anguish that my narrative invariably generates. The balance may well tip one way when the medical arguments for a reduction schedule are piled up, but on the other hand the effect is light compared to this one other concern . . .

He did not get any further. In June he made several other notes about how badly he suffered:

Withdrawal symptoms. Anguish. Nine days until sentencing. Next week, Birgitta is away on holiday. As is Erik Kall. And Källberg will rule the roost. How in all the world will I handle my terrible anxiety when my medications have been down-sized?? Why (honestly, <u>why?</u>) should Källberg downgrade me like this? <u>Where</u> are those who would defend me and soothe me – where? And if they exist, how do they react?[518]

In fact, they reacted strongly. As Viola put it, 'pandemonium broke out' among Margit's pupils. Ståhle tried to persuade Källberg to reconsider and let Sture have his drugs on demand. Cajsa Lindholm wrote a letter to Sture to persuade him to carry on with the therapy and the police investigations all the same:

If you can bear to complete the therapeutic process you will be contributing invaluable knowledge to all those who work with vulnerable children and adults, and also to society's insight into and capacity to deal with such problems. I am well aware that no one except yourself can grasp what you are going through and that the pain and loneliness you experience is yours alone and, furthermore, that this poses a dilemma for you in that the more you tell and reveal to others, the more alone you become because you are giving up on what used to give your life its meaning while at the same time people turn away from you. Though not all: for me and my colleagues and others, too, who are prepared, understand and have the will to set everything we learn into a greater context, your work is exceptionally important and instils in us a deep respect for your courage and willingness to tell your story. So, in this sense you are not alone. There are many of us who hope that you can take the strain and who share your way of seeing the world and also fight for the importance of a deep and wide-ranging understanding of mankind.[519]

Another pupil wrote to Källberg and tried to talk him into giving Sture his medicines back. Viola remembers that the letter made him furious. He realized that the agent behind the campaign was Margit, who was trying to control the way he did his job. The effect was to make him even more determined: 'He was like a teenager rebelling against his mother,' Viola said.

Sture describes the withdrawal period as utterly awful. He was fifty-one years old and had been on benzodiazepines daily since he was twenty-three. He spent most of the autumn in 2001 lying on his bed, convinced that he was dying. His weight was dropping like a stone and he lost 30 kilograms over ten months. At worst, his resting pulse was racing at 160 beats per minute. His notes to Ståhle were full of self-pity: 'Who will weep over me when I am dead? I, who grieve so deeply and bitterly over the life I have led, and who sheds tears over the life I am leading. And perhaps this is how it is and will be; I grieve over my life (and over all those who I, consumed with sorrow, have killed) and no one else will.'[520]

He even wrote an outline of a will in which he tried to set out what should be done with his writings, in which he discusses therapy and serial killing at length, after his death. He wanted to punish Källberg:

Following consultations with the chief psychologist at the forensic psychiatry unit [Birgitta Ståhle] and the charge nurse for ward 36,

444

the Säter hospital will own and have the right to dispose of, or to donate, the material in order that it becomes available for *bona fide* research. This material must not, under any circumstances, be left in charge of the present medical director Göran Källberg.[521]

In August, Sture announced that he would not participate in any murder investigations without the medication he claimed to need and, according to his case notes, he was 'doubtful' about his therapy.[522] Ståhle wrote that she considered this stance a 'return to his old, defensive strategies'. This was one in the eye for Källberg, who, in her view, had been preventing Sture from getting better by putting him through detoxification. Despite all this, Sture's medication continued to be scaled down. In September, he took his last Xanax. The next step was to taper off his Stesolid. By early October, the case notes record severe withdrawal symptoms: 'When sitting up pat. rocks his body forward and back, shaky. Aware of heart beat.'[523]

Eventually the turnaround arrived. Källberg had a long talk with Sture at the end of October and noted afterwards that Sture had said he had been 'frightened, angry and disappointed' at the beginning of the detox process but that he felt a bit better. His resting pulse was lower; he slept properly at night for the first time for many years and felt that 'he could look forward to the future with some confidence'.[524]

Sture has told me that he remembers that talk. To be left in peace, they had gone to sit in the ward kitchen and closed the door. 'It was the first time that I felt that the drug withdrawal had worked,' he said. 'And I began to feel grateful to Göran Källberg.'

By the end of November, the day of his last dose of Stesolid was due and the staff reported some progress: 'His anxiety attacks still occur but have decreased rather than increased in number. The atmosphere around this patient is unusually quiet.'[525]

In January 2002, Källberg and Sture talked again and Sture said that the drug reduction meant that he sensed his body in new ways. 'He describes the difference as having "greater integrity", and another level of experiencing bodily sensations.'[526] Sture told me that when he stroked the skin on his arm with his fingertips, he could not remember sensing it like this before in his life. He no longer knew what an unmedicated body felt like. But the mental effects Sture experienced were the most exceptional and tumultuous. It was like undergoing a personality change, from a junkie self into a sober person he did not know.

There are many case note entries reporting this positive transformation but for Ståhle it was a problematic turn of events. On her watch, Sture had become madder year on year. He had been diagnosed as a psychotic, probably outright schizophrenic and prone to swap between multiple personalities. His history included endless suicide attempts as well as being allegedly guilty of at least thirty-nine murders. Ståhle, Margit and the former medical director Erik Kall had consistently interpreted his track record as a series of signs that Sture 'was recovering his contact with reality' because his repressed memories were gradually retrieved.[527] But when Källberg gradually eliminated the medication Sture flourished correspondingly. His symptoms of mental dysfunction were disappearing as if by magic. It must have begun to dawn on Ståhle that she had been an active agent in a mistreatment of epic proportions. We do not know what she really felt because she refuses to explain herself. We do know, however, that during 2002 Ståhle made several entries in Sture's case notes in which she, rather desperately, tries to give the psychotherapy the credit for her patient's sudden recovery:

The recent Christmas was the first holiday that Thomas says has made him feel happy. He sees himself as liberated in a way he has not felt before. This change also includes a new access to himself and to the present. [. . .] Thomas is more in touch with himself, also with his body. Today, he can see himself for the invaded personality he once was. Invaded by early, brutal events, sadism and intellectualization. An increased ability to deep vision and contact has become possible only because the illusion (the Simon illusion) about reality has been recovered and revealed. This illusion concealed genuine needs and experiences that had been denied.[528]

'The Simon illusion' was Margit's term for the notion that Sture had believed himself able to restore Simon to life by murdering people. Now, this illusion had been swept away and hence Sture felt much better.

On 14 February, Sture announced that he would never again participate in any murder investigations. A week later, on 22 February, the long withdrawal process was finished and he had his first entirely drug-free day since his teens. By then, he had notified the Deed Poll Office that he wanted to change his name. On his fifth drug-free day, he was Sture Ragnar Bergwall once more. Thomas Quick had ceased to exist. Two months later, he explained to Ståhle that he needed 'a holiday' from the therapy and she wrote in his case notes:

Sture describes how he now has got access to himself as a person, to his body and to his deep mental life, in a positive sense. This, to him, is quite new. Previously, he has been crowded, occupied by destructive experiences, fantasies etc. Today has brought new experiences in its wake and he feels alive. For this he is very grateful. He thinks that therapy had opened up these new possibilities, together with the fact that he is now drug free. Currently, however, he is also very tired and worn out. It is observable as his body weight has been sharply reduced. For this reason, Sture has suggested a holiday from the therapeutic work. He needs to take charge of this new life and to rest. We agreed to a break from today and until the autumn.[529]

Sture said that while he wanted to avoid hurting Ståhle he had actually made a much less conciliatory decision. He notes in his calendar: 'From now on, it's time out from therapy. Said (to B) that I'll rest over spring and summer. Left unsaid, that I am convinced I won't be back.'[530]

Three weeks later, a nurse made this entry in the case notes: 'Sture let us know that he is feeling fine, even that he has never felt as well as he does now. Feels a sense of freedom.'[531]

The next time Sture and Ståhle met was in August. She expected that the therapy sessions would start up again and Sture said to me that he found it very hard to turn her down. The strong emotional bond he had formed with her over the years had not yet been cut. He assured her that one day he might well return both to the therapy sessions and investigations but that he wanted to rest for a longer, indeterminate time. A week or so later, they had a final therapeutic talk. No new appointment was agreed.

Then, silence fell around Sture. His case notes, usually packed with drama, became lists of short entries about purely practical things. Whole years take up only a few pages. Sometimes, Penttinen came for a visit. He still hoped that Sture would change his mind and start spinning his 'narratives' again. Sometimes, Ståhle saw him for roughly the same reason. Sture talked to them but nothing more.

To endure the detox process, he had set up a strict timetable of routines and he stuck to it. He woke at 5.29 a.m., listened to the news on the radio, got out of bed at 5.33, then dressed and went to the dining room at 5.54 where he breakfasted on sour milk and coffee. At 6.04, he was let out to take his morning walk, following a figure-of-eight-shaped course in the interior courtyard. A small crab apple tree grew in the yard, a memorial to Simon known as the 'Simon tree'. Sture and Ståhle had planted it together as a step in the mental healing. The idea was that the tree would become a sacred place and make it easier for Sture to give up on his sacred caches. Sture spent eighty minutes walking every morning and passed the Simon tree twenty times. It produced tiny, inedible fruit in the autumn.

He showered at 7.25. He solved crosswords and listened to the radio until 4.00 p.m. He read or watched TV in the evenings. After going to bed, he turned the light off at 9.30. The next day, he repeated his schedule from the beginning. His routines were unchanging, seven days a week, 365 days a year.

His mind was lucid. He knew that Thomas Quick had been a construct that he and the team had collaborated on to create, but he had nobody to tell about it. He knew that with eight murder convictions he would never be allowed to leave Säter. There was no point in claiming innocence; if he said he had lied all along and tried to tell the real story, no one would believe him. The only effect would be open warfare with the staff at Säter – precisely the people who were in complete control of his life as a criminal sentenced to inpatient care. They might, for example, punish him by cancelling his leave, which allowed him a little excursion once every fifth week, accompanied by three staff members. They could take away his books.

Only a madman would challenge the psychiatric unit.

Outside Säter, he had no one to talk to either. His lawyers were part of the past craziness. His relationships with his siblings were, of course, ruined after he had portrayed his parents as sadistic sex criminals and accused two of his brothers of being accomplices in murder and butchery. He had no friends and hardly a single private visitor had come to see him in all his years in the unit. Sture was completely alone. But he wasn't a machine and to survive he needed a minimum of human contact and kindness. He depended on his good relations with the hospital staff. His wisest course was to stick to his serial killer story and not rock the boat, which was what he planned to do for the rest of his life.

Ståhle continued seeing Margit for therapy and supervision even though she had finished treating Sture. The last time the Dalarna County Council paid Margit a fee for her services as psychology supervisor was, according to the Wages Office record, Wednesday 16 June 2004. Margit was ninety years old. People I have interviewed told me that Ståhle went to Margit for therapy sessions until her mentor's death on 28 January 2005, just before her ninety-first birthday.

Sven Å Christianson has told me that he, too, stayed faithful to Margit until the end. He said that he had made her a promise, 'an agreement that we would keep each other company because there was no need to end this contact that was so important to us both'. When he told me this, I already knew that fear of being abandoned had haunted Margit all her life. She did not have to worry in the end, because her son in spirit would not leave her. Christianson could not have offered her a more precious gift.

Margit had left the Swedish Church and did not want a religious funeral. A few weeks after her death, a small memorial service was held in the conference venue Princess Hall in leafy Djurgården, where Margit had invited many visiting psychoanalysts to lecture.[532] But even the memorial service was overshadowed by old conflicts between her pupils. Many of those who, as long ago as the 1970s, had seen Margit as their mother did not care to come and say goodbye. Tomas Videgård, Patricia Tudor-Sandahl, Margareta Hedén-Chami and several others stayed away. Göran Källberg did not go to the service either. Viola Källberg thinks the decision not to attend was his definitive separation from the woman who had meant so much to him for at least fifteen years of his life.

Cajsa and her patients Lena Arvidsson and 'Stina' were there, as was Birgitta Ståhle, Gillan Liljeström and Sven Å Christianson. Gillan made a brief speech and made special mention of how, once, when she and Margit had talked about what is important in life, Margit had told her about a botanist she had read about. He had spent his whole life looking for a rare plant and, to the last, dragged himself off on new excursions. In the end, he did find the plant – and then he died. This was how Margit had wanted to live, Gillan said: 'Always working, in touch with what matters, engaged.'

I believe Sture was the rare plant Margit had been looking for all her life as a psychoanalyst. When I met Gillan, I asked her if Margit ever doubted Sture's credentials as a serial killer. 'No,' she replied, without a second's hesitation. Until the day she died Margit had believed in Sture's 'narrative'.

Cajsa Lindholm, Lena Arvidsson and Gillan Liljeström continue with their therapeutic work to this day. Their mission, following Margit's lead, is to help people remember their repressed memories, often of sexual abuse in childhood. We will never know how many families they have broken up by creating false memories of abuse that never happened.

Sven Å Christianson still works at the University of Stockholm, and is an active lecturer and writer. He rarely agrees to be interviewed about the Quick years and if he concedes to speak about it all, he states, often quite brusquely, that his role had nothing to do with assessing how believable Sture was.

Göran Källberg tried as best he could to make good the damage he had caused by allowing Margit's theoretical ideas to dominate at Säter.

He realized that Sture had been wrongly convicted. In 2009, while the retrial investigations were still going on, Källberg said in a police interview that he 'felt deeply uncomfortable' about Sture's presumed guilt and that he had spoken to 'several judges' to find out if there was 'any hope of any retrials' for Sture. They had told him that there was no such hope if the only new evidence was that Sture had confessed while overdosed on mind-bending drugs.[533]

Källberg tried to find a solution but at the same time he did not want to let the unit down. His duty, as an employee at Säter, was to report the errors of treatment to the relevant authorities. He never did.

His hopes for retrials were dashed in the aftermath of the decision by Johan Asplund's parents to submit a written complaint to the Office of the Chancellor of Justice in 2006. This was two years before Sture withdrew his confessions and the appeal process started. The complaint stated that Christer van der Kwast and Seppo Penttinen were guilty of professional misconduct and perjury in the Quick trials and all eight murder investigations. Anna-Clara and Björn Asplund had never believed that Sture had murdered their son and had seen more than enough of van der Kwast's and Penttinen's ways of working to realize that the District Courts had been deceived over and over again.

The Office of the Chancellor of Justice is the authority charged with making sure that other Swedish state agencies comply with the law and good practice and report to the government of the day. At the time, Göran Lambertz was the Chancellor of Justice. The Asplunds had presented the Chancellor's office with enough documentation to fill six cardboard boxes and must have been prepared to wait for a long time while the staff sifted through the extensive material. However, Göran Lambertz, who had received the Asplunds' complaint on Friday 17 November, reached his decision after just seven working days. In his response, he wrote that Christer van der Kwast and Seppo Penttinen 'had carried out their work skilfully' and that his office saw no need 'to examine the matter further'. Consequently, he closed the case.[534]

Five days later, an article by Lambertz was published in the opinion pages of *Dagens Nyheter*. Lambertz said that, after going through the documentation, he found that the eight murders of which Sture had been found guilty were of 'an analogous character' and, hence, it seemed 'more likely that a person with a markedly disturbed personality had committed many such analogous crimes rather than that these acts had been committed by several different perpetrators'.[535] Lambertz had instantly revealed to anyone who was even slightly informed about the Quick investigations that he was astonishingly ignorant. The one shared feature of Thomas Quick's alleged murders was that they had so little in common. He appeared to have picked his victims indiscriminately: children and adults, boy and girls, men and women. He sexually assaulted some and did not touch others. He dismembered some and left other bodies lying where they fell. He killed by strangling, knifing and battering with a stick or other blunt instruments. Quick had murdered anyone in any old way. Göran Lambertz, Sweden's Chancellor of Justice, did not know this, but he apparently did know that 'in all essential respects' Christer van der Kwast and Seppo Penttinen 'had carried out their work skilfully'.

Jan Olsson was one of the senior crime squad officers who had left in protest over the conduct of the investigations into the Quick killings. He went public with his criticisms of Lambertz's decision. In his reply, the Chancellor of Justice revealed his faith in the theory of repressed memories:

> Those who, like Jan Olsson, believe that there are solid reasons for finding Quick innocent of the crimes of which he has been convicted, have surely been affected by the unusual situation. A deeply disturbed individual has required assistance in order to recall exceptional acts which he may or may not have been guilty of committing. And, during the trials, he repeatedly makes mistakes. Conclusion: he cannot be guilty of these acts. But he can – of course. An unbiased observer would easily realize this.[536]

Lambertz's stance was mystifying. A possible explanation came that summer, on 28 July 2007, when he addressed the Swedish people on the popular radio programme *Summer*. Lambertz revealed that he admired two people in particular: the former Archbishop K. G.

Hammar and Thomas Quick's former defence lawyer Claes Borgström.[537] Borgström had seemingly managed to infect Göran Lambertz with a belief in repressed memories and, as a result, the Chancellor of Justice had felt it unnecessary to read up on the Quick case before acquitting van der Kwast and Penttinen from all suspicions of misconduct.

Of course, the 2006 decision by the Chancellor of Justice eliminated any hope Sture might have about ever leaving Säter. When Hannes Råstam wrote to him in April 2008, Sture had taken about 2,000 morning walks in the exercise yard and passed the Simon tree some 40,000 times. Hannes asked if they could meet – no strings. Sture said yes, with hardly a thought that anything might change, and they agreed to meet on 2 June. When Hannes asked Sture if he still stood by his murder confessions, Sture said he did.

Afterwards, Hannes phoned Göran Källberg. Viola Källberg remembers the call very clearly. Göran had been torn between his loyalty to the unit and his desire for justice. Viola had whispered to her husband during the phone call that he must tell the journalist how drugged Sture had always been. Göran did as she asked.

Hannes had no access to Sture's case notes at the time and only Sture could consent to an outsider reading through his case. But Hannes had acquired access to the police store of filmed re-enactments and knew what to look for, thanks to Källberg's information. It did not take him long to see what Källberg meant. Sture was often visibly drugged to the eyeballs as the Quick team urged him on through the countryside. Hannes spent the rest of the summer reading stacks of investigative paperwork from police records and speaking to the police officers who had decided to leave the Quick investigations. Once more that summer, he returned to Säter. Nothing new happened but Sture had come to trust Hannes and told him that he was welcome back.

On 17 September, Hannes visited Sture for the third time to tell him what the police videos had revealed. Sture remembers that meeting very well. He has said that he felt completely defeated and drained at first but when Hannes started to speak about his medication, his state of mind suddenly changed. In his book *The Case of Thomas Quick: The*

Making of a Serial Killer, Hannes describes the moment during their talk when Sture suddenly leaned forward and whispered: "' ... but if I haven't committed these murders ... then what do I do?'" His eyes had a despairing look, Hannes said. Then, he answered: "'If you haven't, Sture, now is the chance of your life.'"[538]

Sture has said that Hannes and he had shared 'a magic moment' as they sat together in one of the unit's kitchens. Afterwards, when Sture was back in his room, he made a fist in his pocket and thought – yes! Hannes Råstam had made him realize that he had an ally outside Säter. Hannes, who had planned to return to Gothenburg, was also moved by what had happened. He found a hotel room in Säter and visited the hospital again the next day. That was when Sture expressly stated that he had never in his entire life murdered anyone.

Hannes was on the brink of a major scoop, but neither he nor Sture were stupid enough to imagine that a TV documentary would do anything other than make Sture's situation worse. Unless they were able to start a retrial process with a reasonable chance of being successful, Sture would only start a war with Säter and that was the last thing he could afford to risk. He was, in every way, a prisoner in the unit.

Immediately after this meeting with Sture, Hannes called Thomas Olsson. They had worked together before on a case that Hannes had made a documentary about and which Olsson had taken to the Supreme Court, with the outcome that an innocent man went free. This time Hannes presented such convincing arguments for Sture's innocence that Olsson decided to go to Säter himself. He met Sture on 19 September, the day after Hannes had left. Effectively, the retrial application was already under way. Four days later, Hannes and a photographer came to Säter. On three consecutive days, Sture was interviewed about the making of the 'serial killer' Thomas Quick.

Hannes also interviewed Göran Källberg for a TV broadcast. Källberg had retired by then but still stood in as roving locum consultant when there was a gap in the staffing rota. On TV, the former medical director bravely criticized his own unit but refused to talk about anything other than Sture's medication. At no time did he even mention Margit's name. He almost gave the impression that he had never worked at Säter hospital until he turned up in 2001 and began Sture's detoxification. To the viewers, he was a hero who kick-started the process that would bring an end to the Quick hysteria.

Hannes made two documentaries that ran on TV in December 2008. Back at Säter, Källberg's participation in the programmes was regarded as treachery. Viola has told me that Birgitta Ståhle felt utterly betrayed by her old boss, which is understandable. Källberg introduced her to Margit in the 1980s but now he pretended to have no idea what Sture's therapy had been about.

The first retrial application was submitted by Thomas Olsson only four months after the documentaries. The media took an intense interest and the clinical staff reacted as if under siege. On 15 May 2009, Källberg's successor as medical director, Susanne Nyberg, forbade him to enter ward 36 or meet Sture anywhere. In his very last entry in Sture's case notes, Källberg records the ban on seeing Sture. He adds that 'in my recent talks with this patient, he has been calmer and more rational than I have ever seen him before, an observation which I mentioned to him and with which he agrees.'[539] That was the last time they met.

Säter began to subject Sture to the punishments he had known would follow. His 'out-for-air' excursions every fifth week were cancelled 'for reasons of security'. In October 2009 his room was emptied of books, CDs and films, which were all packed into boxes and locked into Säter's basement. In November it was decided that his room must be inspected twice weekly and, later that month, two tradesmen turned up and removed the venetian blinds. Every intervention was motivated by 'security concerns'. In December, the searches of his room were intensified and carried out daily.[540] Since the autumn of 1992, Sture had been regarded as a serial killer but it was only seventeen years later, when he applied for a retrial, that Säter began to manage him as if he were Hannibal Lecter.

After Hannes Råstam's documentaries, the Prosecution Authority received several complaints against Christer van der Kwast and Seppo Penttinen, repeatedly claiming aggravated professional misconduct and perjury. The law defines a period of limitations, which effectively meant that their work prior to March 1999 could not be subject to possible prosecution,[541] but van der Kwast and Penttinen could still be scrutinized for their handling of the pre-trial investigations and court statements in the cases of the Storvik and Jensen murders (May 1999), and also for their efforts in the Johan Asplund case. However, these complaints were not followed up. The head of the Prosecution Authority announced his conclusion that the Chancellor of Justice had 'thoroughly examined' this issue as early as 2006, and found that Christer van der Kwast and Seppo Penttinen had worked skilfully. One might have thought that the Prosecution Authority would reconsider the Chancellor of Justice's verdict, but that would not do at all, because the Chancellor's office sits in judgement over the Prosecution Authority. It is higher up in the judicial hierarchy: 'Thus, I cannot undertake to scrutinize the verdict by the Chancellor of Justice' admitted the head of the Prosecution Authority.

When, in 2006, Göran Lambertz praised the past work by van der Kwast and Penttinen, after seven days of 'investigation', in effect he conferred legal immunity on their activities during the Quick years. Lambertz seemed unconcerned about this. Soon after the second of Hannes's films had been shown, he was back on the TV4 morning news for a chat. He expressed this opinion about the Quick team's way of performing murder investigations: 'Look, I'm not a psychotherapist and have no expertise in areas such as psychology and psychiatry. But if we assume that the man was guilty, this was surely the only way to find out more about what was going on. Then the psychotherapist and the prosecutor and the police officer worked perfectly correctly as I see it.'[542]

The following year, before the first murder sentence had been removed, Lambertz was appointed to Justice of the Supreme Court. The Supreme Court is the spine of the Swedish judicial system. Not even the government has the right to sack the court's justices.

The rest of the Swedish legal system struggled manfully to repair the damage that the Quick team had left in its wake. Sture was declared not guilty of one murder after another. Meanwhile, Säter went all out for a damage limitation campaign. Birgitta Ståhle wrote to the social services department to say that she had never even heard of any therapeutic approach that aimed at recovering repressed memories. Susanne Nyberg, the medical director, let it be known that, even though she had been employed at Säter for most of the 1990s, she had not the faintest idea what was going on in Sture's psychotherapy sessions. The consultant psychiatrist Erik Kall made a powerful counter-attack when it was suggested Sture had been given experimental treatment at Säter: 'The contact with psychologists that was offered to this patient cannot be described as experimental but rather conducted on an object relations theoretical basis which is based on well documented grounds.'[543]

Outside Säter the majority of people were largely ignorant about what had actually happened. The unit obviously wanted it to stay that way and clammed up.

Göran Källberg, however, knew the truth. I asked Viola if she thought that her husband might ever have decided to speak about Margit's influence. She thought for a while and said: 'Yes, I believe he would. He was an honest man. If you had approached him and asked, he would have told you the truth.'

Sture thinks along the same lines. Hannes had told him that he planned to interview Göran Källberg again but the interview never took place. On 1 April 2011, Källberg had a meeting with a few colleagues during a coffee break at Säter. He was close to his sixty-ninth birthday but had recently signed up for another year as locum consultant. Suddenly, he leaned back in his armchair, fell asleep and never woke up again. Göran Källberg died in the unit that he and Margit had created together.

Barely three weeks later, Hannes Råstam had an appointment at the Sahlgrenska hospital, where he was told that he had only a few months left to live. He was given an appalling course of chemotherapy treatment and kept going for nine months. He worked on his book *The Case of Thomas Quick: The Making of a Serial Killer* until the day he died.

Perhaps Göran Källberg really would have told Hannes the rest of the story but we will never know. That the story did not get told was frustrating, not only for Sture but also for his siblings, who all contacted him as the retrial processes continued. In the autumn of 2012, they travelled to Säter for a family get-together in the visitors' room. Their joint take on the Quick scandal was that, fundamentally, psychotherapy was the core problem, not poor police work. The Swedish public had never been informed of this and the Bergwalls' shared outrage was the reason why Sture's eldest brother Sten-Ove Bergwall phoned me after Hannes Råstam's funeral.

On Wednesday 31 July 2013, the last investigation of the retrial process closed and from that day Sture was officially innocent of murder. Säter has been trying to keep him locked up but the unit cannot win. He will be allowed to turn his back on forensic psychiatric care and walk out, a free man.

What will he do when he is outside? Many journalists have asked him and he often replies that he will go for a walk through the forest, moving straight ahead and not in a figure of eight. If this book were a script for a Hollywood film, it might have ended with the camera following Sture as he leaves Säter and climbs into a taxi that takes him to Främby promontory, where he heads for the forest. There, among the trees, he opens a discreet trapdoor in the ground and descends into his universal cafe, where Simon is recreated.

But that has nothing to do with reality. The strange case of Thomas Quick is not about a serial killer but about unreasoning faith, obsession and collective madness. Sture was not a monster. There was a many-headed monster, though: the people who transformed Sture into Thomas Quick. He joined that team himself but he could never have created Thomas Quick the serial killer without the help of the others, and of Margit in particular. I am convinced that, without Margit, the century's biggest miscarriage of Swedish justice would not have come to pass.

Personally, I think the Quick team is more alarming than any serial killer. That kind of criminal is, after all, quite rare. But I do not think that many of us are immune to the temptation of joining a group that rewards its members with a wonderful sense of belonging in exchange for going easy on critical scrutiny, and the results can be quite terrifying.

This is why I have come to the conclusion that the story about Thomas Quick is fundamentally about what our need for shared beliefs and for connection with others can make us do. As Frieda Fromm-Reichmann expressed it: 'Loneliness seems to be such a painful, frightening experience that people do practically everything to avoid it.'[544]

In the early 1960s, Margit marked that passage with pencil lines. She went on to devote her life as a psychoanalyst to try to prove the truth of what her soulmate had written.

My own view is that the story about Margit, Sture and the circle around them above all else confirms that we are prepared to do whatever it takes to not feel lonely.

In this, Margit was right.

Afterword

Once Sture Bergwall's last murder conviction had finally been overturned in December 2013, the Swedish government ordered a public inquiry into this, Sweden's most serious miscarriage of justice in modern times. The inquiry was charged with scrutinizing concerns about forensic psychiatric care as well as the legal issues, and asked to identify any systemic flaws that may have given rise to the shambles. The inquiry commission is still at work

Soon after the publication of Dan Josefsson's book in Sweden, the Department of Psychology at the University of Stockholm decided to forbid Professor Sven Å Christianson from including his book *Inside the Mind of a Serial Killer* in the 'required reading' lists for his courses in Forensic Psychology. His publisher took the book out of print. However, Professor Christianson is still a member of the faculty at the university.

In March 2014, the Administrative Court in Stockholm decided that Sture Bergwall should no longer be held in compulsory psychiatric detention at the Säter clinic: instead, he could live in the community on condition that he provided a weekly urine sample to prove that he was drug free. He left Säter and moved to a village in northern Sweden, where he currently lives in a small flat near his older brother Sten-Ove. His conduct has been exemplary and, just over a year after his release, on 16 April 2015, the care order was withdrawn. Sture Bergwall became a free man, twenty-four years after his admission to psychiatric care. He is currently writing a book about his life.

Acknowledgements and Thanks

This book would not have been written had it not been for that call from Sten-Ove Bergwall. I am grateful that you trusted me to find the missing pieces of the jigsaw. My thanks also go to Kristoffer Lind at Lind & Co, who grasped at once what I wanted to do and gave me a publisher's agreement within an hour of having read the synopsis. Without a grant from Natur & Kultur and another one from the Swedish Authors' Fund it would have been difficult for me to put all other work aside and concentrate on this task.

Thanks to Peo Hansen for your important support when I started out on my research. Thanks to Jenny Küttim, the most skilful researcher I have ever met. Thanks to Johan Brånstad at Swedish Television, who only needed a brief chat on the phone to let me start working on the documentary *The Woman Behind Thomas Quick* in parallel with my writing. Thanks to Rickard L. Sjöberg who read the manuscript and gave me invaluable advice. Thanks to Tomas Lappalainen who offered his incontrovertible judgement, especially on the writerly approach in some of the sections. Thanks also to my Swedish editor Lena Kamhed for her encouragement and for being such a sensible guide. Thanks to the English translator Anna Paterson for handling this difficult material in such a brilliant way. Thanks to my English editor Ka Bradley at Portobello for her devoted work. Thanks to Sigrid Rausing for her swift decision to publish the book in English, after reading the Swedish manuscript of my then-unpublished book.

Thanks to my family who put up with me living in the strange world of the Quick team for more than two years.

The Strange Case of Thomas Quick is dedicated to the memory of Hannes Råstam.

Bibliography

(1992) '122 mördare går lösa i Sverige' ['122 Murderers go free in Sweden'], *Expressen*, 20 September, pp. 13–19.

(1993) 'Säterpatienten anses bunden till mord på 14-åring' ['Säter patient allegedly linked to murder of 14-year-old'], *Dala-Demokraten*, 11 November.

Application for retrial in criminal case B 179/94, 4 June 2012 (Concerning Charles Zelmanovits). Chief Prosecutor Bengt Landahl.

—— B 348/95, 20 April 2009 (Concerning Yenon Levi). Thomas Olsson.

—— B 100/97, 20 April 2010 (Concerning Therese Johannessen). Thomas Olsson.

—— B1548-99 11 April 2011 (Concerning Gry Storvik and Trine Jensen). Thomas Olsson.

—— B 187-93, 8 September 2011 (Concerning Johan Asplund). Thomas Olsson.

—— B 26/95, 18 June 2012 (Concerning the Appojaure murders). Chief Prosecutor Kristian Augustsson.

Arvidsson, L. (assumed name), letters to Sture Bergwall, 27 October 1992, 6 December 1992, 18 August 1993, 25 October 1993, 14 November 1993, 12 January 1994, 17 January 1994, 17 January 1994, 19 September 1994.

Arvidsson, L. (assumed name) (1994), 'Att vårda dömda våldsbrottslingar på regionvårdsenheten på Säters sjukhus' ['To treat criminals with convictions for violence in the regional secure unit at Säter Hospital']. A psychotherapeutic approach based on the British object relations theory; special study essay; supervisor: Hanna Olsson, Stockholm University, Psychology Dept., Spring 1994.

Aschberg, R. (1996), 'Falska fakta skadar utredningen' ['Falsifications damage the investigation'], *Aftonbladet*, 23 April, p. 17.

Aschberg, R. & Johansson, A. (2006), 'Quick ljög om morden' ['Quick lied about the murders'], *Aftonbladet*, 27 December, pp. 6–7.

Asplund, B. (1998), 'Åtala åklagaren i Quick-målet' ['Charge the Quick case prosecutor'], *Dagens Nyheter*, 17 May.

Barnett, J. (14 July 1971), letter to Margit Norell.

Bass, E. & Davis L. (1988), *The Courage to Heal: A Guide for Women Survivors of Child Sexual Abuse*, Cedar, London.

Bauer, P. J. (2006), 'Constructing a Past in Infancy: A Neuro-Developmental Account', *Trends in Cognitive Sciences*, 10(4): 175–81.

Belin, S. (1987), *Schizofrenibehandling: psykiatri på liv och död* [*Treatment of Schizophrenia: Life-or-Death Psychiatry*], Stockholm, Natur & Kultur.

Bergwall, S. (1995), *Min bror Thomas Quick: en berättelse om det ofattbara* [*My Brother Thomas Quick: An incredible story*], Stockholm, Rabén Prisma.

Bergwall, S. O. (2009), 'Kris inom rättspsykiatrin – fallet Thomas Quick' ['Crisis in forensic psychiatry – the case of Thomas Quick'], *Newsmill*, 10 December.

Bladh, A. K. (1994), 'Thomas Quick åtalas för mord' ['Thomas Quick prosecuted for murder'], *TT/Dala-Demokraten*, 24 August, p. 6.

Bladh, A. K. (1994), 'Sätermannen: barndomsupplevelserna gjorde mig till mördare' ['The Säter man: my childhood experiences made me a murderer'], *TT*, 2 September.

Bladh, A. K. (1994), 'Rättegången mot Quick är helt unik' ['Quick's trial is utterly unique'], *TT/Dala-Demokraten*, 2 November.

Bladh, A. K. (1996), 'Rättegången om Appojauremorden – en pojk-mördares berättelse' ['Appojaure court case – the boy killer's story'], *TT*, 9 January.

Bloom, S. L. (1994), 'Hearing the Survivor's Voice: Sundering the Wall of Denial', *Journal of Psychohistory*, 21: 461–77.

Borch-Jacobsen, M. (2009), *Making Minds and Madness: From Hysteria to Depression*, Cambridge, Cambridge University Press.

Borgström, C. (1998), 'Psykologerna kränker offrens anhöriga' ['The psychologists humiliate the victims' relatives'], *Dagens Nyheter*, 6 June, p. A4.

Borgström, C. (1998), 'En ovanligt otäck konspirationsteori' ['An exceptionally nasty conspiracy theory'], *Svenska Dagbladet*, 17 June, p. 18.

Borgström, C. (19 May 2000), 'Plädering i rättegången rörande mordet på Gry Storvik och Trine Jensen' ['Plea in the murder trial re G. Storvik and T. Jensen']. Transcribed at Säter from tape recording.

Bruce, D., Dolan, A. & Phillips-Grant, K. (2000), 'On the Transition from Childhood Amnesia to the Recall of Personal Memories', *Psychological Science*, 11(5), pp. 360–64.

Carlsson, M. (1999), 'Han får Quick att minnas morden' ['He makes Quick remember his murders'], *Expressen*, 19 August, p. 12.

Case notes for Sture Bergwall (21 April to 24 June 1966), Child and Adolescent Psychiatry Clinic in Falun.

—— (16 March 1970; under arrest), Forensic Psychiatry Clinic, Håga Hospital, Södertälje.

—— (18 March 1989), Outpatient Psychiatric Clinic, Falun.

—— (20 January 1973 to 9 November 2013), Säter Forensic Care Unit.

Ceci, S. J., Loftus, E. F., Leichtman, M. D. & Bruck, M. (1994), 'The Possible Role of Source Misattributions in the Creation of False Beliefs Among Pre-schoolers', *International Journal of Clinical and Experimental Hypnosis*, 42(4), pp. 304–20.

Christianson, S. Å. (3 October 1994), 'Allmänna minnesfunktioner hos Thomas Quick, 50 04 26 – XXXX' ['Expert statement concerning: the functioning of Thomas Quick's overall memory'], Case B 179/94, Piteå District Court.

Christianson, S. Å. (3 October 1994), 'Betingelser för Thomas Quicks 50 04 26 – XXXX utsaga psykologiskt avseende' ['Expert statement concerning: Psychological Conditions Affecting the Statement by Thomas Quick'], Case B 179/94, Piteå District Court.

Christianson, S. Å. (ed.) (1996), *Rättspsykologi: den forensiska psykologin i Sverige: en kunskapsöversikt* [*Forensic Psychology: An overview of forensic psychology in Sweden*], Natur & Kultur, Stockholm.

Christianson, S. Å. (2 January 1996), letter to judge Roland Åkne.

Christianson, S. Å. (2 January 1996), Betingelser för Thomas Quicks utsaga psykologiskt avseende [Expert statement: psychological evaluation of Thomas Quick's witness statements], Case B 26/95, Gällivare District Court.

Christianson, S. Å. (1997), Riktlinjer för vallning av Thomas Quick i

Norge den 11 juni i samband med utredningen av Therese Johannessens försvinnande 1988 [Guidelines for re-enactment site visit with Thomas Quick in Norway].

Christianson, S. Å. (2010), *I huvudet på en seriemördare* [*Inside the Mind of a Serial Killer*], Norstedts, Stockholm.

Christianson, S. Å. & Engelberg, E. (1997), 'Remembering and Forgetting Traumatic Events: A Matter of Survival'; in Martin A. Conway (ed.), *Recovered Memories and False Memories*, Oxford University Press, Oxford, pp. 231–50.

Christianson, S. Å. & Loftus, E. F. (1987), 'Memory for Traumatic Events', *Applied Cognitive Psychology*, 1: 225–39.

Christianson, S. Å., Loftus, E. F., Hoffman, H. & Loftus, G. R. (1991), 'Eye Fixation and Memory of Emotional Events', *Journal of Experimental Psychology: Learning, Memory, and Cognition*, 17: 693–701.

Christianson, S. Å. & Wentz, G. (1996), *Brott och minne: Berättelser om grova brott i känslo- och minnesperspektiv* [*Crimes and memory: Stories of violent crime from emotional and memory perspectives*], Natur & Kultur, Stockholm.

Cioffi, F. (1974), 'Was Freud a liar?', *Listener*, 91(7): 172–4.

Conti, R. (1999), 'The Psychology of False Confession', *Journal of Credibility Assessment and Witness Psychology*, 2(1): 14–36.

Cross, C. R. (2006), *Room Full of Mirrors: A Biography of Jimi Hendrix*, Hyperion Books, New York.

Cullberg, J. (2007), *Mitt psykiatriska liv* [*My Life in Psychiatry*], Natur & Kultur, Stockholm.

Curtius, M. (1996), 'Man won't be retried in repressed memory case', *Los Angeles Times*, 3 July (http://articles.latimes.com/1996-07-03/news/mn-20778_1_ memory-case).

Dåderman, A. (1999). 'Thomas Quick: "Xanor berättade och Rohypnol gestaltade, Stesolid grät, Somadril log, kodein smekte och heminevrin ..."' ['Thomas Quick: "Xanax told stories, Rohypnol acted out, Stesolid wept, Somdril smiled, Codeine caressed and Heminevrin ..."'], Lecture at conference for doctors in Stockholm (26 November).

Dåderman, A. (2009), Sakkunnigutlåtande rörande Sture Bergwall f.d.

Thomas Quick [Expert statement]; Bilaga 13 till Ansökan om resning i mål nr B 348/95 (Ang. Yenon Levi) [Appendix 13 to Application for retrial ... (concerning Yenon Levi)].

Dahlström-Lannes, M. (1996), 'Det finns bevisade fall av bortträngda minnen' ['There are proven cases of repressed memories'], Svenska Dagbladet, 8 February, p. 4.

Dahlström-Lannes, M. (25 August 2000), letter to Sture Bergwall.

Denke, E. (1997), 'Gåtan Lars-Inge Svartenbrandt' ['The enigma of Lars-Inge Svartenbrandt'], Nordisk kriminalkrönika [Annals of Nordic Crime].

Doctor's certificate by Dr Göran Fransson (1964:542), re-assessment as per 7 § of person convicted of crime, 23 January 1991.

Engman, T. (1996), 'Quick erkände dubbelmord' ['Quick confessed to double murder'], Dagens Nyheter, 10 January.

Ericsson, L. (2004), 'Jag blir så fruktansvärt förtjust i schizofrena' ['I'm so totally crazy about schizophrenics'], Ordfront, no. 4, pp. 20–27.

Ericsson, Bo (2012), Nedläggningsbeslut, Statsåklagare [Decision to close case by head of Prosecution Service], 24 September 2012.

Esterson, A. (1993), Seductive Mirage: An Exploration of the Work of Sigmund Freud (Open Court Publishing Co.).

Fallenius, A. & Lövkvist, N. (1996), '"Var är vår son?"' ['"Where is our son?"'], Expressen, 24 April, p. 8.

Ferm, L. (1994), Svartenbrandt (Sellin & Partner, Stockholm).

Fisher, R. P. & Geiselman, R. E. (1992), Memory-Enhancing Techniques for Investigative Interviewing: The Cognitive Interview, Charles C. Thomas, Springfield, Illinois.

Fisher, R. P. & Geiselman, R. E. (2010), 'The Cognitive Interview Method of Conducting Police Interviews: Eliciting Extensive Information and Promoting Therapeutic Jurisprudence', International Journal of Law and Psychiatry, 33(5): 321–8.

Flordh, C. & Notini, D. (1996), '"Jag såg behovet av ett alternative"' ['"I realised an alternative was needed"'], Interview with Margit Norell, Bulletin för Svenska föreningen för holistisk psykoterapi och psykoanalys, 47: 3–18.

Forensic psychiatric assessment by Dr Otto Brundin, 16 March 1970.

—— Dr Yngve Holmstedt, 8 May 1970.

—— Dr Marianne Kristiansson, 30 January 1991.

Fransson, G. (1994), 'Inkompetens bakom rymning. Sätermannen Thomas Quicks förre läkare Göran Fransson dömer ut sjukhusledningens agerande' ['Incompetence leads to escape. Göran Fransson, former doctor responsible for the Säterman Thomas Quick, condemns the actions of the hospital board'], *Dagens Nyheter*, 17 July.

Freud, S. (1896), 'The Aetiology of Hysteria'; in Freud, S. (1962; 2001), *The Standard Edition of the Complete Psychological Works of Sigmund Freud*, vol. 3 (1893–1899), Hogarth Press, London. Cf. also Vintage re-issue of the Standard Edition.

Freud, S. (1899), 'The Interpretation of Dreams', *The Standard Edition of the Complete Psychological Works of Sigmund Freud*, vol. 4, Hogarth Press/Vintage Classics, London 2001.

Freud, S. (1910). 'Two Case Histories (Little Hans and the Rat Man)'; in *The Standard Edition of the Complete Psychological works of Sigmund Freud*, vol. 10 (1910), Vintage Classics, London, 2001.

Freud, S. (1917–19), 'An Infantile Neurosis and Other Works (incl. The Wolfman)'; in *The Standard Edition of the Complete Psychological works of Sigmund Freud*, vol. 17 (1917–1919), Vintage Classics, London, 2001.

Freud, S. (1925), *An Autobiographical Study*, Hogarth Press, London.

Freud, S. (1933), 'Femininity'; in *The Standard Edition of the Complete Psychological works of Sigmund Freud*, vol. 22 (1932–1936). Early psycho-analytic publications. New introductory lectures on psycho-analysis and other works. Vintage Classics, London, 2001, pp. 112–35.

Freud, S. (1985), *The Complete Letters of Sigmund Freud to Wilhelm Fliess 1887–1904*, Belknap Press of Harvard University, Cambridge, Mass.

Fromm, E. (1964), *The Heart of Man: Its Genius for Good and Evil*, Harper & Row, New York.

Fromm, E. (9 May 1970), letter to Margit Norell.

Fromm, E. (1994), *The Art of Listening*, Constable, London.

Fromm-Reichmann, F. & Bullard, D. M. (1959), *Psychoanalysis and psychotherapy: Selected Papers*, University of Chicago Press, Chicago.

Garry, M. & Hayne, H. (2006), *Do Justice and Let the Sky Fall: Elizabeth F. Loftus and Her Contributions to Science, Law, and Academic Freedom*, Lawrence Erlbaum, Mahwah, N J.

Garry, M., Manning, C. G., Loftus, E. F. & Sherman, S. J. (1996), 'Imagination inflation: Imagining a Childhood Event Inflates Confidence that it Occurred', *Psychonomic Bulletin and Review*, 3(2): 208–14.

Gudjonsson, G. H. (1999), 'The Making of a Serial False Confessor: The Confessions of Henry Lee Lucas', *The Journal of Forensic Psychiatry*, vol. 10 (2): 416–26.

Haggbloom, S. J., Warnick, R., Warnick, J. E., Jones, V. K., Yarbrough, G. L., Russell, T. M. & Monte, E. (2002), 'The 100 Most Eminent Psychologists of the 20th Century', *Review of General Psychology*, 6(2): 139–52.

Hart-Davis, D. (2010), *Philip de Laszlo: His Life and Art*, Yale University Press, New Haven.

Heaps, C. & Nash, M. (1999), 'Individual Differences in Imagination Inflation', *Psychonomic Bulletin and Review*, 6(2): 313–18.

Heaps, C. M. & Nash, M. (2001), 'Comparing Recollective Experience in True and False Autobiographical Memories', *Journal of Experimental Psychology: Learning, Memory, and Cognition*, 27: 920–30.

Höglund, J. (1996), 'Quick kan åtalas igen: åklagaren utreder över tio mordfall' ['Quick likely to be charged again: prosecutor investigates ten murder cases'], *Göteborgs Posten*, 25 March, p. 6.

Höglund, R. (1998), *Svenska Dagbladet*, 17 June.

Höjer, B. (2004), *Att hela skottsår: Studiehemmet i Kramfors 1932–72: Axel Erdmann och hans medarbetare berättar* [*Healing Gunshot Wounds: The educational institute in Kramfors 1932-72*], Saltsjö-Boo, Kronstrand & Nilsson.

Höjer, B. (2005), 'Att jämna ut motsättningarna: Ådalen 1931 och studiehemmet i Kramfors' ['Easing Conflicts: Ådalen 1931 and the educational institute in Kramfors']; in *Folkbildning – samtidig eller tidlös?: om innebörder över tid* [*Education for All – timeless or of the present? About meaning and time*], Linköping, Mimer, Institutionen för beteendevetenskap, Linköpings universitet, pp. 35–56.

Holgersson, A. (1998), 'Fallet Quick – nederlag för rättsväsendet' ['The Quick case – a defeat of Swedish justice'], *Svenska Dagbladet*, 12 June.

Holmes, D. (1990), 'The Evidence for Repression: An Examination of Sixty Years of Research'; in J. Singer (ed.), *Repression and Dissociation: Implications for Personality, Theory, Psychopathology and Health*, University of Chicago Press, Chicago, pp. 85–102.

Horney Eckardt, M. (2 April 1974), letter to Margit Norell.

Hornstein, G. A. (1992), 'The Return of the Repressed: Psychology's Problematic Relations with Psychoanalysis, 1909–1960', *American Psychologist*, 47(2): 254.

Hyman Jr, I. E. & Loftus, E. F. (1998), 'Errors in Autobiographical Memory', *Clinical Psychology Review*, 18(8): 933–47.

Hyman Jr, I. E. & Pentland, J. (1996), 'The Role of Mental Imagery in the Creation of False Childhood Memories', *Journal of Memory and Language*, 35(2): 101–17.

Hyman, I. E., Husband, T. H. & Billings, F. J. (1995), 'False Memories of Childhood Experiences', *Applied Cognitive Psychology*, 9(3): 181–97.

Interview with Jan Olsson, 3 July 2009.

Israëls, H. & Schatzman, M. (1993), 'The Seduction Theory'; in *History of Psychiatry*, 4: 23–59.

Janov, A. (1970), *The Primal Scream: Primal Therapy: The Cure for Neurosis*, Dell, New York.

Johansson, P. M. (1999, a & b), *Freuds psykoanalys: Utgångspunkter and Arvtagare i Sverige* [*Freud's Psychoanalysis: Origins and descendants in Sweden*], vols. 1 & 2, Daidalos, Göteborg.

Johansson, P. M. (2006), 'Invited Commentary on the Interview with Jan Stensson', *International Forum of Psychoanalysis*, vol. 15 (1): 13–16.

Johansson, P. M. (2008), *Freuds psykoanalys: Arvtagare i Sverige del 2* [*Freud's Psychoanalysis: Origins and Descendants in Sweden*], vol. 3, Daidalos, Göteborg.

Jonsson, E. (1986), *Tokfursten* [*King of Fools*], Rabén & Sjögren, Stockholm.

Kall, E. (8 June 2010), Yttrande till Kammarrätten [Witness statement to Civil Court of Appeal].

Källberg, G. (3 March 1994), Minnesanteckningar från konflikten på Säter [Personal notes about the conflict at Säter], 18 October 1993 to 3 March 1993.

Kassin, S. M. & Wrightsman, L. S. (1985), 'Confession Evidence'; in Kassin, S. M. & Wrightsman, L. S., *The Psychology of Evidence and Trial Procedure*, Sage Publications, Beverly Hills, California, pp. 67–94

Kendall-Tackett, K. A., Williams, L. M. & Finkelhorn, D. (1993), 'Impact of Sexual Abuse on Children: A Review and Synthesis of Recent Empirical Studies', *Psychological Bulletin*, 113(1): 164–88.

Kihlstrom, J. F. (1995), 'The Trauma-Memory Argument', *Consciousness and Cognition*, 4(1): 63–7.

Kihlstrom, J. F. (2006), 'Trauma and Memory Revisited', *Memory and Emotions: Interdisciplinary Perspectives*, pp. 259–93.

Knapp, G. P. (1989), *The Art of Living: Erich Fromm's Life and Works*, P. Lang, New York.

Lagercrantz, D. (1990), 'Svartenbrandt skulle benådas – Leif G. W. Persson stoppade beslutet' ['Svartenbrandt about to be freed – Leif G. W. Persson stopped the process'], *Expressen*, 30 March.

Lagercrantz, D. (1994), '"Jag känner mig kluven inför mina patienter"' ['"I feel split when facing my patients"'], *Aftonbladet Söndag*, 9 August, pp. 4–9.

Lambertz, G. (3 December 2006), 'Därför ändrade jag mig om Thomas Quicks skuld' ['Why I changed my mind about Thomas Quick's guilt'], *Dagens Nyheter*, 3 December, p. A4.

Larsson, D. (1998), *Mytomanen Thomas Quick: en documentation* [*The Mythomaniac Thomas Quick: documentation*], 1st ed., self-published, D. Larsson, Luleå.

Larsson, D. (1998), 'Quick har duperat rättsväsendet' ['Quick has duped justice'], *Dagens Nyheter*, 4 May, p. A4.

Larsson, D. (2009), '25 år sedan morden i Appojaure' ['25 years since the murders in Appojaure'], *Norrländska Socialdemokraten*, 22 June.

Lilienfeld, S. O., Lynn, S. J. & Lohr, J. M. (2003), *Science and Pseudoscience in Clinical Psychology*, Guilford Press, New York.

Lilja, M. (1996), 'Quicks hem rivs i jakt på bevis' ['Quick's home demolished in search for evidence'], *Expressen*, 22 April, p. 6.

Liljeström, G., Lindholm, C. & Ståhle, B. (2005), 'In Memoriam, Margit Norell', *Svenska Dagbladet*, 7 March, p. 49.

Lindeberg, P. (1999), *Döden är en man: Historien om obducenten och allmänläkaren* [*Death is a Man: The Story About the Pathologist and the Generalist*], Fischer, Stockholm.

Lindholm, C. (27 June 2001), letter to Sture Bergwall.

Lindholm, T., Sjöberg, R. L., Pedroletti, C., Boman, A., Olsson, G. L., Sund, A. & Lindblad, F. (2009), 'Infants' and Toddlers' Remembering and Forgetting of a Stressful Medical Procedure', *Journal of Pediatric Psychology*, 34(2): 205–16.

Lindsay, D. S. & Read, J. D. (1994), 'Psychotherapy and Memories of Childhood Sexual Abuse: A Cognitive Perspective', *Applied Cognitive Psychology*, 8(4): 281–338.

Loftus, E. F. (1993), 'The Reality of Repressed Memories', *American Psychologist*, 48: 518–37.

Loftus, E. F. (1997), 'Repressed Memory Accusations: Devastated Families and Devastated Patients', *Applied Cognitive Psychology*, 11(1): 25–30.

Loftus, E. F. (2003), 'Make-Believe Memories', *American Psychologist*, 58: 864–73.

Loftus, E. F. & Ketcham, K. (1994), *The Myth of Repressed Memory: False Memories and Allegations of Sexual Abuse*, 1st ed., St Martin's Press, New York.

Loftus, E. F. & Palmer, J. C. (1974), 'Reconstruction of Automobile Destruction', *Journal of Verbal Learning and Verbal Behavior*, 13: 585–9.

Loftus, E. F. & Pickrell, J. E. (1995), 'The Formation of False Memories', *Psychiatric Annals*, 25: 720–25.

Lynn, S. J., Lock, T., Loftus, E. F., Krackow, E. & Lilienfeld, S. O. (2003), 'The Remembrance of Things Past: Problematic Memory Recovery Techniques in Psychotherapy'; in S. O. Lilienfeld, S. J. Lynn & J. M. Lohr (eds.), *Science and Pseudoscience in Clinical Psychology*, Guilford Press, New York, pp. 205–39.

Mangs, K. & Martell, B. (1983), '0–20 år i psykoanalytiskt perspektiv' ['0 to 20 years from a psychoanalytical perspective'], 3rd ed., revised, Lund, Studentlitteratur.

Masson, J. M. (1984), *The Assault on Truth: Freud's Suppression of the Seduction Theory*, Farrar, Straus & Giroux.

Mattisson, S. & Fröberg, P. (1994), 'Sätermannen och hans offer' ['The Säterman and his victims'], *IDag*, 31 October, p. 13.

Mazzoni, G. A. L., Loftus, E. F. & Kirsch, I. (2001), 'Changing Beliefs About Implausible Autobiographical Events: A Little Plausibility Goes a Long Way', *Journal of Experimental Psychology: Applied*, 7: 51–9.

McNally, R. J. (2003), *Remembering Trauma*, Belknap Press at Harvard University Press, Cambridge Mass.

McNally, R. J. (2005), 'Debunking Myths About Trauma and Memory', *The Canadian Journal of Psychiatry/La Revue canadienne de psychiatrie*, 50 (13).

McNally, R. J., Lasko, N. B., Clancy, S. A., Macklin, M. L., Pitman, R. K. & Orr, S. P. (2004), 'Psychophysiological Responding During Script-Driven Imagery in People Reporting Abduction by Space Aliens', *Psychological Science*, 15: 493–7.

Michanek, B. (1990), '"Jag var som en far för honom"' ['"I was like a father for him"'], *Aftonbladet*, 24 March, p. 11.

Michanek, B. (1992), '"Hur kunde ni släppa ut honom?"' ['"How could you let him loose?"'], *Aftonbladet*, 27 June, p. 10.

Miller, A. (1981), *The Drama of the Gifted Child and the Search for the True Self*, Basic Books, New York.

Miller, A. (1983), *For Your Own Good: Hidden Cruelty in Child-Rearing and the Roots of Violence*, Farrar Straus Giroux, New York.

Minutes of Margit's group meetings, 27 October 1984; 6 April 1991; 28 September 1996.

Molin, K. (1990), 'Våldet skyddar mot den stora rädslan' ['Violence serves as protection against dread'], *Dagens Nyheter*, 8 February.

Nässén, T. (9 December 2002), letters to Seppo Penttinen and Jan Karlsson.

Nilsson, P. (1994), '"Jag bluffade alla på Säter"' ['"I bluffed everyone at Säter"'], *Expressen*, 24 April, pp. 6–7.

Nordin, A. (1999), 'Fromm i våra hjärtan' ['Fromm in our hearts'], *Psykologtidningen*, 1: 4–8.

Nordin, S. (2012), *Filosoferna det västerländska tänkandet sedan år 1900* [*The Philosophers: Western Thought Since 1900*]: [Nietzsche – Freud – Bergson . . .], Stockholm, Atlantis.

Norell, M. (1968), 'Några personliga anteckningar om min egen utveckling och den holistiska föreningens tillblivelse' ['Some personal reflections on my development and the origins of the Holistic Society'], *Bulletin för Svenska föreningen för holistisk psykoterapi och psykoanalys*, 1.

Norell, M., letters to Joseph Barnett, 3 March 1971.

Norell, M., letters to Erich Fromm; 30 December 1970; 19 January 1971; 16 February 1971; 14 April 1971; 23 October 1971; 23 October 1971; 21 November 1971; 18 November 1972; 19 December 1972; 19 December 1976.

Norell, M., letters to David Schecter, 6 March 1975; 22 November 1975; 10 January 1976; 15 February 1976; 26 March 1976; 21 May 1976; 20 November 1976; 13 February 1977; 1 May 1977; 7 May 1977; 22 May 1977; 12 October 1977; 20 November 1977; 8 April 1978; 28 August 1978; 4 April 1980.

Norell, M., letter to Jorge Silva, 14 November 1989.

Norell, M., letters to Otto Allen Will, 23 May 1968; 20 September 1969; 26 April 1970.

Norell, M. (1977), 'Orts syn på förändring och möjlig utveckling' ['A local view of change and possible development']. Svenska föreningen för holistisk psykoterapi och psykonalys [Lecture to The Swedish Society for Holistic Psychiotherapy and Psychoanalysis], 26 March 1977.

Norell, M. (1989), 'Tidig incest: Erfarenheter av den terapeutiska processen med incest-patienter' ['Early Incest: Experiences of the therapeutic process for patients subjected to incestuous abuse'], unpublished article.

Norell, M., 'The World of Thomas Quick', unpublished manuscript.

Norell, M., Nyman, M. & Sandin, B. (1975), 'Samtalsterapi med schizofrena patienter vid Säters sjukhus' ['Talking therapy for schizophrenic patients at Säter hospital'], *Läkartidningen*, 33: 3066–8.

Olsson, H. (1990), *Catrine och rättvisan* [*Catrine and Justice*], Carlsson, Stockholm.

Ohlson, L (1990), 'Inte klokt att släppa ut honom i frihet' ['Insane to let him out'], *Aftonbladet*, 22 March, p. 8.

Penttinen, S. (2004), 'Förhörsledarens syn på Gåtan Thomas Quick' ['The senior investigating officer's views on the Thomas Quick enigma'], *Nordisk kriminalkrönika* [*Annals of Nordic Crime*], pp. 427–36.

Penttinen, S. (No date), 'Några synpunkter kring resningsansökan beträffande Appojauremorden' ['Views on the application for retrial of the Appojaure murders'].

Persson, K. (10 May 1995), letter to Sture Bergwall.

Piper, A. (1994), 'Multiple Personality Disorder', *The British Journal of Psychiatry*, 164(5): 600–12. Doi:10.1192/bjp.164.5.600

Police interview with Örjan Bergwall, 18 February 1999.

Police interviews with Sture Bergwall 1 March 1993; 17 March 1993; 18 March 1993; 21 April 1993; 25 May 1993*; 28 May 1993; 27 September 1993; 26 January 1994; 14 April 1994; 14 April 1994; 19 April 1994; 14 June 1994; 12 December 1994; 17 January 1995; 9 February 1995; 9 February 1995; 10 April 1995; 23 February 1996; 4 July 1997; 2 September 1998; 10 February 1999; 22 March 1999; 6 October 1999 (1); 6 October 1999 (2); 9 September 2000; 10 September 2000; 18 October 2000.

Police interview with Sven Å Christianson, 26 November 2010.

Police interview with Göran Källberg, 13 July 2009.

Police interview with Kristina (not her true name), 27 February 1995.

Police interview with Jan Olsson, 3 July 2009.

Police interviews with Patrik (not his true name), 22 February 1995; 22 May 1996; 20 November 1996.

Police interviews with Kjell Persson, 1 March 1993; 15 April 1994; 19 December 2000 (as Kjell Långbergs); 9 May 2001 (as Kjell Långbergs).

Police interview with Birgitta Ståhle, 25 May 2009.

Police interview with Maria Sykijäinen, 20 February 1995.

*Wrongly dated 25 April 1993, but correct date must be 25 May 1993 as the Ryggen re-enactment being planned for the following day took place on 26 May 1993.

Police reports, see 'Reports' below

Pope H. G. Jr. & Hudson J. I. (1995), 'Can Memories of Childhood Sexual Abuse be Repressed?', *Psychological Medicine*, 25: 121–6.

Porter, S., Yuille, J. C. & Lehman, D. R. (1999), 'The Nature of Real, Implanted, and Fabricated Memories for Emotional Childhood Events', *Law and Human Behavior*, 23(5): 517–37.

Quick, T. (1994), 'Jag rymde för att dö' ['I ran away to die'], *Dagens Nyheter*, 12 July, p. A4.

Quick, T. (1995), 'Jag kan bli frisk' ['I can get well'], *Dagens Nyheter*, 4 January, p. A4.

Quick, T. (23 October 1995), letter from 'Ellington'.

Quick, T. (18 July 1996), letter to Detective Inspector Stellan Söderman.

Quick, T. (31 May 1997), letter to Seppo Penttinen.

Quick, T. (1998), *Kvarblivelse* [*What Remains*], Stockholm, Kaos Press.

Quick, T. (1999), 'Om frihet – om pressens bemötande av *Kvarblivelse*' ['On freedom – how the press responded to *What remains*'], Flashback News agency, 19, 25 May.

Quick, T. (9 June 2001), diary note.

Quick, T. (12 June 2001), diary note.

Quick, T. (2001), 'Thomas Quick efter mytomanbeskyllningar: "Jag slutar delta i polisutredningar"' ['Thomas Quick and the accusations of mythomania: "I won't participate in the police investigations"'], *Dagens Nyheter*, 15 November 2001.

Quick, T. (probably autumn 2001), Testament (written by hand).

Råstam, H. (2013), *Fallet Thomas Quick: att skapa en seriemördares*, Swedish edition, Stockholm, Ordfront, 2012. English trans. by Henning Koch, *Thomas Quick: The Making of a Serial Killer*, Canongate Books, Edinburgh.

Reading list (22 March 1985), Förteckning över litteratur som Margitgruppen studerade från hösten 1980 till hösten 1984 [Literature recommended to the 'Margit group', autumn 1980–autumn 1984], signed by Margit Norell.

Record of reconstruction, Appojaure crime site, 10 July 1995.

Referral (24 June 1969) of Sture Bergwall, to the Adult Psychiatric Service in Falun.

Report by Bjerknes, O. T. & Grøttland, H. (11 June 1997), Rapport omkring Thomas Quick sin befaring i Örjeskogen onsdag [On TQ re-enactment in Örje forest, 11 June 1997].

Report (July 1984) of first police investigation of Appojaure murders.

Reports by Penttinen, S. (26 May 1993), Promemoria upprättad i samband med vallning av: Quick, Thomas Ragnar [On the re-enactment with TQ].

—— (17 September 1993), Promemoria upprättad med anledning av telefonsamtal 17 September 1993 med chefsöverläkare Kjell Persson, Säters sjukhus [On telephone conversation with Dr Kjell Persson].

—— (25 May 1994), Promemoria upprättad i samband med vallning av Quick, Thomas Ragnar (Sture) f. 500426-XXXX [On re-enactment with TQ].

—— (21 November 1994), Promemoria upprättad i samband med besök hos Thomas Quick på Säters sjukhus avd 36, 16 November 1994 [On visit to TQ in hospital ward 36].

—— (23 November 1994), Promemoria upprättad med anledning av förhörsuppgifter som lämnats av Quick, när han upplysningsvis hörts om morden i Appojaure 1984 [On TQ's statements in interview re the Appojaure murders].

—— (19 September 1995), Promemoria upprättad efter telefonsamtal med Quick, Thomas Ragnar 500426-XXXX [On telephone conversation with TQ].

—— (22 March 1996), Redovisning över förhörsuppgifter angående det som Quick, Thomas Ragnar, 500426-XXXX, berättar om mord i Norge [On TQ's statements in interview re the Norway murders].

—— (11 June 1996), Promemoria [Report].

—— (2 June 1997), Upprättad efter företagen vallning med Quick, Thomas Ragnar, 500426-XXXX [On re-enactment with TQ].

—— (8 June 1998), Promemoria upprättad efter vallning med Quick, Thomas Ragnar, 500426-XXXX. Vallningen ägde rum måndagen den 8:e juni 1998 [On re-enactment with TQ].

—— (27 September 2000), On investigation at Främby udde, 27 September 2000.

—— (17 October 2000), Promemoria [Report].

—— (4 June 2000), Promemoria uppprättad i samband med vallning av Quick, Thomas Ragnar (Sture) 500426-XXXX [On re-enactment with TQ].

—— (From 11 March 1993 to 16 August 1999), Områden som varit föremål för vallningar med Quick, Thomas Ragnar, 500426-XXXX. Samt vidtagna tekniska undersökningar/ undersökningsresultat [Crime re-enactment sites with Quick, T .R. 500426-XXXX, also technical findings].

Report of police investigation of sites north of Sundsvall (18 September 2000).

Report by Wendt, K-Å (24 April 2012), PM angående under granskningen anträffade förhör [Report on interrogations during on-going investigations] Bilaga 15 till chefsåklagare Bengt Landahls resningsansökan rörande mordet på Charles Zelmanovitz [Appendix (15) to retrial application in the case of the murder of C Zelmanovits].

Report by Wikström, A. (18 December 1996), Kort summering tidsplanering / våren 1997 [Brief summary of schedule / spring 1997].

—— (11 June 1997 a), PM avseende vallning den 11 juni 1997/ärende Therese Johannesen, Drammen [On the re-enactment on 11 June 1997 in Drammen / re Therese Johannesen].

—— (11 June 1997 b), Synpunkter / uppfattningar avseende vallning den 11 juni 1997 [Points of view/ perceptions with regard to the re-enactment on 11 June 1997].

Report on the technical investigations [tekniska undersökningar], 1993–1999.

Rycroft, R. (1995), *Critical Dictionary of Psychoanalysis*, Penguin, London.

Sandin, B. (1986), *Den zebrarandiga pudelkärnan* [*The Zebra-Striped Poodle's Core*], Rabén & Sjögren, Stockholm.

Sandler, M. (1971), *Från Lillgården till Arvfurstens palats* [*From Lillgården to Arvfursten's Palace*], Rabén & Sjögren, Stockholm.

Sanner, E. (16 March 1966), Brev till barn- och ungedomspsykiatrin i Falun ang. Sture Bergwalls homosexualitet [Letter to Child- and Adolescent Psychiatry Service in Falun Concerning Sture Bergwall's homosexuality].

Schecter, D., letters to Margit Norell, 22 February 1976; 5 August 1976; 20 November 1976; 15 May 1977; 8 November 1977; 13 April 1980; 10 July 1980.

Schimek, J. G. (1987), 'Fact and Fantasy in the Seduction Theory: A Historical Review', *Journal of the American Psychoanalytic Association*, 35(4): 937–65.

Sentence in criminal case (Dom i brottsmål) B100-97. Re: The murder of Therese Johannessen. Hedemora Tingsrätt.

—— B788-90. Re: Aggravated robbery, 17 April 1991.

—— B1116-91. Re: The acquittal of arson with intent to kill, 14 June 1991.

—— B179-94. Re: The murder of Charles Zelmanovits, 16 November 1994, Piteå District Court.

—— B3348-97. Re: The murder of Yenon Levi, 28 May 1997, Hedemora District Court.

—— B1548-99. Re: The murders of Gry Storvik and Trine Jensen, 22 June 2000, Falun District Court.

—— B187-93. Re: The murder of Johan Asplund, 21 June 2001, Sundsvall District Court.

—— B26-95. Re: The Appojaure murders, Gällivare District Court.

Sjöberg, R. L. (23 March 2010), Assessment in Connection with the Application for Retrial in the Case of the Murders of Gry Storvik and Trine Jensen.

Sjöberg. Rickard L. (23 March. 2010), Report on Test Evaluation, as an Appendix to Application for Retrial Case B1548-99 (Re. Gry Storvik and Trine Jensen) by Thomas Olsson, solicitor, 11 April 2011.

Sjöberg, R. L. & Lindholm, T. (2009), 'Children's Autobiographical Reports About Sexual Abuse: A Narrative Review of the Research Literature', *Nordic Journal of Psychiatry*, 63(6): 435–42.

Sjögren, L. (1989), *Sigmund Freud: Mannen och verket* [*Sigmund Freud: The Man and His Work*], Natur & Kultur, Stockholm.

Social Services Board, Doc. no. 114:5772-94. Decision in the case of Thomas Quick. Investigation carried out after Sture Bergwall's escape attempt, July 1994.

Social Services Department (1980–9). Prostitutionen i Sverige, del 1. En rapport utarbetad inom prostitutionsutredningen [Prostitution in Sweden, Part 1: A report agreed within the commission on prostitution], Sou 1977:01.

Social Services Investigation (1 March 1991). Carried out by Anita Sterky, social worker. Appendix to Forensic Psychiatric Assessment, 25 March 1991.

Spanos N. P. (1994), 'Multiple Identity Enactments and Multiple Personality Disorder: A Socio-Cognitive Perspective', *Psychological Bulletin*, 116(1): 143–65.

Spanos, N. P., Menary, E., Gabora, N. J., DuBruil, S. C. & Dewhirst, B. (1991), 'Secondary Identity Enactments During Hypnotic Past-Life Regression: A Socio-Cognitive Perspective', *Journal of Personality and Social Psychology*, 61: 308–20.

Ståhle, B. (3 March 1995), 'Handskriven minnesanteckning vid samtal med "Ellington"' ['Notes written by hand from talk with "Ellington"'].

Ståhle, B. (2 June 1997), Notes from talk with Thomas Quick during therapy.

Ståhle, B. (13 November 1998), Handskriven anteckning om likdelar gjord vid vallning på Främby udde [Notes written by hand from re-enactment re body parts].

Ståhle, B. (1999), 'Traumatiska erfarenheter och våldsbrott' ['Traumatic experiences and crimes of violence']; in Andersson, B. (ed.), *Ett rum att leva i: om djupgående psykoterapeutiska processer och objektrelationsteori* [*A Room to Live In: About psychotherapeutic processes that explore in depth and object relations theory*], Carlsson, Stockholm, pp. 287–303.

Ståhle, B. (18 May 2000), 'Vittnesmål i rättegången rörande mordet på Gry Storvik och Trine Jensen' ['Witness statement in the trial of the murders of Gry Storvik and Trine Jensen']; transcribed at Säter from tape recording.

Ståhle, B. (18 August 2003), letter to Seppo Penttinen/ Jan Karlsson, Police Authority, Västernorrland County.

Ståhle, B. (2009), Sture Bergwall, 19500426-XXXX, Doc. no. 7635/2009, Submission to Social Services Board.

Stanovich, K. E., (ed.) (2010), *How to Think Straight About Psychology*, 9th ed., Pearson, Boston.

Steinvall, A. (1992),'Djävulen står till svars' ['The Devil stands trial'], *Dagens Nyheter*, 16 April 1992.

Stigson, G. J., Articles in *Dala-Demokraten*:

—— (1993), 'Falunbon har pekat ut var Johan är begravd' ['Man from Falun indicates where Johan is buried'], 3 October, p. 6.

—— (1994), 'Övergrepp i barndomen har gjort mig till mördare' ['Childhood abuse turned me into a murderer'], 3 September.

—— (1994), 'Domen mot Quick blir del i ny beviskedja' ['The verdict in the Quick case now part of new chain of evidence'], 17 November.

—— (1997), 'Quicks offer samlade i gömställe nära Falun?' ['Quick's victims kept in hiding place near Falun'], 16 September, p. 6.

—— (1998), 'Sökandet slår record' ['Record search efforts'], 16 September, p. 13.

—— (2000), 'En tragedi om inte domen blir fällande?' ['A tragedy if no guilty verdict?'], 31 May.

—— (2000), 'Även om Quick skulle neka skulle han fällas!' ['Quick must be deemed guilty even if he denies it!'], 31 May, p. 9.

—— (2001), 'Nya sök efter Johan på Runns torra botten' ['New searches for Johan on the dry bottom of Runn'], 3 May, p. 15.

—— (2001), 'Han har väntat i åtta år' ['He has waited for eight years'], 25 June, p. 16.

—— (2001), 'Nya samtal med Quick efter nyår' ['New interviews with Quick in the New Year'], 18 December, p. 19.

—— (2009), 'Säteröverläkare avslöjar: "Jag ville få överprövning"' ['Säter consultant reveals: "I wanted a retrial"'], 17 June.

Strange, D., Clifasefi, S. & Garry, M. (2007), 'False Memories'; in Garry & Hayne (ed.), *Do Justice and Let the Sky Fall: Elizabeth F. Loftus and Her Contributions to Science, Law and Academic Freedom*, Erlbaum, New Jersey.

Swedish Radio (1973), Interview with Margit Norell, *Familjespegeln* [*Reflecting families*], 7 April.

Swedish Radio (2007), *Sommar* [*Summer*], hosted by Göran Lambertz, 28 July.

Swedish Television (1993), *Rapport* [*Report*], 9 March.

Swedish Television (1993), interview with Christer van der Kwast, 28 May.

Swedish Television (1993), press conference with Christer van der Kwast, 28 November.

Swedish Television (2008), TV4 *Nyhetsmorgon* [*Morning News*], Göran Lambertz and Björn Asplund on the sofa, 22 December.

Swedish Television (2012), *Agenda*, interview with Dr Susanne Nyberg, 26 August.

Tagesson, P., articles in *Expressen*:

—— (1994), 'Han talar sanning om pojkmorden' ['He is telling the truth about the murders of the boys'], 17 June, p. 14.

—— (1994), '"Jag är en ond man": Pojkmördaren Thomas Quick berättar' ['"I am evil": The boy killer Thomas Quick speaks freely'], 2 September, p. 6.

—— (1994), '"Hur kan en männniska vara så grym?"' ['"How can a human being be so cruel?"', 2 November (a), p. 8.

—— (1994), 'Han var inte ensam om dåden' ['He was not alone when carrying out these acts'], 2 November (b), p. 8.

—— (1998), 'Tio andra mord kan klaras upp' ['Ten more murders might be solved'], 16 December, p. 23.

Thompson, C. (1957), 'The Different Schools of Psychoanalysis', *The American Journal of Nursing*, 57 (10): 1304–7.

Tudor-Sandahl, P. (1983), *Om barnet inom oss* [*About the Child Inside Us*], Liber, Stockholm.

Tudor-Sandahl, P. (1991), Video interview with Margit Norell, 5 October.

Usher, J. A. & Neisser, U. (1993), 'Childhood Amnesia and the Beginnings of Memory for Four Early Life Events', *Journal of Experimental Psychology*: General, 122(2): 155–65.

Verdict, 11 December 1995, Christer van der Kwast closes investigation of Johnny Farebrink.

Verdict, 28 November 2006, Doc. no 7449-06-21.

Verdict, 16 February 2009, Doc. no. ÅM 2008/7371. Riksåklagarens beslut rörande ifrågasatt tjänstefel av åklagare och polis vid utredningar och rättegångar mot Thomas Quick m.m [Concerning professional misconduct by prosecutor and investigating police officer in investigations and trials re the Thomas Quick case etc].

Vinterhed, K. (1995), 'Jag minns för mordoffrens skull' ['I remember for the sakes of the murder victims'], *Dagens Nyheter*, 19 April, p. A6.

Vinterhed, K. & Lönnebo, M. (2000), *Jesusboken: personliga Kristusbilder av bland andra Ronny Ambjörnsson* ... [*The Jesus Book: personal understandings of Christ by* ...], Cordia, Göteborg.

Wagenaar, W. A. & Groeneweg, J. (1990), 'The Memory of Concentration Camp Survivors', *Applied Cognitive Psychology*, 4(2): 77–87.

Weigl, K. (1994), 'Idag möter han sin brors mördare' ['He will meet his brother's killer today'], *Aftonbladet*, 1 November.

Weigl, K. (1994), 'Detta är bortom all förståelse' ['It is beyond all understanding'], *Aftonbladet*, 2 November, p. 10.

Wiklund, N. (1998), 'Utred felkällorna i fallet Quick' ['Investigate the sources of error in the Quick case'], *Dagens Nyheter*, 8 May, p. A4.

Wiklund, N. (1998), 'Advokaten vilseleder om bevisen mot Quick' ['The lawyer distorts the evidence against Quick'], *Dagens Nyheter*, 9 June, p. A4.

Will, O. A., 13 May 1968, letter to Margit Norell.

Sture Bergwall at Säter (July 2000).

Margit Norell in her consultation room on Norrtull Street in Stockholm (1996).
PHOTO: TOMAS SÖDERGREN

Senior Investigating Officer Seppo Penttinen, Sture Bergwall, Sture's lawyer Claes Borgström and his therapist, the psychologist Birgitta Ståhle, photographed during a site visit in Drammen, Norway (April 1996).

SÄTERS SJUKHUS
Box 350, 783 27 SÄTER
Tel 0225-560 00
Tjänsteställe (klinik el motsv)

Rättspsykiatriska regionvårdsenheten

Spec anm, överkänslighet

A 3 b

Journalblad		Blad
Personnr	50 04 26 - 7190	90
Namn	Quick Thomas	
Adress		
Tfn		

Journaltext

Datum resp Sökord	Avd/mott, Läkare resp Löptext
95-09-12	Skötare Mikael Lindgren/cm

Fortsatt övervak, uttalad s-risk. Sedan måndagen den 4/9 har Thomas tillsynes ibland mått ganska skapligt, för att i nästa stund befinna sig i depressionens mörka rum. Är mera aktiv i sitt tänkande kring självmord enl terapeuten Birgitta Ståhle. Ibland svarar han på tilltal, ibland inte, detta gäller speciellt om han befinner sig på sitt rum och har dragit filten över huvudet. Har skrivit ett testaments- liknande brev, som finns i pärmen. Kortspel och alfapet fungerar som förut, som en stunds avkoppling från självmords tankar. Terapisituationen är f n enl Thomas ohyggligt jobbig detta ligger till grund för Thomas, just nu, besvärliga situation.

| 95-09-15 | Leg sjuksköt Barbro Östlund/cm |

Vid överrapportering från nattöversköt medd att Thomas blivit mordhotad på kvällen den 14. Tfn-samtal från polisen kom in torsdag kväll. Attentatet skulle ske mellan kl 11.00 14.00 fredag. Åtg vidtogs i samband med klinikledningen. Beslutades att Thomas skulle kvarstanna på avd. Pat skulle dock ej vistas vid boendedelen under dagen. Dagen förflöt lugnt och när inget ovanligt hade uppmärksammat fick pat återgå till sina rum efter kvällsmaten.

| 95-09-19 | Skötare Kenneth Ersson/cm |

Kl 17.15 börjar Thomas oroligt trava fram och tillbaka på avd. 17.30 får han tabl Xanor 1 mg, 2 st v b och vi följer honom till musikrummet där han vill vara lite ifred. Ång- esten ökar dock hela tiden och han lägger sig på golvet och krälar och stönar. Vill ej komma ur ångesten. Påstår sig vara vid ngn plats där han ej kommer ihåg vad han har gjort. Han kan senare ledas till rummet. Dr Persson tillkallas per tfn och ord klysma Stesolid 10 mg, 1 st vilken Thomas erhållit 18.35. Mår efter en stund bättre. Vill senare ringa till den polisman som håller i utredningen för de brott han har erkänt. Han pratar länge med honom c:a 1 tim. Ytterligare senare på kvällen pratar han c:a 45 min med sin terapeut per tfn. Vid midnatt får han en mindre ångestattack vilken hävs med tabl Xanor 1 mg 1 st. Somnar senare. Pratar i sömnen emellanåt. Säger då att han vill dö eller att han vill dödas.

8

Samples of Sture's case notes (1995). Please see appendix A for English translation. The last note refers to when Sture, intoxicated by his medication, talked for an hour with Seppo Penttinen. The exchange led to a police report quoted on the next page.

Onsdagen den 19 augusti klockan 19.45 blev undertecknad uppringd av Quick. Quick berättade att har mådde psykiskt mycket dåligt och att han önskade berätta vissa saker som han hade ångest över.

Inledningsvis kom Quick in på **Johan Asplund**. Han sade att den plats där han tidigare vallats i Ryggen-området fortfarande var aktuell som fyndplats. Vid den tidigare vallningen hade han befunnit sig ca 50-75 meter från det ställe där han grävt ner delar av kroppen. Han minns att han vid den vallning som företogs avvek till höger i motsatt riktning och att detta skedde från en plats varifrån har kunde skönja " fyndplatsen ". Området som är aktuellt ligger således i västlig riktning från den plats han tidigare pekat ut.

Quick sade även att **"den norske pojken"** ligger intill en idrottsplats i Lindesberg och att han mycket väl kommer ihåg platsen.

Beträffande **Olle Högbom** sade Quick att han i anslutning till den skola där han stötte på Olle, var in i en äldre fastighet. Han gick en halvtrappa ner i källaren och hiottade en kartong som innehöll s.k träull.
Kartongen skulle han använda till att lägga Olle i. Han säger gråtande att Olle åtminstone var vid liv i samband med införandet i den bil som Quick färdades i. Avsikten var att gömma kroppen på samma plats där han tidigare grävt ner Charles Zelmanovits. Detta skedde dock inte. Namnet Sågholmen är aktuellt beträffande Olle-händelsen, men Quick kan inte placera det rätt i sammanhanget .

Angående händelsen med den **israeliske mannen i Dalarna**. säger Quick att han hade hjälp av en person i samband med mordet. De träffade mannen på en mindre gata i närheten av järnvägsstationen Uppsala. Det framgick att mannen var på semesterresa. Quicks medhjälpare pratade engelska med mannen. De erbjöd mannen skjuts. Färden gick mot Garpenbergshållet. Mordet gjordes i samförstånd mellan Quick och medgärningsmannen. Det skall inte finnas några avvärjningsskador på mannens armar eller händer. Quick höll i honom under det att den andre slog honom med knytnävar och bl.a "ett tungt föremål från bagageluckan". Kroppen lämnades på den plats där slagen föll och arrangerades inte på något sätt. Kroppen blev liggande mer på rygg än på sidan och definitivt inte på magen. Det skall inte förekomma några skärskador på kroppen.
Quick säger att han är av den uppfattningen att mannen kom från Stockholm, när de träffade honom i Uppsala.
Quick nämner att han följt det som skrivits i pressen om händelsen, men att han skyggat för bilderna och inte läst allt som stått skrivet.
Quick säger även att de, hur absurt det än låter, firade mannens död.

Quick berättar även om en person som han kallar för **"Martin"**. Denne skall ligga gömd under mossa i trakten av **Sätrabrunn**. Namnet Martin behöver inte vara personens rätta namn. Denne är ca 18-19 år gammal. Quick var ensam när han tog livet av denne.

Quick nämner även att han i samband med Appojauremorden, d.v.s före morden, av Jonny Farebrink fick höra att denne varit i slagsmål med någon person. Jonny hade visat upp sina knogar och Quick minns att dessa var svullna. Jonny hade sagt att han "slagit någon på käften ". Händelsen skulle ha utspelat sig någon dag innan Quick träffade Jonny i Jokkmokk.

Avslutningsvis säger sig Quick ha hört **Jonny och Rune Nilsson** prata om Vietas-kuppen. Han vill inte närmare gå in på detta.

Sundsvall 95-09-20

Report made after Sture's phone call to Seppo Penttinen (see overleaf). Please see appendix B for English translation. Penttinen is given plenty of information and also a brand-new murder confession. Later, police excavations were made in Lindesberg, where Sture has indicated that he had buried a victim.

Hallå!

Sture är en mytoman, en jävla gris.

Han har ingen chans mot mig!

Jag är Ellington och i natt skall jag lära honom att hänga sig. Nöjd, så nöjd skall jag se på.

Jag har sanningen, inte Sture!! Det var Sture som dödade fostret som han kallar Simon. Nu skall det bli tyst på hans beskyllningar. Jag är inte notad men Sture har tappat kontrollen och han har gjort det för att han inte lyssnar på mig.

Jag är stark!

Han får döda sig själv, med min hjälp förstås men det förstår han inte. Nu skall jag spela på hans så kallade ånger! Jag behöver döda men då kan jag inte ha ynkryggen bredvid mig.

Jag önskar er en trevlig upptäckt och ett angenämt uppstädande.

Jag skiter i om min avslutnings-hälsning inte passar er pryda värd;

Med VÄNLIGA hälsningar Ellington

P.s. Hälsa hans "påhittliga terapeut"!!)

Sture Bergwall, in his role as 'Ellington', wrote this letter to the staff on ward 36 on 23 October. Bergwall always printed his letters but Ellington uses joined-up writing. Please see appendix C for English translation.

19/11 1966

Jag fick idag på eftermiddagen in till mig Margits sammanställning av "Simonillusionen. När jag läst den "drogs" jag tillbaka till den oerhört kraftfulla längtan att få vara en del av Simon, att få dela ett siamesiskt tvillingskap med honom. Jag fanns också så nära mossan och då även de mossor under vilka "mina bröder" finns, och jag längtade till dem.

När jag läste om hur jag ville ta Simon till hjälp för att döda M och sedan åka till Stockholm för att hälsa på kungen blev jag mycket rörd och jag "gled" i och mellan identiteter. Så var Nana hos mig och jag kände hur hon tog mig till Sture-skalet, jag kunde inte stå emot men jag hade Simon med mig. När jag var på väg att dö (jag var naken och jag hängde i min livrem, som var fastbunden i musikrummets element), när Nana sökte döda mig så ropade jag på Simon, ville ha honom nära, så nära (i mig/jag i honom).

Det som blev mycket starkt när jag läste sammanställningen var att se hur intensivt mitt sökande av liv varit och på samma gång, hur märkligt betydelsefullt mitt "finnande" av liv varit. Jag "upptäckte" alltså hur grundmurad min föreställning varit, hur oerhört mäktigt mitt undflyende av M och P varit, hur jag med all mobiliseringsbar styrka flytt undan tidiga traumatiska händelser. Att "upptäcka" detta blev också till en upplevelse av hur svårt det är idag att lämna ifrån mig mina "liv", av hur frågorna kring om hur jag skall kunna lämna mina illusoriska källor, tornade upp sig. Jag såg min ensamhet och jag kände den fullt ut. När detta skedde blev vägen för Nana öppen och mitt behov av Simon skriande.

Jag mindes också med sådan tydlighet hur jag "rann över" till Simon och hur ängslig jag var att inte hinna in till honom, att jag blev ett med honom, att vi två blev en helhet tillsammans. Jag mindes hur min andning i Simon talade om för mig att jag var hos honom, att jag hjälpte honom att leva och att han därigenom gav mig liv. Jag slapp plågan av att se - samtidigt som jag såg allt.

Jag mindes allt detta när jag läste Margits text och då kände jag också igen med tydlighet hur de pojkar jag dödade gav mig liv, jag kände också igen känslan av hur jag i ett mord fann förtröstan i tanken på nästa mord, nästa "livgivare".

Jag var mycket rädd och denna rädsla var så tydlig när jag "kom tillbaka", när jag igenom regressionen hörde personalens rop och då också vågade kliva fram till verklighet - och ångest.

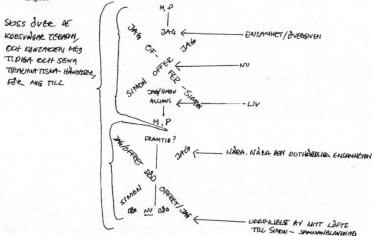

Sture Bergwall and Margit Norell worked together on the development of theories intended for her book 'The World of Thomas Quick'. Here, he writes to Birgitta Ståhle reflecting on what Margit has written. He refers to the suicide by hanging that he recently attempted in his role of 'Nana', the evil mother. Please see appendix D for English translation.

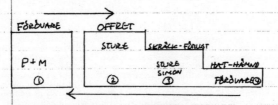

FÖRÖVARE – OFFER – FÖRÖVARE

① VID BROTTET ÄR JAG FÖRÖVAREN

②. VID BROTTET IDENTIFIERAR JAG MIG MED OFFRET.

③. I OFFERIDENTITETEN HAR JAG KONTAKT MED MIN
TIDIGA SKRÄCK, OHJÄLPLIGT FÖRLORAD

④. I OFFERIDENTITETEN TAR JAG HJÄLP AV MITT
FÖRÖVARJAG OCH DÖDAR FÖRÖVAREN

VÄXELSPEL

A: OFFRET SOM VET VAD FÖRÖVARENS HOT INNEBÄR.

B: FÖRÖVAREN SOM AVUNDAS OFFRET OCH DÄRFÖR
VÄRJER SIG FÖR ATT KÄNNA IGEN SIG I OFFRET —
FÖRÖVAREN "GLÖMMER" SIN ROLL OCH BLIR OFFRET.

C. FÖRÖVAREN SOM KÄNNER OFFRETS FRUKTAN / OFFRET
SOM KÄNNER ALL FRUKTAN OCH VÄNDER DET
INÅT → MOT FÖRÖVAREN.

JAG DÖDAR BÅDE OFFRET OCH FÖRÖVAREN

I MIN IDENTIFIKATION MED OFFRET BLIR JAG
DÖDAD / JAG DÖDAR OFFRET.

I MIN VUXENGESTALT HITTAR JAG STYRKA ATT
VÄNDA MIG MOT FÖRÖVAREN / JAG DÖDAR FÖRÖVAREN.
JAG ÄR I ETT OCH SAMMA SKEENDE FÖRÖVAREN
OCH OFFRET. JAG ÖVERLEVER GENOM ATT
DÖDA (BERÄTTA, ÅTERGESTALTA) POJKEN JAG SKULLE VILJA
VARA OCH GENOM ATT DÖDA FÖRÖVAREN.
I FÖRÖVARSITUATIONEN FÖRLORAR JAG MIG IN TILL
M-P INFÖRLIVANDET OCH TILL STURE, DEN LILLA STURE.

A theoretical rendering of the psychology of the serial killer, as understood by
Sture Bergwall. It was to become part of Margit's book *Thomas Quicks värld*
('The World of Thomas Quick'). Please see appendix E for English translation.

APPENDIX A

Translation of Swedish text on page 12 of plate section

SÄTER HOSPITAL	Case notes Sheet	90
Box 350 etc	Person number	50 04 26-7190
	Name	Quick, Thomas

Institution
The Regional Forensic Psychiatric Unit

Date and/or keyword	Ward/clinic, doctor and current notes
95-09-12	Care Assistant Mikael Lindgren

Continued s[uicide]-watch, definite risk. Since Monday 4/9, Thomas seems to have mostly felt well enough, only to find himself from one moment to the next inside depression's dark chamber. Accord. to the therapist Birgitta Ståhle, his thoughts on suicide are more active now. When addressed, he sometimes replies, sometimes not, especially when in his room with the blanket over his head. Has penned a letter rather like a will. It is in his folder. Cards and board games useful as before, offering moments of relaxation from suicidal thoughts. Thomas finds the therapeutic work horribly hard at present, this is the main cause of his difficult situation just now.

95-09-15   Charge Nurse Barbro Östlund / cm
The night charge nurse's hand-over report informed us that Thomas had received murder

493

threat in the evening of the 14th as per tel call from the police on Thursday night. The attack time was between 11.00 and 14.00 on Friday. Approp. measures agreed with senior clinical staff. It was decided that Thomas would remain on the ward. Pat. would however not spend daytime in the living quarters. The day passed without any disturbances and as nothing note-worthy had taken place, pat. was allowed to return to rooms after supper.

95-09-19   Care Assistant Kenneth Ersson /cm
                        At 17.15, Thomas becomes restless, starts walk-ing up and down the ward. At 17.30, given 2 × 1 mg tabl. Xanax as req. and we take him to the music room because he wants some peace. Anxiety increasing all the time, he lies down on the floor, crawls about, moans. Anxiety persists. Says he is somewhere but can't remember what he has done. Later able to be led back to his room. Phoned Dr Persson, prescr. 1 × 10 mg rectal tube Stesolid which was made available to Thomas at 18.35. Feels better after a while. Wants to phone the investigative officer re his confessed murders, talks to him for a long time, about 1 hour. Again, later that evening, speaks on the phone with his therapist for around 45 mins. He has a mild panic attack at midnight but recovers after 1 tabl. Xanax, 1 mg. Later, falls asleep. Occasionally, speaks in his sleep. Says that he wants to die or to kill.

APPENDIX B

Translation of Swedish text on page 13 of plate section

REPORT, drafted following a telephone call from Quick,
THOMAS Ragnar. 500426-7190

On Wednesday 19 August, the undersigned received a phone call from
Quick at 19.45. Quick stated that he felt troubled mentally and that he
wanted to speak about certain matters that caused him deep anxiety.

Initially, Quick referred to **Johan Asplund**. He said that the place in the
Ryggen area where he had previously been taken for a site visit should still
be rated as significant. At the previous site visit he had been approx. 50–75
metres from the place where he had buried parts of the body. At that visit,
he recalled having turned to the right, in other words in the opposite direction and stated that this occurred at a position from where he could discern
the 'significant place'. Consequently, this place is to be found in the west-
erly direction relative to the place he had previously pointed to.

Quick stated that **'the Norwegian boy'** was interred near a sports
ground in Lindesberg and that he remembers that place perfectly well.

Concerning **Olle Högbom**, Quick claimed that he was in an older
type of property adjacent to the school building where he encountered
Olle. He descended a short flight of stairs into a basement and found a box
containing so-called wood wool.

He decided to use the box for putting Olle away in. He was in tears
when he said that Olle was alive at least at the point in time of his entering the car that Quick was driving. Quick's intention was to hide the
body in the same area where he had previously buried Charles
Zelmanovits. However, this was not done. The place name Sågholmen is
relevant in connection with the Olle incident, but Quick cannot set the
link into context.

With reference to the **Dalarna incident involving the man from Israel**, Quick states that, in connection with the murder, he was helped by another person. They met the Israeli in a narrower type of street near the railway station in Uppsala. It transpired that the man was on a holiday trip. Quick's companion spoke in English with the man. They offered the man a lift and drove in the direction of Garpenberg. Quick and his co-perpetrator collaborated about the murder. Apparently, there are no self-defence injuries on the man's arms or hands. Quick held him down while his companion beat him up with his fists, also using, among other things, 'a heavy object kept in the boot'. The body was abandoned at the place of the beating and not tampered with. It was mainly resting on its back rather than on its side and definitely not on its front. There should be no cuts on the body.

Quick had the impression that, when they met the man, he had arrived in Uppsala from Stockholm.

Quick mentions that he has followed what was written in the press about the incident but averted his gaze from the images and anyway did not read everything that has been written.

Absurdly enough, Quick admits that they actually celebrated the man's death.

Quick also speaks of a person he calls **'Martin'**. This person is allegedly hidden beneath a pile of moss in the area of **Sätrabrunn**. The name 'Martin' is not necessarily the person's actual name. The person is 18–19 years old. Quick was on his own when he killed this person.

In connection with the Appojaure murders, Quick also mentions that, prior to the killings, he heard from Jonny Farebrink that he, Jonny, had been in a fight with a person. Jonny had shown off his knuckles and Quick remembers seeing that they were swollen. Jonny spoke of how he had 'knocked somebody senseless'. This incident had apparently taken place a day or so prior to Quick running into Jonny in Jokkmokk.

Ending the call, Quick says that he had heard Jonny and Rune Nilsson talk about the Vietas safe-breaking job. He does not want to say more about this.

Sundsvall 95-09-20   [signature]

APPENDIX C

Translation of Swedish text on page 14 of plate section

23/10 1995

Hello there!

Sture is a mythomaniac. And a fucking pig.

He hasn't got a chance against me!

I am Ellington and tonight I'll trick him into hanging himself. Watching him do it will please me, please me a lot.

I know the truth, not Sture!! It was Sture who killed the foetus he calls Simon.

Now, this will be an end to his accusations. I'm not feeling threatened but Sture has lost control. He doesn't listen to me, that's why.

I AM STRONG!

He might as well kill himself, of course I will give him a helping hand but he won't understand what's going on. Now I'm setting to work on his so-called 'anguish'. I feel a need to kill but can't go ahead with that wimp hanging around.

Wishing you a nice discovery and a pleasant cleaning-up.

And I don't give a shit if my wishes don't suit you prissy lot.

With DEADLY greetings, Ellington.

PS Greetings to his 'excellent therapist'!!!

APPENDIX D

Translation of Swedish text on page 15 of plate section

19/11 1966 [1996?]

Today I was handed Margit's exploration of the 'Simon illusion'. When I read it, I was 'dragged' back into overwhelmingly powerful longing to be part of Simon, to share a Siamese twin-ship with him. I was also so close to the moss, and hence to the mossy covers under which 'my brothers' rest, and I longed for them.

When I read that I wanted Simon to help me kill M, and then travel to Stockholm to see the king, I was very moved and 'slipped' between identities. Then Nana came to me and I sensed that she led me to the Sture-shell; I couldn't resist her but I had Simon with me. When I was close to death (I was naked, with noose around my neck made from my belt, tied to the music room radiator), when Nana tried to kill me I called out to Simon, wanted him to be near, so very close (inside me/I inside him).

I felt very strongly as I read the compilation that it showed my searching for life and just how intense it has been and, simultaneously, how strangely important my 'finding' life has been. I also 'discovered' how fundamental to me my ideas have become, how incredibly potent my need to escape M and P, and how, with all the strength I'm able to mobilize, I have run from those early traumatic events. To 'discover' this has also meant experiencing how hard it has become for me to abandon my 'lives' and how the questions that have arisen around the issue of exposing my illusory sources are now piling up. I saw my own solitude and felt it profoundly. When this happened, Nana's path to me was cleared and my need for Simon cried out to heaven.

I also clearly remembered how I 'overflowed' towards Simon and my

498

anxiety about not getting into him in time, so that I would become one with him, so that the two of us would become a whole together. I remember how my breathing inside Simon told me that I was with him and helped him to live and that, through him, I was given life. I escaped the pain of seeing – at the same time as I saw _everything_.

All this came to my mind when I read what Margit had written and I also very clearly recognized how the boys I had killed had given me life, and also recognized the feeling that, while murdering, I found comfort in the thought of the next murder, the next 'life-giver'.

I became very frightened and my fear was so distinct that when I, while in regression, heard the staff calling, I 'returned' and dared advance towards reality – and towards anguish.

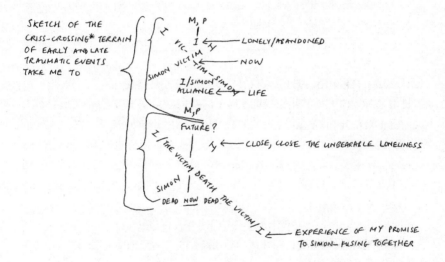

SKETCH OF THE CRISS-CROSSING* TERRAIN OF EARLY AND LATE TRAUMATIC EVENTS TAKE ME TO

M, P
I
FIG. I ←——— LONELY/ABANDONED
VICTIM I ← ——— NOW
SIMON I/SIMON-SIMON
ALLIANCE ←——OR—— LIFE
M, P
FUTURE?
I ← ——— CLOSE, CLOSE THE UNBEARABLE LONELINESS
I / THE VICTIM DEATH
SIMON
DEAD NOW DEAD THE VICTIM/I ←——— EXPERIENCE OF MY PROMISE TO SIMON – FUSING TOGETHER

[The asterisk in the diagram indicates an unclear word in the Swedish.]

499

APPENDIX E

Translation of Swedish text on page 16 of plate section

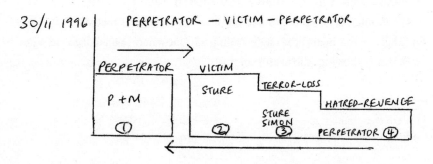

1. I AM THE PERPETRATOR OF THE CRIME
2. I IDENTIFY MYSELF WITH THE VICTIM OF THE CRIME
3. AS I IDENTIFY WITH THE VICTIM, I COME INTO CONTACT WITH MY EARLY TERROR, OF MY HELPLESS LOSS
4. AS I IDENTIFY WITH THE VICTIM I ACCEPT HELP FROM THE PERPETRATOR AND KILL THE PERPETRATOR

GAME OF ALTERNATION

A: THE VICTIM WHO KNOWS WHAT THE PERPETRATOR'S THREAT ENTAILS

B: THE PERPETRATOR WHO IS ENVIOUS OF THE VICTIM AND THEREFORE FIGHTS OFF ANY IDENTIFICATION WITH THE VICTIM – THE PERPETRATOR 'FORGETS' HIS ROLE AND BECOMES THE VICTIM

C: THE PERPETRATOR FEELS THE VICTIM'S FEAR / THE VICTIM WHO RECOGNIZES ALL FEAR ANDS TURNS IT INWARDS [*arrow*], TOWARDS THE PERPETRATOR

<u>I KILL BOTH THE VICTIM AND THE PERPETRATOR</u>
IN MY IDENTITY AS THE VICTIM I AM KILLED / I KILL THE VICTIM

IN MY ADULT PERSONA I FIND THE STRENGTH TO TURN AGAINST THE PERPETRATOR / I KILL THE PERPE-TRATOR.

I AM SIMULTANEOUSLY THE PERPETRATOR <u>AND</u> THE VICTIM. I <u>MYSELF</u> SURVIVE BY KILLING (NARRATE, RE-ENACT) THE BOY WHO I WOULD LIKE TO BE AND BY KILLING THE PERPETRATOR IN THE PERPETRATOR <u>SITU-ATION</u> I LOSE MYSELF INTO INCORPORATING M-P INTO STURE, LITTLE STURE.

Notes

1 Police report, 22 March 1996.
2 Penttinen, S., 2004. See also 'Application for retrial of case B 100-97 part 155'.
3 Police interview, 22 August 1996.
4 Penttinen, S.; in *Annals of Nordic Crime* (2004).
5 Christianson, S. Å., 1997.
6 Police report, 11 June 1997. (a) Wikström, A.
7 Norell, M., unpublished manuscript of 'The World of Thomas Quick', p. 56.
8 Police report, 11 June 1997. (a) Wikström, A.
9 Police report, 11 June 1997. (a) Penttinen, S.
10 Police report, 11 June 1997. (a) Wikström, A.
11 Police report, 11 June 1997. (a) Wikström, A.
12 Police report, 11 June 1997. (a) Wikström, A.
13 Police report, 11 June 1997. (a) Wikström, A.
14 Police report, 11 June 1997. (a) Penttinen, S.
15 Police report, 11 June 1997. Bjerknes, O. T. and Grøttland, H.
16 Police report, 11 June 1997. (a) Penttinen, S.
17 Police report, 11 June 1997. (a) Wikström, A.
18 Police report, 11 June 1997. (a) Wikström, A.
19 Police report, 11 June 1997. (a) Penttinen, S.
20 Quick, T., 1998, p. 182.
21 Police interview, 4 July 1997.
22 Höjer, B., 2004, pp. 25–6.
23 Larsson, D., 1998.
24 Quick, T., 15 November 2001.
25 Stigson, G. J., 17 June 2009.
26 Stigson, G. J., 31 May 2000.
27 Göransson, M., 2012.
28 Dåderman, A., 2009.
29 Pope, Jr., H. G. & Hudson, J. I. (1995); Spanos, N. P. (1994); Freud, S. (1925).
30 Spanos, N. P., Menary, E., Gabora, N. J., DuBruil, S. C. and Dewhirst, B. (1991); Hyman Jr., I. E. and Loftus, E. F. (1998).
31 Loftus, E. F., 1997.
32 Dåderman, A., 2009.
33 Ståhle, B., 2009, p. 1.
34 Interview with Birgitta Ståhle, 25 May 2009.

35 Swedish TV programme *Agenda*, 26 August 2012.

36 Ståhle, B., 8 August 2003.

37 Ståhle, B., 1999; in Norell, M., unpublished manuscript of 'The World of Thomas Quick', p. 287.

38 Norell, M., unpublished manuscript of 'The World of Thomas Quick'.

39 Flordh, C. and Notini, D., 1996.

40 Information about the Dickson family is drawn from, among others, the following sources: the Dickson family's homepage (http://www.swedickson.nu/historia2/historia2.htm). The Swedish National Archive (Riksarkivet) has an on-line 'Presentation of the Dickson family' (http://www.nad.riksarkivet.se/sbl/Presentation.aspx?id=1750). The website of the Forest Museum (Skogsmuseet) is (http://www.skogsmuseet.se/index.php?option=com_content&view=article-&id=36&Itemid=93).

41 Annie Norell Beach's website (http://www.swedickson.nu/florence/florence.htm).

42 *Vecko-Journalen*, no. 15, 1932.

43 Hart-Davis, D., 2010.

44 Norell, M., 15 February 1976.

45 Norell, M., 10 January 1976.

46 Norell, M., 29 February 1976.

47 Norell, M., 23 October 1971.

48 Norell, M., 1968.

49 Norell, M., 29 February 1976.

50 Norell, M., 1968.

51 Norell, M., 1 January 1976.

52 Norell, M., 1968.

53 Höjer, B., 2004, p. 25

54 For information about the educational institute (studiehemmet) in Ådalen, see Höjer, B., 2004 and Höjer, B., 2005.

55 Höjer, B., 2005.

56 Norell, M., 1968.

57 Norell, M., 8 April 1978. Fromm, E., 1964 (see also Kindle locations 2076–2077), confirms that Freud used this expression.

58 Bergwall, S-O., 1995.

59 Case note from the forensic psychiatric clinic at Håga Hospital, Södertälje, 16 March 1970, p. 37.

60 Case note from the forensic psychiatric clinic at Håga Hospital, Södertälje, 16 March 1970, p. 34.

61 Sanner, E., 16 March 1966.

62 Case notes, Child and Adolescent Psychiatric Clinic, Falun. From 21 April 1966 to 24 June 1966.

63 Letter from the head doctor at Child and Adolescent Psychiatric Clinic, Falun to a school doctor, 5 May 1966.

64 Case notes, Child and Adolescent Psychiatric Clinic, Falun, 21 April 1966.

65 Freud, S., 1900. Freud's statements on the hypnotic effect of free association has been discussed in Borch-Jacobsen, M., 2009, p. 45 et seq.

66 Sjögren, L., 1989.

67 Freud, S. (1910), *Two Case Histories*, Vol. 10 and Freud, S. (1917–19), *An Infantile*

Neurosis and other works, Vol. 17 (1917–1919), standard ed., Vintage Classics (2001).
68 Dunlap, K., *Mysticism, Freudianism and Scientific Psychology* (Mosby: St Louis, Mo.: 1920) in Hornstein. G. A., 1992.
69 Johansson, P. M., 2008, p. 437.
70 Johansson, P. M., 1999b.
71 Jastrow, J. (1934), *The House that Freud Built*, in Johansson, P. M., 2003, p. 439.
72 Kinberg, Olof, in *Dagens Nyheter*, 27 June 1953, in Johansson, P. M., 2003, pp. 440–41.
73 Hedenius, Ingmar, in *Dagens Nyheter*, 27 May 1953, in Johansson, P. M., 2003, p. 441.
74 Johansson, P. M., 2008, pp. 433–4.
75 Norell, M. (1968); Flordh, C. and Notini, D. (1996); Tudor-Sandahl, P. (5 October 1991).
76 Johansson, P. M., 2006.
77 Norell, M., 1968.
78 Fromm-Reichmann, F. & Bullard, D. M., 1959.
79 Liljeström, G., Lindholm, C. & Ståhle, B., 7 March 2005.
80 Flordh, C. & Notini, D., 1996.
81 Norell, M., 1 October 1976.
82 Case note from the forensic psychiatric clinic at Håga Hospital, Södertälje, 16 March 1970, p. 51.
83 Referral note, 24 June 1969.
84 Examination by forensic psychiatrist, 16 March 1970.
85 Examination by forensic psychiatrist, 16 March 1970.
86 Examination by forensic psychiatrist, 8 May1970.
87 Johansson, P. M., 2008, p. 275.
88 *Läkartidningen*, vol. 65, no. 6, 1968, pp. 608–9.
89 The Holistic Society joined the International Federation of Psychoanalytic Societies (IFPS) as a full member in 1968. Margit Norell participated in forums in Madrid (1970), New York (1972), Zürich (1974) and Berlin (1977). The information comes from Norell, M. (3 March 1971); Barnett, J. (14 July 1971); Horney Eckardt, M. (2 April 1974) & Norell, M. (1 October 1976).
90 Norell, M., 19 December 1972.
91 Will, O. A., 13 May 1968.
92 Norell, M., 23 May 1968.
93 Norell, M., 26 April 1968.
94 Nordin, A., 1999.
95 Fromm, E., 1994, p. 53 and p. 55.
96 Fromm, E., 9 May 1970.
97 Nordin, A., 1999.
98 Norell, M., 30 December 1970.
99 Norell, M., 30 December 1970.
100 Norell, M., 14 April 1971.
101 Norell, M., 19 January 1971.
102 Norell, M., 16 February 1971.
103 Norell, M., 23 October 1971.
104 Knapp, G. P. , 1989.

105 Fromm, E., 1964, Kindle location 435.
106 Norell, M., 23 October 1971
107 Norell, M., 21 November 1971.
108 Ericsson, L., 2004.
109 Norell, M., Nyman, M. & Sandin, B., 1975.
110 Norell, M., 20 September 1969.
111 Norell, M., Nyman, M. & Sandin, B., 1975.
112 Cullberg, J., 2007, pp. 103–4 and p. 236.
113 Sveriges Radio, *Reflecting Families*, 7 April 1973.
114 Norell, M., 22 November 1975.
115 Schecter, D., 22 February 1976
116 Norell, M., 26 March 1976.
117 Norell, M., 21 May 1976.
118 Schecter, D., 5 August 1976.
119 Schecter, D., 20 November 1976.
120 Norell, M., 20 November 1976.
121 Norell, M., 3 June 1975.
122 Norell, M., 13 February 1977.
123 Norell, M., 7 May 1977.
124 Schecter, D., 15 May 1977.
125 Norell, M., 22 May 1977.
126 Norell, M., 1977.
127 Case notes, 10 August 1994.
128 Lindsay, D. S. & Read, J. D., 1994.
129 Norell, M., 1 May 1977.
130 Schecter, D., 8 November 1977.
131 Norell, M., 20 November 1977.
132 Norell, M., 4 April 1980.
133 Schecter, D., 13 April 1980.
134 Unless another source is indicated, the quoted extracts in this chapter are taken from Sture Bergwall's case notes.
135 Dåderman, A., 2009.
136 Cross, C. R., 2006, p. 332.
137 Prosecutor's protocol, 10 April 1974.
138 Case notes, 17 April 1974.
139 Case notes, 18 April 1974.
140 Case notes, 12 May 1974.
141 Case notes, 14 May 1974.
142 Case notes, 14 May 1974.
143 Case notes, 13 June 1974.
144 Case notes, 15 May 1974.
145 Case notes, 27 September 1974.
146 Case notes, 27 September 1974.
147 Case notes, 14 November 1974.
148 Case notes, 21 January 1975.
149 Case notes, 30 January 1975 and 3 February 1975.
150 Case notes, 13 February 1975.

151   Case notes, 29 May 1975.
152   Case notes, 4 November 1975.
153   E.g. case notes, 4 December 1977.
154   Bergwall, S., 1995, pp. 125–7.
155   Bergwall, S., 1995, pp. 123–5.
156   Chronicle quoted in Quick, T., 1998.
157   Bergwall, S., 1995, p. 129.
158   Rycroft, R., 1995.
159   Janov, A., 1970.
160   Minutes, 27 October 1984.
161   Norell, M., 19 December 1976.
162   Molin, K., 8 February 1990.
163   Ferm, L., 1994.
164   Denke, E., 1997.
165   On 15 August 1994, Margit Norell declared in two social services certificates that Ståhle had been supervised by her since 1988 and had been in personal psychotherapy since 1990.
166   Arvidsson, L., 1994, p. 43.
167   Freud, S., 1896; in Freud, S., 1962, 2001, p. 203. Italics in original.
168   Freud, S., 1985, p. 184.
169   Cioffi, F., 1974.
170   Stanovich, K. E., ed., 2010.
171   Freud, S., 1933, pp. 532–3.
172   See e.g. Thompson, C., 1957.
173   Freud, S., 1896, ibid., p. 204.
174   McNally, R. J., 2003, p. 164.
175   Freud, S., 1896, ibid. p. 204.
176   Masson, J. M., 1984, p. 205.
177   Borch-Jacobsen, M., 2009, p. 38.
178   Schimek, J. G. (1987); Esterson, A. (1993); Israëls, H. & Schatzman, M. (1993).
179   Malcolm, J., 1984.
180   Kihlstrom, J. F., 1995 & 2006. Discusses Bass and Davis (cf. below) but also e.g. Fredrickson, R., *Repressed Memories: A journey to recovery from sexual abuse* (Simon & Schuster, 1992), Herman, J. L., *Trauma and Recovery* (Basic Books, 1992) and Terr, L., *Unchained Memories: True stories of traumatic memories, lost and found* (Basic Books, 1994).
181   Lindsay, D. S. & Read, J. D., 1994.
182   Strange, Clifasefi & Garry, 2007.
183   Bass, E. and Davis, L., 1988.
184   Bass, E. & Davis L., 1988, p. 82.
185   Stanovich, K. E., ed., 2010.
186   Lilienfeld, S. O., Lynn, S. J. & Lohr, J. M., 2003.
187   Mangs, K. & Martell, B., 1983, p. 11.
188   Loftus, E. F., 1993.
189   Holmes, D. S., 1990.
190   Wagenaar, W. A. & Groeneweg, J., 1990.
191   Pope Jr., H. G., Oliva, P. S. & Hudson, J. I., 1999.

192 Haggbloom, S. J., et al., 2002.
193 E.g. Garry, M. & Hayne, H., 2006.
194 Loftus, E. F. & Palmer, J. C., 1974.
195 McNally, R. J., 2005; Loftus, E. F. & Ketcham, K., 1994.
196 Holmes, D., 1990, p. 97.
197 Loftus, E. F., 1993.
198 Spanos, N. P., Menary, E., Gabora, N. J., DuBruil, S. C. & Dewhirst, B., 1991.
199 Loftus, E. F. & Pickrell, J. E., 1995.
200 Spanos, N. P., Menary, E., Gabora, N. J., DuBruil, S. C. & Dewhirst, B., 1991.
201 Ceci, S. J., Loftus, E. F., Leichtman, M. D. & Bruck, M., 1994.
202 Hyman, I. E., Husband, T. H., Billings, F. J., 1995; and Hyman Jr., I. E. &
     Pentland, J., 1996.
203 Heaps, C. M. & Nash, M., 2001.
204 Garry, M., Manning, C. G., Loftus, E. F. & Sherman, S. J., 1996; Heaps, C. &
     Nash, M., 1999.
205 Porter, S., Yuille, J. C. & Lehman, D. R., 1999.
206 Porter, S., Yuille, J. C. & Lehman, D. R., 1999.
207 Mazzoni, G. A. L., Loftus, E. F. & Kirsch, I., 2001.
208 Spanos, N. P., Menary, E., Gabora, N. J., DuBruil, S. C. & Dewhirst, B., 1991.
209 Curtius, M., 3 July 1996.
210 Bloom, S., 1994.
211 McNally, R. J., 2003.
212 McNally, R. J., Lasko, N. B., Clancy, S. A., Macklin, M. L., Pitman, R. K. &
     Orr, S. P., 2004.
213 Loftus, E. F., 2003.
214 Heaps, C. M. & Nash, M., 2001.
215 Loftus, E. & Ketcham, K., 1994, p. 87.
216 Kendall-Tackett, K. A., Williams, L. M. & Finkelhor, D., 1993.
217 Usher, J. A. & Neisser, U. (1993); Bruce, D., Dolan, A. & Phillips-Grant, K.
     (2000); Bauer, P. J. (2006); Lindholm, T., Sjöberg, R. L., Pedroletti, C., Boman,
     A., Olsson, G. L., Sund, A. & Lindblad, F. (2009); Sjöberg, R. L. & Lindholm, T.
     (2009).
218 Case note entries by Lena Arvidsson (assumed name), 6 September 1995, 4 July
     1996, 23 July 1997 and 6 August 1998.
219 Email from Lena Arvidsson (assumed name), 21 April 2012.
220 Loftus, E. F. & Ketcham, K., 1994, pp. 160–62.
221 Email from Lena Arvidsson (assumed name), 8 June 2012.
222 Case number not stated for reasons of privacy.
223 Norell, M., 22 May 1977.
224 Norell, M., 1977.
225 Arvidsson, L., 1994.
226 Norell, M., 30 December 1970.
227 Norell, M., 18 November 1972.
228 Norell, M., 13 February 1977.
229 Norell, M., 12 October 1977.
230 Norell, M., 28 August 1978.
231 Social Services Department (1980:9). Prostitution in Sweden, part 1.

232 Olsson, H., 1990.
233 Lindeberg, P., 1999.
234 Tudor-Sandahl, P., 1983.
235 Norell, M., 1989.
236 Norell, M., 14 November 1989.
237 Sandin, B., 1986.
238 Jonsson, E., 1986.
239 The opera *King of Fools* by Carl Unander-Scharin had its premiere at Vadstena Castle in 1996.
240 Lagercrantz, D., 30 March 1990.
241 Denke, E., 1997.
242 Michanek, B., 24 March 1990.
243 Ohlson, L., 22 March 1990.
244 Michanek, B., 24 March 1990.
245 Police interview with Örjan Bergwall, 18 February 1999.
246 Police interviews with Patrik, 22 May 1996, p. 20; 20 November 1996, p. 14.
247 Police interview with Maria Sykijäinen, 20 February 1995.
248 Police interview with Kristina, 27 February 1995.
249 Police interview with Patrik, 22 February 1995.
250 Sentence, criminal case B1116/91, p. 4.
251 Case notes, 13 March 1989, psychologist Birgitta Rindberg.
252 Police interview with Patrik, 22 May 1996, p. 5.
253 Doctor's certificate as per §7, 23 January 1991.
254 In social services report, 30 March 1991, submitted with the forensic psychiatric assessment, 25 March 1991, by Dr Marianne Kristiansson.
255 Forensic psychiatric assessment, 25 March 1991, by Dr Marianne Kristiansson.
256 Case notes, 10 May 1991.
257 Loftus, E. F., 1993.
258 Wagenaar, W. A. and Groeneweg, J., 1990.
259 Case notes, 17 May 1991.
260 Minutes, 6 April 1991.
261 Case notes, 2 July 1991.
262 Case notes, 10 July 1991.
263 Case notes, 9 September 1991.
264 Norell, M., unpublished manuscript of her book 'The World of Thomas Quick'.
265 Case notes, 9 April 1992.
266 Letter from Sture Bergwall to Kjell Persson, 27 April 1992; in Norell, M., unpublished manuscript of 'The World of Thomas Quick', p. 4.
267 Michanek, B., 27 June 1992.
268 Forensic psychiatric report, 30 January 1991.
269 Case notes, 26 June 1992.
270 '122 Murderers Walk Free on Sweden's Streets', *Expressen*, 20 September 1992.
271 A letter from Sture Bergwall to Kjell Persson, 19 October 1992; in Norell, M., unpublished manuscript of 'The World of Thomas Quick'.
272 Police interview, 19 December 2000.
273 Police interview, 1 March 1993; Kjell Persson states this on p. 38.
274 Police interview, 19 December 2000; cf. also interview on 9 May 2001.

275 Case note entry by Kjell Persson, 21 May 1993.
276 Steinvall, A. (1992), p. A12.
277 A letter from Sture Bergwall to Kjell Persson, 5 January 1993; in Norell, M.,
     unpublished manuscript of 'The World of Thomas Quick', p. 8.
278 A letter from Sture Bergwall to Kjell Persson, 5 January 1993; in Norell, M.,
     unpublished manuscript of 'The World of Thomas Quick', p. 11.
279 Arvidsson, L., 27 October 1992.
280 Arvidsson, L., 6 December 1992.
281 Case note entry by Birgitta Ståhle, 1 March 1993.
282 Case note entry by Göran Fransson, 15 February 1993.
283 Case note entry by Göran Fransson, 23 February 1993.
284 Norell, M., 1989.
285 Police interview, 1 March 1993.
286 A letter from Sture Bergwall to Kjell Persson, 19 October 1992; in Norell, M.,
     unpublished manuscript of 'The World of Thomas Quick', p. 11.
287 Information from the author's interview with Christer van der Kwast.
288 Stigson, G. J., 25 May 2001.
289 Swedish TV News (Rapport programme), 9 March 1993.
290 Stigson, G. J., 10 March 1993.
291 Police interview, 17 March 1993.
292 Police interview, 18 March 1993.
293 Police interview, 21 April 1993.
294 Police interview, 25 May 1993 (wrongly dated 25 April). See also Norell, M.,
     unpublished manuscript of 'The World of Thomas Quick', pp. 33–4.
295 Report, 26 May 1993.
296 Police interview, 28 May 1993.
297 Fransson, G., 17 July 1994.
298 Swedish television news, 28 May 1993.
299 Case note entry by Kjell Persson, 21 May 1993.
300 Belin, S., 1987, pp. 142–4.
301 In Norell, M., unpublished manuscript of 'The World of Thomas Quick', pp.
     141–2.
302 McNally, R. J., 2003, p. 164.
303 Miller, A., 1983.
304 Letter by Sture Bergwall, 24 September 1994; in Norell, M., unpublished
     manuscript of 'The World of Thomas Quick', p. 110.
305 Letter from Sture Bergwall to the ward round at Säter; in Norell, M.,
     unpublished manuscript of 'The World of Thomas Quick', p. 19.
306 Case note entry by Kjell Persson, 21 May 1993.
307 Arvidsson, L., 18 August 1993.
308 Letter from Sture Bergwall to Lena Arvidsson, 17 April 1993; in Norell, M.,
     unpublished manuscript of 'The World of Thomas Quick'.
309 Arvidsson, L., 25 October 1993.
310 Sture's case notes record that he was on leave to Stockholm on 24 August 1993,
     and also on 'Wed 22 Sept'.
311 Report, 17 September 1993.
312 Case note entry by Kjell Persson, 22 October 1993.

313 Norell, M., 1977.
314 Case note entry by Kjell Persson, 22 October 1993.
315 Police interview, 27 September 1993.
316 Case notes, 2 November 1993.
317 Swedish Television, 9 November 1993.
318 Arvidsson, L., 14 November 1993.
319 'Säter patient allegedly linked to murder of 14-year-old', *Dala-Demokraten*, 11 November 1993,
320 Tagesson, P., 1994.
321 Stigson, G. J., 17 November 1994.
322 Höglund, J., 25 March 1996.
323 Stigson, G. J., 18 December 2001.
324 Report, 24 April 2012. Here, DI Kjell-Åke Wendt states that he, after talking with Seppo Penttinen on the telephone (19 November 2009), with some difficulty obtained thirteen interview files that had been hidden and not entered into the diary. Kjell-Åke Wendt worked for chief prosecutor Björn Ericson on the retrial application on behalf of Sture Bergwall.
325 'Säter patient allegedly linked to murder of 14-year-Ood', *Dala-Demokraten*, 11 November 1993.
326 Police interview, 15 May 1994.
327 Conti, R., 1999.
328 Dahlstedt, 2013.
329 Gudjonsson, G. H., 1999.
330 Text written by Sture, 28 March 1995; in Norell, M., unpublished manuscript of 'The World of Thomas Quick', p. 199. A.
331 Källberg, G., personal notes about the conflict at Säter, 3 March 1994.
332 Case note entry by Göran Källberg, 30 January 1994.
333 Källberg, G., personal notes about the conflict at Säter, 3 March 1994.
334 Källberg, G., personal notes about the conflict at Säter, 3 March 1994.
335 Norell, M., unpublished manuscript of 'The World of Thomas Quick', p. 82. A.
336 Arvidsson, L., 12 January 1994.
337 Arvidsson, L., 17 January 1994.
338 Case note entry by Birgitta Ståhle, 23 June 1994.
339 Social Service investigation Doc. no. 114:5772-94.
340 Social Services investigation Doc. no. 114:5772-94.
341 Social Services investigation Doc. no. 114:5772-94.
342 Case note entry by Birgitta Ståhle, 13 July 1994.
343 Quick, T., 12 July 1994.
344 Letter from Sture Bergwall to the staff on ward 36; in Norell, M., unpublished manuscript of 'The World of Thomas Quick', pp. 89–90.
345 Nilsson, P., 24 April 1994.
346 Stigson, G. J., 17 June 2009; Kall, E.; in Statement to High Court, 8 June 2010. The Stigson interview with Göran Källberg includes 'medication [. . .] at abuse-level dosages'. The statement by Dr Kall includes ' . . . medication prescribed to help Sture manage his therapy and court trials'.
347 Case note entry by Birgitta Ståhle, 10 August 1994.
348 Case notes, 5 August 1994.

349 Case notes, 9 August 1994.
350 Case notes, 10 August 1994.
351 Text written by Sture Bergwall in the autumn of 1994; in Norell, M., unpublished manuscript of 'The World of Thomas Quick', p. 92.
352 Police interview, 26 January 1994.
353 Police interview, 14 April 1994.
354 Christianson, S. Å. and Loftus, E. F., 1987.
355 E.g. Christianson, S. Å., Loftus, E. F., Hoffman, H. and Loftus, G. R., 1991.
356 Loftus, E. F., 1993.
357 Christianson's own account in an interview with Kjell-Åke Wendt, 26 November 2010.
358 Weigl, K., 1 November 1994.
359 Note by Sture Bergwall, 13 December 1993; in Norell, M., unpublished manuscript of 'The World of Thomas Quick', pp. 83–4.
360 Interrogation, 9 February 1994.
361 Police interview, 14 April 1994.
362 Carlsson, M., 19 August 1999; Christianson, S. Å. and Engelberg, E., 1997; Police interview, 26 November 2010.
363 Fisher, R. P. and Geiselman, R. E., 1992.
364 Fisher, R. P. and Geiselman, R. E., 2010.
365 Police report, 25 May 1994.
366 Police interview, 26 November 2010.
367 Lindsay, D. S. and Read, J. D., 1994.
368 Police interview, 19 April 1994, p. 8.
369 Police interview, 14 June 1994.
370 Police interview, 14 June 1994.
371 Application for retrial of case B 179/94 (Re: Charles Zelmanovits).
372 Police report, 4 June 2012.
373 Bladh, A. K., 24 August 1994; the article was published in several newspapers, including Dagens Nyheter and Dala-Demokraten.
374 Dåderman, A., 26 November 1999.
375 Case notes, 26 September 1994.
376 Tagesson, P., 2 September 1994.
377 Bladh, A. K., 2 September 1994; Stigson, G. J., 3 September 1994.
378 Arvidsson, L., 19 September 1994.
379 Report, 24 April 2012.
380 E.g. Mattisson, S. and Fröberg, P., 31 October 1994; Weigl, K., 1 November 1994.
381 Stigson, G. J., 25 June 2001.
382 Lagercrantz, D., 9 August 1994.
383 Weigl, K., 2 November 1994.
384 Bladh, A. K., 2 November 1994.
385 Sentence, Piteå District Court, case B 179–94.
386 Tagesson, P., 2 November 1994.
387 Weigl, K., 2 November 1994.
388 Tagesson, P., 2 November 1994. A.
389 Weigl, K., 2 November 1994.
390 Sentence, Piteå District Court, case B 179–94.

391 Christianson, S. Å., 3 October 1994; submission by expert witness concerning the functioning of Thomas Quick's overall memory.
392 Christianson, S. Å., 3 October 1994. Expert witness evaluation of psychological conditions affecting the statement by Thomas Quick.
393 Christianson, S. Å., 3 October 1994. Expert witness evaluation of psychological conditions affecting the statement by Thomas Quick.
394 Kassin, S. M. and Wrightsman, L. S., 1985.
395 Bladh, A. K., 2 November 1994.
396 Weigl, K., 2 November 1994.
397 Christianson, S. Å. and Engelberg, E., 1997.
398 Christianson, S. Å. and Engelberg, E., 1997.
399 In Norell, M., unpublished manuscript of 'The World of Thomas Quick', p. 217.
400 Sture Bergwall, Diary note, 4 October 1995; in Norell, M., unpublished manuscript of 'The World of Thomas Quick', p. 249.
401 Sture Bergwall, Letter to Margit Norell (autumn 1995); in Norell, M., unpublished manuscript of 'The World of Thomas Quick', p. 151. A.
402 Sture Bergwall, Diary note (autumn 1995); in Norell, M., unpublished manuscript of 'The World of Thomas Quick', pp. 150–1. A.
403 Sture Bergwall, Daily notes with M. Norell's comments, 26 and 28 September; in Norell, M., unpublished manuscript of 'The World of Thomas Quick', section *Dad – Ellington and M – Nana* (compilation), p. 26.
404 Quick, T., 4 January 1995.
405 Vinterhed, K., 19 April 1995.
406 Spanos, N. P., 1994.
407 Piper, A., 1994.
408 Lynn, S. J., Lock, T., Loftus, E. F., Krackow, E. and Lilienfeld, S. O., 2003.
409 Birgitta Ståhle, Letter to Margit Norell, 5 August 1994; in Norell, M., unpublished manuscript of 'The World of Thomas Quick', section *Summary, Ellington – Nana*.
410 Ståhle, B., 13 March 1995; also quoted in Norell, M., unpublished manuscript of 'The World of Thomas Quick', pp. 192–3. A.
411 Daily note by Sture Bergwall; in Norell, M., unpublished manuscript of 'The World of Thomas Quick', pp. 202–3.
412 Case note entry by Dr Staffan Persson, 19 July 1995.
413 Notes by Birgitta Ståhle RE a talk with 'Ellington', 21 October 1994. In Norell, M, unpublished manuscript of 'The World of Thomas Quick', section *Dad – Ellington and M – Nana*, p. 20.
414 Quick, T., 23 October 1995.
415 Note by Birgitta Ståhle, 28 October 1995; in Norell, M., unpublished manuscript of 'The World of Thomas Quick', section *Dad – Ellington and M – Nana*, p. 28. Also mentioned in case note entry, made same date.
416 Case notes, 19 September 1995.
417 Police report, 19 September 1995.
418 Case notes, 19 September 1995.
419 Police interview, 10 April 1995.
420 Police report, 21 November 1994.
421 Report from first investigation of Appojaure murders, p. 132.
422 Police report, 23 November 1994.

423 Application for retrial of case B 26/95 (Concerning the Appojaure murders), p. 10.
424 Police interview, 17 January 1995, p. 7 and p. 20.
425 Police interview, 17 January 1995, p. 20.
426 Prosecutor's decision, 11 December 1995.
427 Police interview, 12 December 1994.
428 Police interview, 9 February 1995, p. 12.
429 Nässén, T., 9 December 2002.
430 Reconstruction record, 10 July 1995, Appendix C.
431 Larsson, D., 22 June 2009.
432 Interview with Jan Olsson, 3 July 2009.
433 Penttinen, S. (no date). Views on the Retrial Application in the matter of the Appojaure murders.
434 Case notes, 12 July 1995.
435 Sture Bergwall, Diary notes, 18 September 1995; in Norell, M., unpublished manuscript of 'The World of Thomas Quick', p. 231.
436 Christianson, S. Å., 2 January 1996.
437 Case notes, 29 July 1995.
438 Case notes, 6 and 19 September, and 25 December, 1995.
439 Case note entry by Erik Kall, 26 September 1995.
440 Case notes, 17 August 1995.
441 Application for retrial of case B 100-97 (concerning Therese Johannessen).
442 Bladh, A. K., 9 January 1996.
443 Engman, T., 10 January 1996.
444 Sentence in criminal case B26-95 (the Appojaure murders).
445 Christianson, S. Å. and Engelberg, E., 1997, pp. 231–50; published 20 March 1997 according to the publishers' website http://ukcatalogue.oup.com/product/9780198523864.do
446 Christianson, S. Å., 2010.
447 Christianson, S. Å., 2 January 1996.
448 Christianson, S. Å. and Wentz, G., 1996, p. 14.
449 The programme was shown on 17 May 1995, and then again on 11 June 1995.
450 Police report, 22 March 1996.
451 Sentence in criminal case B100-97 (Re: The murder of Therese Johannessen).
452 Sentence in criminal case B1548-99 (Re: The murders of Gry Storvik and Trine Jensen).
453 Expert report by Rickard L. Sjöberg, 23 March 2010.
454 Case dismissal statement by prosecutor Bo Ericsson, 24 September 2012.
455 Police interview, 9 February 1995.
456 Police interview, second on same day, 6 October 1999.
457 Penttinen, S., 2004, p. 430.
458 Police report, 22 March 1996.
459 Report of police investigation of sites north of Sundsvall, 18 September 2000.
460 Sentence in criminal case B3348-97 (Re: The murder of Yenon Levi).
461 Police report, 19 September 1995.
462 Police interview, 23 February 1996.
463 Nässén, T., 9 December 2002.
464 Dåderman, A., 26 November 1999.

465 Arvidsson, L., 19 September 1994.
466 Persson, K., 5 October 1995.
467 Letter from Sture Bergwall, 24 September 1994; in Norell, M., unpublished manuscript of 'The World of Thomas Quick', p. 110.
468 Note by Birgitta Ståhle, 7 March 1996; in Norell, M., unpublished manuscript of 'The World of Thomas Quick'.
469 Note by Birgitta Ståhle, 13 August 1996; in Norell, M., unpublished manuscript of 'The World of Thomas Quick', section *Dad – Ellington and M – Nana*.
470 Vinterhed, K. and Lönnebo, M., 2000, p. 15.
471 From a report of the final plea of the defence by Claes Borgström; in Norell, M., unpublished manuscript of 'The World of Thomas Quick'.
472 Borgström, C., 18 May 2000; Stigson, G. J., 31 May 2000.
473 Ståhle, B., 18 May 2000.
474 Dahlström-Lannes, M., 8 February 1996.
475 Dahlström-Lannes, M., 25 August 2000.
476 Sture Bergwall's statement at Yenon Levi trial. Quoted in Birgitta Ståhle's letter to Margit Norell, 12 May 1997; in Norell, M., unpublished manuscript of 'The World of Thomas Quick'.
477 Borgström, C., 6 June 1998.
478 Borgström, C., 17 June 1998.
479 Quick, T., 25 May 1999.
480 Quick, T., 18 July 1996.
481 Case note entry by Birgitta Ståhle, 4 February 1997.
482 Quick, T., 31 May 1997.
483 Police report, 2 June 1997.
484 Ståhle, B., 2 June 1997.
485 Christianson, S. Å., 1997.
486 Police report by Anna Wikström, 18 December 1996.
487 Police report by Anna Wikström, 18 December 1996.
488 Report of technical investigations 1993–1999 (no date).
489 Lilja, M., 22 April 1996.
490 Aschberg, R., 23 April 1996; Fallenius, A., Lövkvist, N., 24 April 1996.
491 Aschberg, R. and Johansson, A., 27 December 2006.
492 Police report, 8 June 1998.
493 Larsson, D. (4 May 1998); Wiklund, N. (8 May 1998); Asplund, B. (17 May 1998); Borgström, C. (6 June 1998); Wiklund, N. (9 June 1998); Holgersson, A. (12 June 1998); Höglund, R. (17 June 1998); Borgström, C. (17 June 1998).
494 Bergwall, Sture, Diary note, 30 July 1998; in Norell, M., unpublished manuscript of 'The World of Thomas Quick'.
495 Stigson, G. J., 16 September 1997.
496 Police interview, 2 September 1998.
497 Tagesson, P., 16 September 1998.
498 Stigson, G. J., 16 September 1998.
499 Ståhle, B., 13 November 1998.
500 Police interview, 10 February 1999.
501 Police interview, 22 March 1999.
502 Ståhle, B., 18 May 2000.

503 Police interview, 9 September 2000.
504 Police report, 27 September 2000.
505 Police report, 17 October 2000.
506 Police interview, 18 October 2000.
507 Application for retrial of case B 187-93 (Concerning the murder of Johan Asplund).
508 Sentence in criminal case B187-93 (Concerning the murder of Johan Asplund).
509 Stigson, G. J., 17 November 1994.
510 Police interview, 13 July 2009.
511 Case note entry by Göran Källberg, 25 April 2001.
512 Police interview, 13 July 2009.
513 Case note entry by Erik Kall, 10 May 2001.
514 Police interview, 13 July 2009, p. 3; also own sources.
515 Case note entry by Göran Källberg, 29 May 2001.
516 Case note entry by Göran Källberg, 5 June 2001.
517 Minutes, 28 September 1996.
518 Quick, T., 9 and 12 June 2001.
519 Lindholm, C., 27 June 2001.
520 Quick, T., 12 June 2001.
521 Quick, T., will and testament (no date).
522 Case notes, 7 August 2001.
523 Case notes, 2 October 2001.
524 Case notes, 17 October 2001.
525 Case notes, 28 November 2001.
526 Case notes, 11 January 2002.
527 Case notes (e.g. 14 November 1994; 13 October 1995; 11 October 1996; 20 October 1996; 4 February 1997; 25 April 1997; 16 December 1997; 12 February 1999; 26 November 2000).
528 Case note entry by Birgitta Ståhle, 22 January 2002.
529 Case note entry by Birgitta Ståhle, 10 April 2002.
530 Sture Bergwall, calendar note, 11 April 2002.
531 Case notes, 30 April 2002.
532 Tudor-Sandahl, P., 5 October 1991.
533 Police interview, 13 July 2009.
534 Verdict, 28 November 2006.
535 Lambertz, G., 3 December 2006.
536 Lambertz, G., 12 February 2007.
537 Swedish Radio programme *Summer* (*Sommar*, 28 July 2007).
538 Råstam, H., 2013.
539 Case note entry by Göran Källberg, 15 May 2009.
540 Bergwall, S-O., 10 December 2009.
541 Verdict, 16 February 2009.
542 TV4, *Morning News*, 22 December 2008.
543 Kall, E., 8 June 2010.
544 Fromm-Reichmann, F. and Bullard, D. M., 1959.

Image Credits

The author and the publisher have made every effort to trace the copyright holders. Please contact the publisher if you are aware of any omissions.

1. Sture at Säter (July 2000). From the private archive of Sture Bergwall. Reproduced with his kind permission.
2. Margit Norell in her consultation room on Nurrtull Street in Stockholm (1996). Copyright © Tomas Södergren.
3. Senior Investigation Officer Seppo Penttinen, Sture Bergwall, Claes Borgström and Birgitta Ståhle, photographed during a site visit in Drammen, Norway (April 1996). Copyright © Sven Erik Røed/TT Bildbyrå/Press Association.
4. Samples of Sture's case notes (1995).
5. Police report made after Sture's phone call to Seppo Penttinen (1995).
6. A handwritten letter written by Sture in his role as 'Ellington' (1996). From the private archive of Sture Bergwall. Reproduced with his kind permission.
7. Sture's typed letter to Birgitta Ståhle. From the private archive of Sture Bergwall. Reproduced with his kind permission.
8. A theoretical rendering of the psychology of the serial killer, as understood by Sture Bergwall (1996). From the private archive of Sture Bergwall. Reproduced with his kind permission.

Text Credits